ANO[...] NOISE

Ryoko Fukuyama

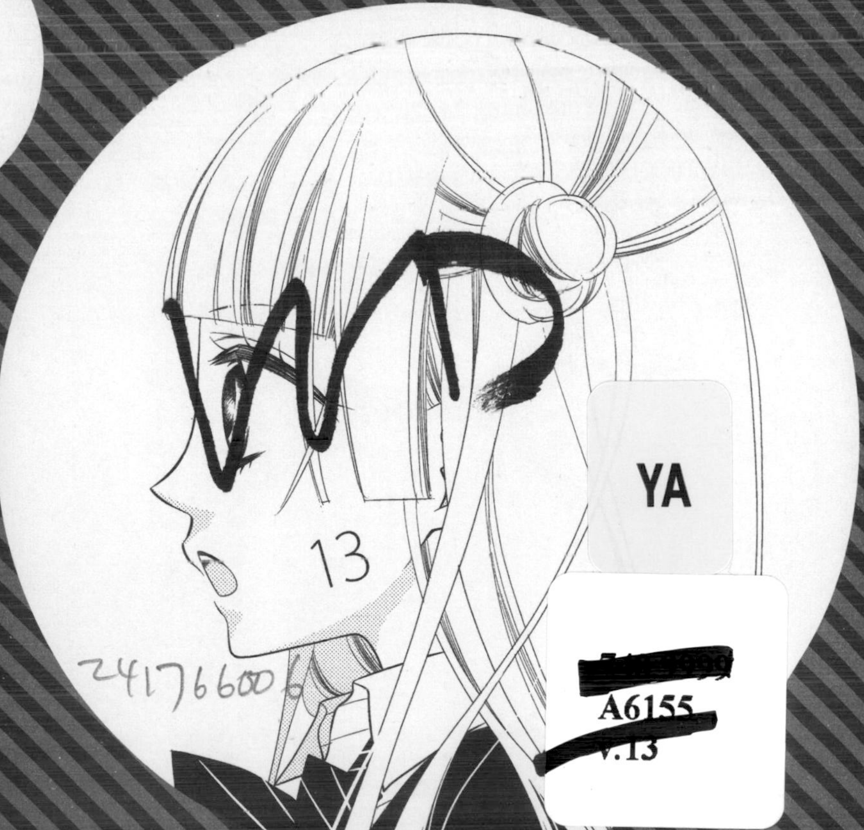

13

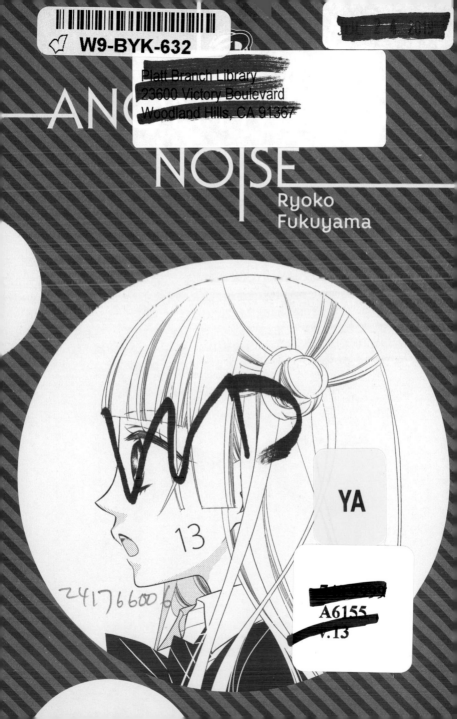

Anonymous Noise
Volume 13

CONTENTS

Song 71...............3

Song 72...............33

Song 73...............65

Song 74...............97

Song 75...............117

Spilled Gelatin.....138

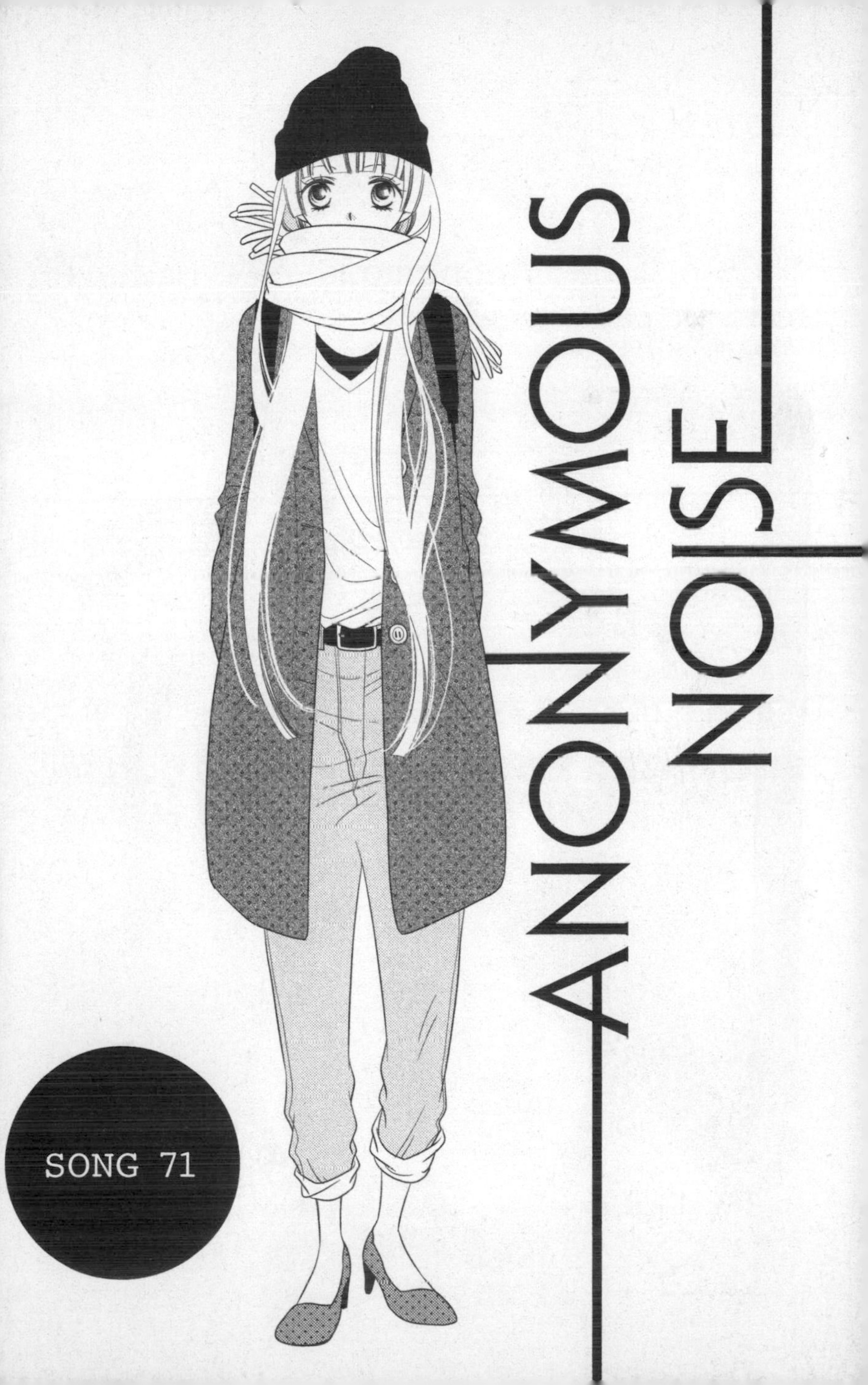
ANONYMOUS NOISE
SONG 71

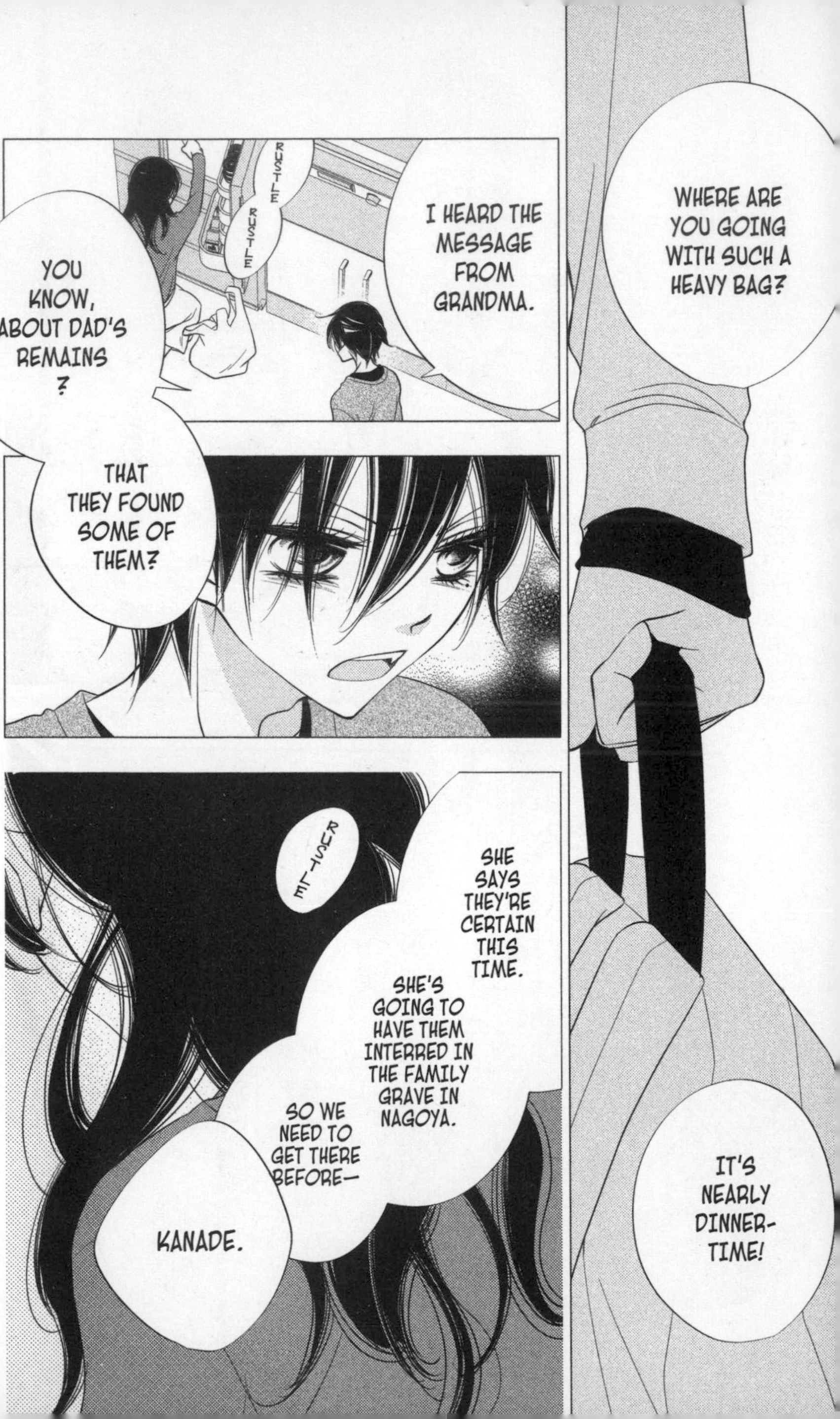
WHERE ARE YOU GOING WITH SUCH A HEAVY BAG?
IT'S NEARLY DINNER-TIME!
I HEARD THE MESSAGE FROM GRANDMA.
RUSTLE
RUSTLE
YOU KNOW, ABOUT DAD'S REMAINS?
THAT THEY FOUND SOME OF THEM?
RUSTLE
SHE SAYS THEY'RE CERTAIN THIS TIME.
SHE'S GOING TO HAVE THEM INTERRED IN THE FAMILY GRAVE IN NAGOYA.
SO WE NEED TO GET THERE BEFORE—
KANADE.

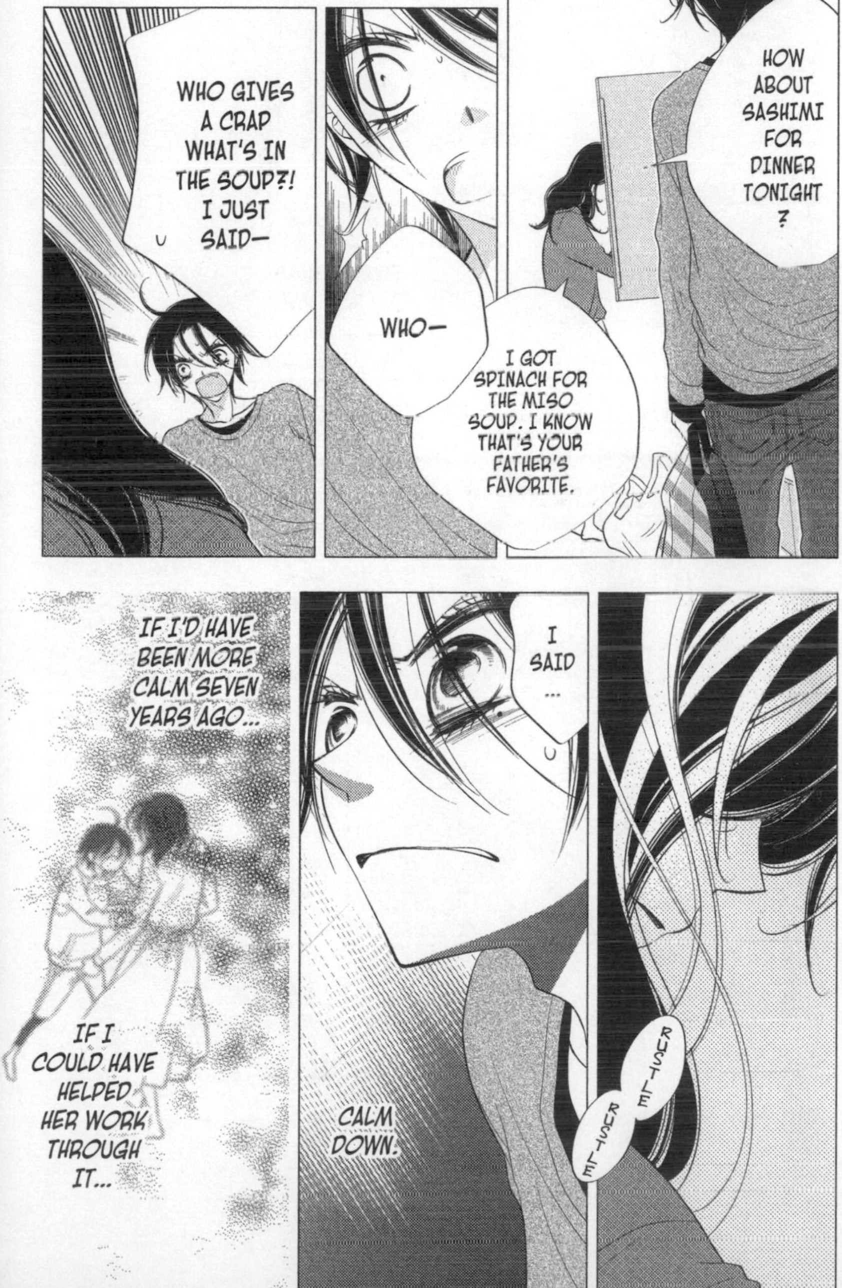
HOW ABOUT SASHIMI FOR DINNER TONIGHT?
I GOT SPINACH FOR THE MISO SOUP. I KNOW THAT'S YOUR FATHER'S FAVORITE.
WHO—
WHO GIVES A CRAP WHAT'S IN THE SOUP?! I JUST SAID—
RUSTLE
RUSTLE
I SAID...
CALM DOWN.
IF I'D HAVE BEEN MORE CALM SEVEN YEARS AGO...
IF I COULD HAVE HELPED HER WORK THROUGH IT...

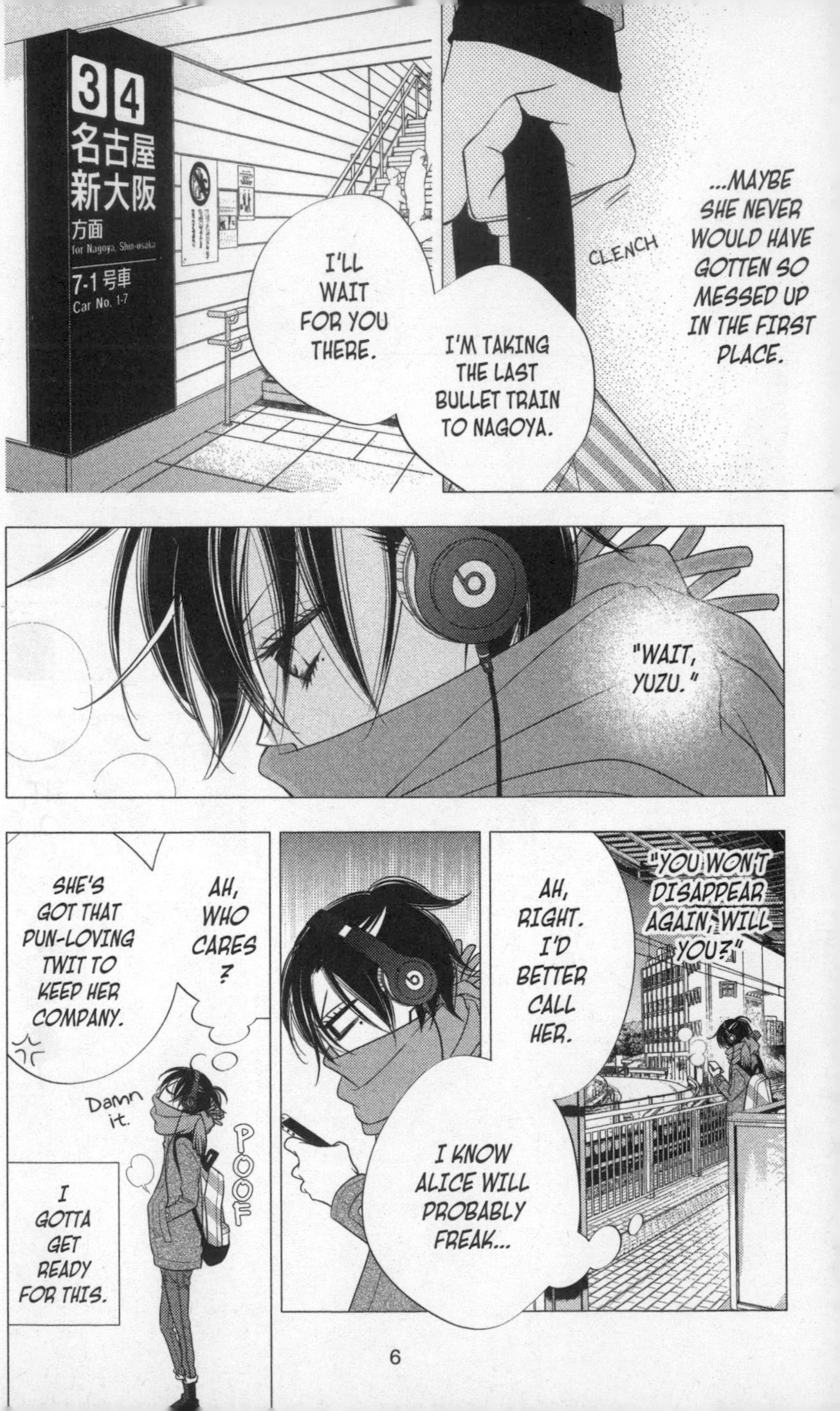
CLENCH
...MAYBE SHE NEVER WOULD HAVE GOTTEN SO MESSED UP IN THE FIRST PLACE.
3 4
名古屋 新大阪 方面
for Nagoya, Shin-osaka
7-1 号車
Car No. 1-7
I'M TAKING THE LAST BULLET TRAIN TO NAGOYA.
I'LL WAIT FOR YOU THERE.
"WAIT, YUZU."
"YOU WON'T DISAPPEAR AGAIN, WILL YOU?"
AH, RIGHT. I'D BETTER CALL HER.
I KNOW ALICE WILL PROBABLY FREAK...
AH, WHO CARES?
SHE'S GOT THAT PUN-LOVING TWIT TO KEEP HER COMPANY.
Damn it.
POOF
I GOTTA GET READY FOR THIS.

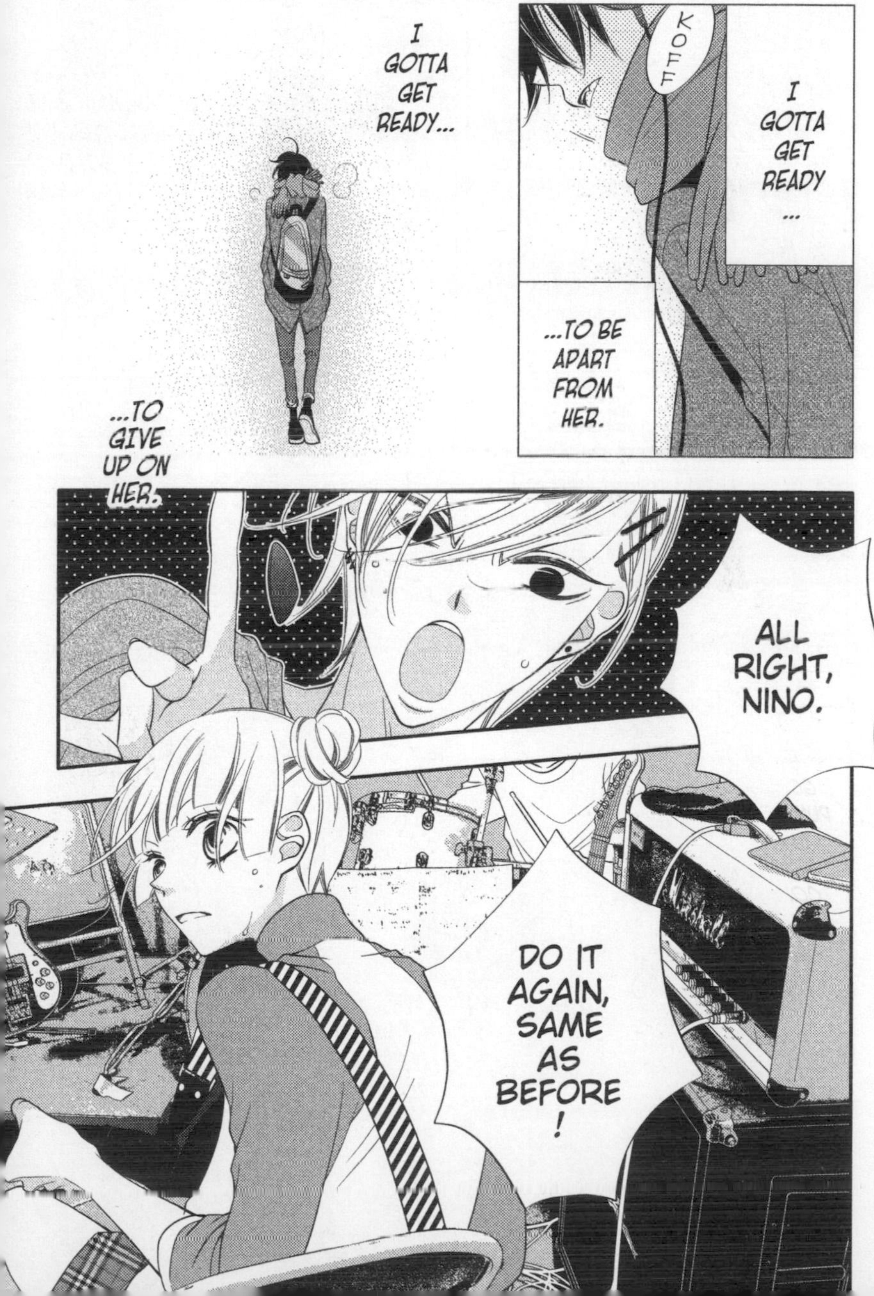
KOFF
I GOTTA GET READY ...
...TO BE APART FROM HER.
I GOTTA GET READY...
...TO GIVE UP ON HER.
ALL RIGHT, NINO.
DO IT AGAIN, SAME AS BEFORE!

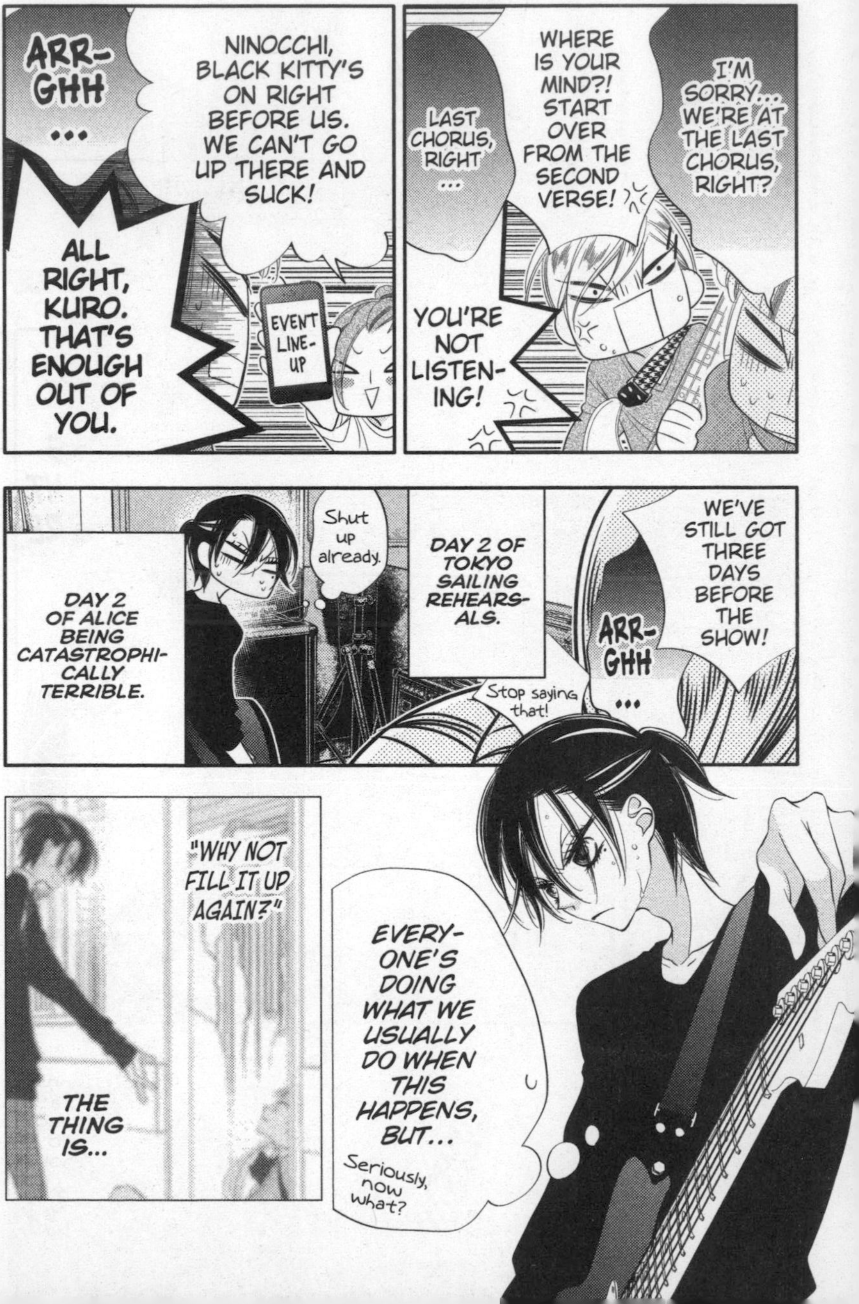
I'M SORRY... WE'RE AT THE LAST CHORUS, RIGHT?
WHERE IS YOUR MIND?! START OVER FROM THE SECOND VERSE!
LAST CHORUS, RIGHT...
YOU'RE NOT LISTENING!
NINOCCHI, BLACK KITTY'S ON RIGHT BEFORE US. WE CAN'T GO UP THERE AND SUCK!
EVENT LINE-UP
ARR-GHH...
ALL RIGHT, KURO. THAT'S ENOUGH OUT OF YOU.
WE'VE STILL GOT THREE DAYS BEFORE THE SHOW!
ARR-GHH...
Stop saying that!
DAY 2 OF TOKYO SAILING REHEARSALS.
Shut up already.
DAY 2 OF ALICE BEING CATASTROPHICALLY TERRIBLE.
EVERYONE'S DOING WHAT WE USUALLY DO WHEN THIS HAPPENS, BUT...
Seriously, now what?
"WHY NOT FILL IT UP AGAIN?"
THE THING IS...

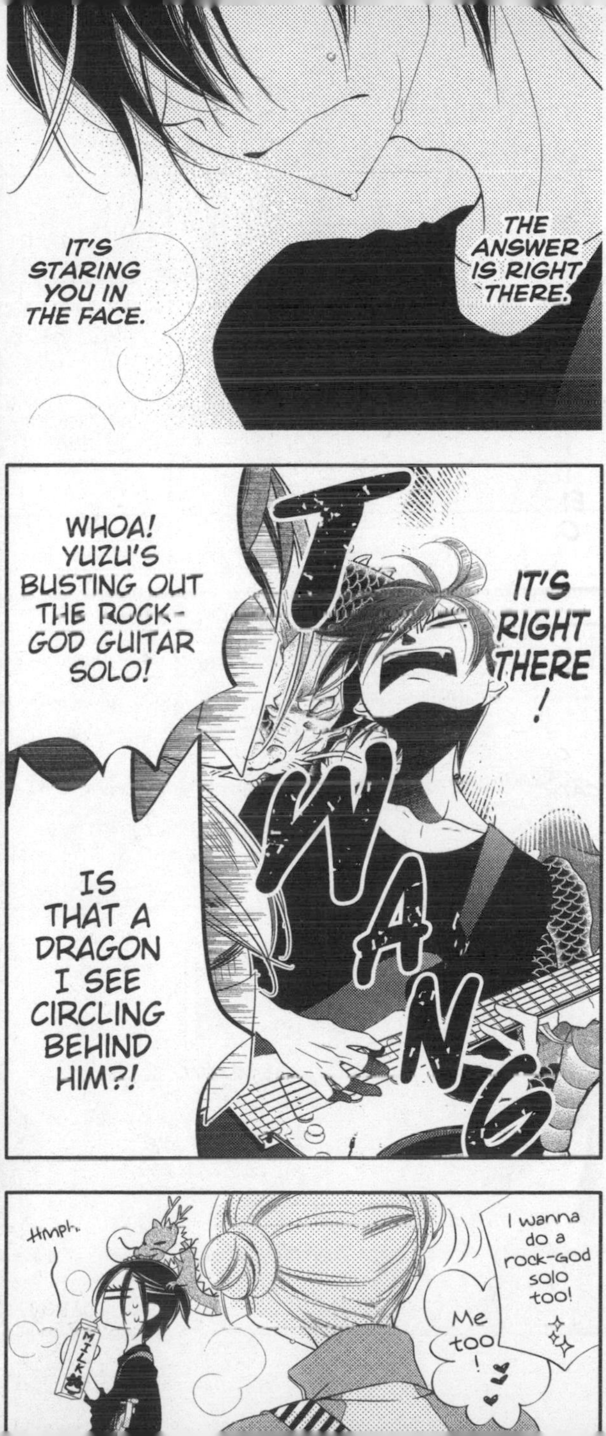
THE ANSWER IS RIGHT THERE.
IT'S STARING YOU IN THE FACE.
IT'S RIGHT THERE!
WHOA! YUZU'S BUSTING OUT THE ROCK-GOD GUITAR SOLO!
IS THAT A DRAGON I SEE CIRCLING BEHIND HIM?!
JWANG
I wanna do a rock-God solo too!
Me too!
Hmph.
MILK

1

Hello, and welcome! I'm Ryoko Fukuyama. Thank you so much for picking up a copy of *Anonymous Noise* volume 13! Once again, I must apologize for not writing out my author's note by hand—I plan to resume doing that in the next volume. Have you finally come to miss my chicken scratches?

HEH HEH HEH

I decided to start the third series of covers once again with Nino. And this time, with a white background! I've been wanting to go white for a long time, so I'm happy I finally could.
I haven't decided if I'll keep it for volume 14, though. Hmmm...
Anyway, I hope you enjoy volume 13 of *Anonymous Noise*!

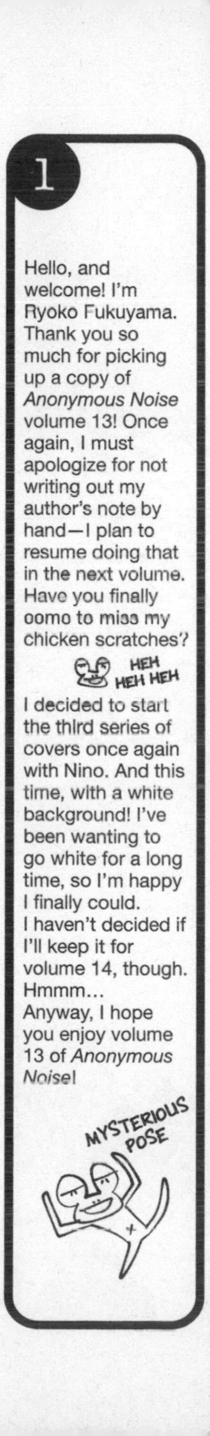
MYSTERIOUS POSE

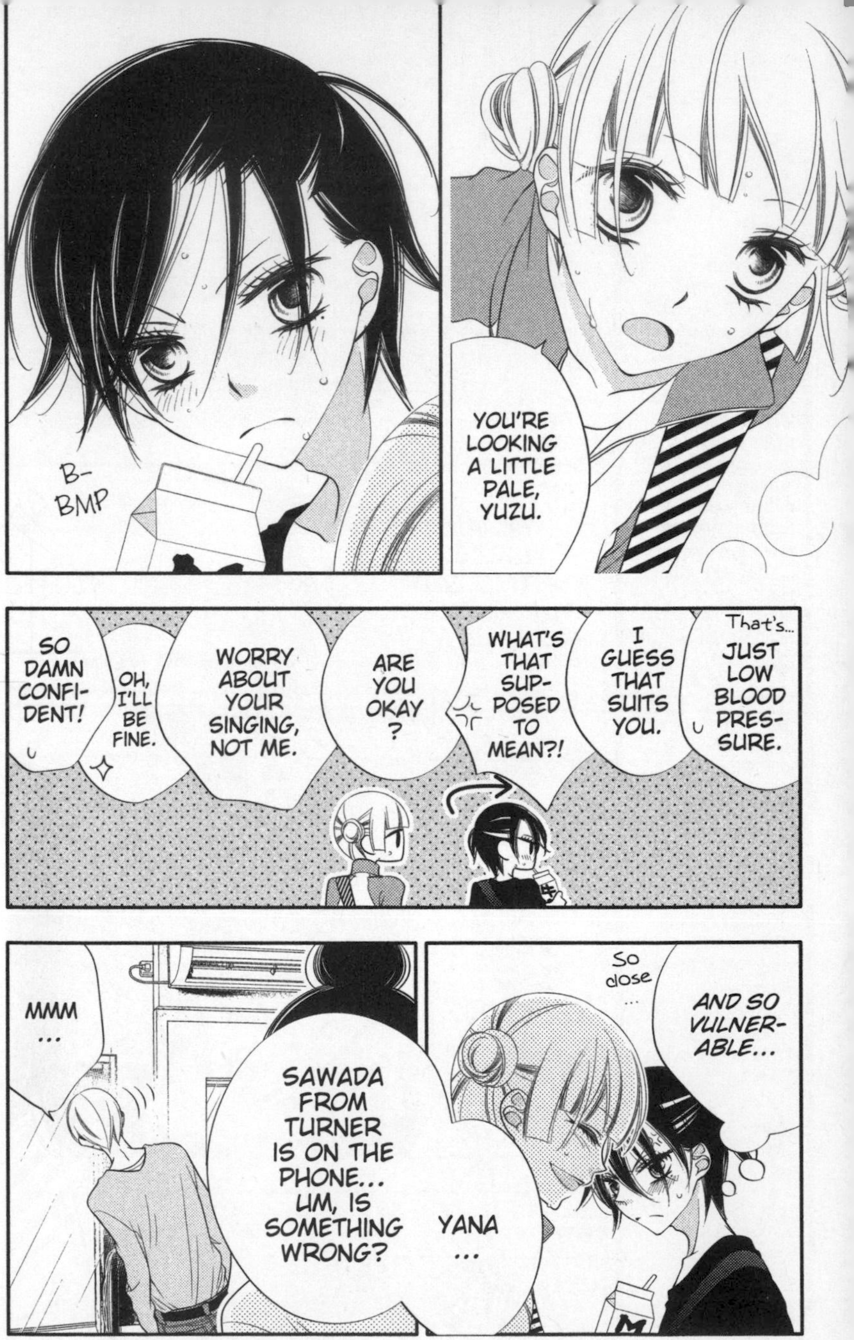
YOU'RE LOOKING A LITTLE PALE, YUZU.
B-BMP
That's... JUST LOW BLOOD PRESSURE.
I GUESS THAT SUITS YOU.
WHAT'S THAT SUP-POSED TO MEAN?!
ARE YOU OKAY?
WORRY ABOUT YOUR SINGING, NOT ME.
OH, I'LL BE FINE.
SO DAMN CONFI-DENT!
So close...
AND SO VULNER-ABLE...
YANA...
SAWADA FROM TURNER IS ON THE PHONE... UM, IS SOMETHING WRONG?
MMM...

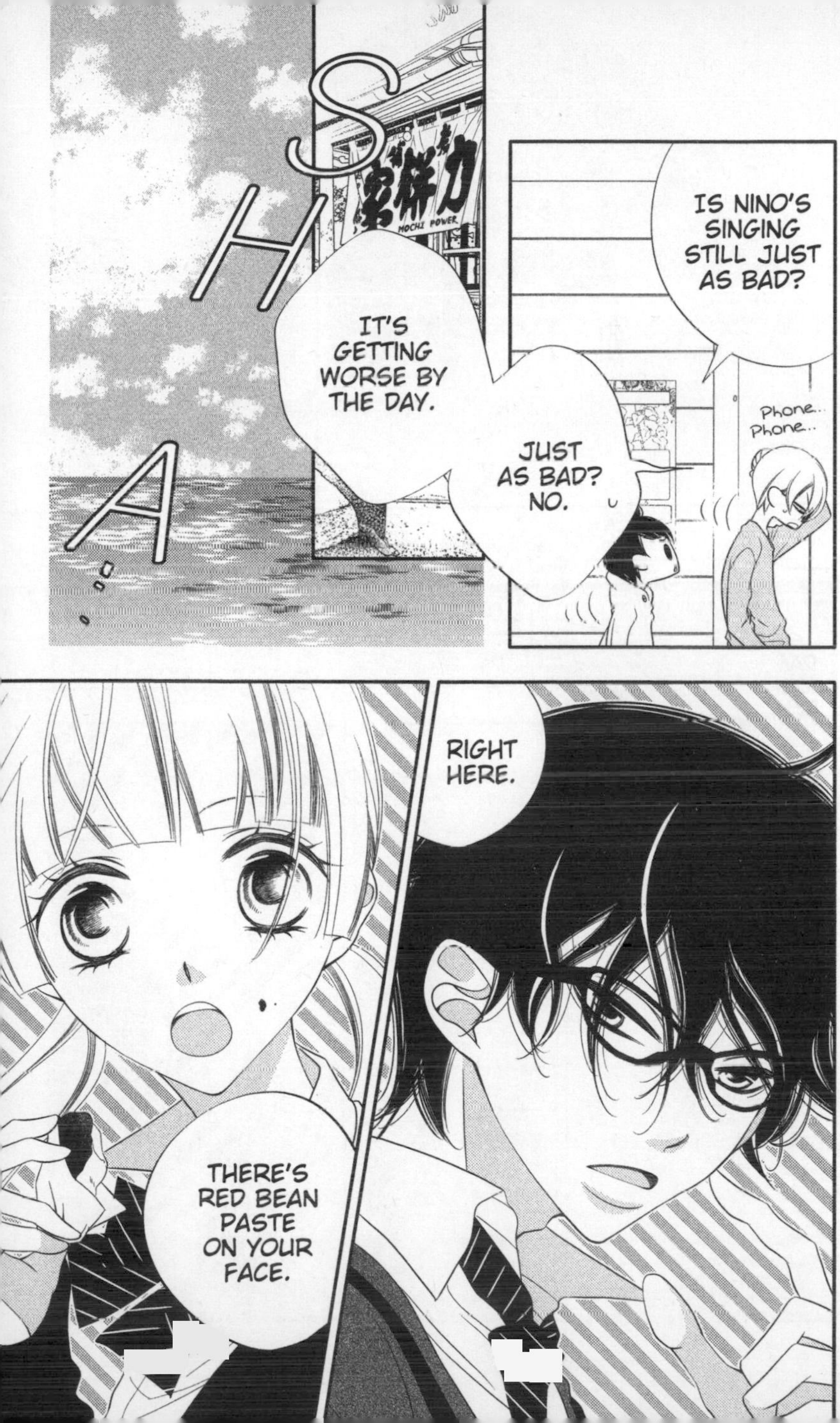
IS NINO'S SINGING STILL JUST AS BAD?
Phone.. Phone..
JUST AS BAD? NO.
SHA
MOCHI POWER
IT'S GETTING WORSE BY THE DAY.
RIGHT HERE.
THERE'S RED BEAN PASTE ON YOUR FACE.

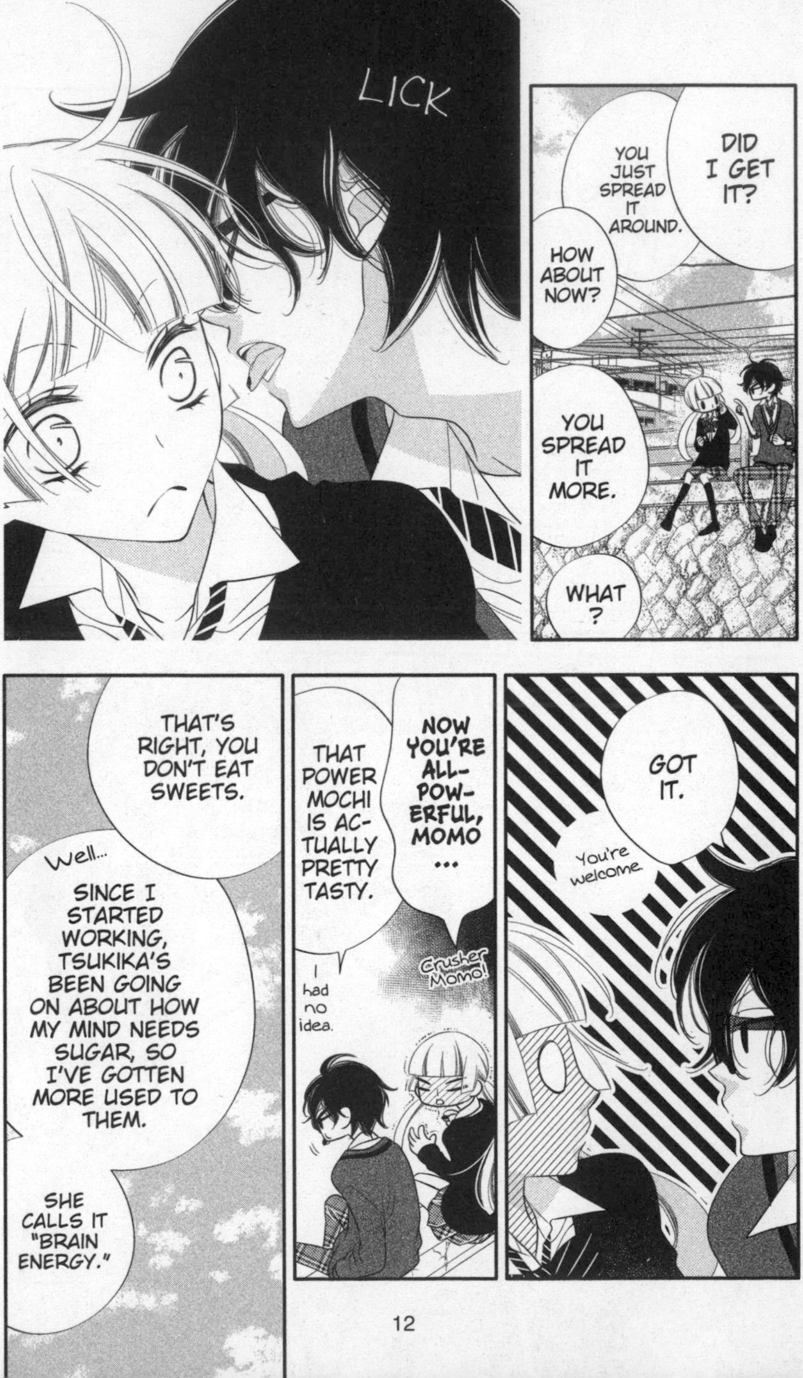
DID I GET IT?
YOU JUST SPREAD IT AROUND.
HOW ABOUT NOW?
YOU SPREAD IT MORE.
WHAT?
LICK
GOT IT.
You're welcome.
NOW YOU'RE ALL-POWERFUL, MOMO...
Crusher Momo!
THAT POWER MOCHI IS ACTUALLY PRETTY TASTY.
I had no idea.
THAT'S RIGHT, YOU DON'T EAT SWEETS.
Well...
SINCE I STARTED WORKING, TSUKIKA'S BEEN GOING ON ABOUT HOW MY MIND NEEDS SUGAR, SO I'VE GOTTEN MORE USED TO THEM.
SHE CALLS IT "BRAIN ENERGY."

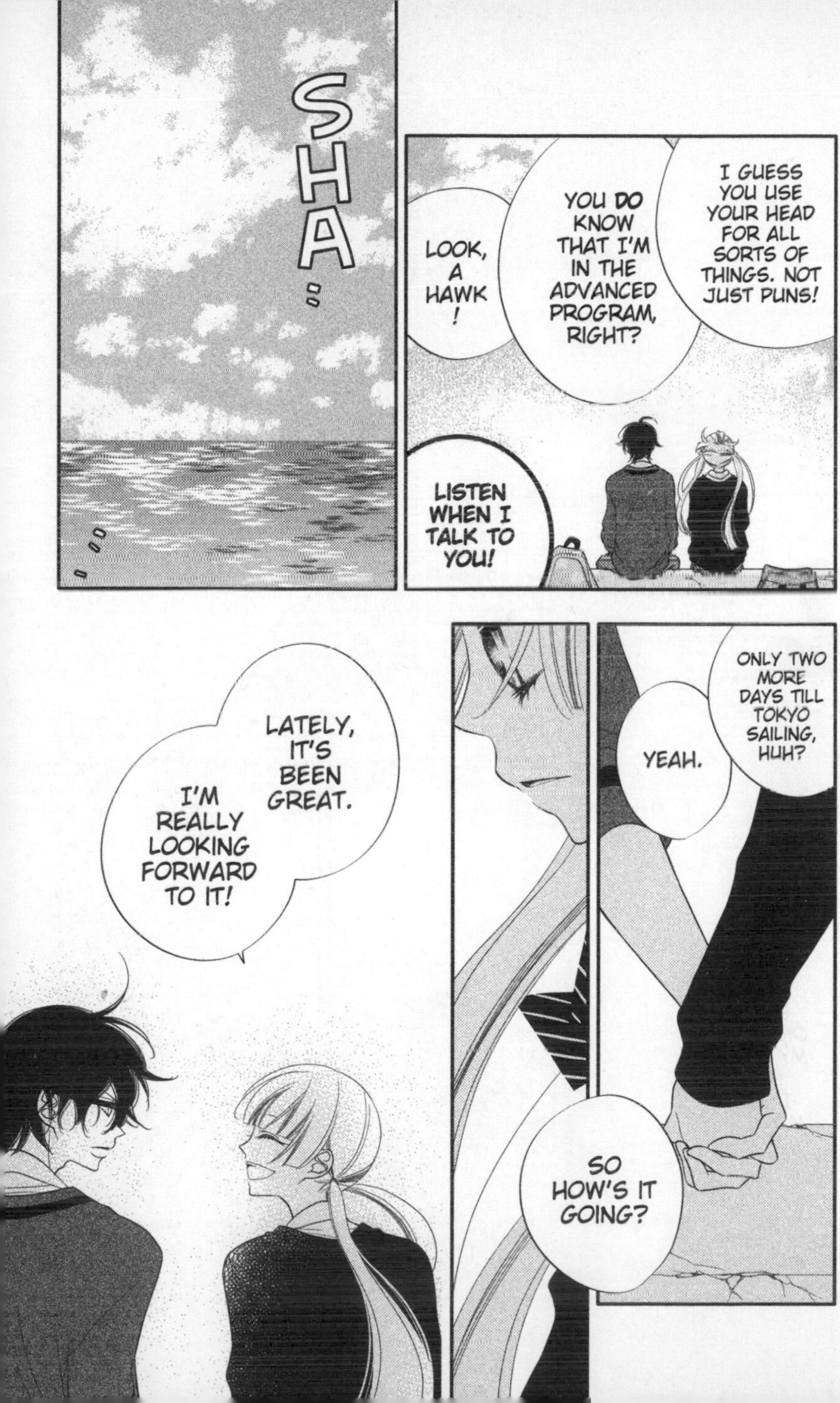
I GUESS YOU USE YOUR HEAD FOR ALL SORTS OF THINGS. NOT JUST PUNS!
YOU DO KNOW THAT I'M IN THE ADVANCED PROGRAM, RIGHT?
LOOK, A HAWK!
LISTEN WHEN I TALK TO YOU!
SHA...
ONLY TWO MORE DAYS TILL TOKYO SAILING, HUH?
YEAH.
SO HOW'S IT GOING?
LATELY, IT'S BEEN GREAT.
I'M REALLY LOOKING FORWARD TO IT!

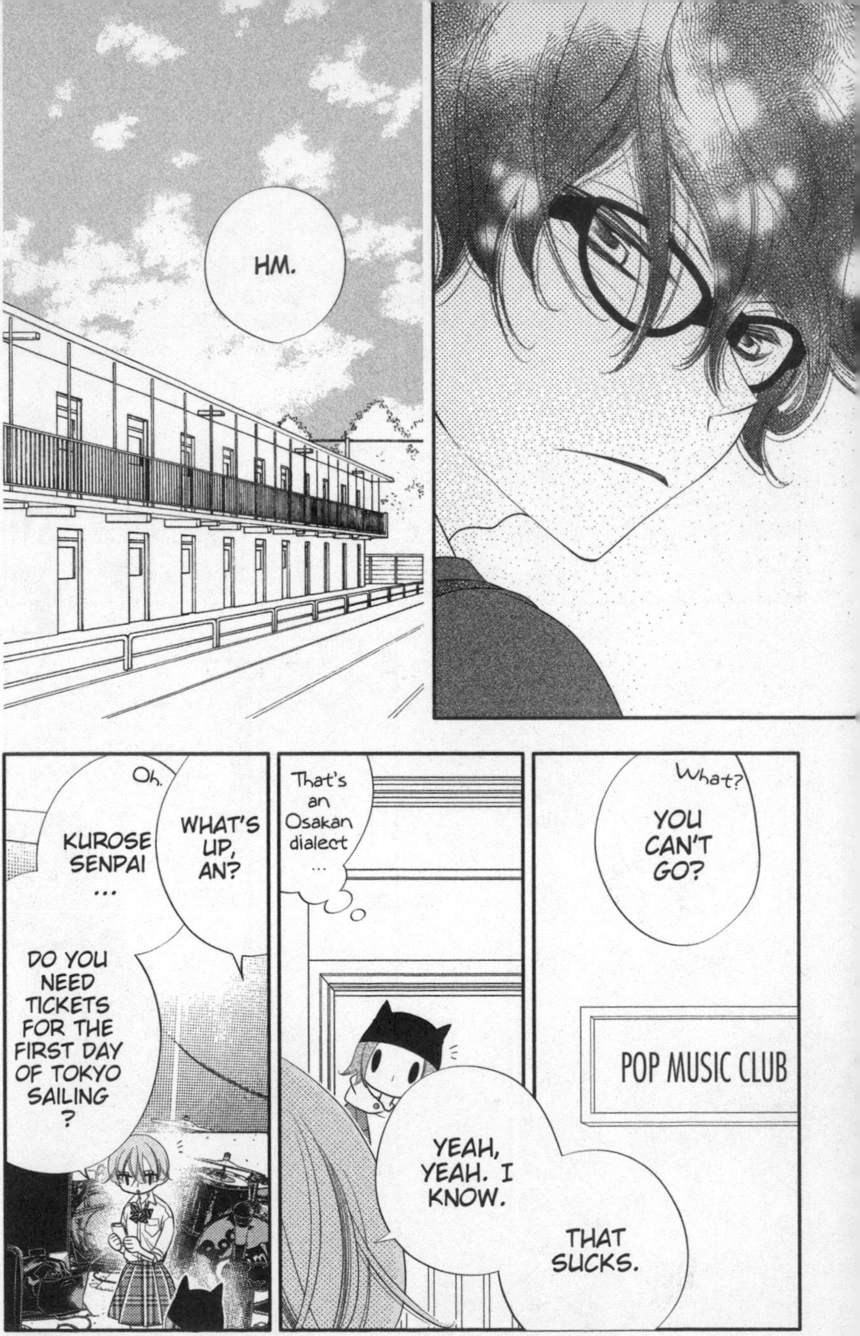
HM.
What?
YOU CAN'T GO?
POP MUSIC CLUB
That's an Osakan dialect ...
YEAH, YEAH. I KNOW.
THAT SUCKS.
Oh.
WHAT'S UP, AN?
KUROSE SENPAI ...
DO YOU NEED TICKETS FOR THE FIRST DAY OF TOKYO SAILING?

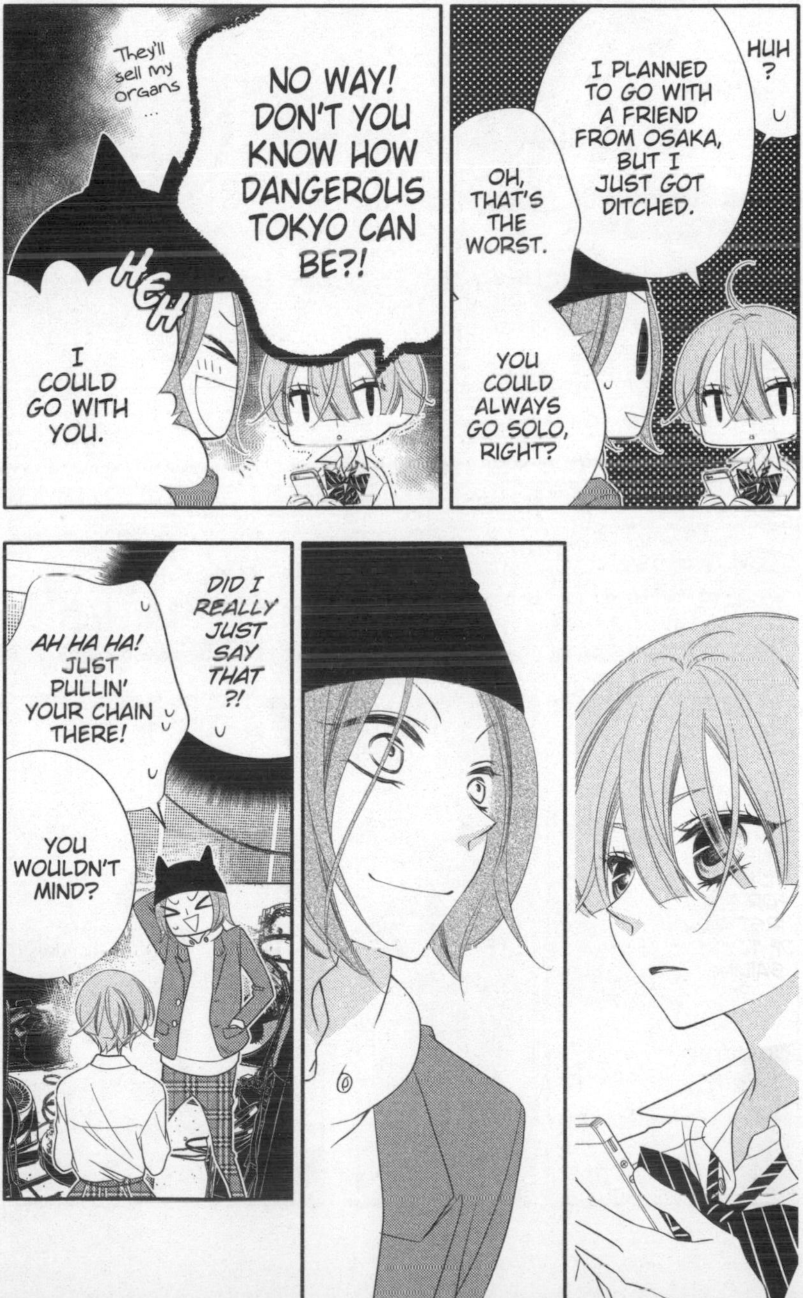
HUH?
I PLANNED TO GO WITH A FRIEND FROM OSAKA, BUT I JUST GOT DITCHED.
OH, THAT'S THE WORST.
YOU COULD ALWAYS GO SOLO, RIGHT?
NO WAY! DON'T YOU KNOW HOW DANGEROUS TOKYO CAN BE?!
They'll sell my organs ...
HEH
I COULD GO WITH YOU.
DID I REALLY JUST SAY THAT?!
AH HA HA! JUST PULLIN' YOUR CHAIN THERE!
YOU WOULDN'T MIND?

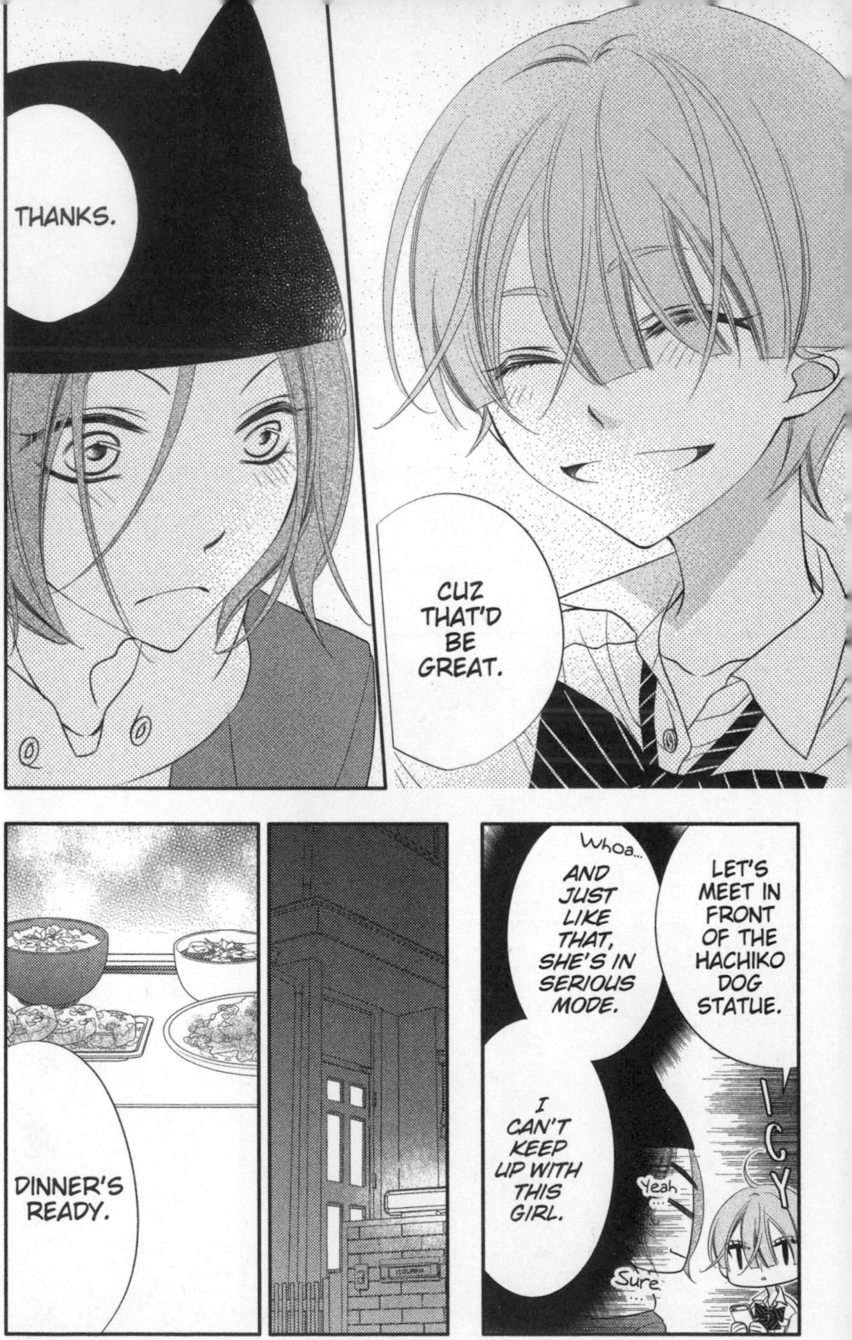
CUZ THAT'D BE GREAT.
THANKS.
LET'S MEET IN FRONT OF THE HACHIKO DOG STATUE.
Whoa...
AND JUST LIKE THAT, SHE'S IN SERIOUS MODE.
ICY
I CAN'T KEEP UP WITH THIS GIRL.
Yeah...
Sure...
DINNER'S READY.

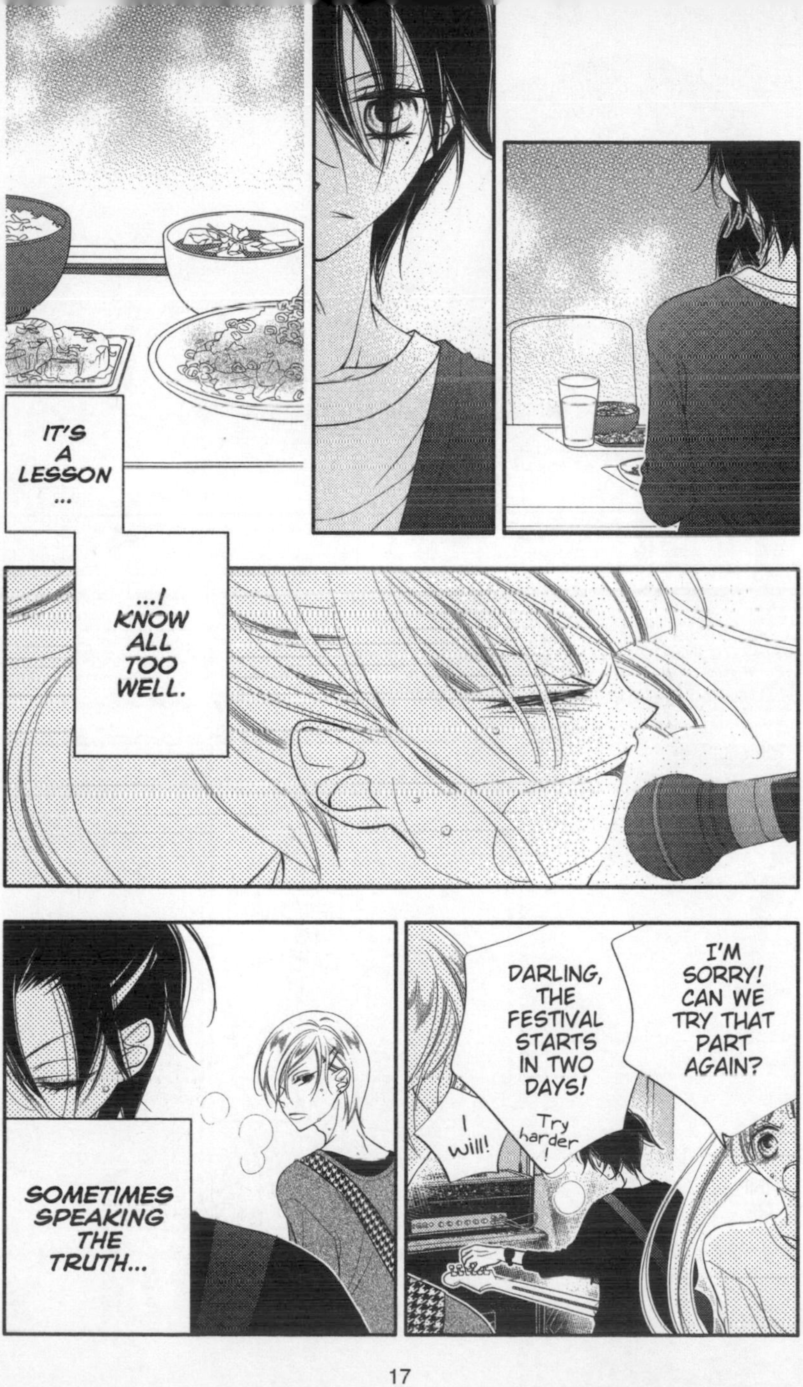
IT'S A LESSON...
...I KNOW ALL TOO WELL.
I'M SORRY! CAN WE TRY THAT PART AGAIN?
DARLING, THE FESTIVAL STARTS IN TWO DAYS!
Try harder!
I will!
SOMETIMES SPEAKING THE TRUTH...

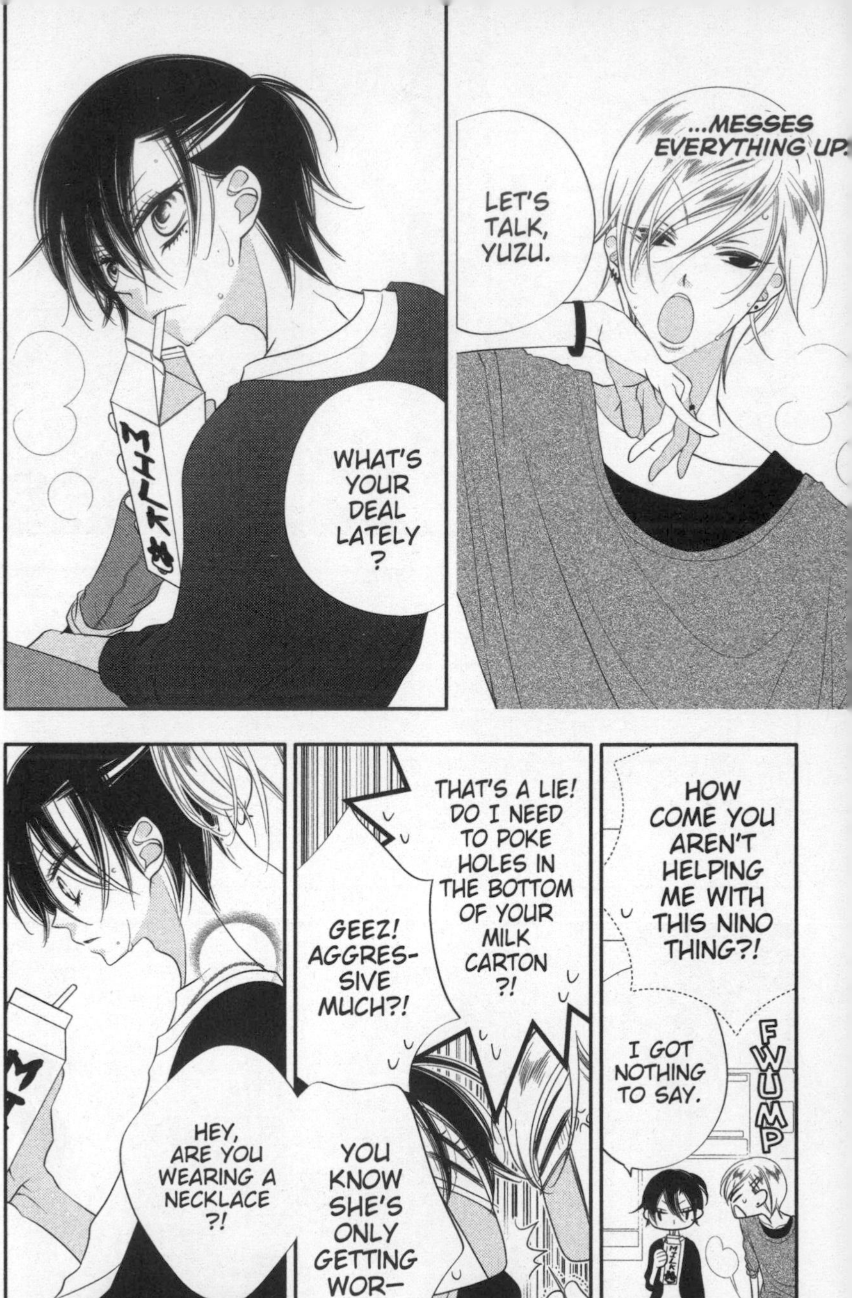
...MESSES EVERYTHING UP.
LET'S TALK, YUZU.
MILK
WHAT'S YOUR DEAL LATELY?
HOW COME YOU AREN'T HELPING ME WITH THIS NINO THING?!
FWUMP
I GOT NOTHING TO SAY.
THAT'S A LIE! DO I NEED TO POKE HOLES IN THE BOTTOM OF YOUR MILK CARTON?!
GEEZ! AGGRES-SIVE MUCH?!
YOU KNOW SHE'S ONLY GETTING WOR—
HEY, ARE YOU WEARING A NECKLACE?!

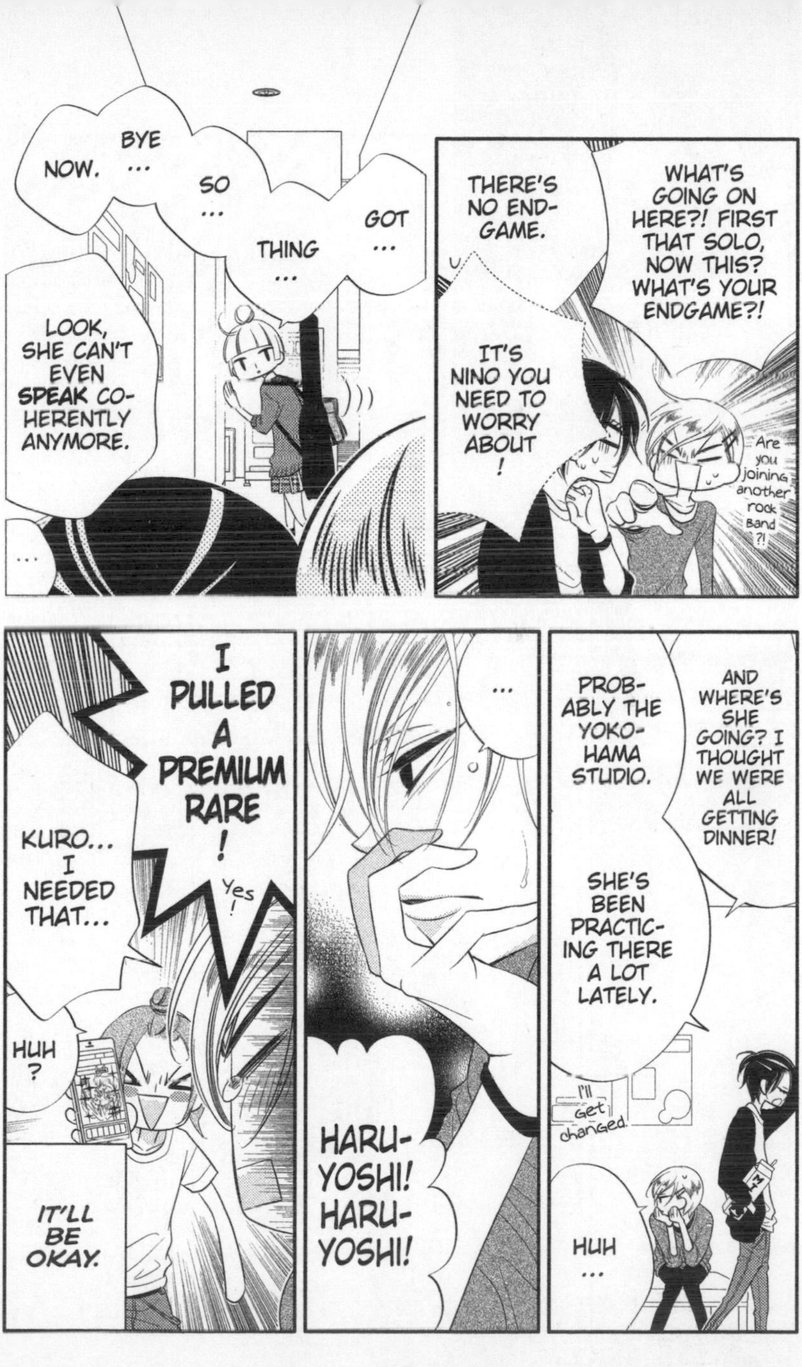
WHAT'S GOING ON HERE?! FIRST THAT SOLO, NOW THIS? WHAT'S YOUR ENDGAME?!
Are you joining another rock band?!
THERE'S NO END-GAME.
IT'S NINO YOU NEED TO WORRY ABOUT!
GOT ... THING ... SO ... BYE ... NOW.
LOOK, SHE CAN'T EVEN SPEAK CO-HERENTLY ANYMORE.
...
AND WHERE'S SHE GOING? I THOUGHT WE WERE ALL GETTING DINNER!
PROB-ABLY THE YOKO-HAMA STUDIO.
SHE'S BEEN PRACTIC-ING THERE A LOT LATELY.
I'll get changed.
HUH ...
...
HARU-YOSHI! HARU-YOSHI!
I PULLED A PREMIUM RARE!
Yes!
KURO... I NEEDED THAT...
HUH?
IT'LL BE OKAY.

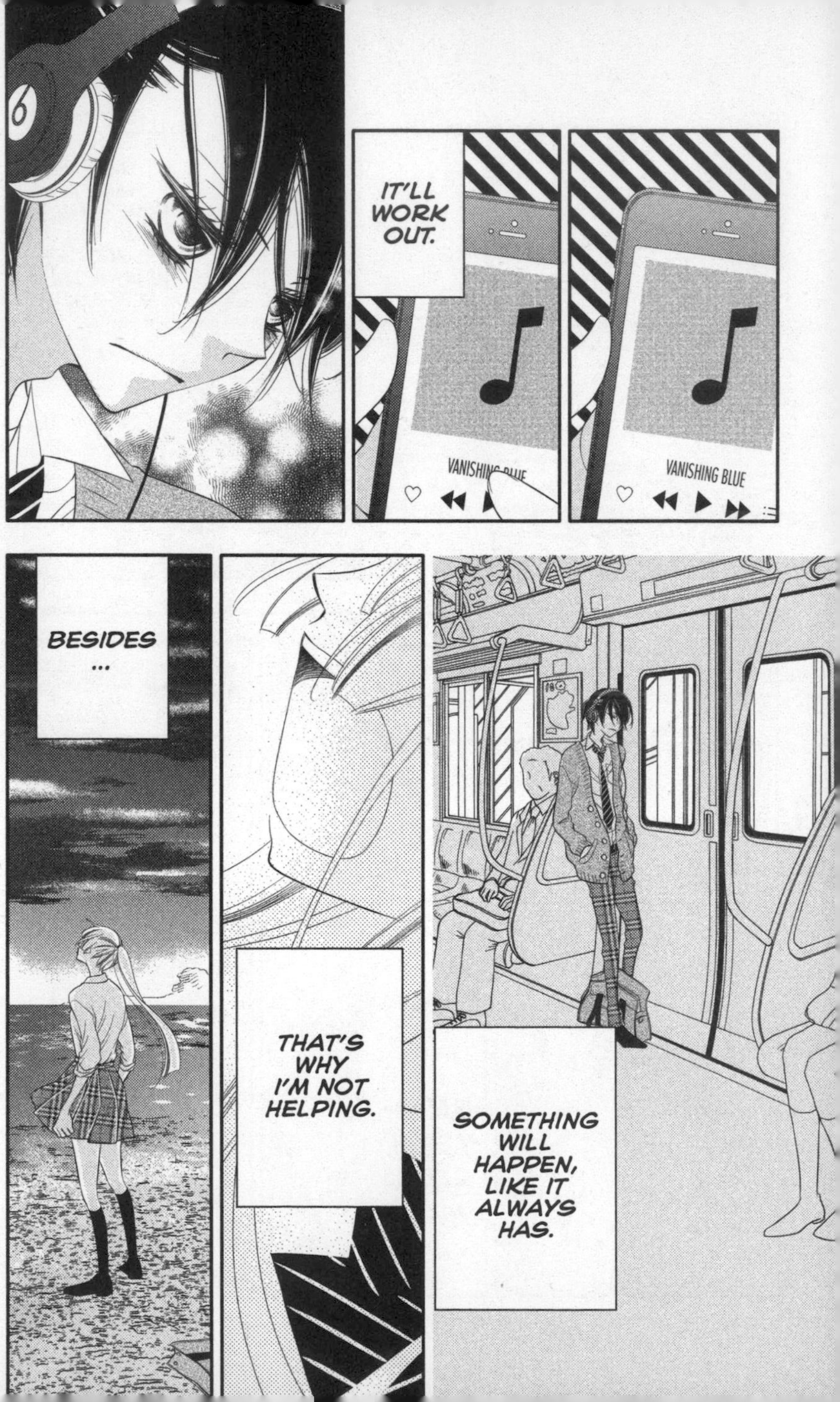
VANISHING BLUE
IT'LL WORK OUT.
SOMETHING WILL HAPPEN, LIKE IT ALWAYS HAS.
THAT'S WHY I'M NOT HELPING.
BESIDES ...

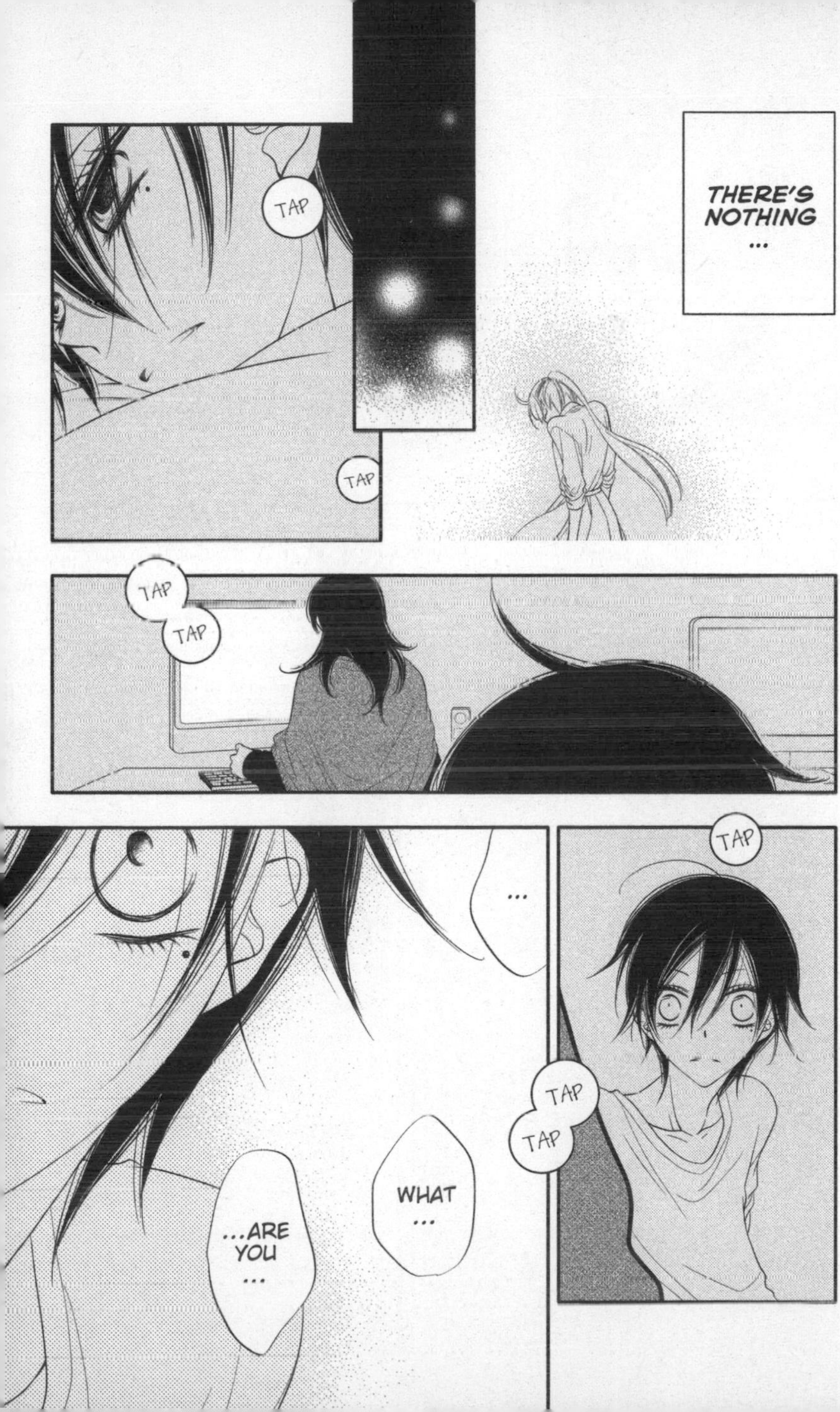
THERE'S NOTHING ...
TAP
TAP
TAP
TAP
TAP
TAP
TAP
...
WHAT ...
...ARE YOU ...

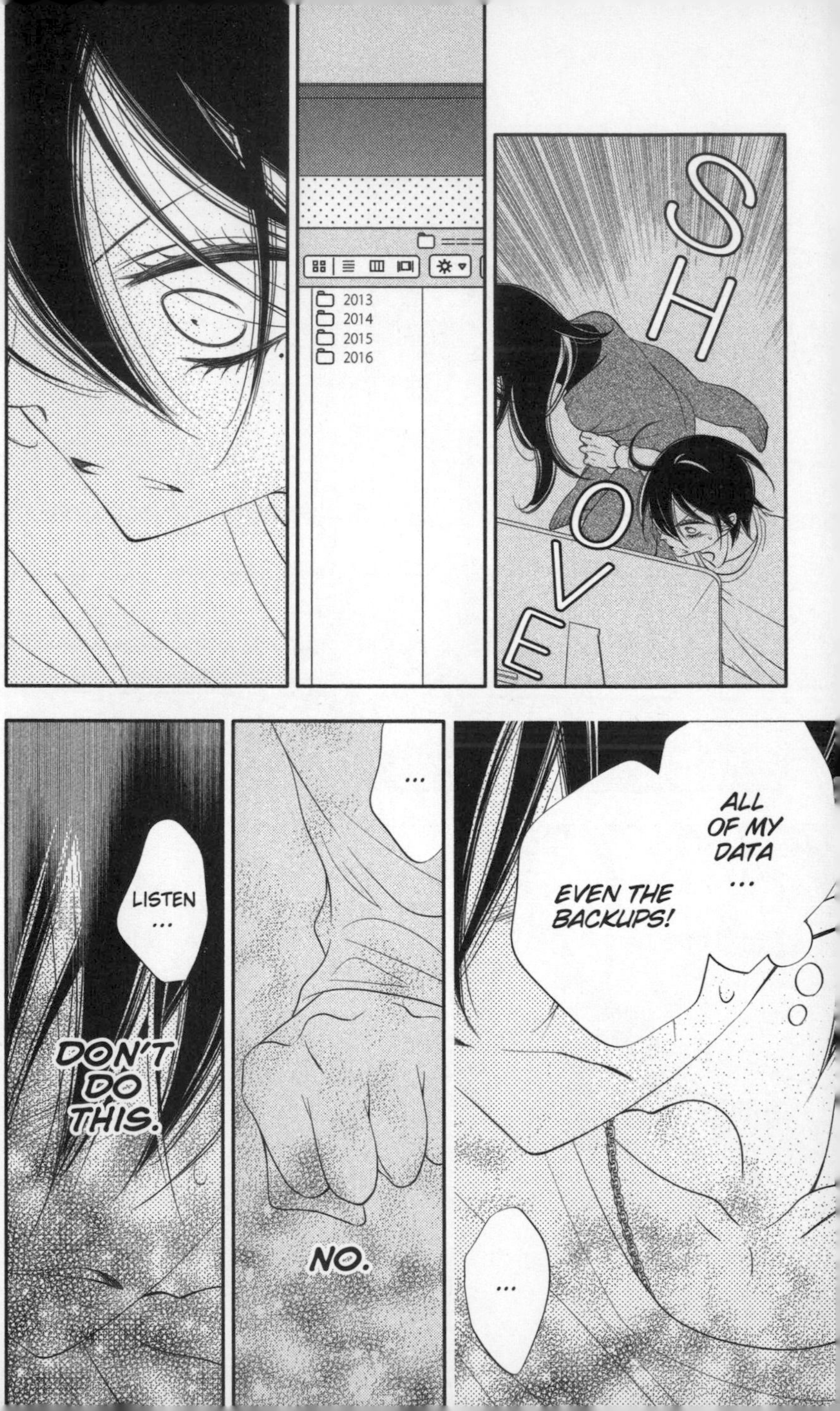
SHOVE
2013
2014
2015
2016
ALL OF MY DATA ...
EVEN THE BACKUPS!
...
...
NO.
LISTEN ...
DON'T DO THIS.

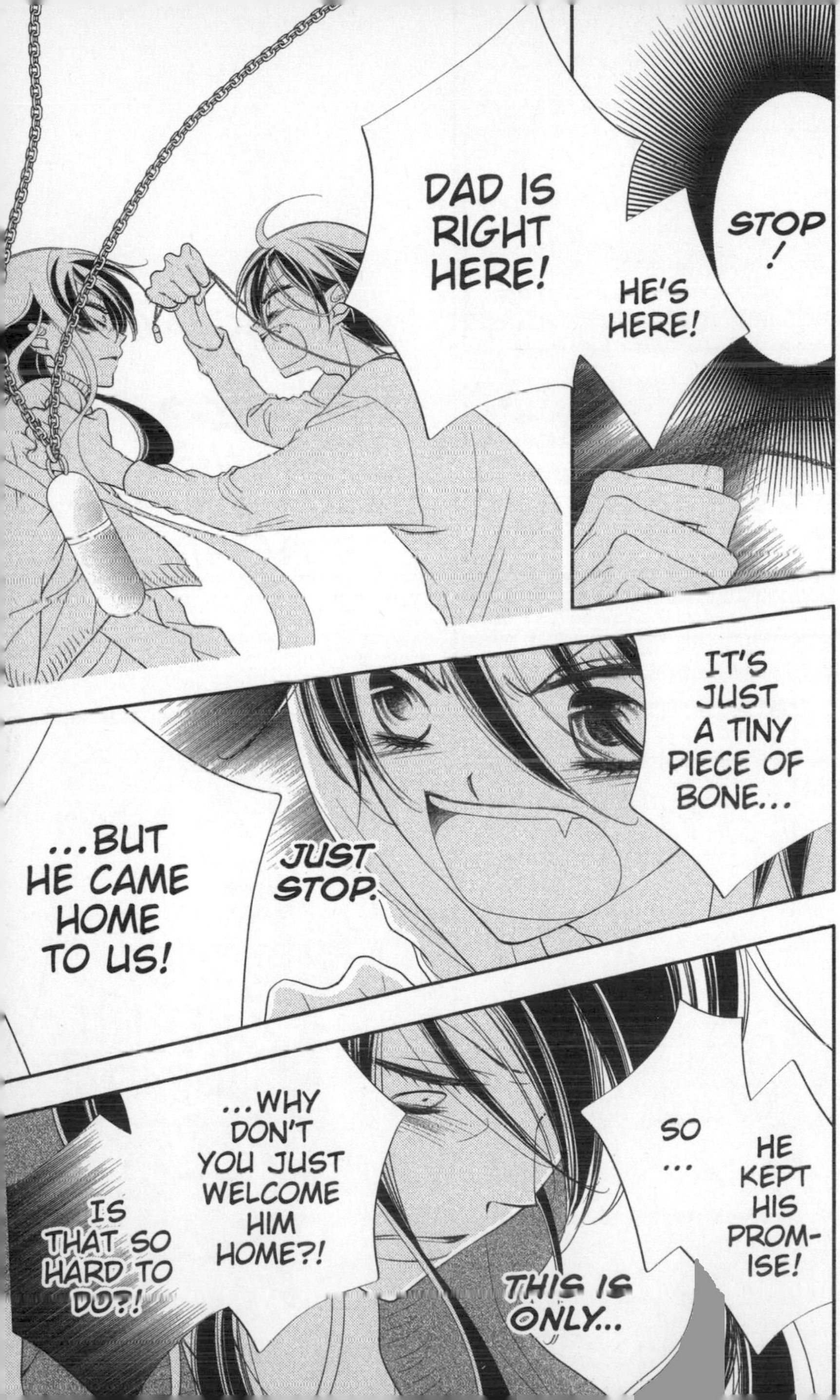
STOP!
HE'S HERE!
DAD IS RIGHT HERE!
IT'S JUST A TINY PIECE OF BONE...
JUST STOP.
...BUT HE CAME HOME TO US!
HE KEPT HIS PROMISE!
SO...
THIS IS ONLY...
...WHY DON'T YOU JUST WELCOME HIM HOME?!
IS THAT SO HARD TO DO?!

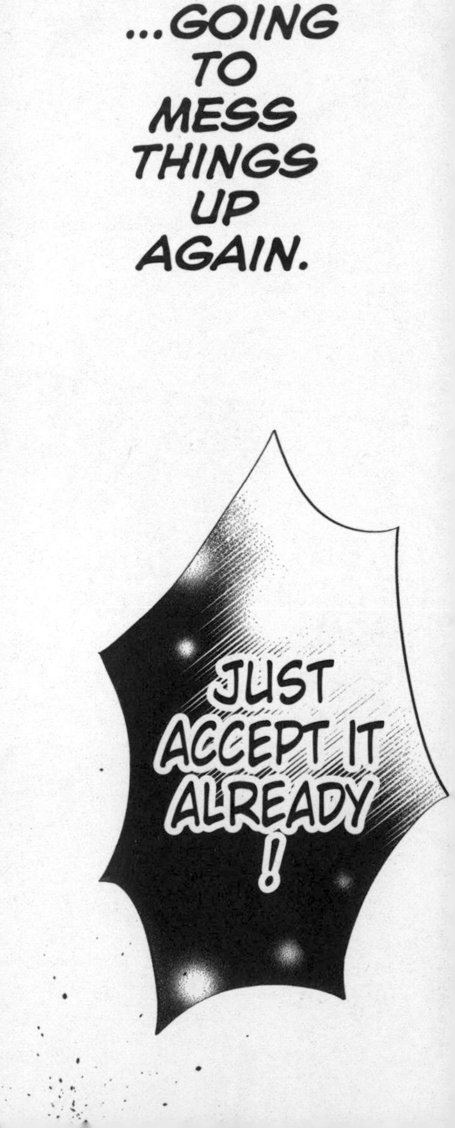
...GOING TO MESS THINGS UP AGAIN.
JUST ACCEPT IT ALREADY!
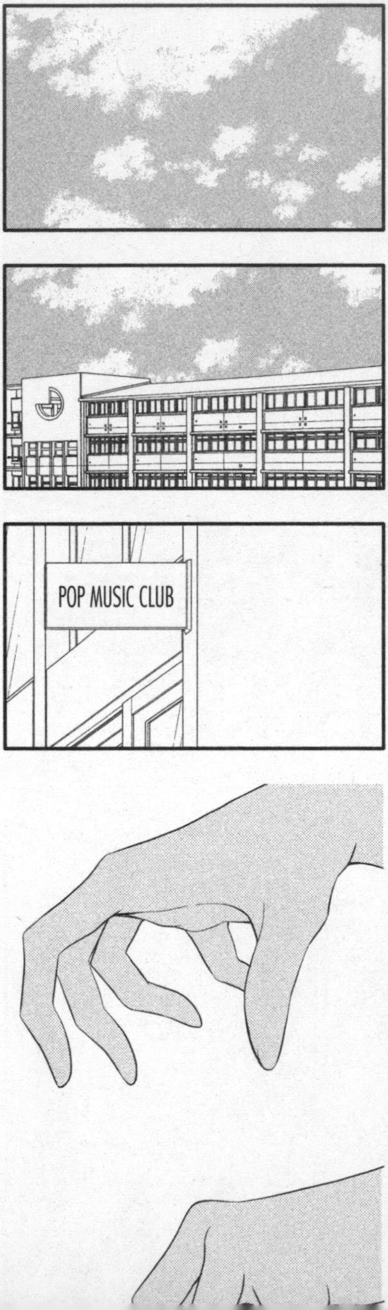
POP MUSIC CLUB

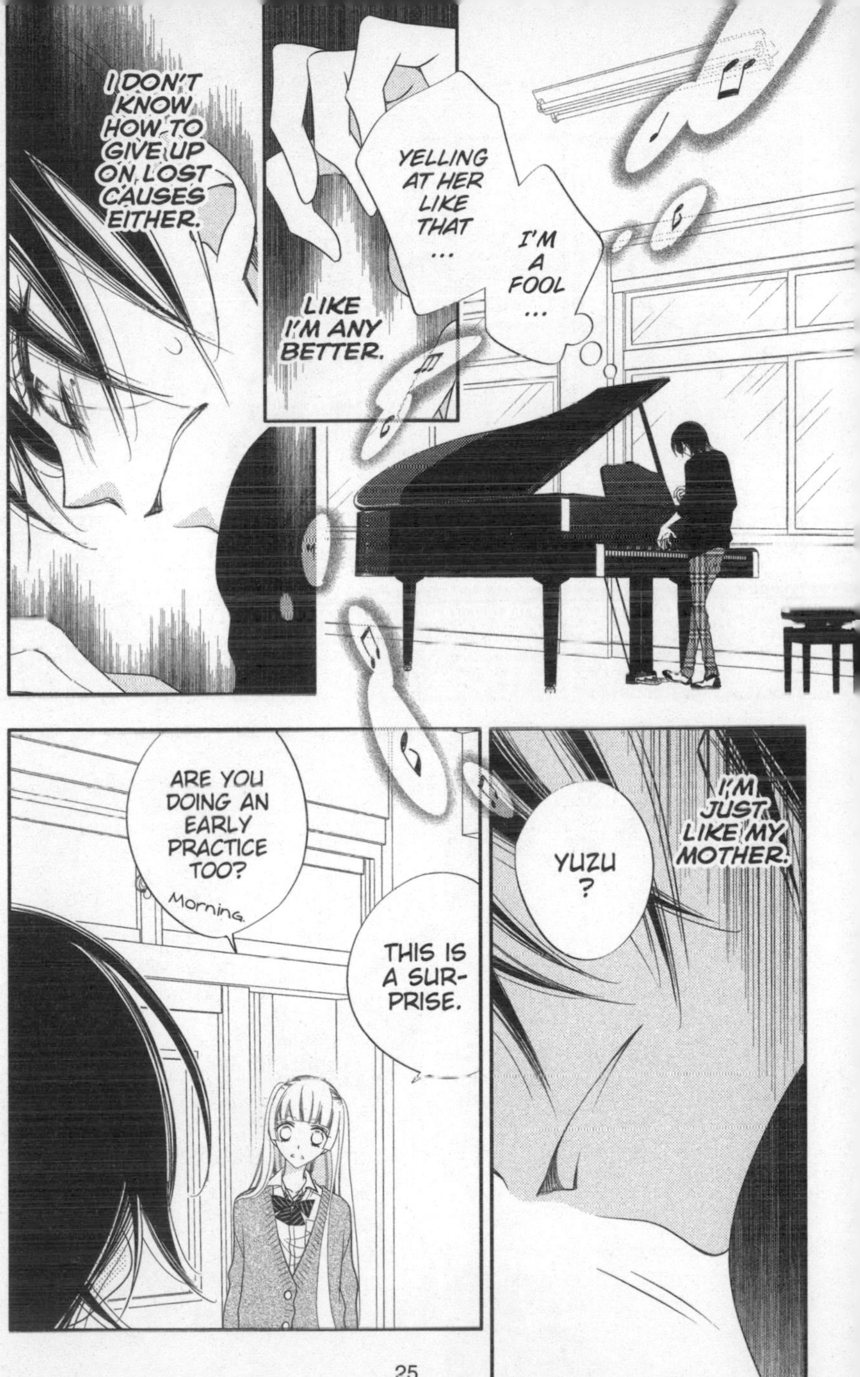
YELLING AT HER LIKE THAT ...
I'M A FOOL ...
LIKE I'M ANY BETTER.
I DON'T KNOW HOW TO GIVE UP ON LOST CAUSES EITHER.
I'M JUST LIKE MY MOTHER.
YUZU?
ARE YOU DOING AN EARLY PRACTICE TOO?
Morning.
THIS IS A SURPRISE.

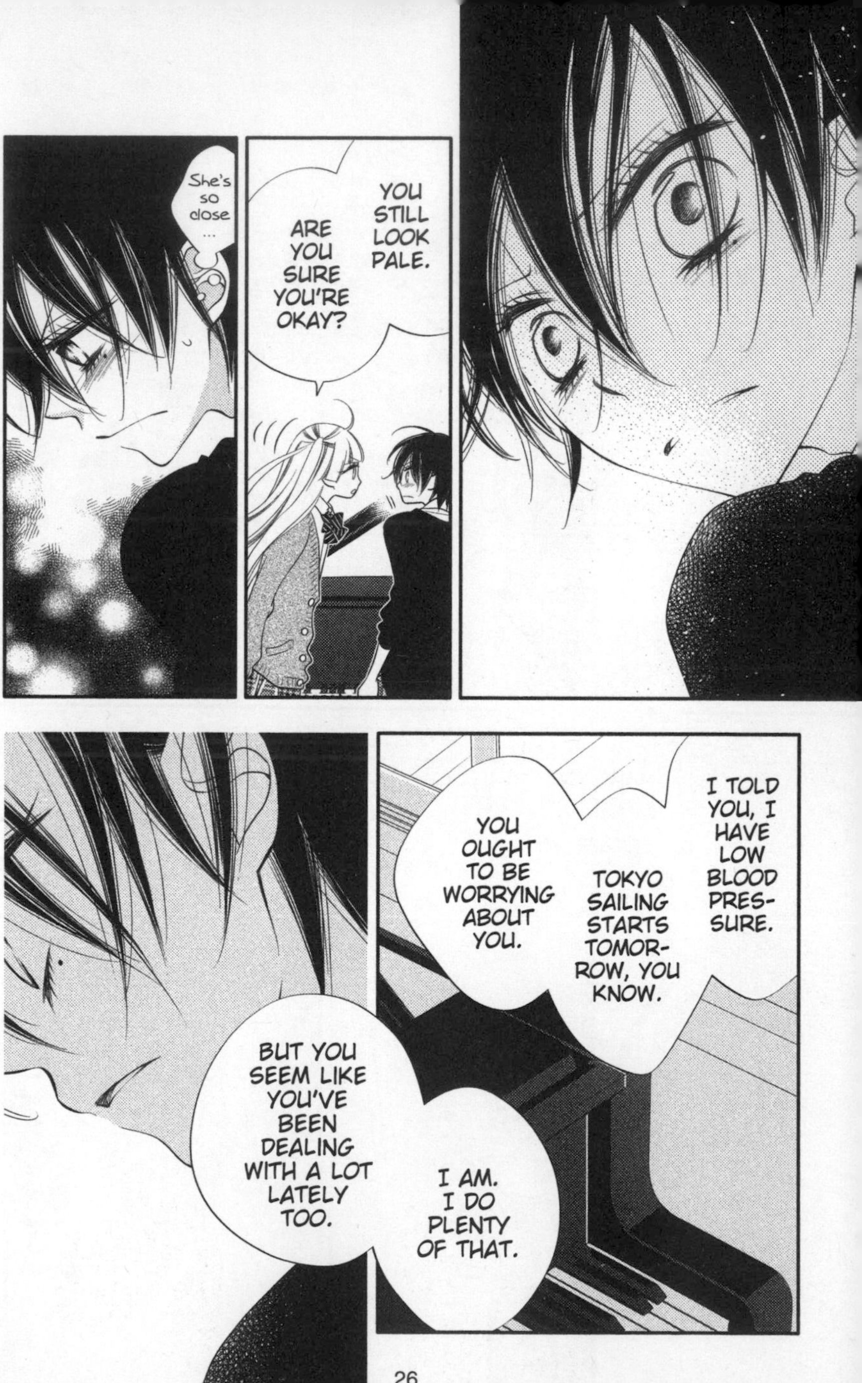
YOU STILL LOOK PALE.
ARE YOU SURE YOU'RE OKAY?
She's so close ...
I TOLD YOU, I HAVE LOW BLOOD PRES-SURE.
TOKYO SAILING STARTS TOMOR-ROW, YOU KNOW.
YOU OUGHT TO BE WORRYING ABOUT YOU.
BUT YOU SEEM LIKE YOU'VE BEEN DEALING WITH A LOT LATELY TOO.
I AM. I DO PLENTY OF THAT.

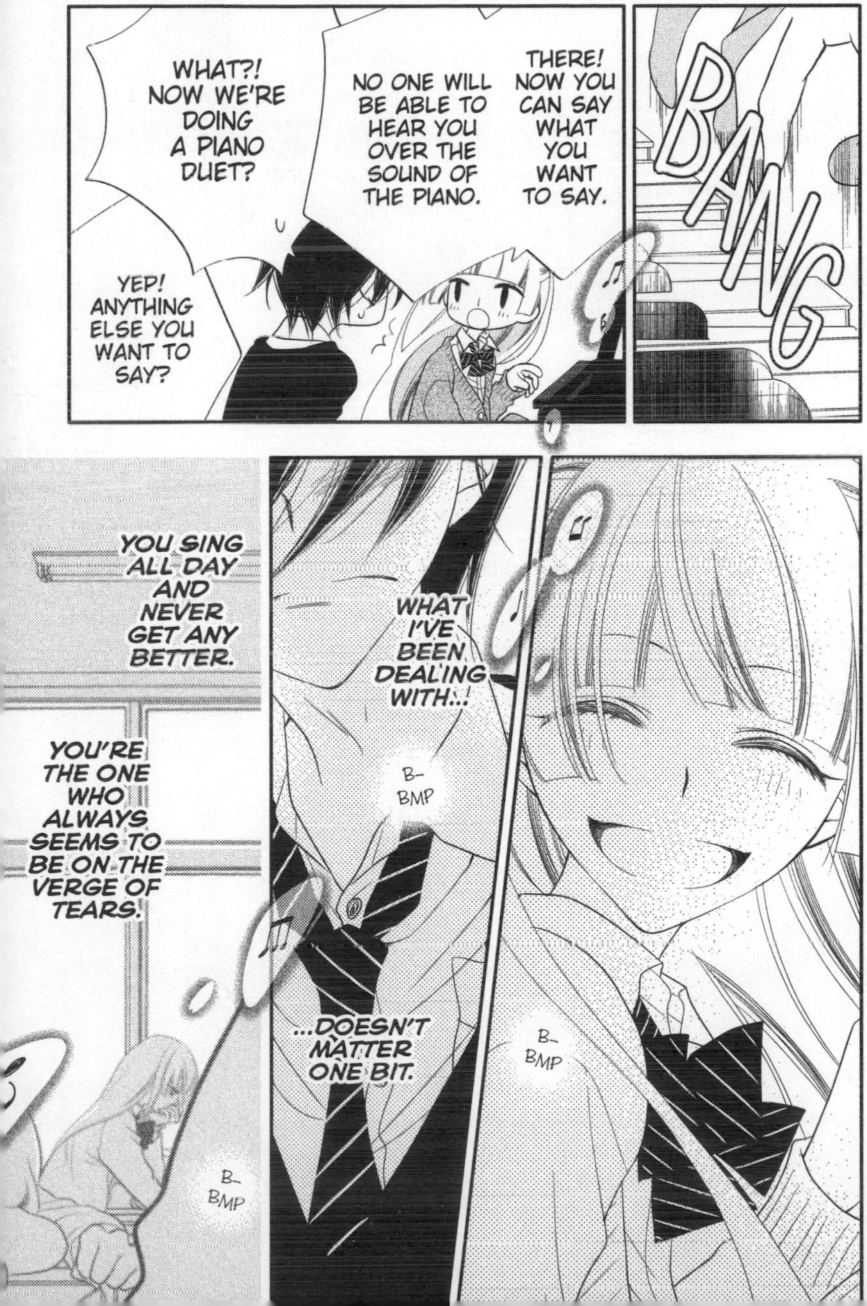
BANG
THERE! NOW YOU CAN SAY WHAT YOU WANT TO SAY.
NO ONE WILL BE ABLE TO HEAR YOU OVER THE SOUND OF THE PIANO.
WHAT?! NOW WE'RE DOING A PIANO DUET?
YEP! ANYTHING ELSE YOU WANT TO SAY?
B-BMP
WHAT I'VE BEEN DEALING WITH...
B-BMP
...DOESN'T MATTER ONE BIT.
YOU SING ALL DAY AND NEVER GET ANY BETTER.
YOU'RE THE ONE WHO ALWAYS SEEMS TO BE ON THE VERGE OF TEARS.
B-BMP

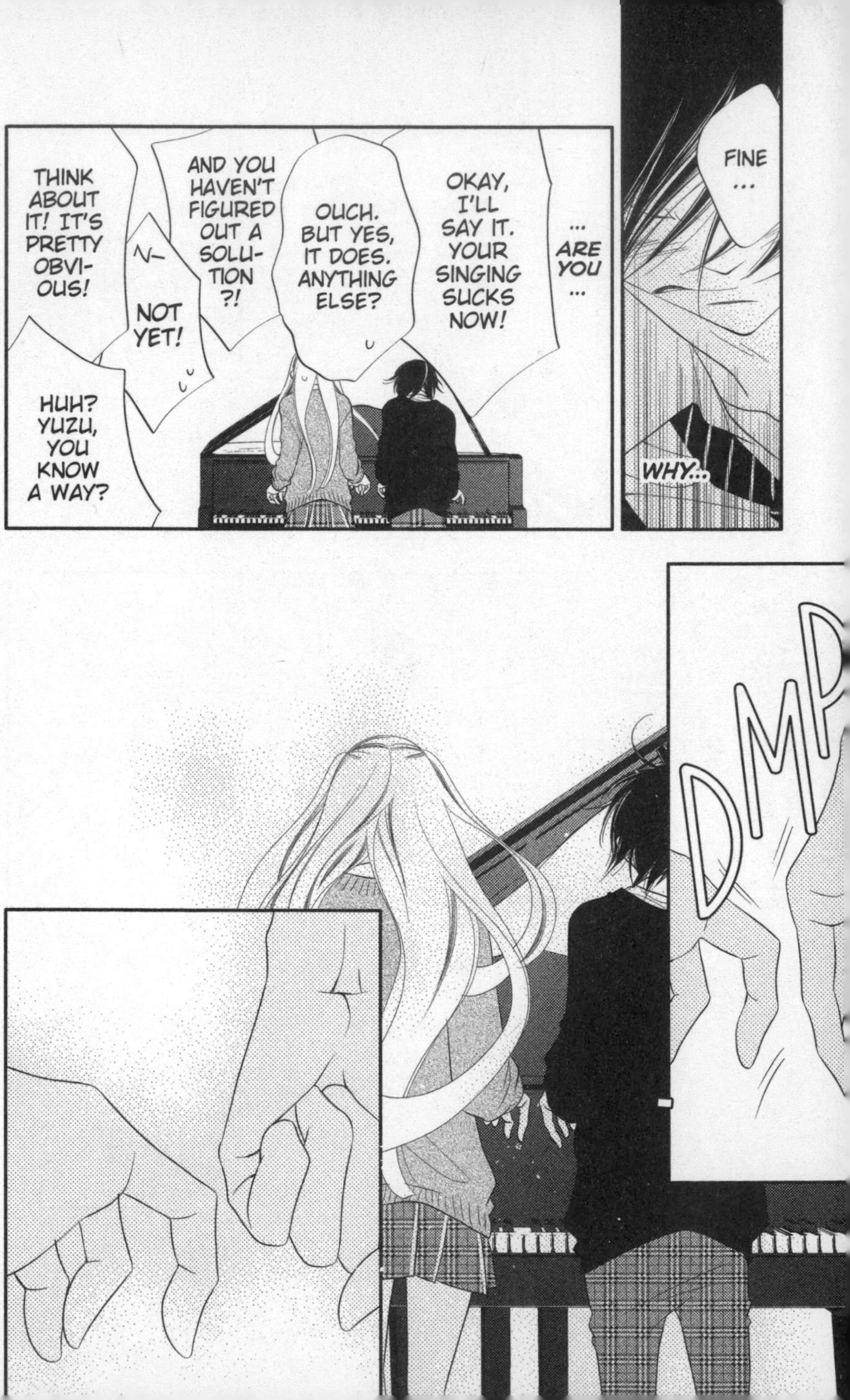
FINE ...
WHY...
... ARE YOU ...
OKAY, I'LL SAY IT. YOUR SINGING SUCKS NOW!
OUCH. BUT YES, IT DOES. ANYTHING ELSE?
AND YOU HAVEN'T FIGURED OUT A SOLUTION?!
N— NOT YET!
THINK ABOUT IT! IT'S PRETTY OBVIOUS!
HUH? YUZU, YOU KNOW A WAY?
DMP

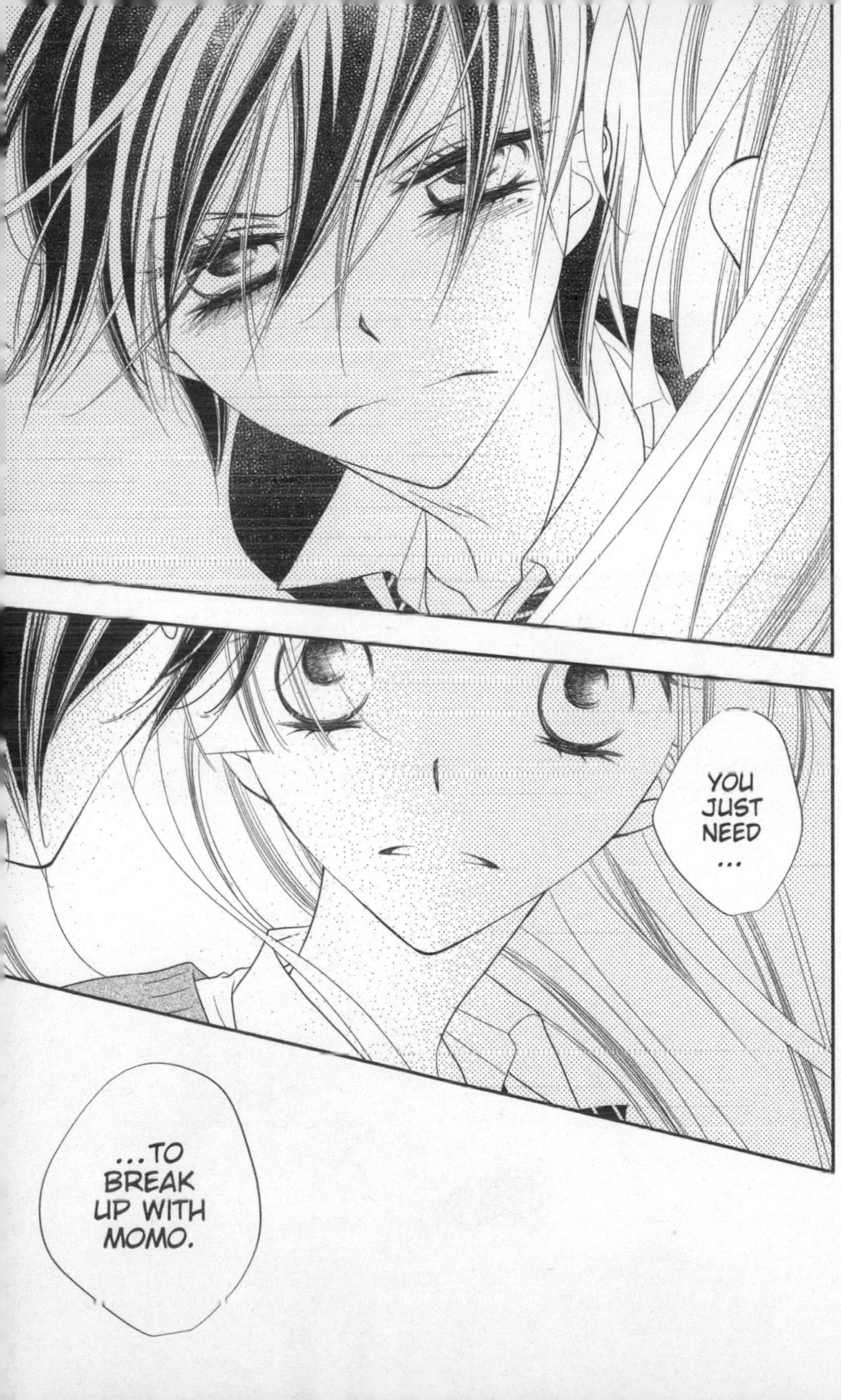
YOU JUST NEED ...
...TO BREAK UP WITH MOMO.

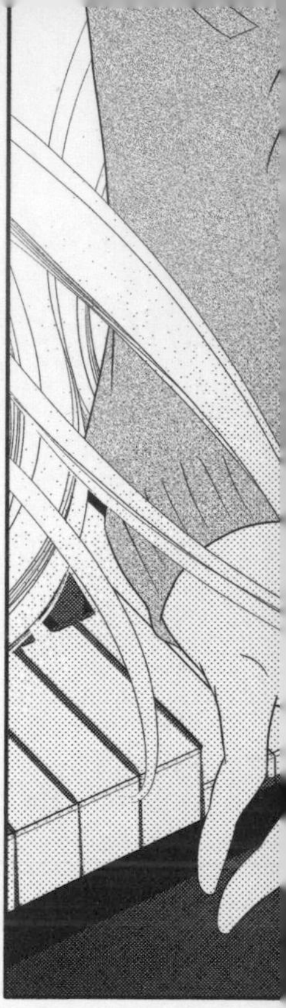
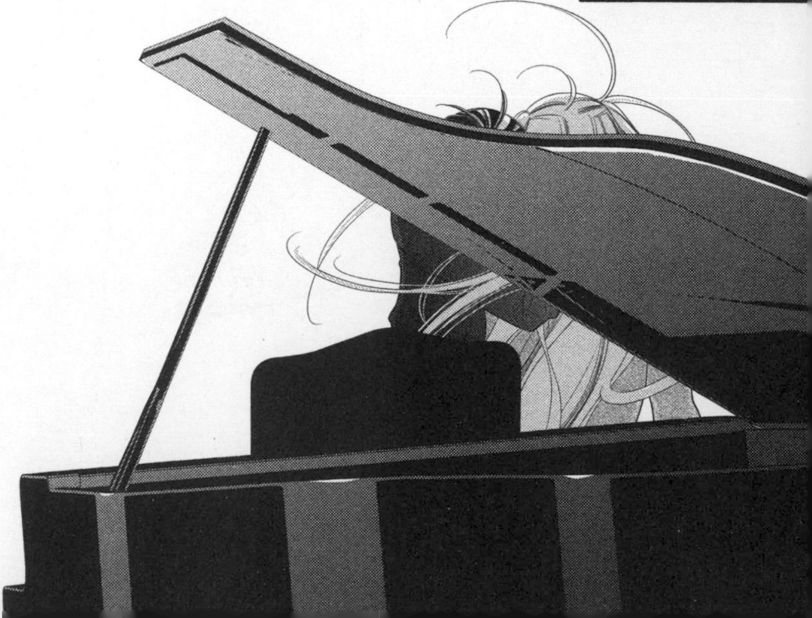

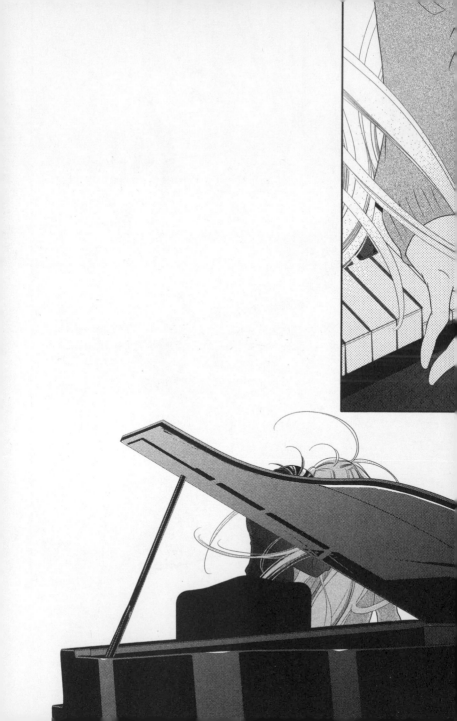

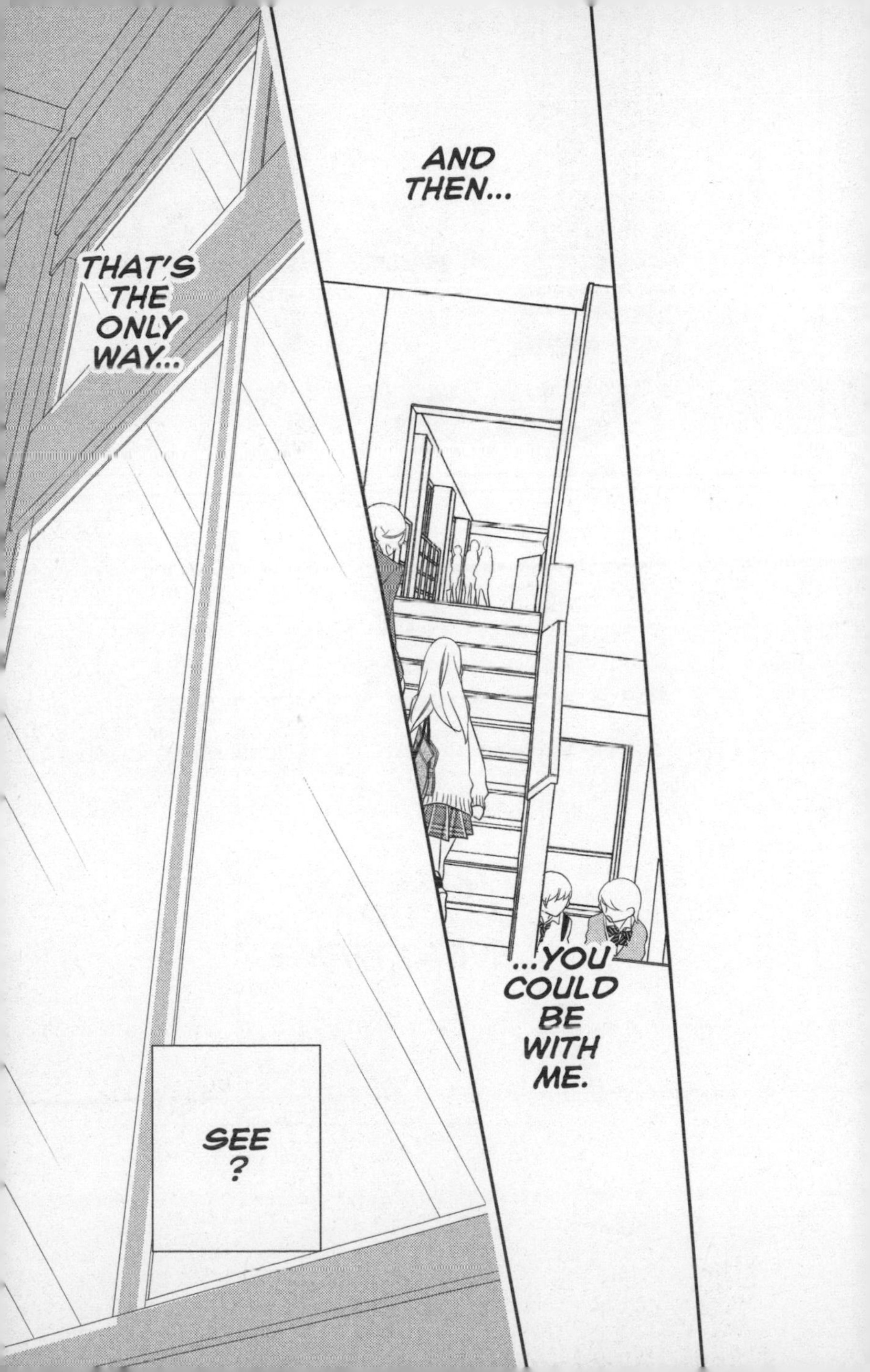
AND THEN...
...YOU COULD BE WITH ME.
THAT'S THE ONLY WAY...
SEE?

THEN YOUR VOICE ...

...WILL COME BACK.

IT MESSES UP EVERYTHING.

SONG 72

NORTHERN JAPAN'S FIRST MAJOR LIVE CIRCUIT

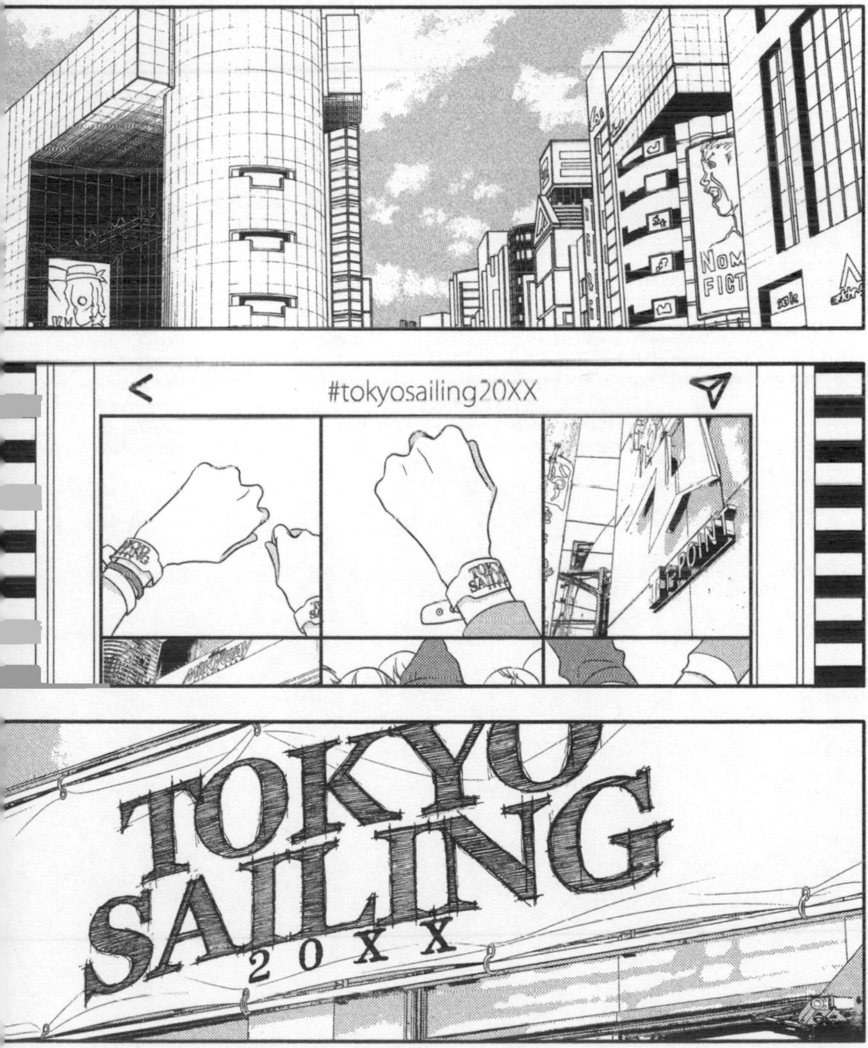
#tokyosailing20XX
TOKYO SAILING
20XX

TOKYO SAILING

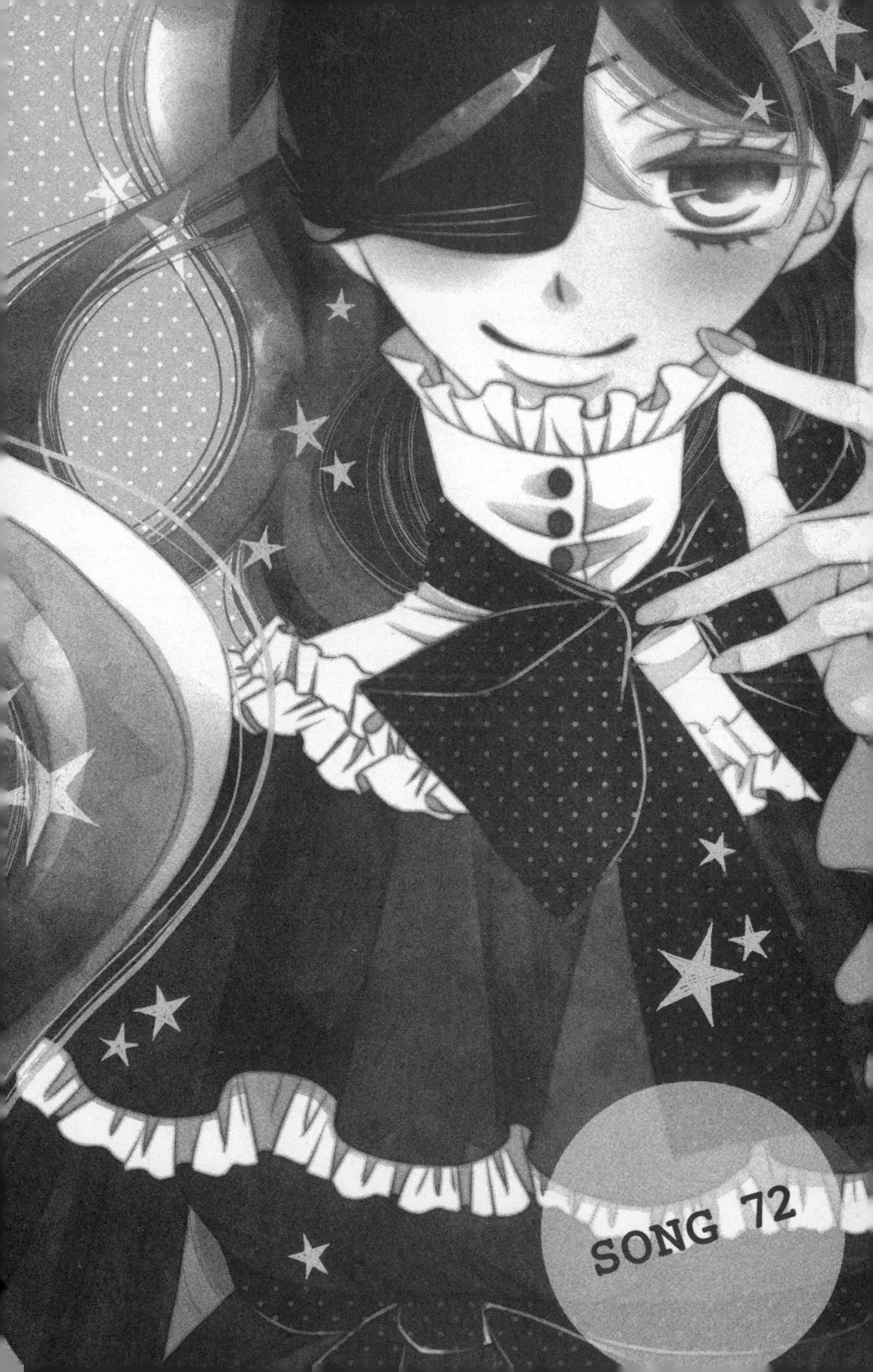
SONG 72

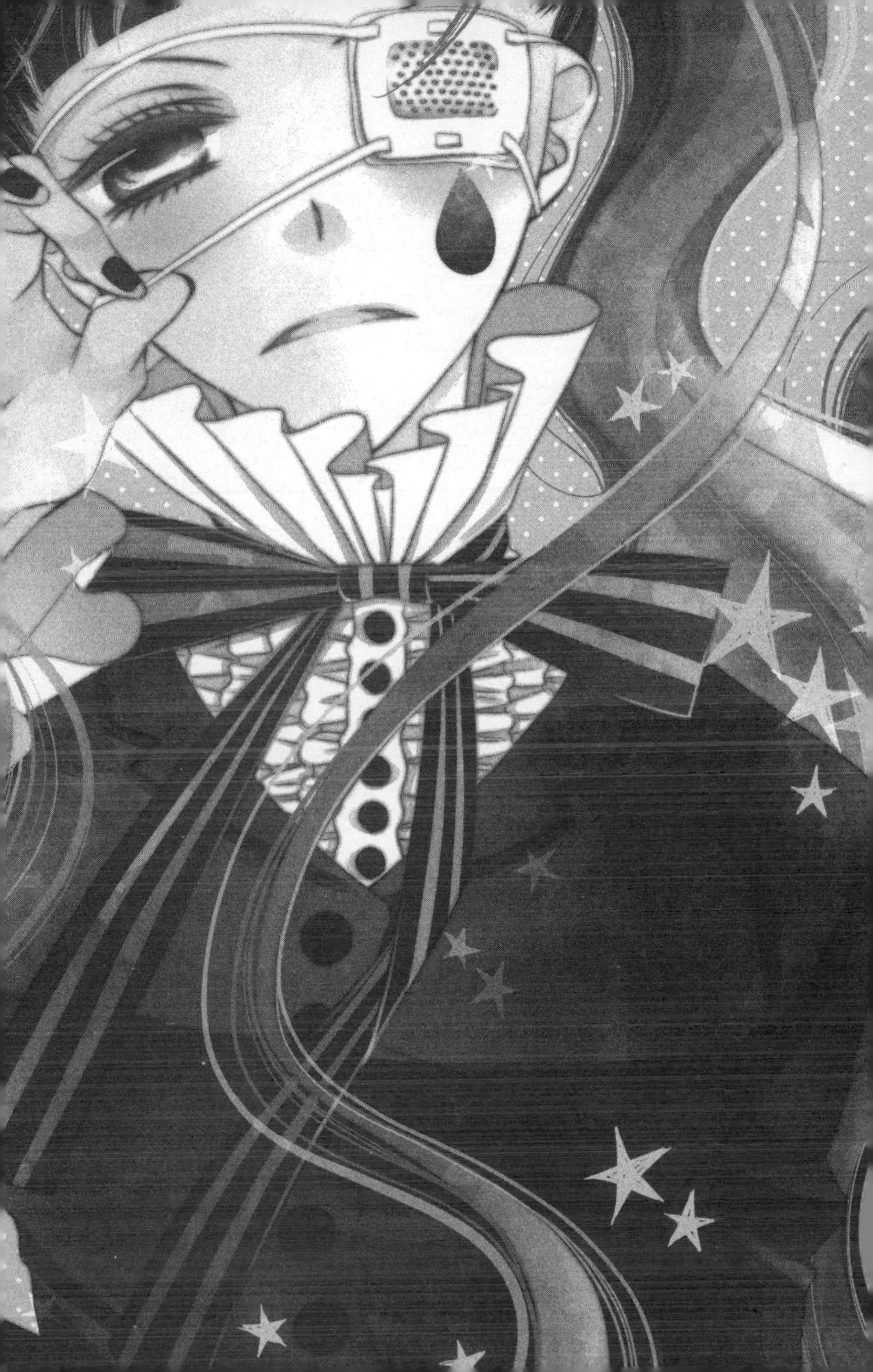

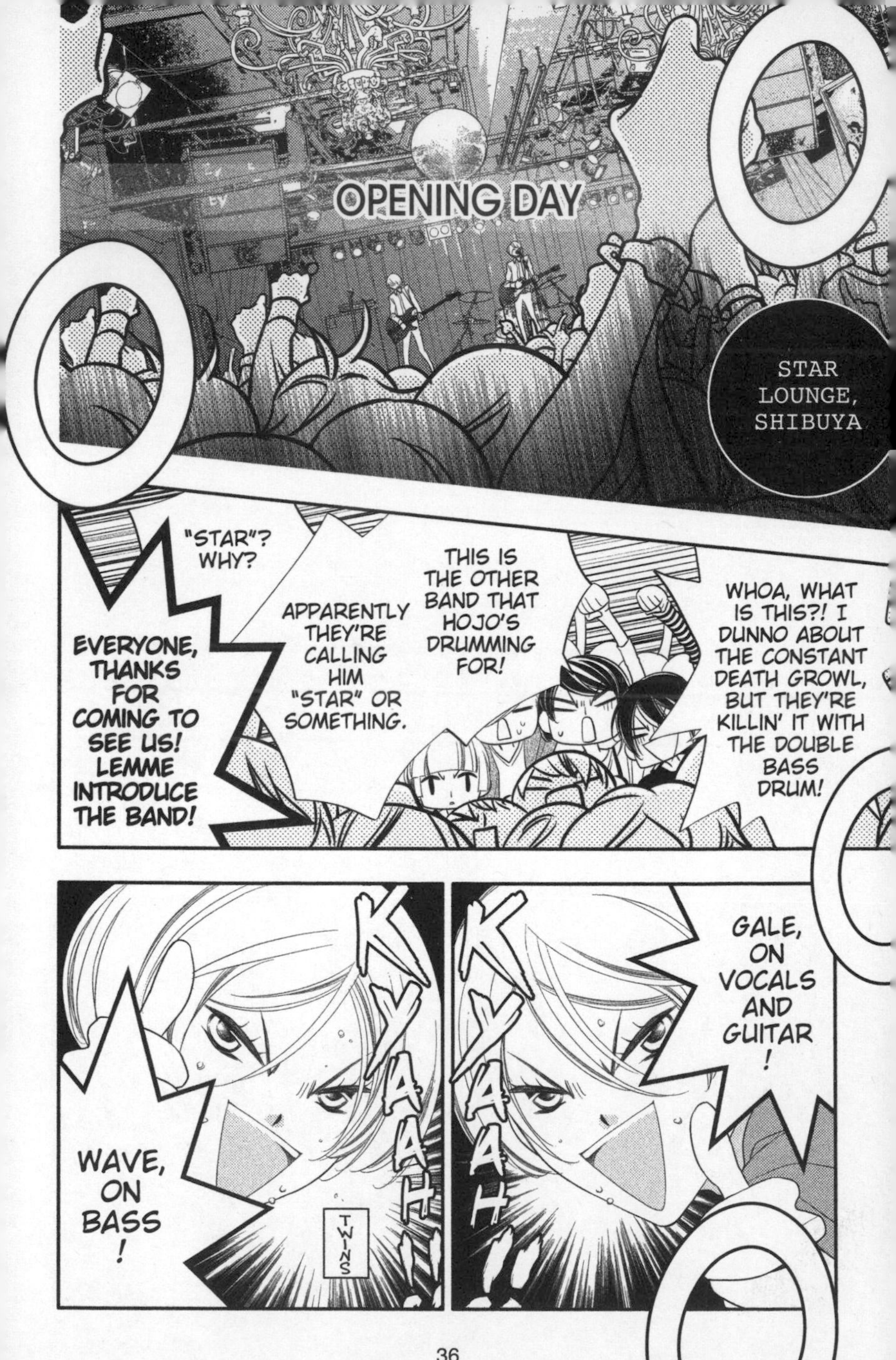

OPENING DAY
STAR LOUNGE, SHIBUYA
WHOA, WHAT IS THIS?! I DUNNO ABOUT THE CONSTANT DEATH GROWL, BUT THEY'RE KILLIN' IT WITH THE DOUBLE BASS DRUM!
THIS IS THE OTHER BAND THAT HOJO'S DRUMMING FOR!
"STAR"? WHY?
APPARENTLY THEY'RE CALLING HIM "STAR" OR SOMETHING.
EVERYONE, THANKS FOR COMING TO SEE US! LEMME INTRODUCE THE BAND!
GALE, ON VOCALS AND GUITAR!
KYAAAH!!
KYAAAH!!
WAVE, ON BASS!
TWINS

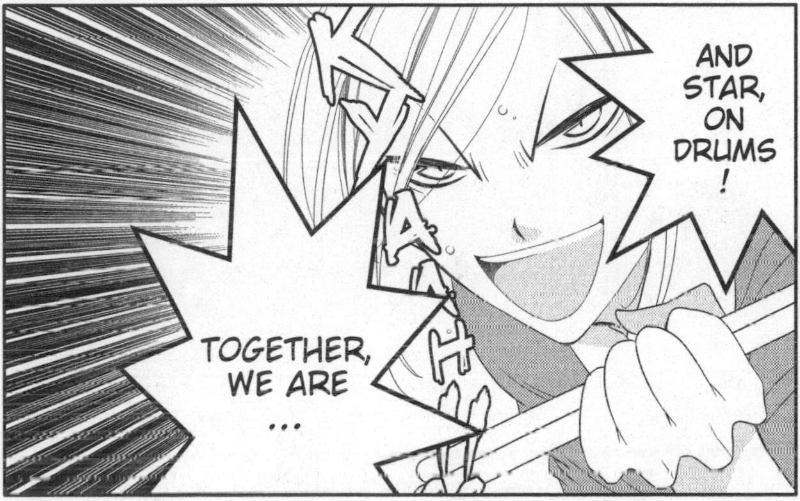
AND STAR, ON DRUMS!
TOGETHER, WE ARE ...

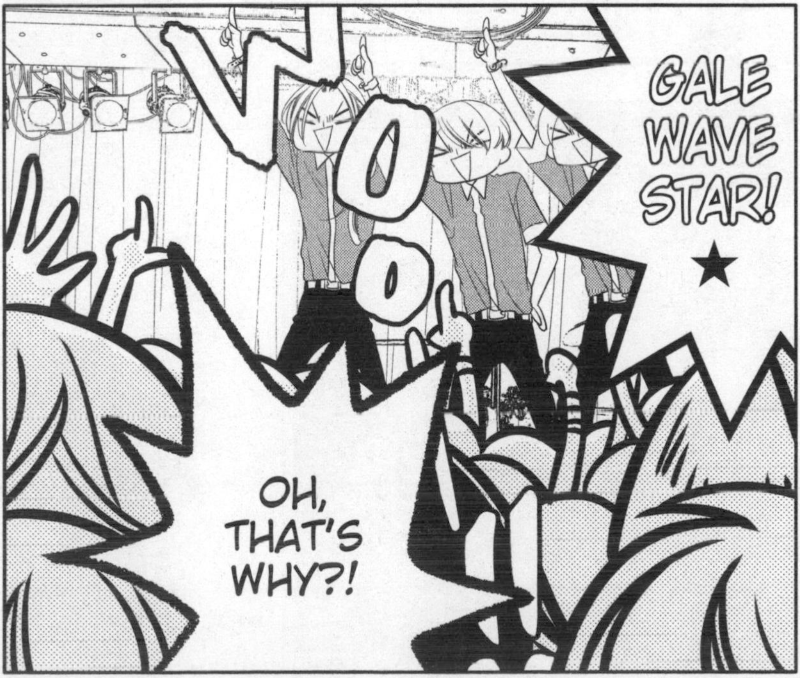
GALE WAVE STAR! ★
OH, THAT'S WHY?!

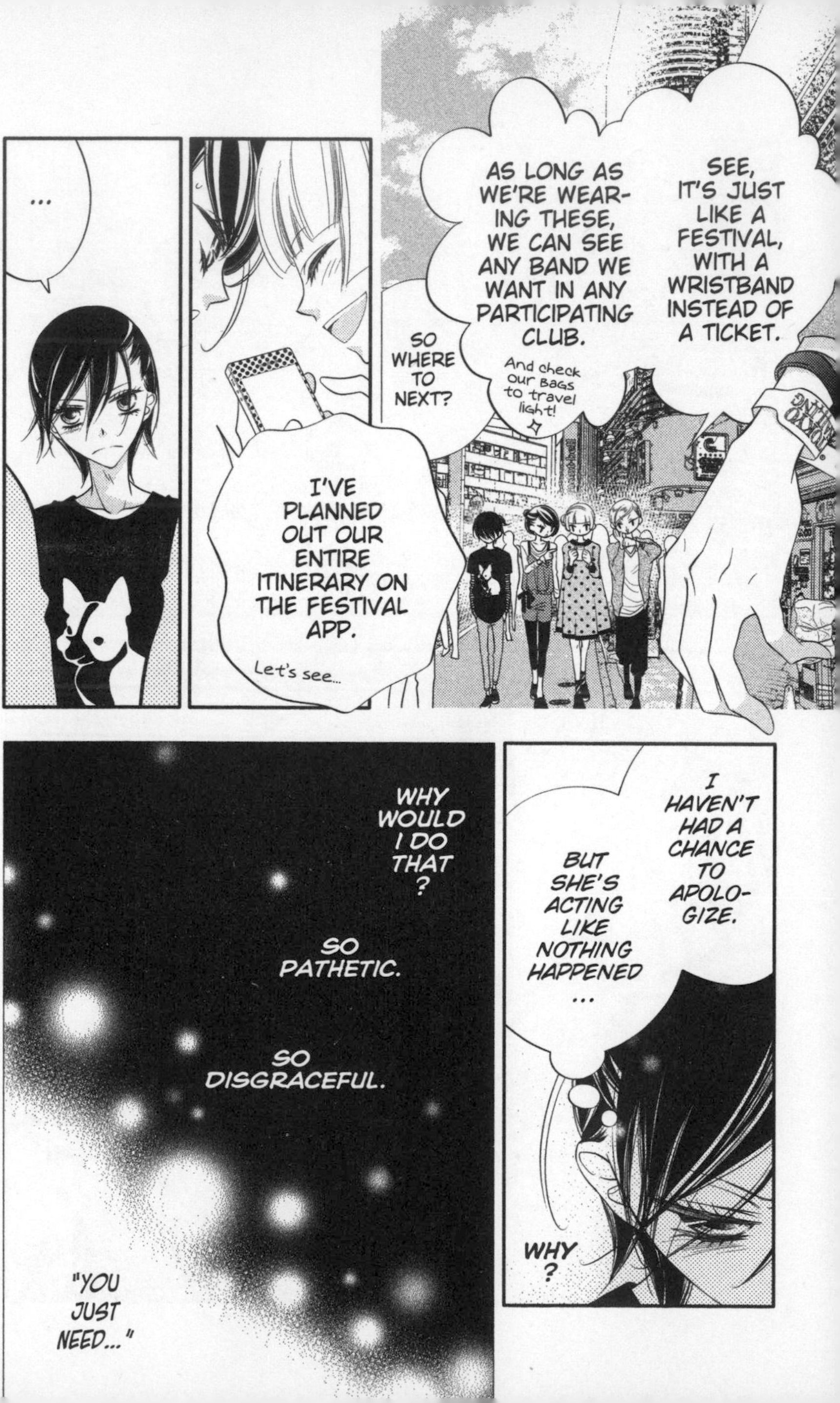
SEE, IT'S JUST LIKE A FESTIVAL, WITH A WRISTBAND INSTEAD OF A TICKET.
AS LONG AS WE'RE WEARING THESE, WE CAN SEE ANY BAND WE WANT IN ANY PARTICIPATING CLUB.
And check our bags to travel light!
SO WHERE TO NEXT?
I'VE PLANNED OUT OUR ENTIRE ITINERARY ON THE FESTIVAL APP.
Let's see...
...
I HAVEN'T HAD A CHANCE TO APOLOGIZE.
BUT SHE'S ACTING LIKE NOTHING HAPPENED...
WHY?
WHY WOULD I DO THAT?
SO PATHETIC.
SO DISGRACEFUL.
"YOU JUST NEED..."

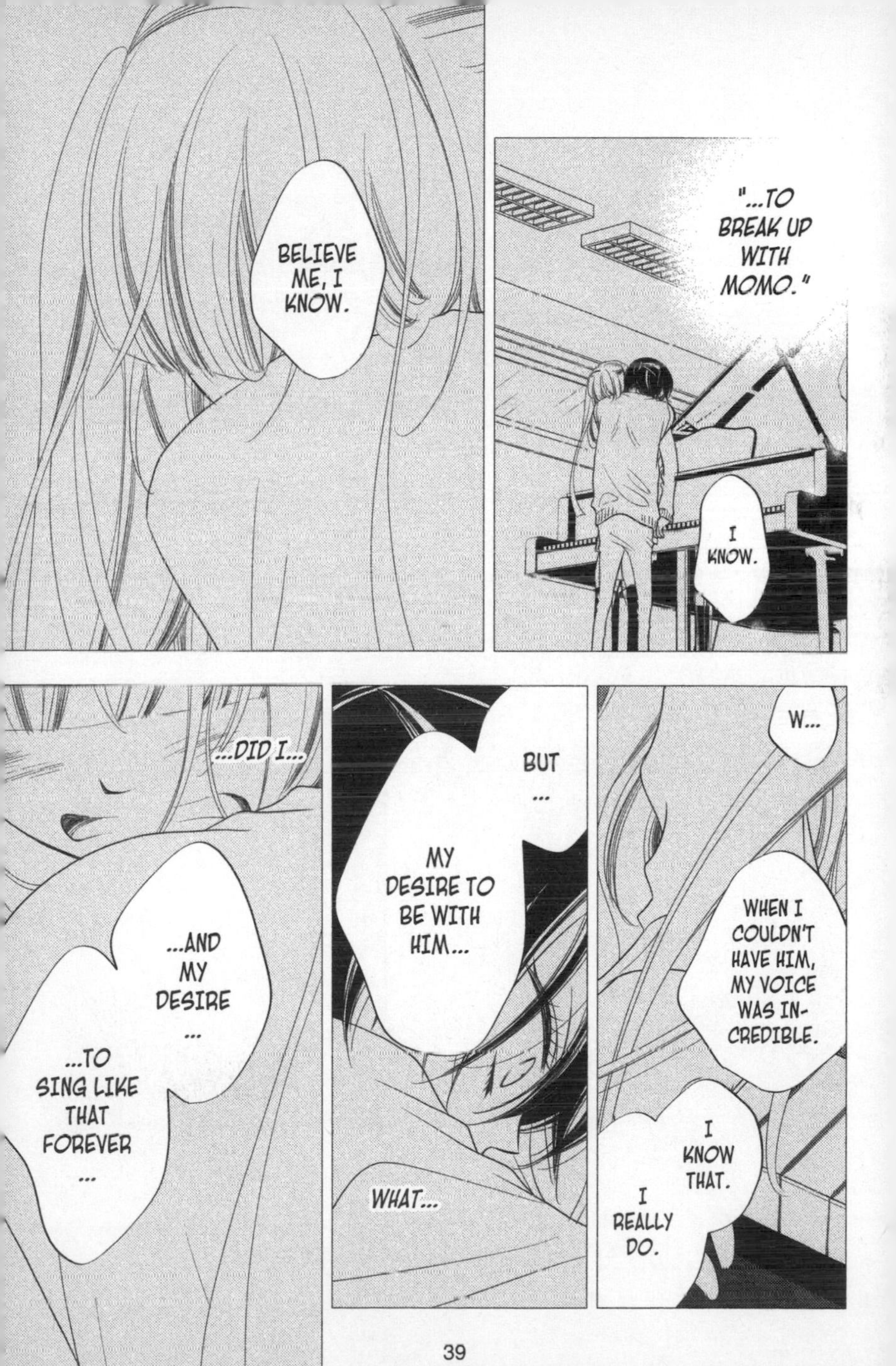
"...TO BREAK UP WITH MOMO."
I KNOW.
BELIEVE ME, I KNOW.
W...
WHEN I COULDN'T HAVE HIM, MY VOICE WAS INCREDIBLE.
I KNOW THAT.
I REALLY DO.
BUT ...
MY DESIRE TO BE WITH HIM...
WHAT...
...DID I...
...AND MY DESIRE ...
...TO SING LIKE THAT FOREVER ...

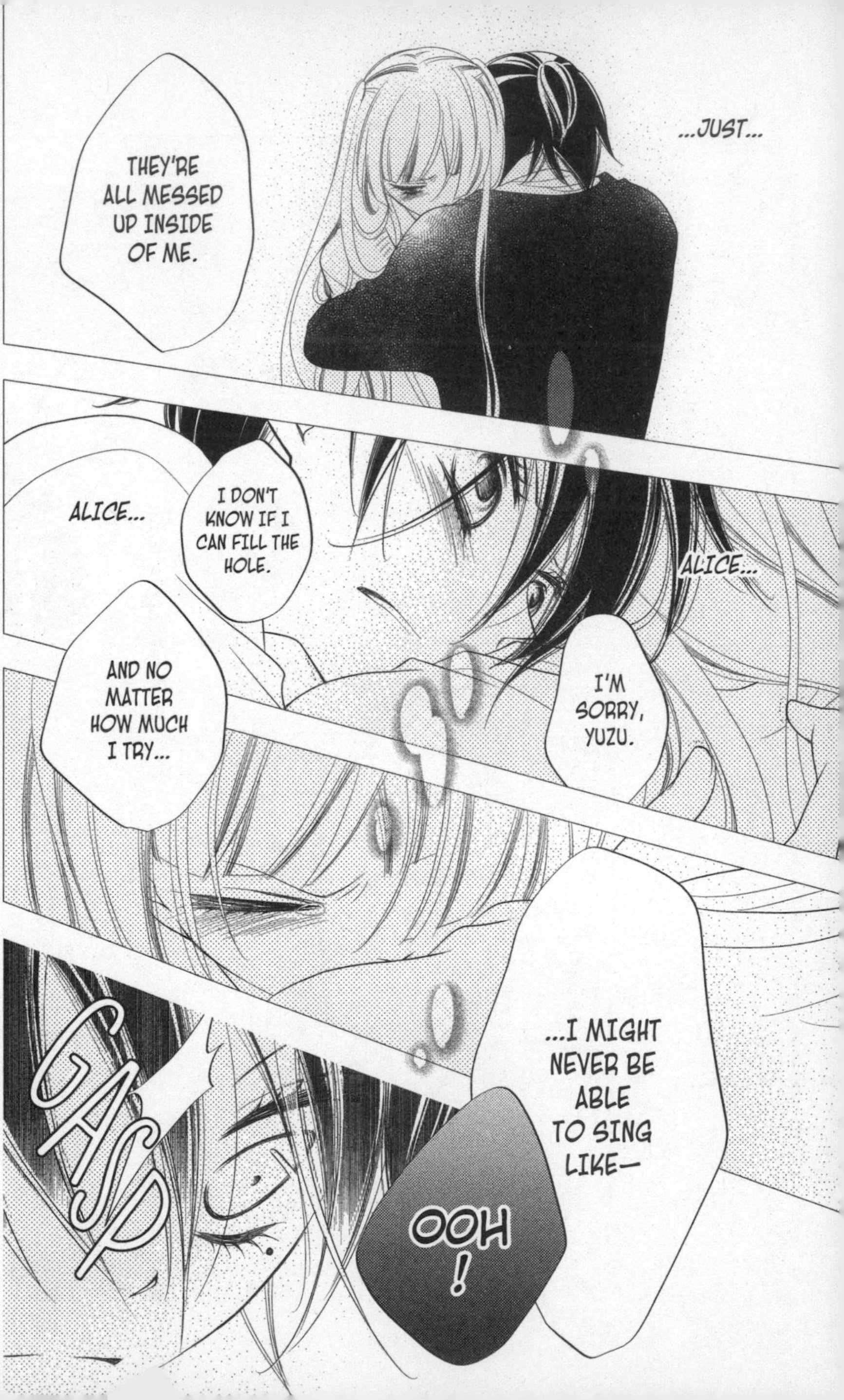
...JUST...
THEY'RE ALL MESSED UP INSIDE OF ME.
ALICE...
I DON'T KNOW IF I CAN FILL THE HOLE.
ALICE...
I'M SORRY, YUZU.
AND NO MATTER HOW MUCH I TRY...
...I MIGHT NEVER BE ABLE TO SING LIKE—
OOH!
GASP.

2

When this volume releases, the anime should be nearing the end of its run. In fact, I think this book's release date is the exact airdate as episode 11. Is everyone watching the anime? Are you enjoying it? I've managed to attend the voice-over session for every episode. When I agreed to do the anime, I wanted to make sure I didn't have any regrets about it, so I asked to attend all the production meetings, including all the voice-over sessions. And I'm really glad I did. I had a lot of fun and left satisfied every time. The people working on the show are kind, funny and a lot of fun to be with. The cast members were always friendly and really brought the anime to life with their incredible performances. I can't thank all of them enough.

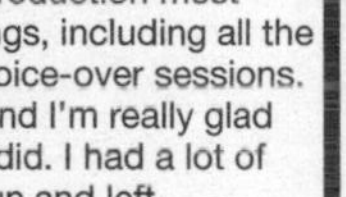
WHEE

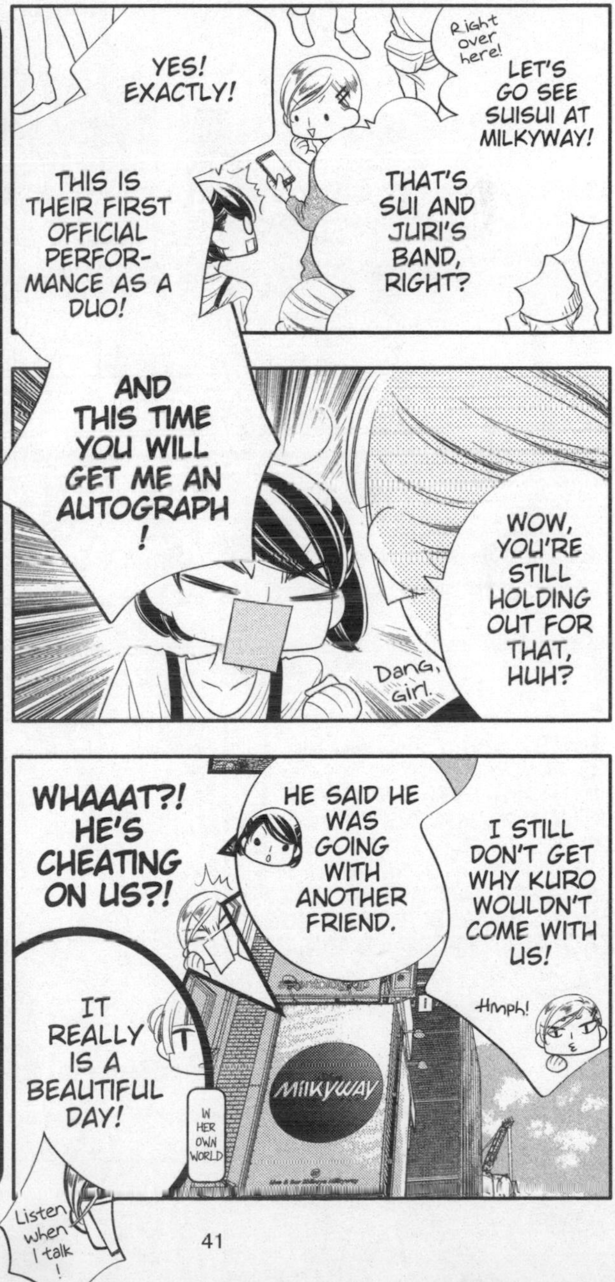
Right over here!
LET'S GO SEE SUISUI AT MILKYWAY!
THAT'S SUI AND JURI'S BAND, RIGHT?
YES! EXACTLY!
THIS IS THEIR FIRST OFFICIAL PERFORMANCE AS A DUO!
AND THIS TIME YOU WILL GET ME AN AUTOGRAPH!
WOW, YOU'RE STILL HOLDING OUT FOR THAT, HUH?
Dang, Girl.
I STILL DON'T GET WHY KURO WOULDN'T COME WITH US!
Hmph!
HE SAID HE WAS GOING WITH ANOTHER FRIEND.
WHAAAT?! HE'S CHEATING ON US?!
IT REALLY IS A BEAUTIFUL DAY!
IN HER OWN WORLD
MilkyWay
Listen when I talk!

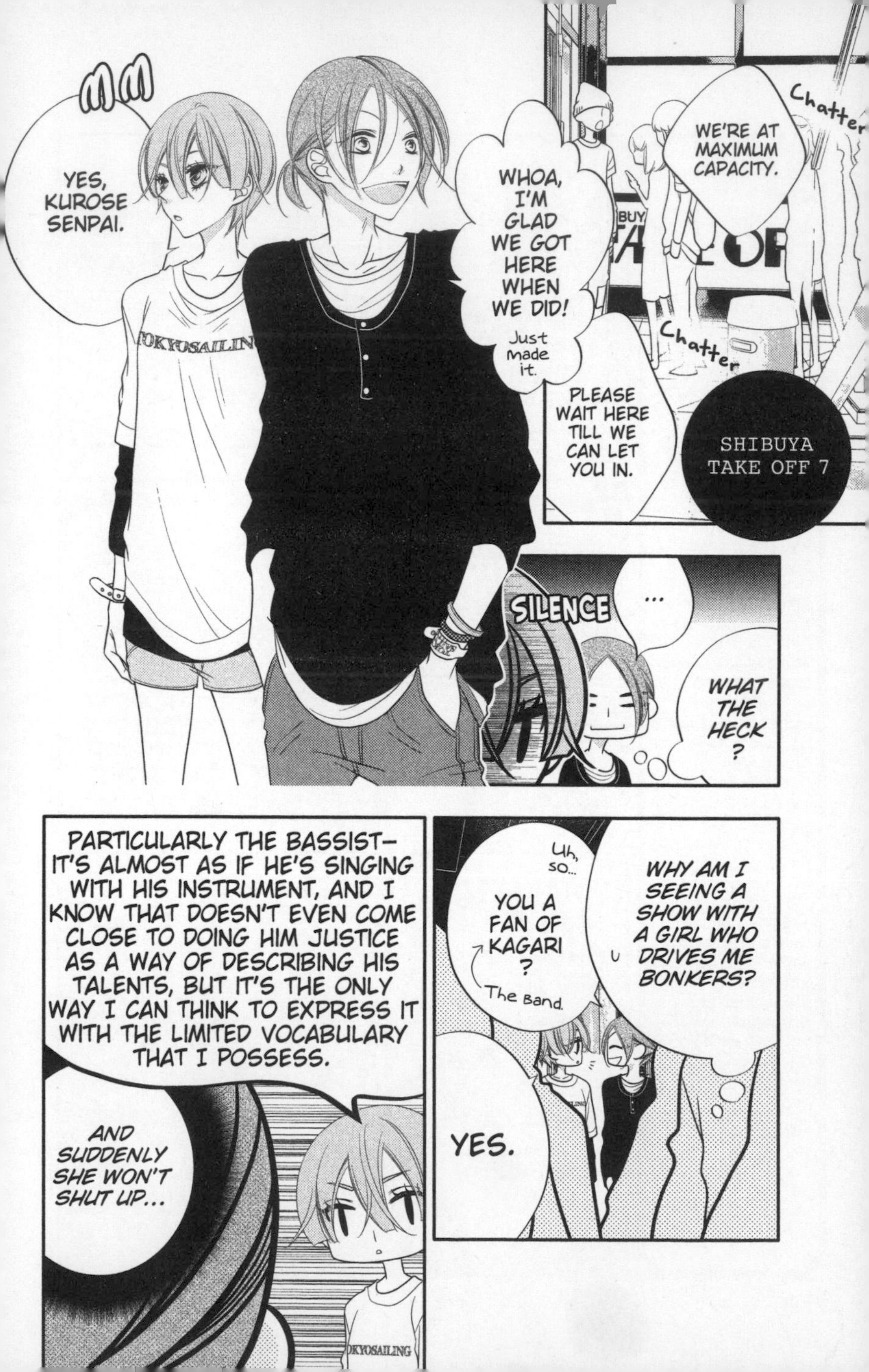
Chatter
WE'RE AT MAXIMUM CAPACITY.
Chatter
PLEASE WAIT HERE TILL WE CAN LET YOU IN.
SHIBUYA TAKE OFF 7
SILENCE
...
WHAT THE HECK?
WHOA, I'M GLAD WE GOT HERE WHEN WE DID!
Just made it.
MM
YES, KUROSE SENPAI.
WHY AM I SEEING A SHOW WITH A GIRL WHO DRIVES ME BONKERS?
Uh, so...
YOU A FAN OF KAGARI?
The band.
YES.
PARTICULARLY THE BASSIST—IT'S ALMOST AS IF HE'S SINGING WITH HIS INSTRUMENT, AND I KNOW THAT DOESN'T EVEN COME CLOSE TO DOING HIM JUSTICE AS A WAY OF DESCRIBING HIS TALENTS, BUT IT'S THE ONLY WAY I CAN THINK TO EXPRESS IT WITH THE LIMITED VOCABULARY THAT I POSSESS.
AND SUDDENLY SHE WON'T SHUT UP...

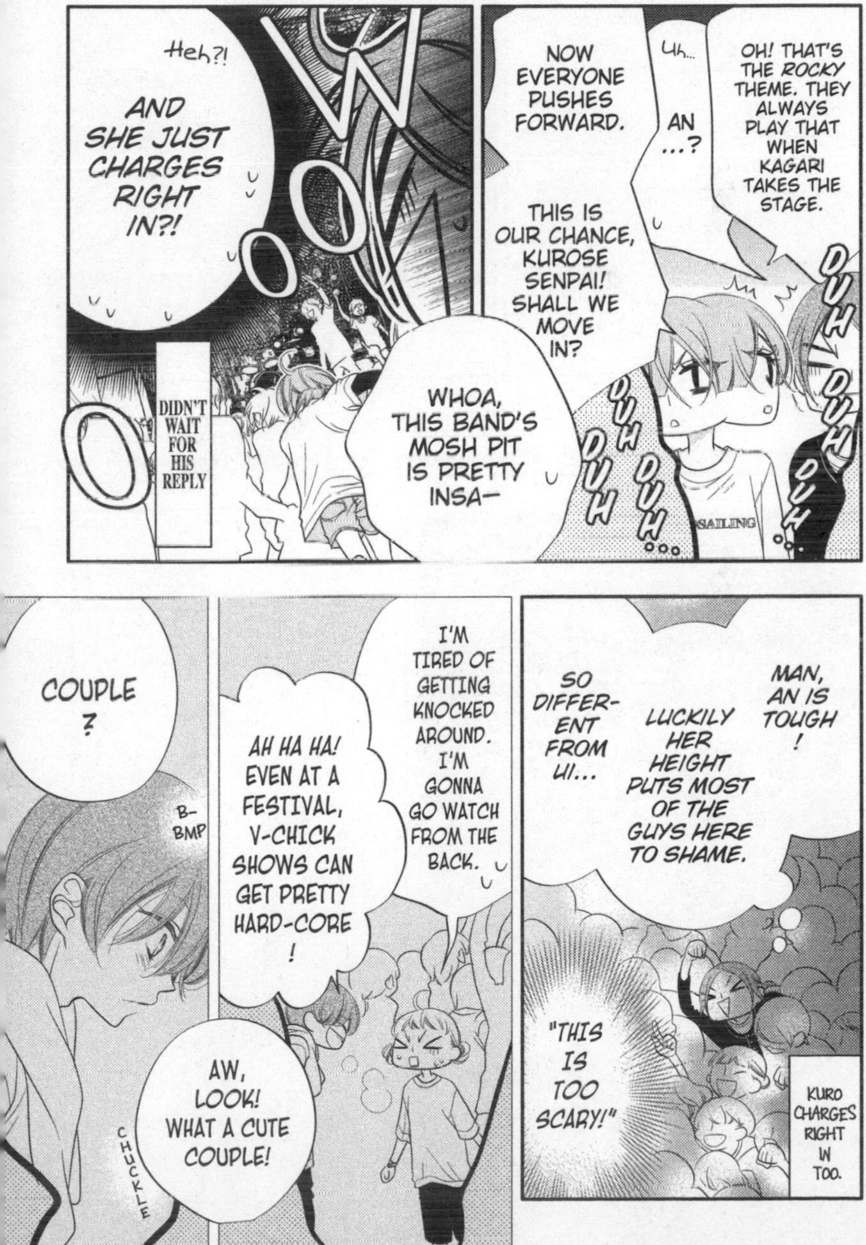
OH! THAT'S THE *ROCKY* THEME. THEY ALWAYS PLAY THAT WHEN KAGARI TAKES THE STAGE.
Uh...
AN ...?
NOW EVERYONE PUSHES FORWARD.
THIS IS OUR CHANCE, KUROSE SENPAI! SHALL WE MOVE IN?
DUH DUH DUH...
DUH DUH DUH...
SAILING
WHOA, THIS BAND'S MOSH PIT IS PRETTY INSA—
Heh?!
AND SHE JUST CHARGES RIGHT IN?!
WOOOO
DIDN'T WAIT FOR HIS REPLY
MAN, AN IS TOUGH!
LUCKILY HER HEIGHT PUTS MOST OF THE GUYS HERE TO SHAME.
SO DIFFER-ENT FROM UI...
KURO CHARGES RIGHT IN TOO.
"THIS IS TOO SCARY!"
I'M TIRED OF GETTING KNOCKED AROUND. I'M GONNA GO WATCH FROM THE BACK.
AH HA HA! EVEN AT A FESTIVAL, V-CHICK SHOWS CAN GET PRETTY HARD-CORE!
COUPLE?
B-BMP
AW, LOOK! WHAT A CUTE COUPLE!
CHUCKLE

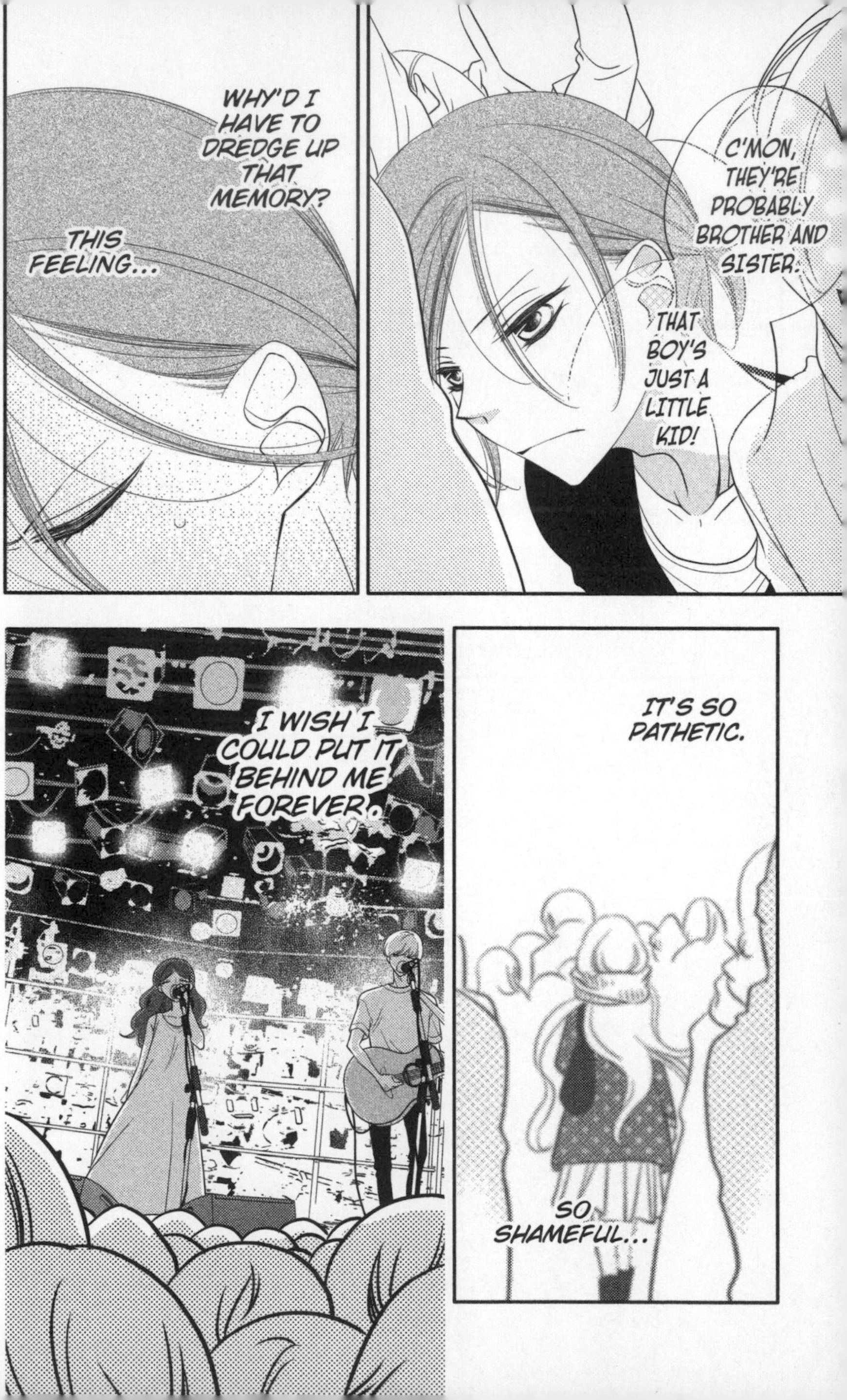
C'MON, THEY'RE PROBABLY BROTHER AND SISTER.
THAT BOY'S JUST A LITTLE KID!
WHY'D I HAVE TO DREDGE UP THAT MEMORY?
THIS FEELING...
IT'S SO PATHETIC.
SO SHAMEFUL...
I WISH I COULD PUT IT BEHIND ME FOREVER.

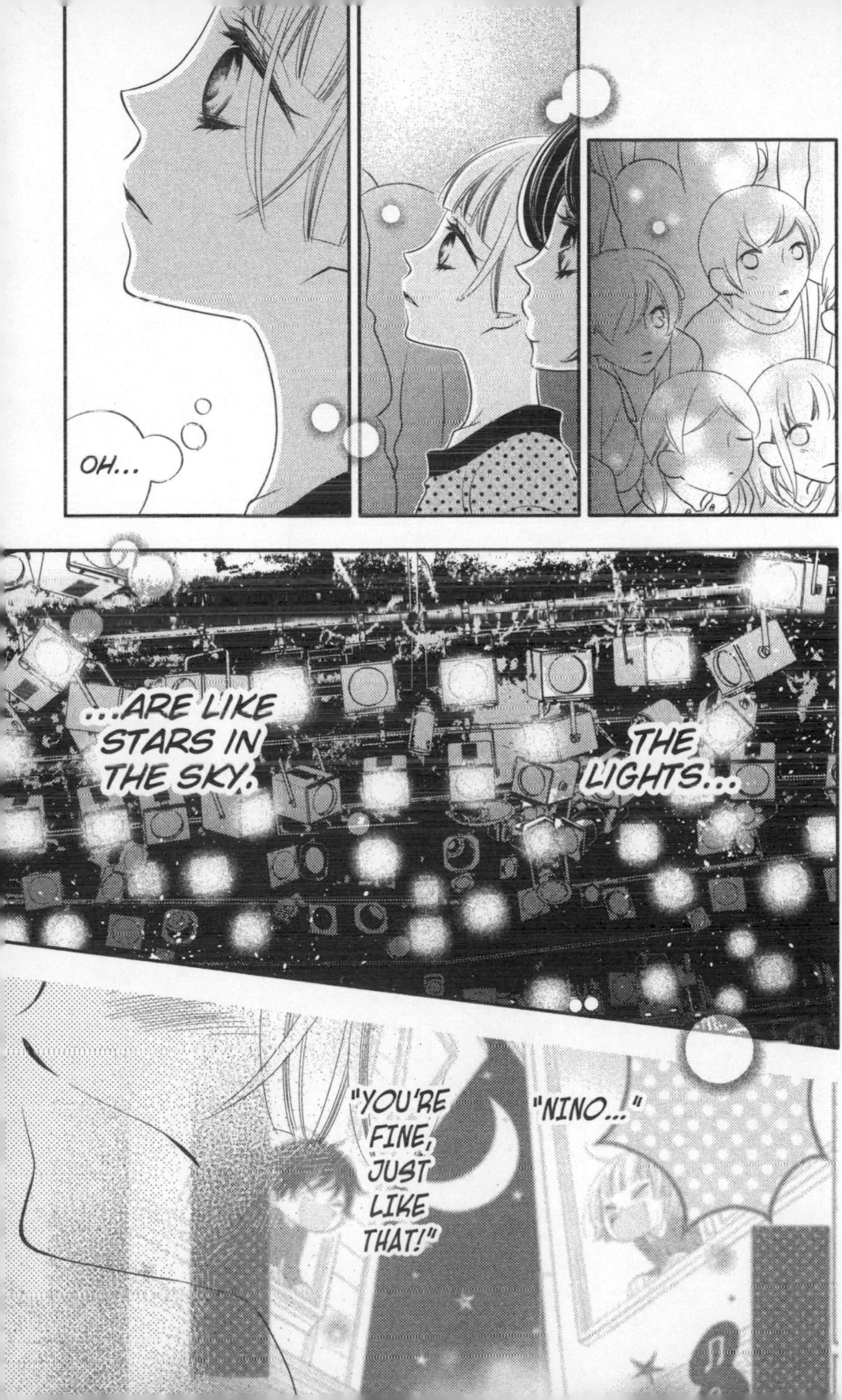
OH...
THE LIGHTS...
...ARE LIKE STARS IN THE SKY.
"NINO..."
"YOU'RE FINE, JUST LIKE THAT!"

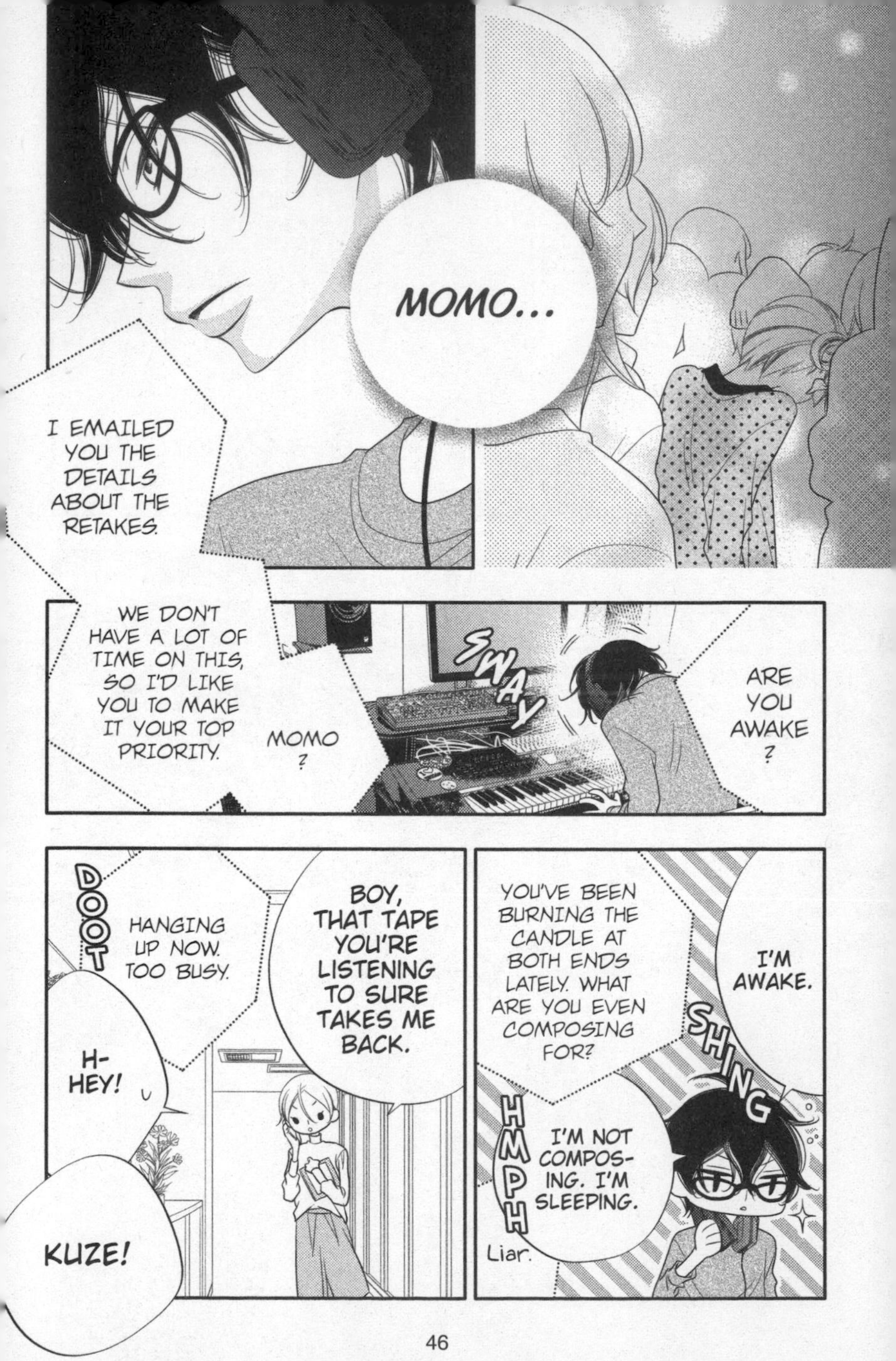
MOMO...
I EMAILED YOU THE DETAILS ABOUT THE RETAKES.
WE DON'T HAVE A LOT OF TIME ON THIS, SO I'D LIKE YOU TO MAKE IT YOUR TOP PRIORITY.
ARE YOU AWAKE?
SWAY
MOMO?
I'M AWAKE.
SHING
YOU'VE BEEN BURNING THE CANDLE AT BOTH ENDS LATELY. WHAT ARE YOU EVEN COMPOSING FOR?
I'M NOT COMPOSING. I'M SLEEPING.
HMPH
Liar.
BOY, THAT TAPE YOU'RE LISTENING TO SURE TAKES ME BACK.
HANGING UP NOW. TOO BUSY.
DOOT
H-HEY!
KUZE!

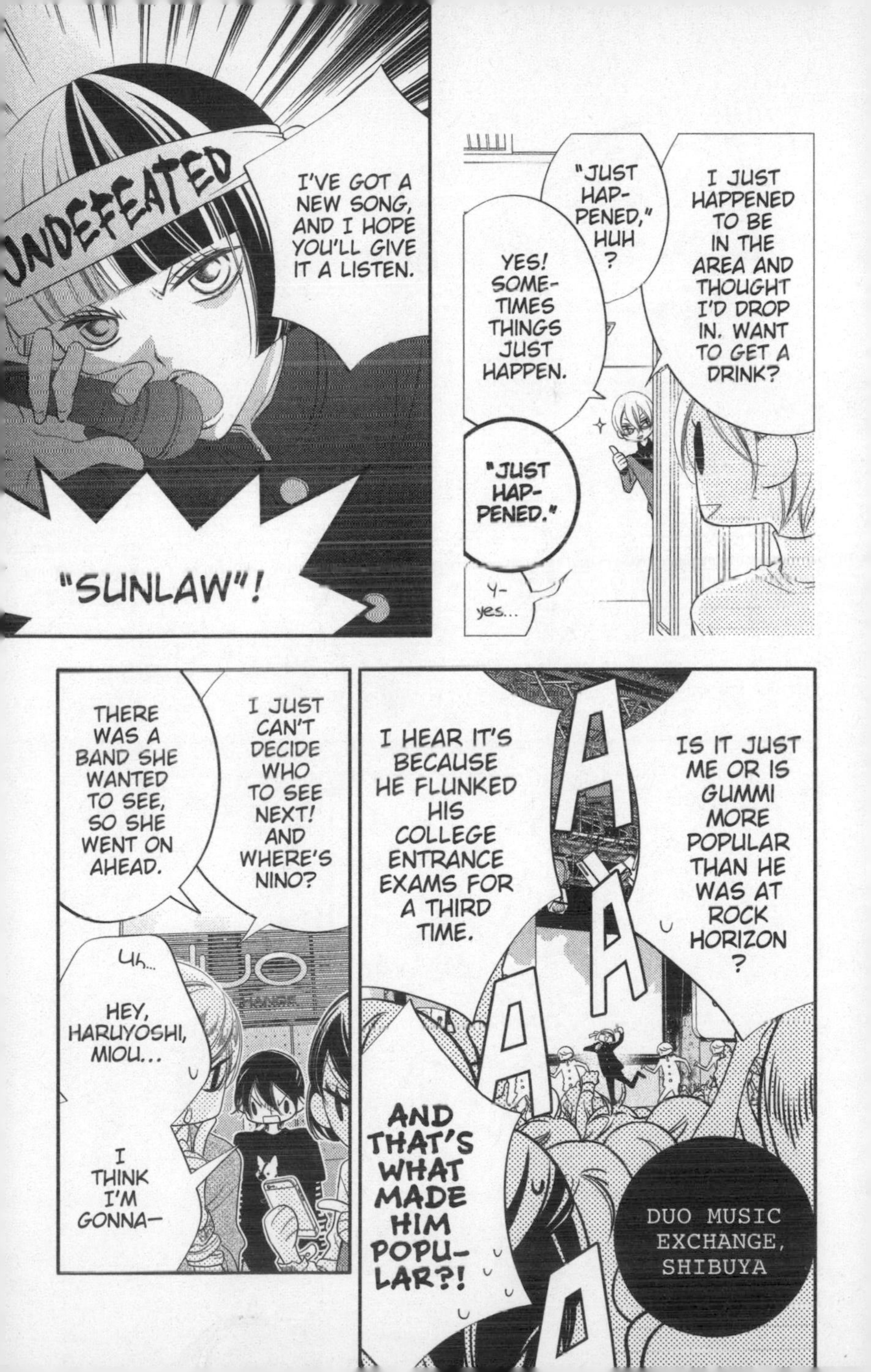
I JUST HAPPENED TO BE IN THE AREA AND THOUGHT I'D DROP IN. WANT TO GET A DRINK?
"JUST HAPPENED," HUH?
YES! SOMETIMES THINGS JUST HAPPEN.
"JUST HAPPENED."
Y-yes...
UNDEFEATED
I'VE GOT A NEW SONG, AND I HOPE YOU'LL GIVE IT A LISTEN.
"SUNLAW"!
IS IT JUST ME OR IS GUMMI MORE POPULAR THAN HE WAS AT ROCK HORIZON?
I HEAR IT'S BECAUSE HE FLUNKED HIS COLLEGE ENTRANCE EXAMS FOR A THIRD TIME.
AAAAA
AND THAT'S WHAT MADE HIM POPULAR?!
DUO MUSIC EXCHANGE, SHIBUYA
I JUST CAN'T DECIDE WHO TO SEE NEXT! AND WHERE'S NINO?
THERE WAS A BAND SHE WANTED TO SEE, SO SHE WENT ON AHEAD.
Uh...
HEY, HARUYOSHI, MIOU...
I THINK I'M GONNA—

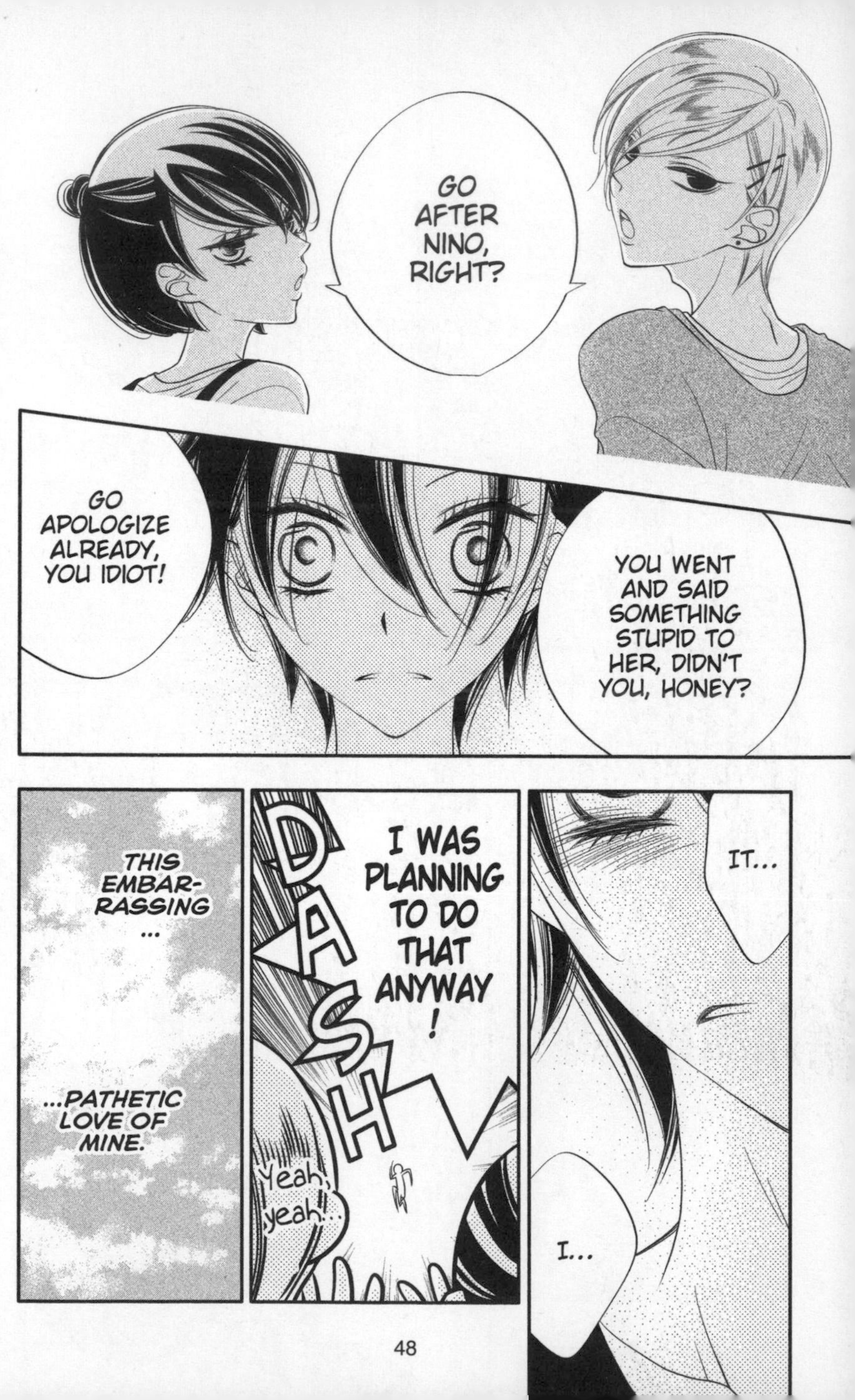
GO AFTER NINO, RIGHT?
YOU WENT AND SAID SOMETHING STUPID TO HER, DIDN'T YOU, HONEY?
GO APOLOGIZE ALREADY, YOU IDIOT!
IT...
I...
I WAS PLANNING TO DO THAT ANYWAY!
DASH
Yeah, yeah!...
THIS EMBARRASSING...
...PATHETIC LOVE OF MINE.

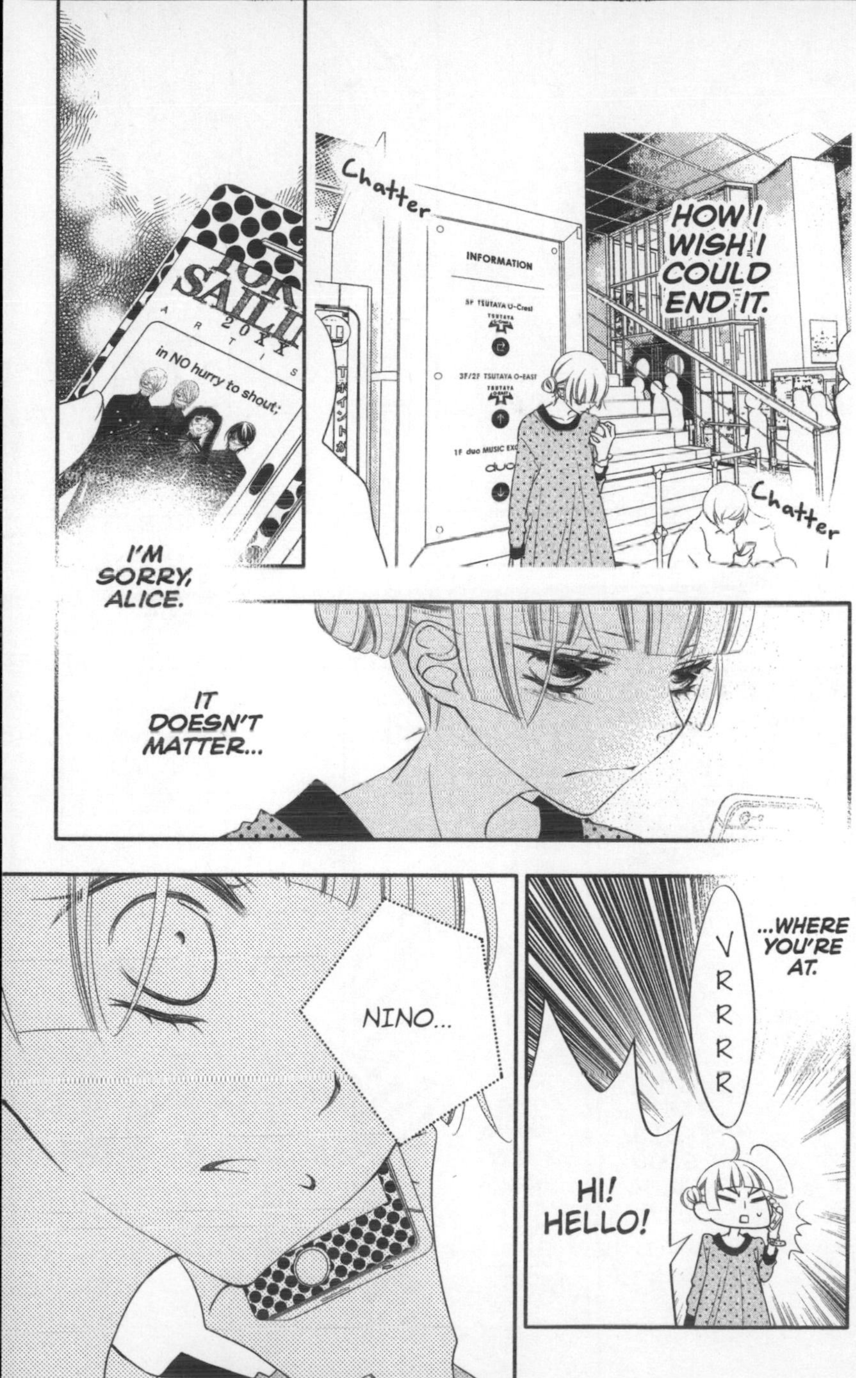
Chatter
INFORMATION
5F TSUTAYA O-Crest
3F/2F TSUTAYA O-EAST
HOW I WISH I COULD END IT.
Chatter
20XX
in NO hurry to shout;
I'M SORRY, ALICE.
IT DOESN'T MATTER...
...WHERE YOU'RE AT.
VRRRR
HI! HELLO!
NINO...

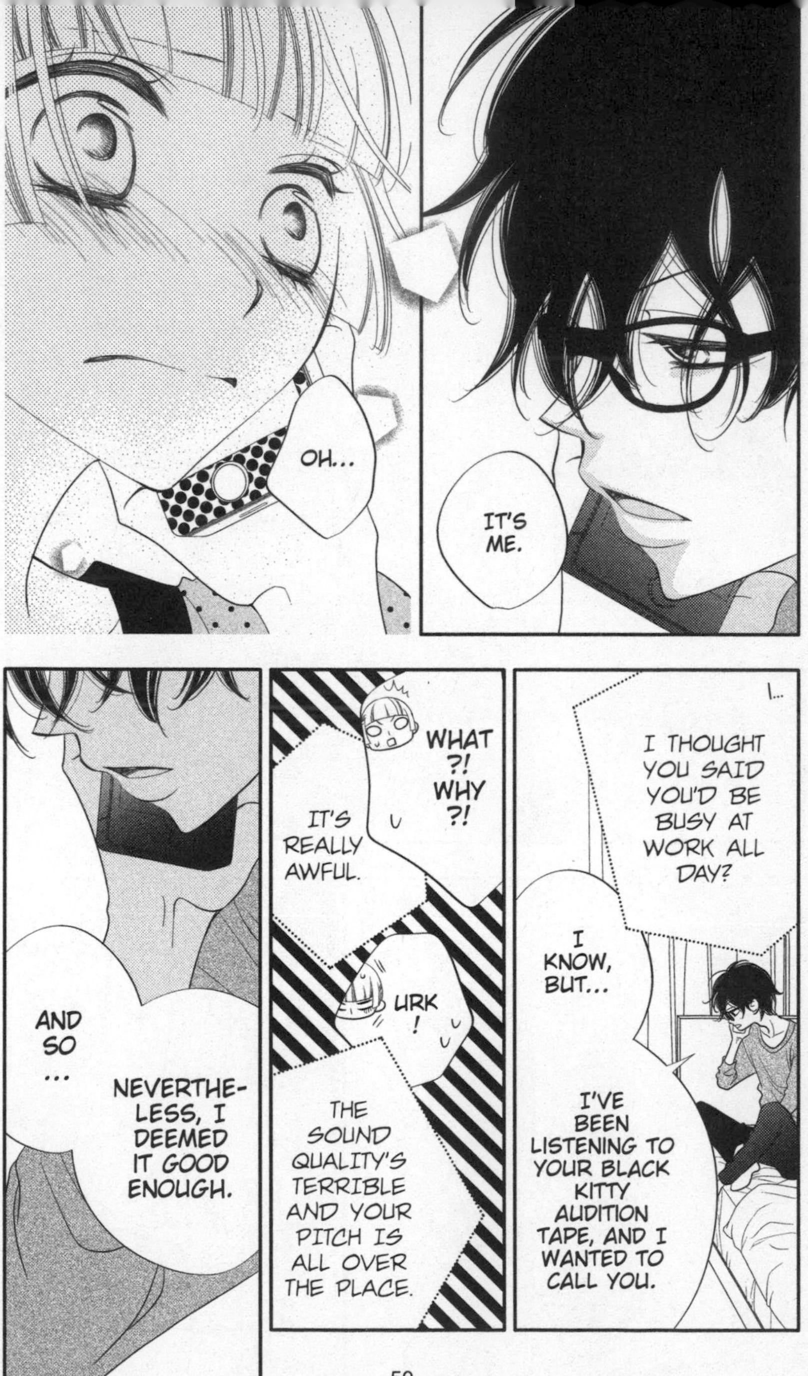
IT'S ME.
OH...
I...
I THOUGHT YOU SAID YOU'D BE BUSY AT WORK ALL DAY?
I KNOW, BUT...
I'VE BEEN LISTENING TO YOUR BLACK KITTY AUDITION TAPE, AND I WANTED TO CALL YOU.
WHAT?! WHY?!
IT'S REALLY AWFUL.
URK!
THE SOUND QUALITY'S TERRIBLE AND YOUR PITCH IS ALL OVER THE PLACE.
NEVERTHE-LESS, I DEEMED IT GOOD ENOUGH.
AND SO...

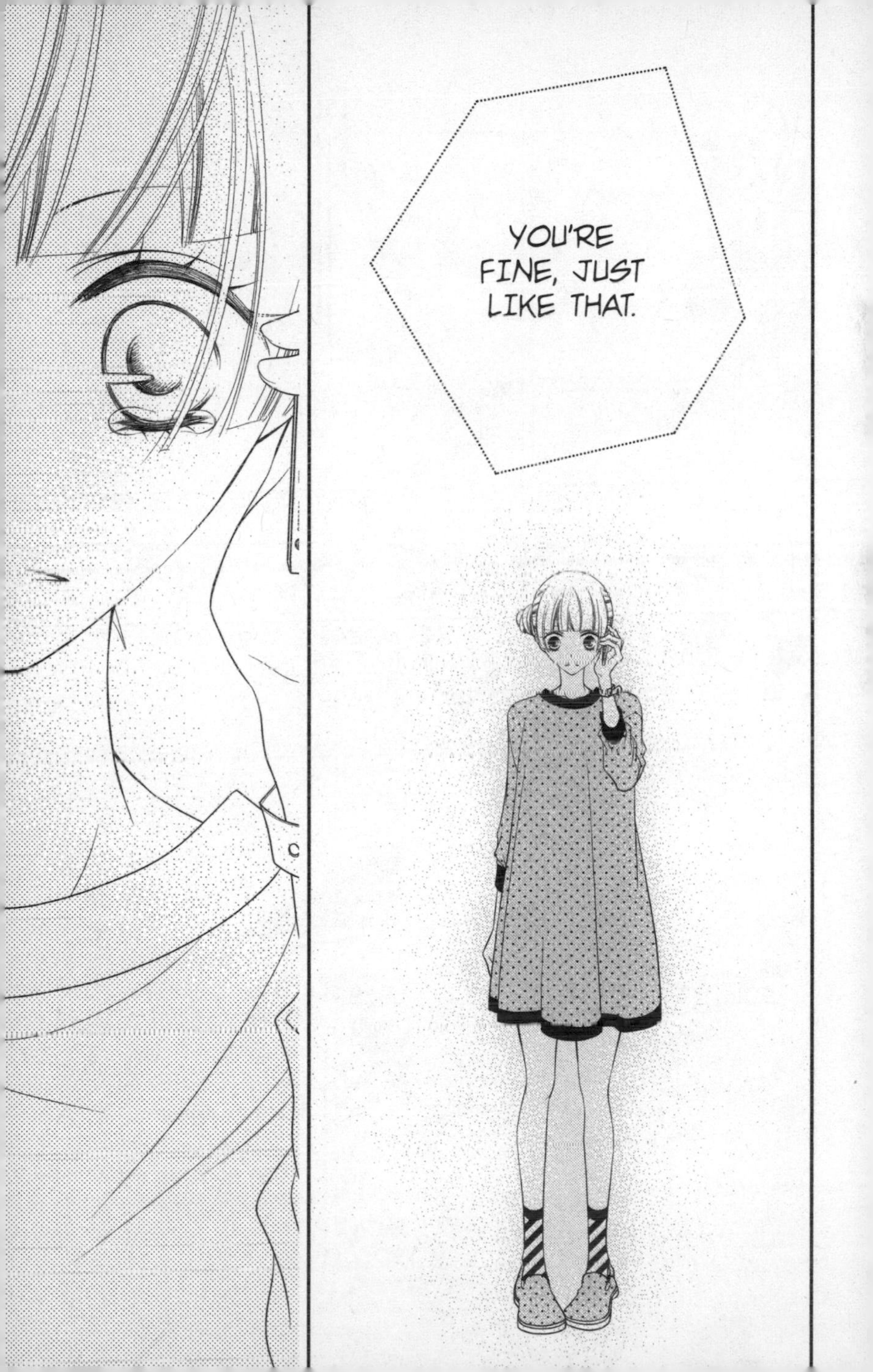
YOU'RE FINE, JUST LIKE THAT.

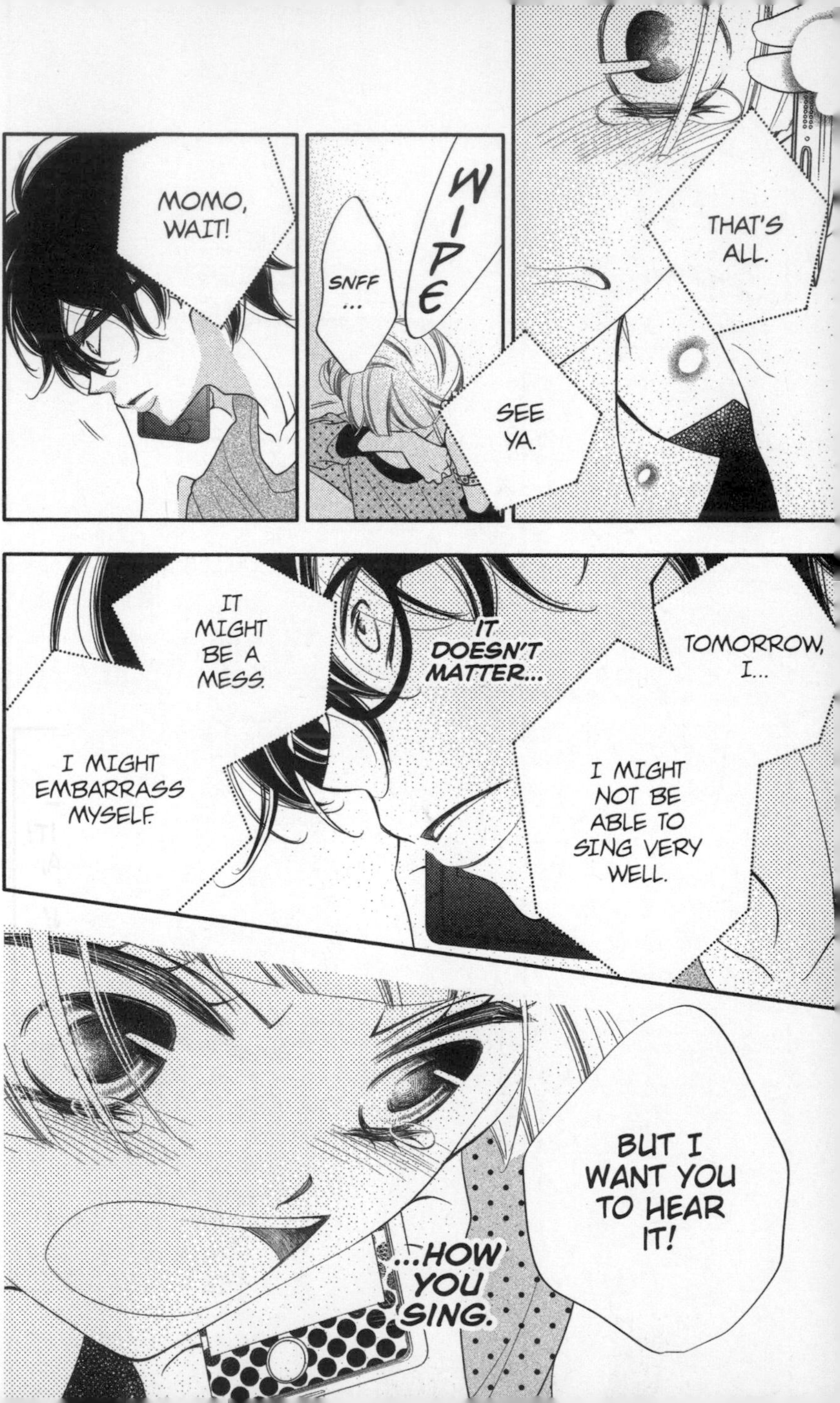
THAT'S ALL.
SEE YA.
WIPE
SNFF ...
MOMO, WAIT!
TOMORROW, I...
I MIGHT NOT BE ABLE TO SING VERY WELL.
IT DOESN'T MATTER...
IT MIGHT BE A MESS.
I MIGHT EMBARRASS MYSELF.
BUT I WANT YOU TO HEAR IT!
...HOW YOU SING.

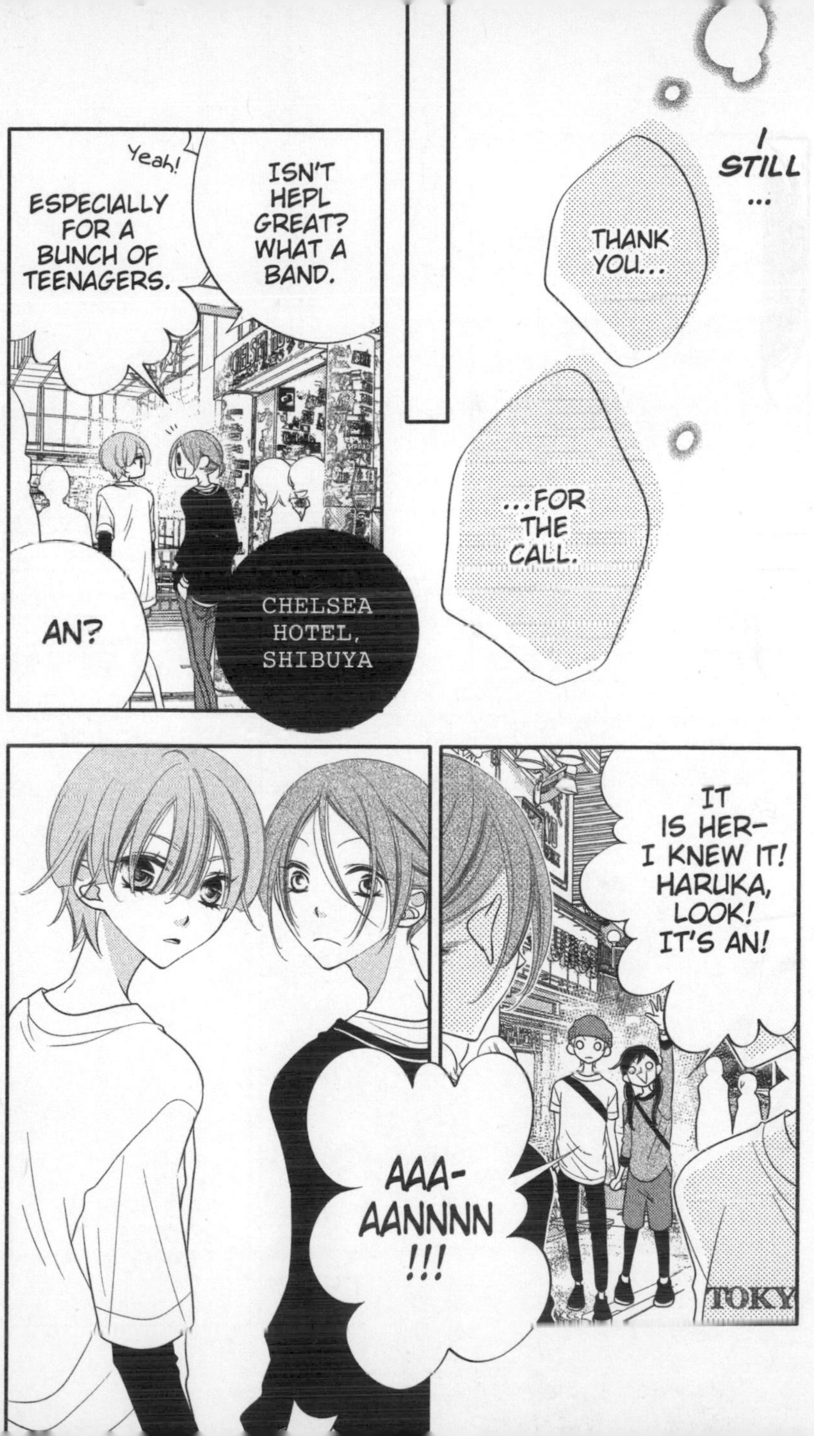
I STILL...
THANK YOU...
...FOR THE CALL.
ISN'T HEPL GREAT? WHAT A BAND.
Yeah!
ESPECIALLY FOR A BUNCH OF TEENAGERS.
CHELSEA HOTEL, SHIBUYA
AN?
IT IS HER- I KNEW IT! HARUKA, LOOK! IT'S AN!
TOKY
AAA-AANNNN!!!

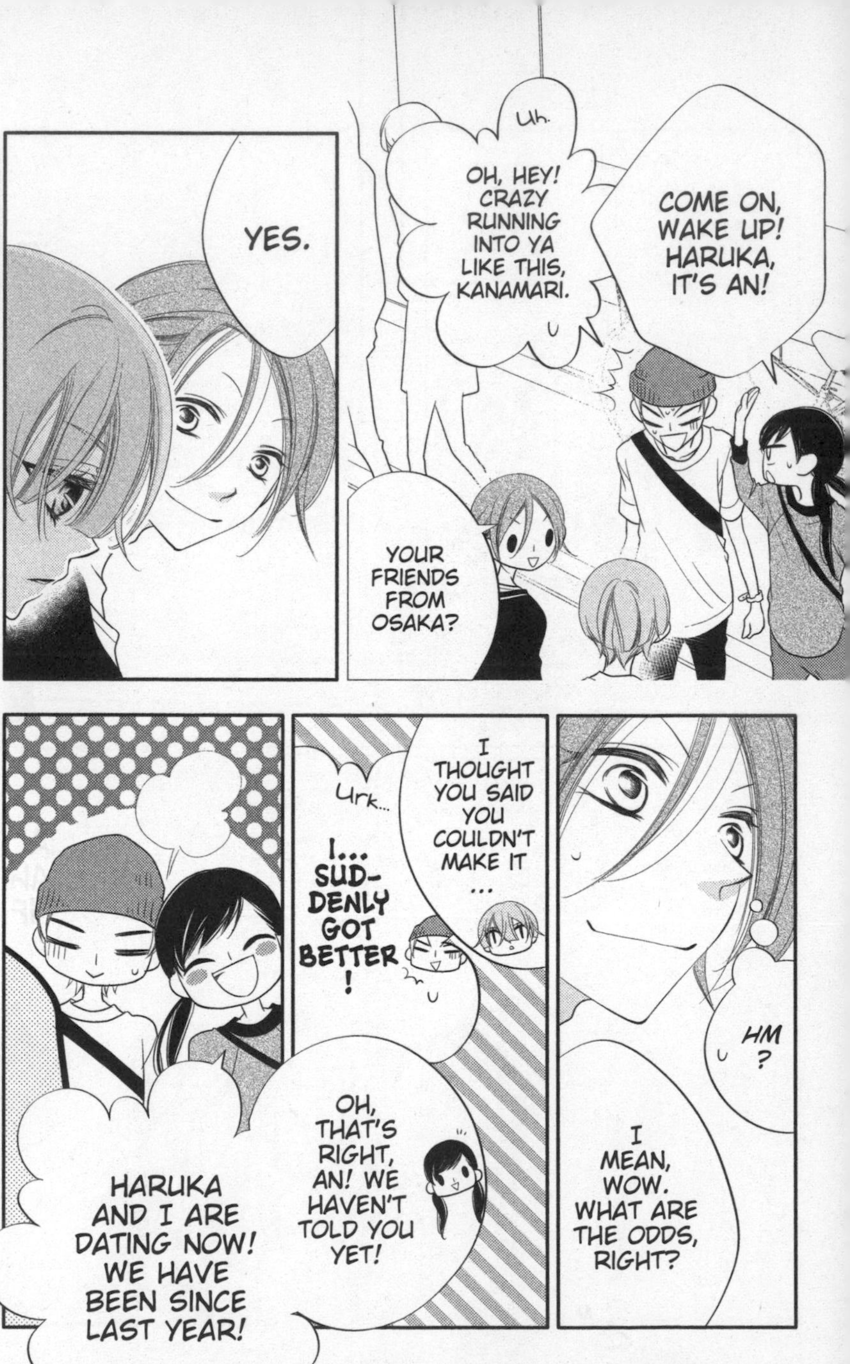
COME ON, WAKE UP! HARUKA, IT'S AN!
Uh.
OH, HEY! CRAZY RUNNING INTO YA LIKE THIS, KANAMARI.
YOUR FRIENDS FROM OSAKA?
YES.
HM?
I MEAN, WOW. WHAT ARE THE ODDS, RIGHT?
I THOUGHT YOU SAID YOU COULDN'T MAKE IT...
Urk...
I... SUD-DENLY GOT BETTER!
OH, THAT'S RIGHT, AN! WE HAVEN'T TOLD YOU YET!
HARUKA AND I ARE DATING NOW! WE HAVE BEEN SINCE LAST YEAR!

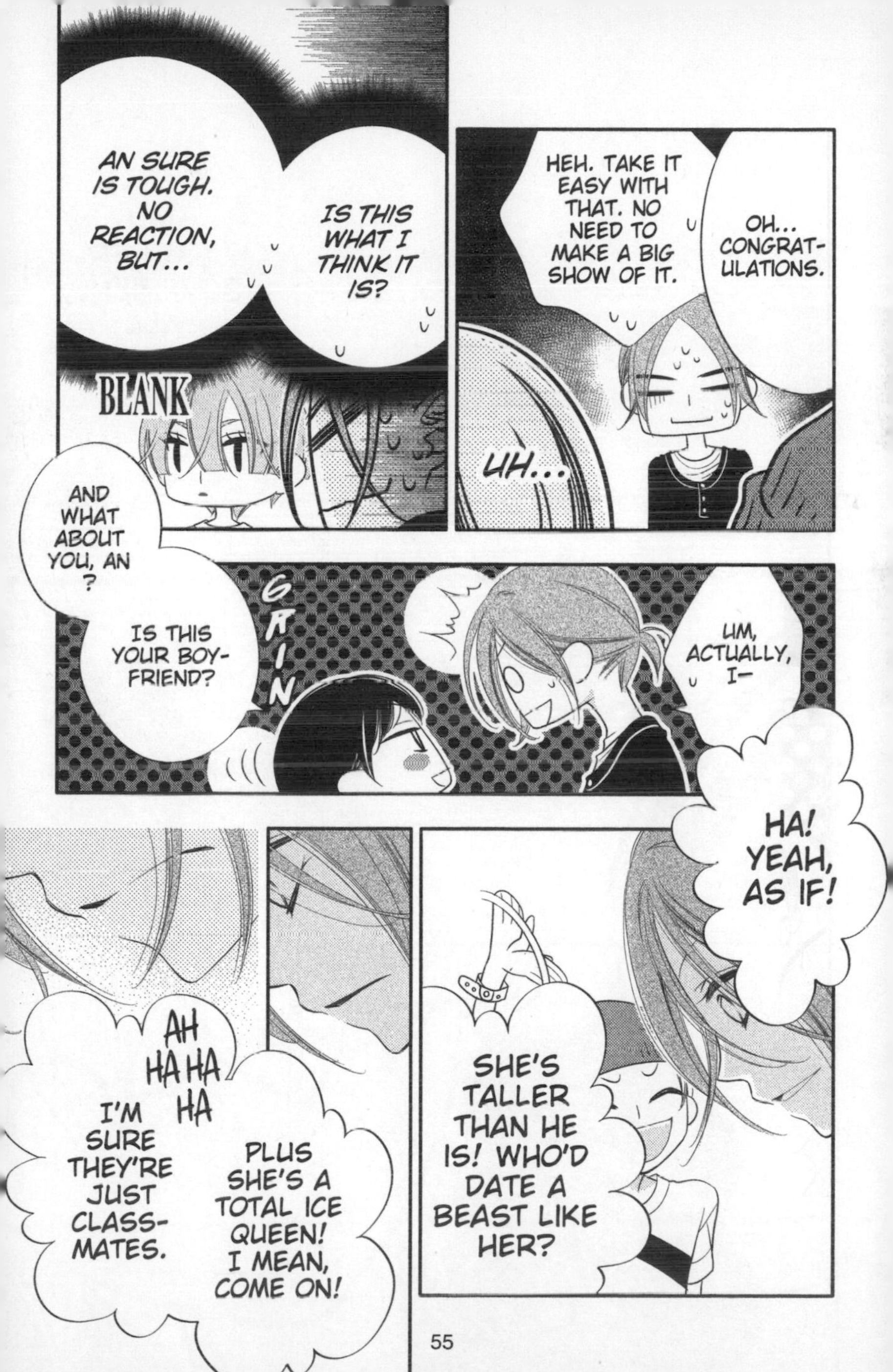
OH... CONGRAT-ULATIONS.
HEH. TAKE IT EASY WITH THAT. NO NEED TO MAKE A BIG SHOW OF IT.
UH...
IS THIS WHAT I THINK IT IS?
AN SURE IS TOUGH. NO REACTION, BUT...
BLANK
AND WHAT ABOUT YOU, AN?
UM, ACTUALLY, I—
GRIN
IS THIS YOUR BOY-FRIEND?
HA! YEAH, AS IF!
SHE'S TALLER THAN HE IS! WHO'D DATE A BEAST LIKE HER?
AH HA HA HA HA
PLUS SHE'S A TOTAL ICE QUEEN! I MEAN, COME ON!
I'M SURE THEY'RE JUST CLASS-MATES.

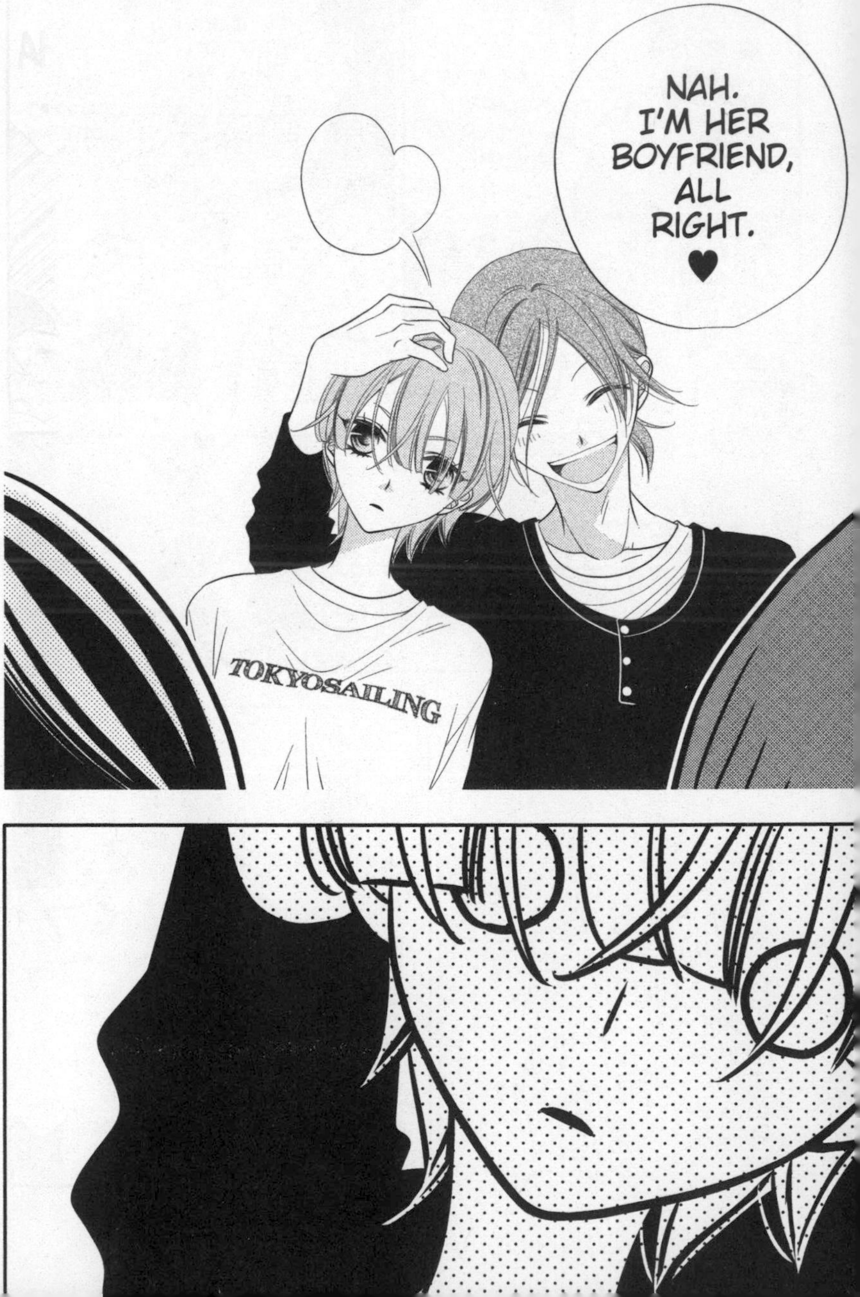
NAH. I'M HER BOYFRIEND, ALL RIGHT. ♥
TOKYOSAILING

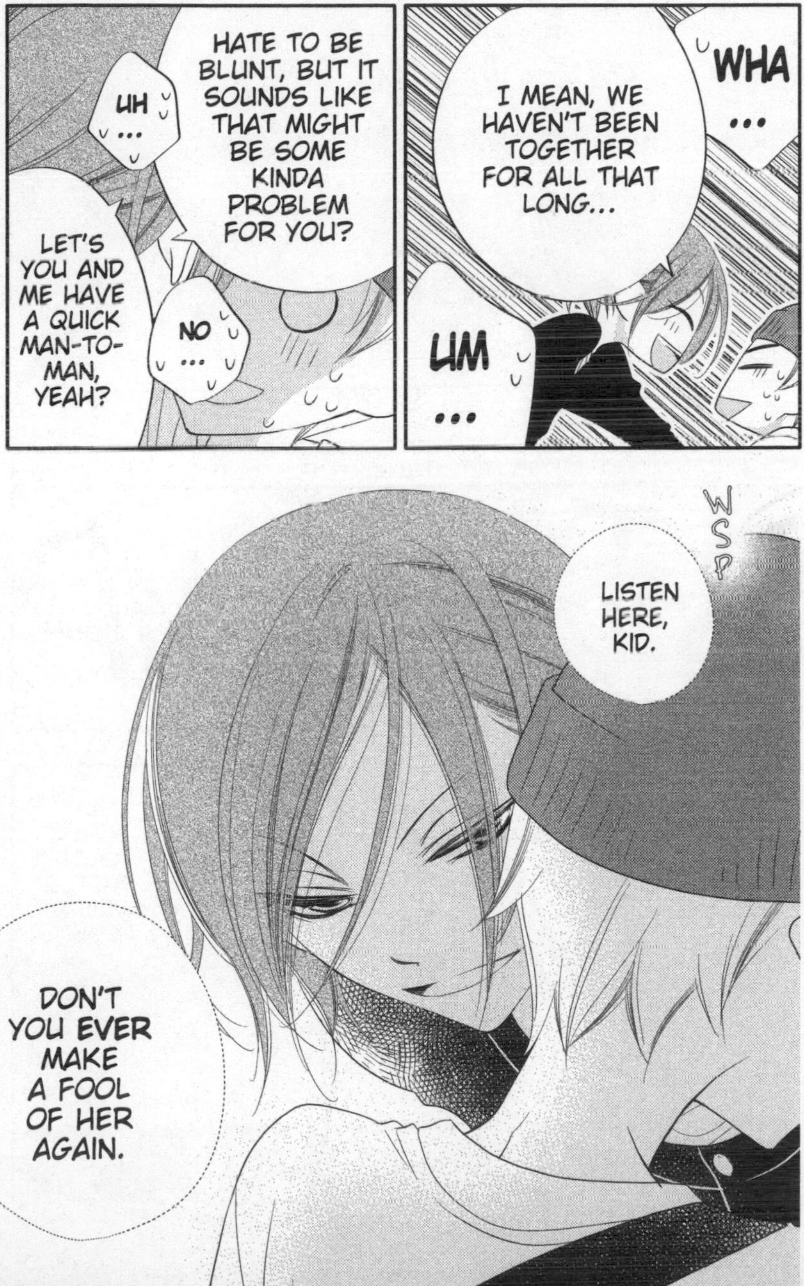
WHA ...
I MEAN, WE HAVEN'T BEEN TOGETHER FOR ALL THAT LONG...
UM ...
HATE TO BE BLUNT, BUT IT SOUNDS LIKE THAT MIGHT BE SOME KINDA PROBLEM FOR YOU?
UH ...
LET'S YOU AND ME HAVE A QUICK MAN-TO-MAN, YEAH?
NO ...
WSP
LISTEN HERE, KID.
DON'T YOU EVER MAKE A FOOL OF HER AGAIN.

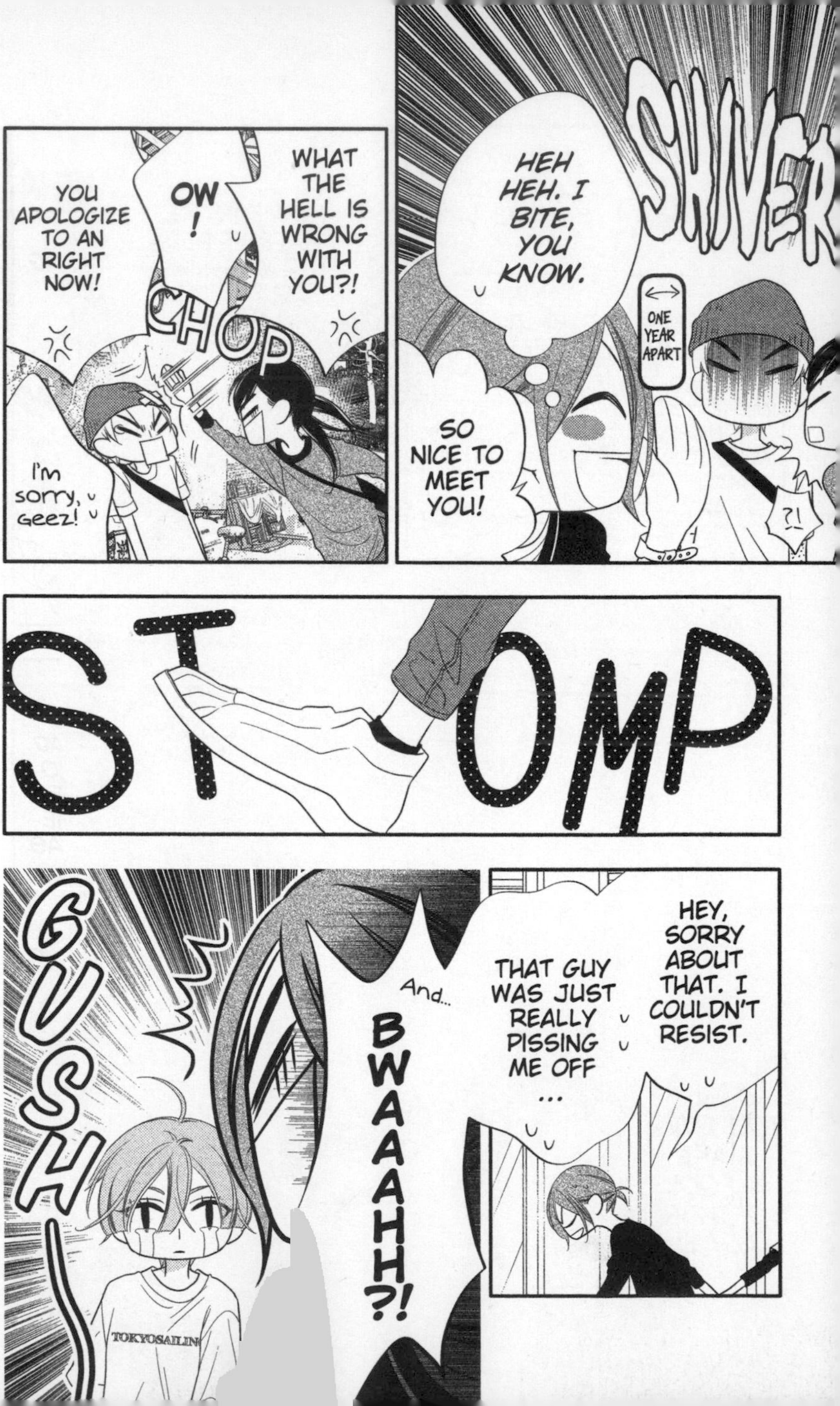
SHIVER
HEH HEH. I BITE, YOU KNOW.
ONE YEAR APART
SO NICE TO MEET YOU!
?!
WHAT THE HELL IS WRONG WITH YOU?!
OW!
YOU APOLOGIZE TO AN RIGHT NOW!
CHOP
I'm sorry, geez!
STOMP
HEY, SORRY ABOUT THAT. I COULDN'T RESIST.
THAT GUY WAS JUST REALLY PISSING ME OFF...
And...
BWAAAAHH?!
GUSH
TOKYOSAILIN

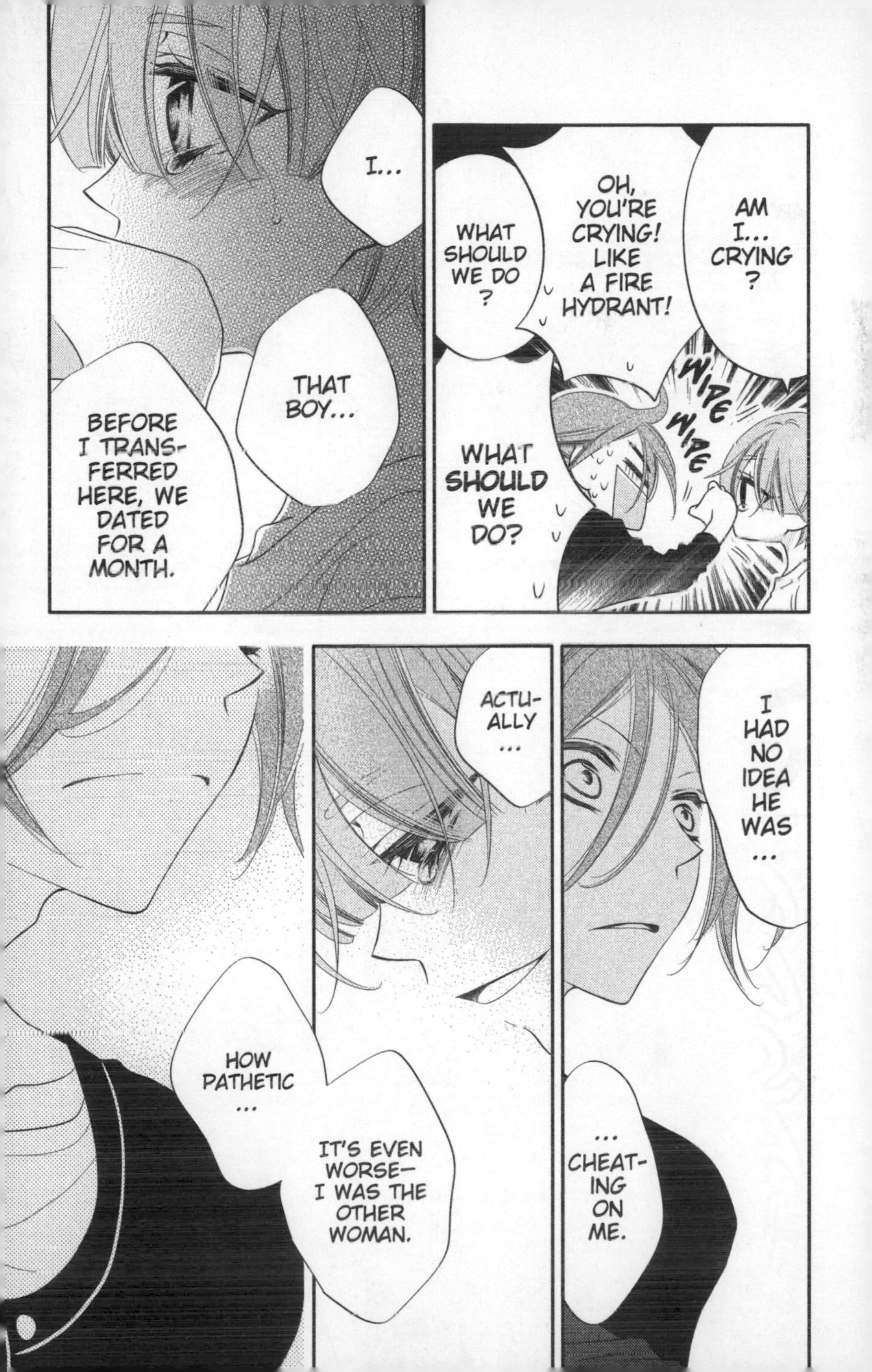
AM I... CRYING?
OH, YOU'RE CRYING! LIKE A FIRE HYDRANT!
WHAT SHOULD WE DO?
WIPE WIPE
WHAT SHOULD WE DO?
I...
THAT BOY...
BEFORE I TRANSFERRED HERE, WE DATED FOR A MONTH.
I HAD NO IDEA HE WAS...
...CHEATING ON ME.
ACTUALLY...
HOW PATHETIC...
IT'S EVEN WORSE— I WAS THE OTHER WOMAN.

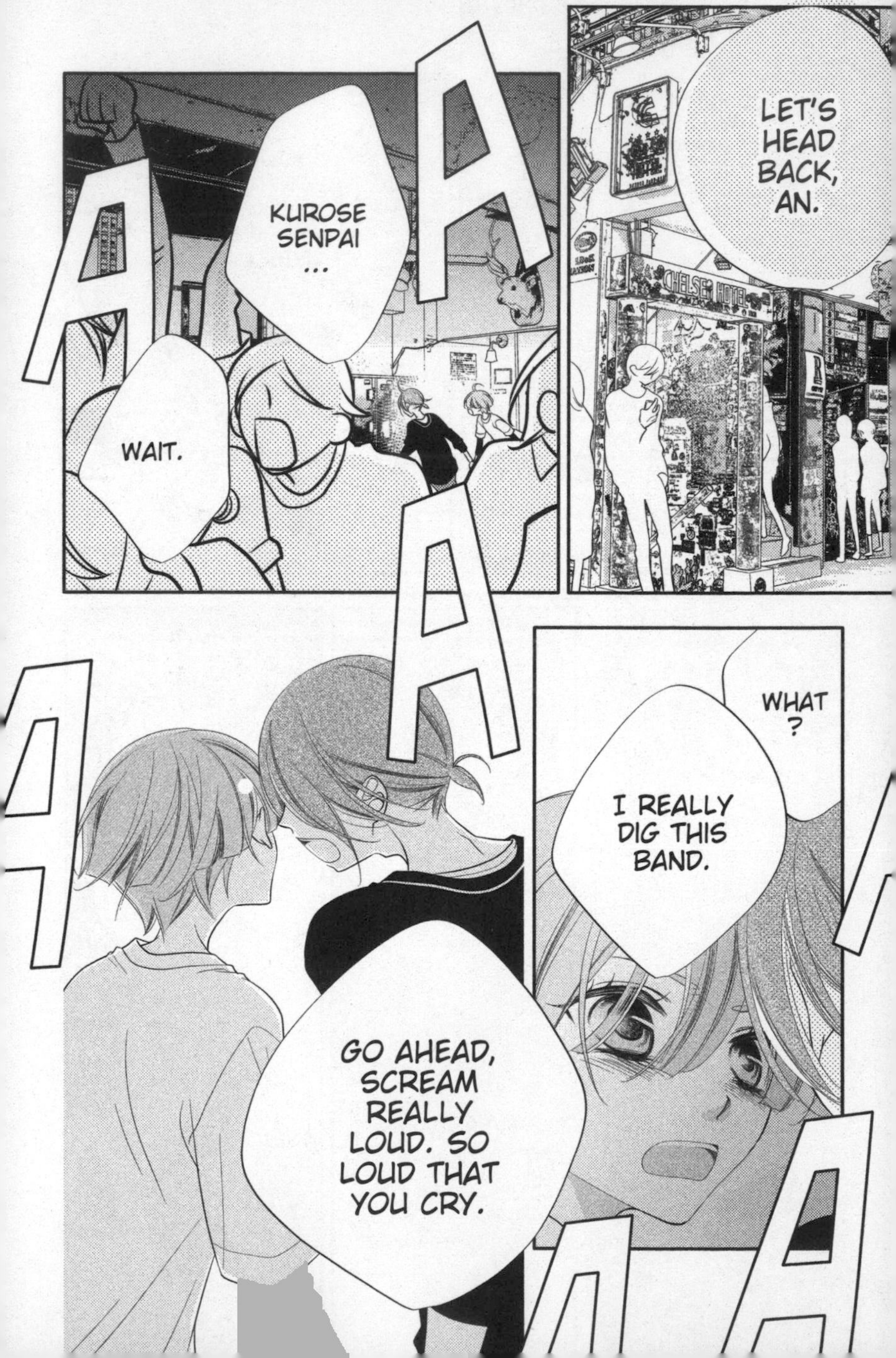
LET'S HEAD BACK, AN.
KUROSE SENPAI ...
WAIT.
AAAA
WHAT?
I REALLY DIG THIS BAND.
GO AHEAD, SCREAM REALLY LOUD. SO LOUD THAT YOU CRY.
AAAA

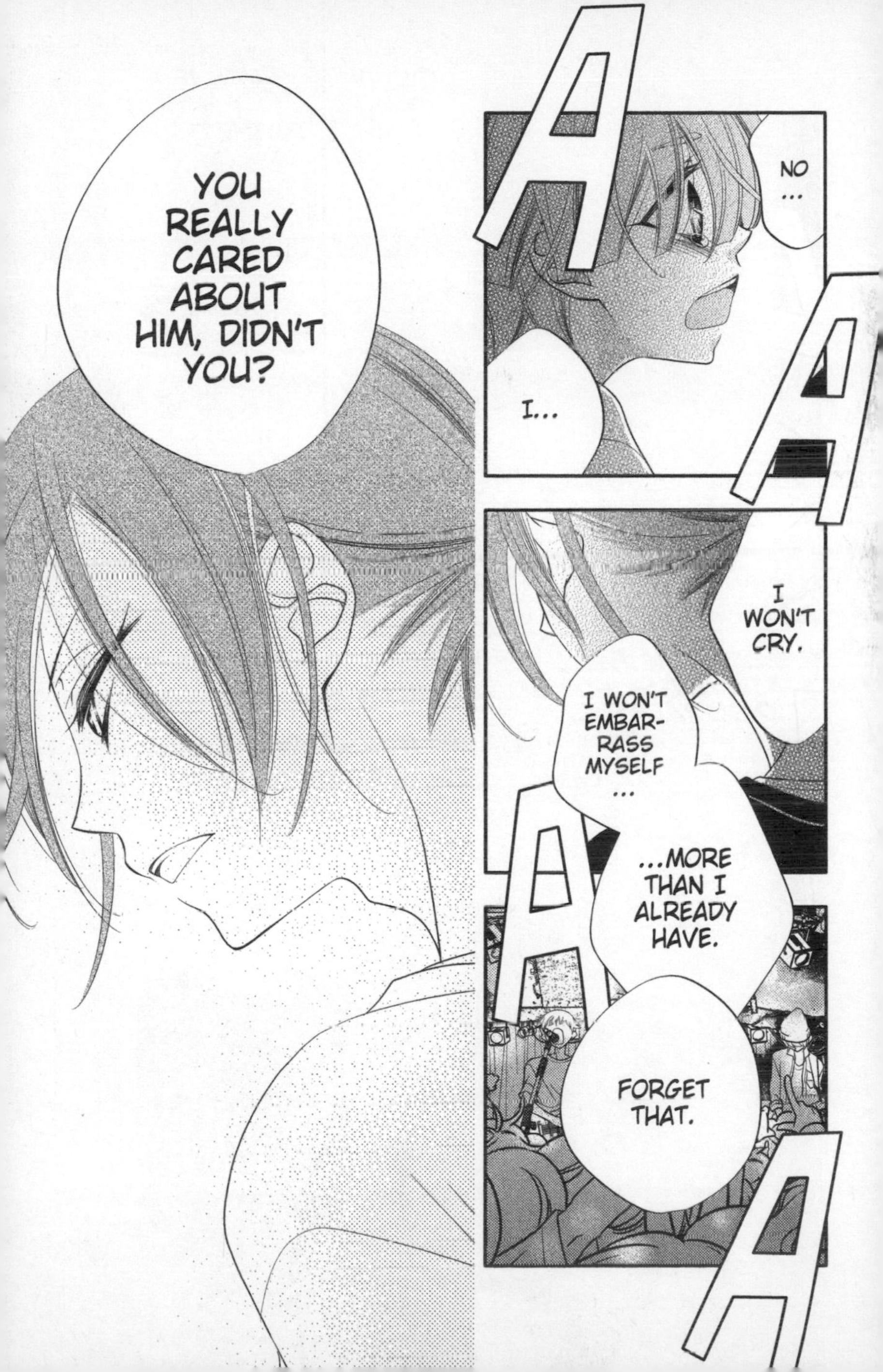
AAAA
NO ...
I...
I WON'T CRY.
I WON'T EMBAR-RASS MYSELF ...
...MORE THAN I ALREADY HAVE.
FORGET THAT.
YOU REALLY CARED ABOUT HIM, DIDN'T YOU?

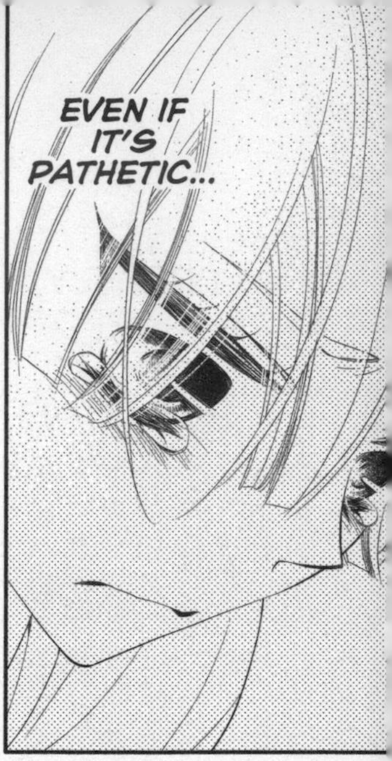
EVEN IF IT'S PATHETIC...
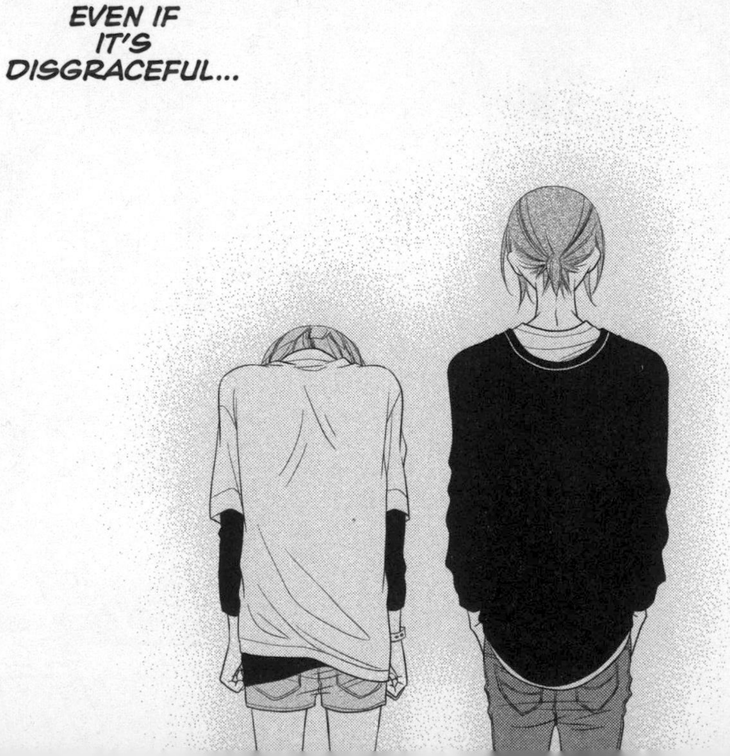
EVEN IF IT'S DISGRACEFUL...

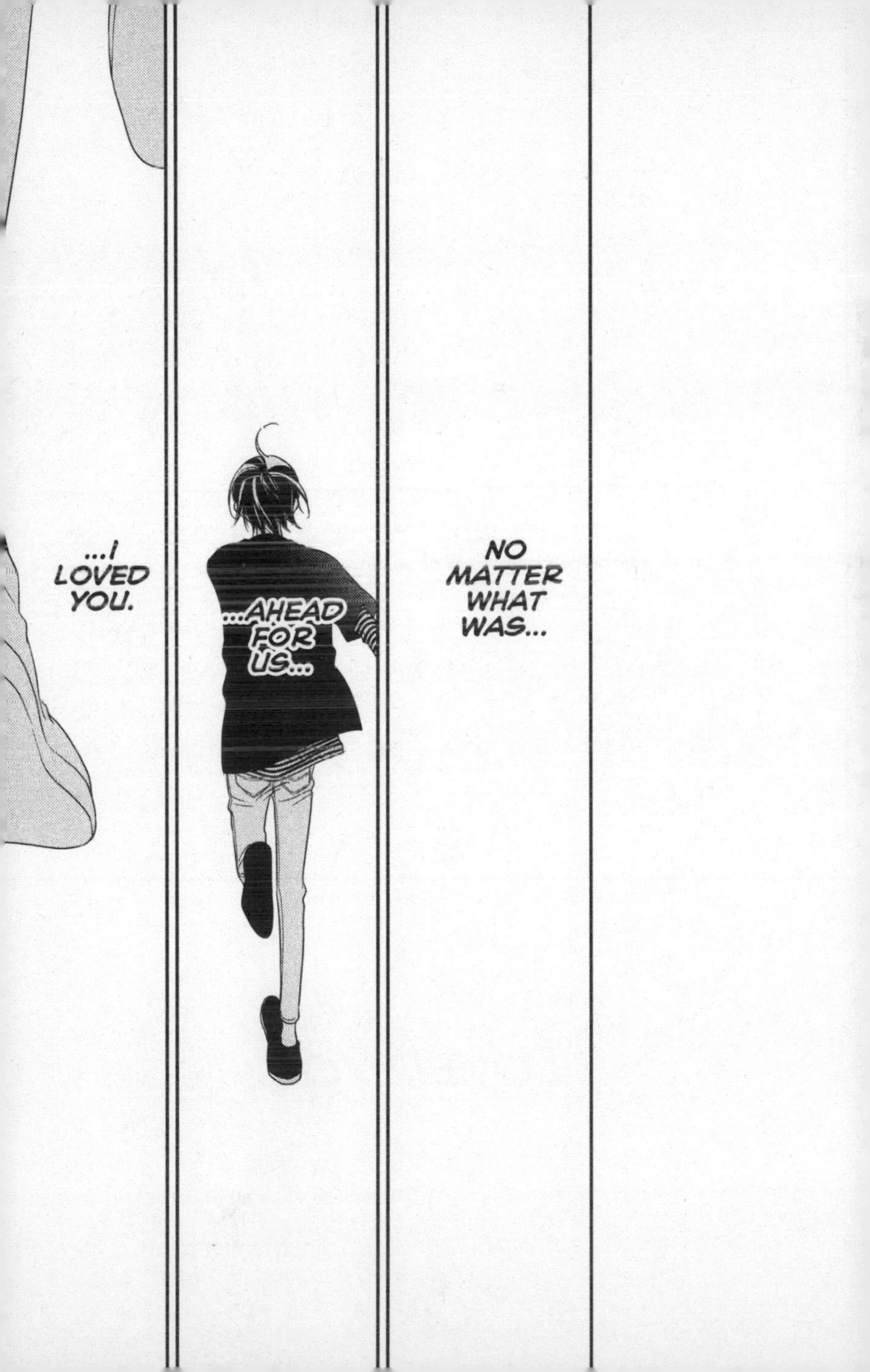
NO MATTER WHAT WAS...
...AHEAD FOR US...
...I LOVED YOU.

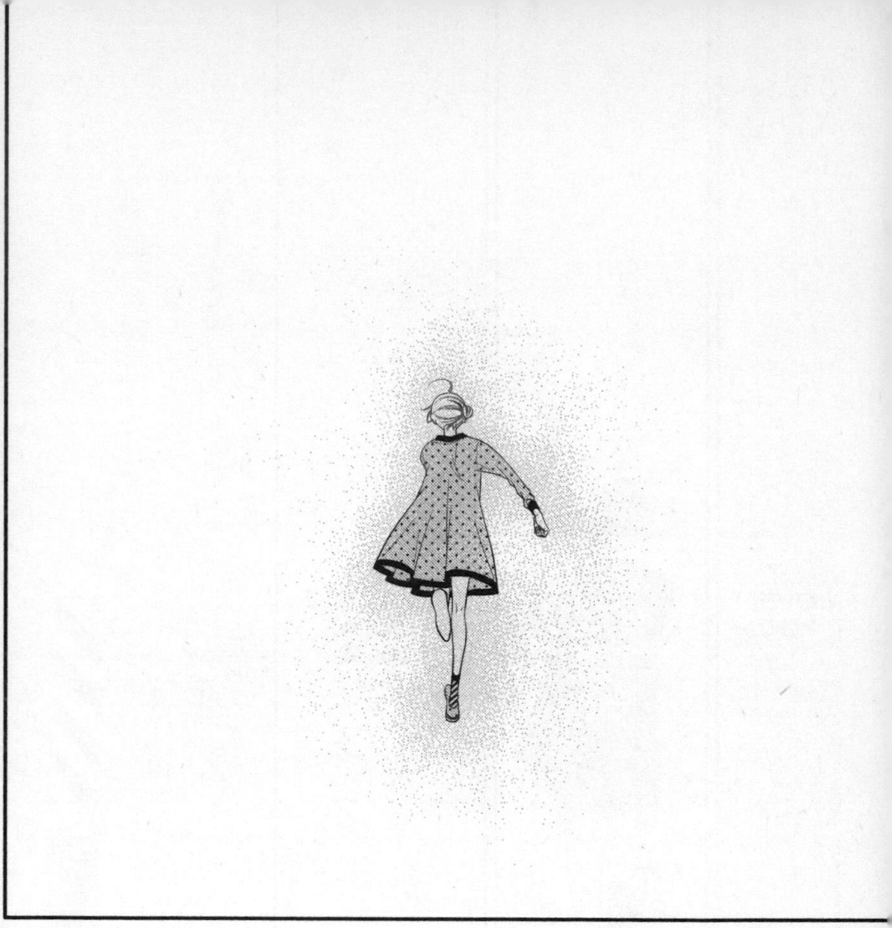

I LOVED YOU.

SONG 73

PLEASE...

...GOD...

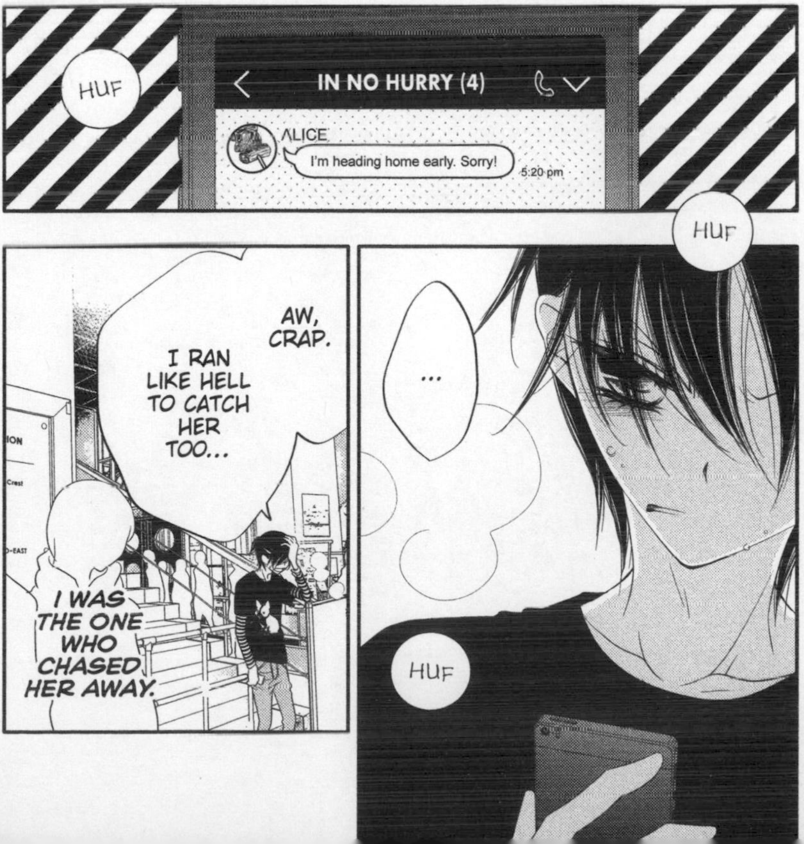
HUF
IN NO HURRY (4)
ALICE
I'm heading home early. Sorry!
5:20 pm
HUF
...
HUF
AW, CRAP.
I RAN LIKE HELL TO CATCH HER TOO...
I WAS THE ONE WHO CHASED HER AWAY.

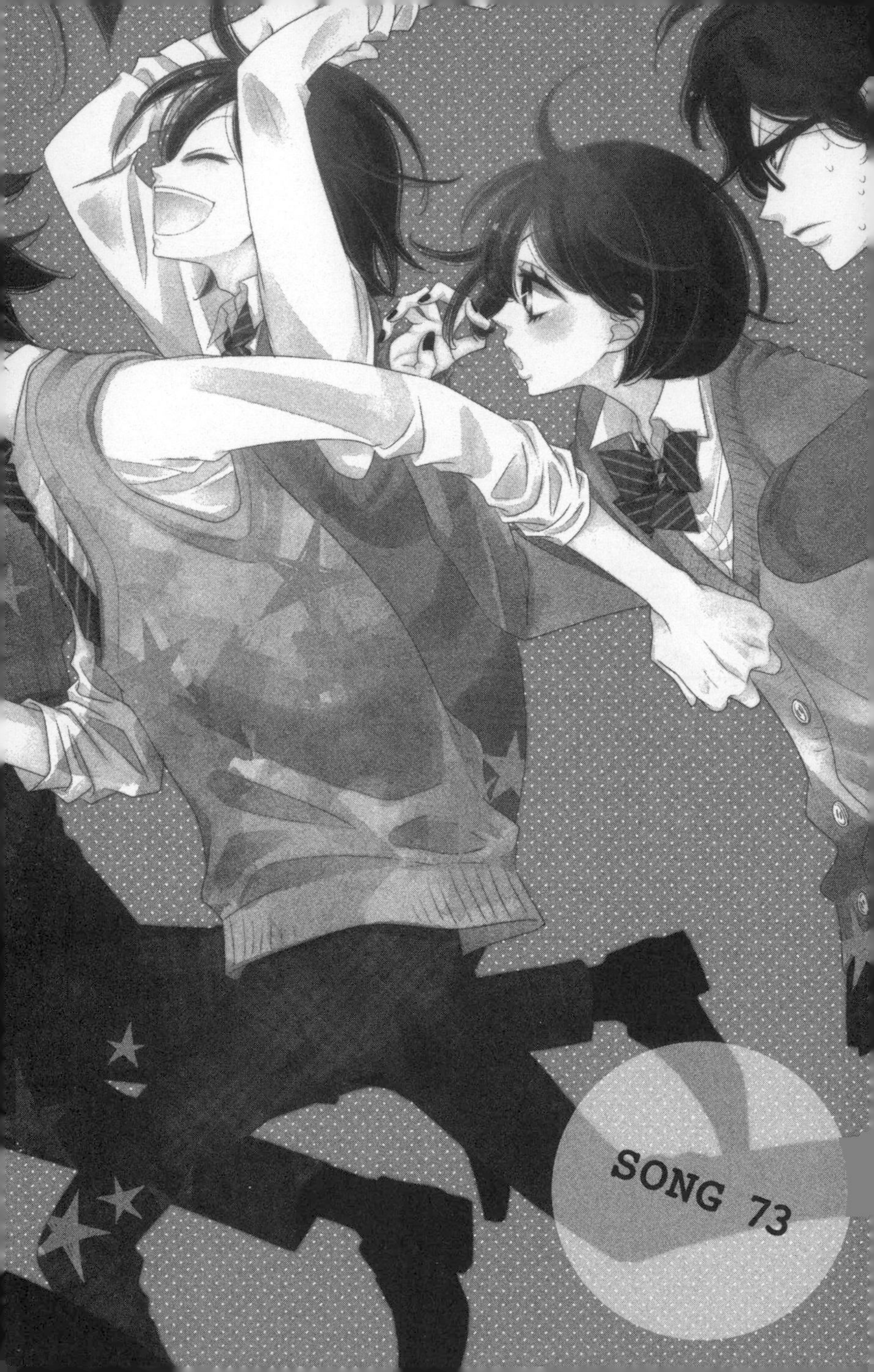
SONG 73

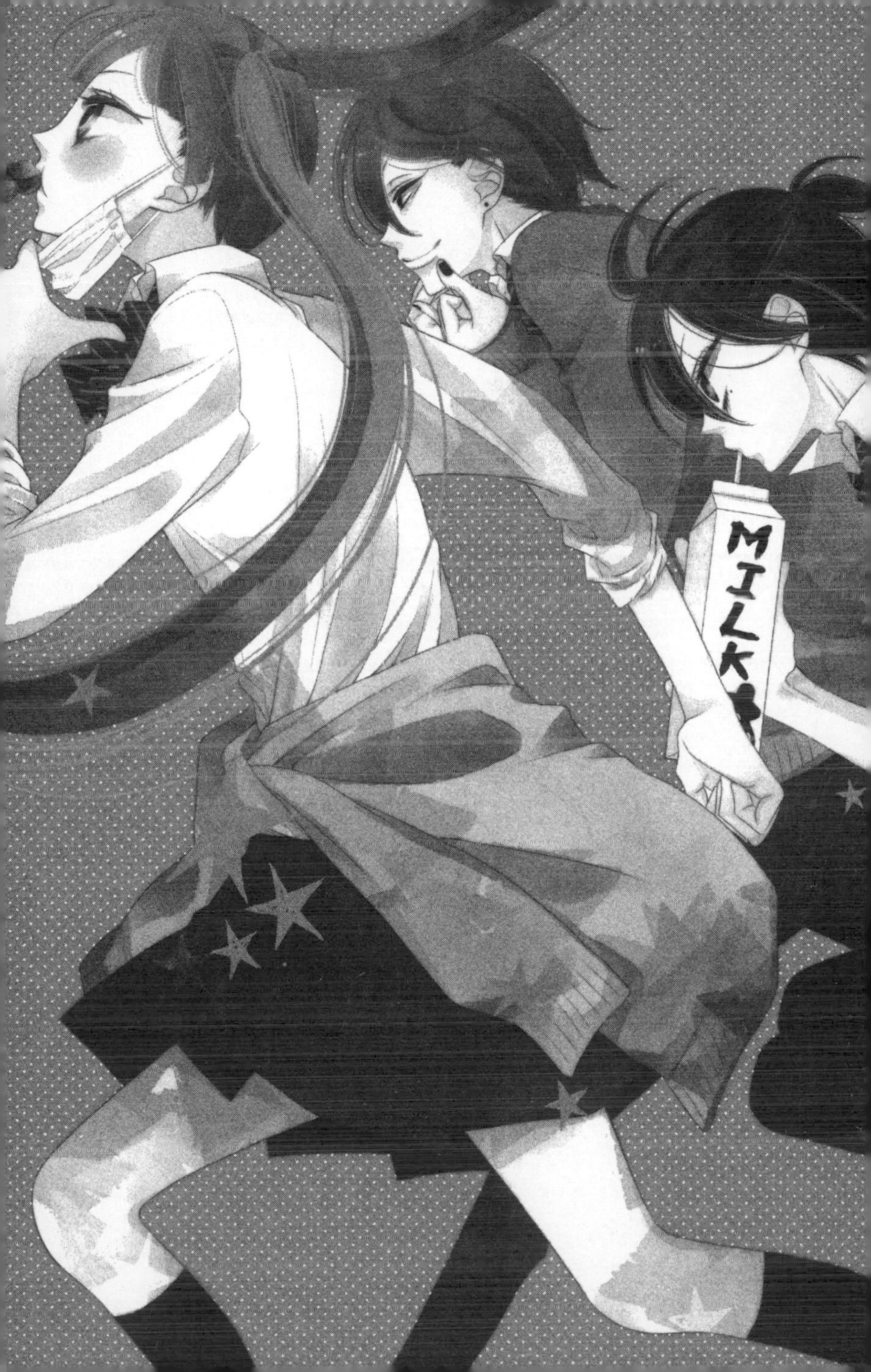
MILK

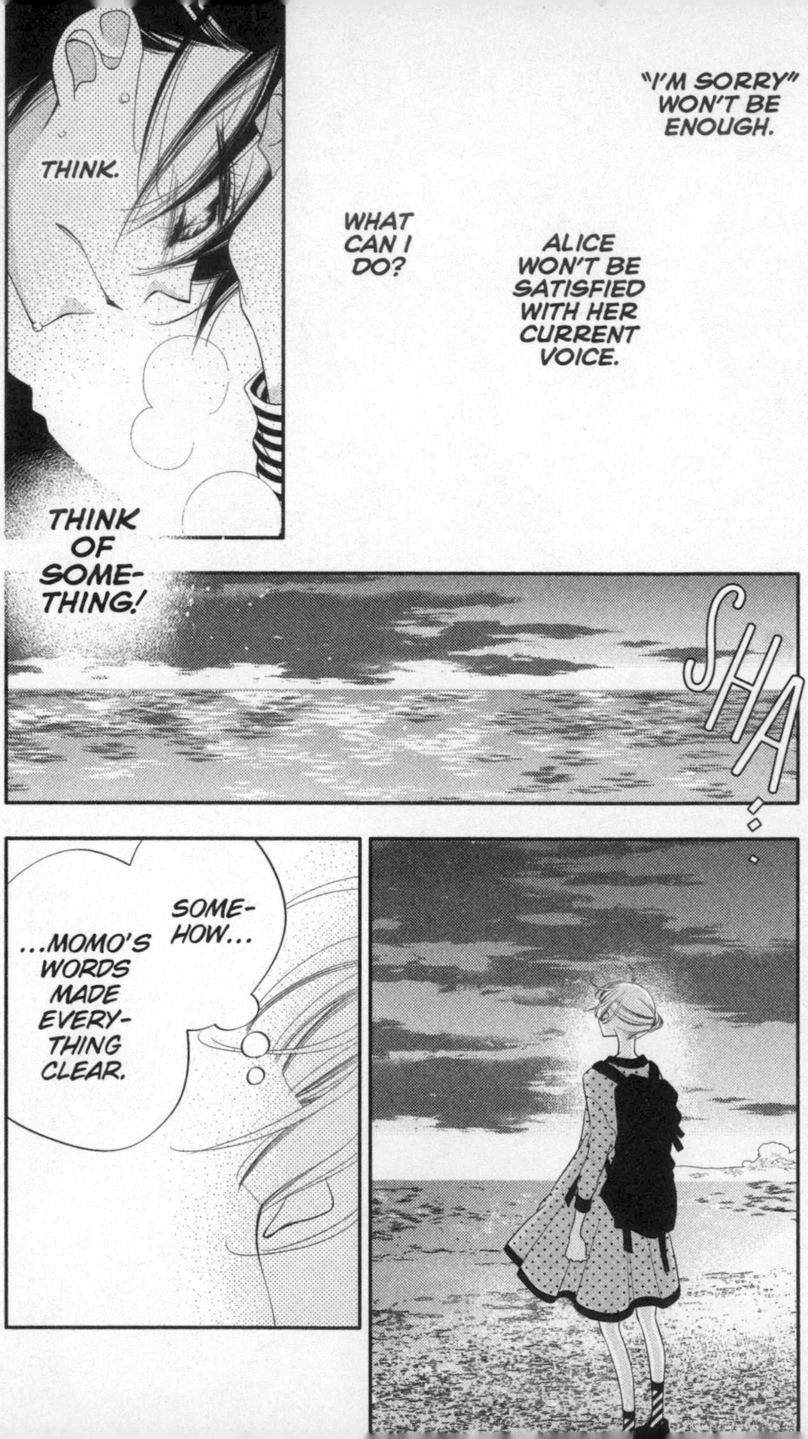
"I'M SORRY" WON'T BE ENOUGH.
ALICE WON'T BE SATISFIED WITH HER CURRENT VOICE.
WHAT CAN I DO?
THINK.
THINK OF SOME-THING!
SHA
SOME-HOW...
...MOMO'S WORDS MADE EVERY-THING CLEAR.

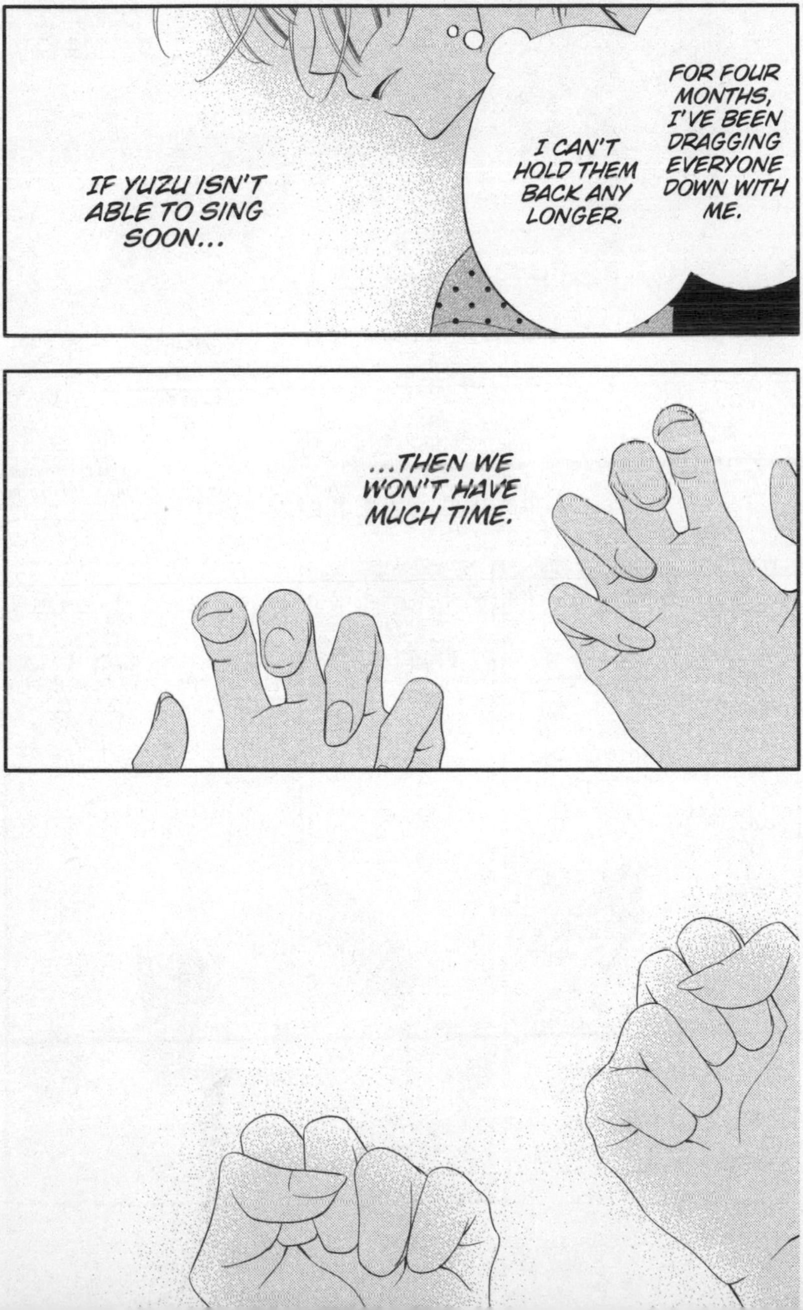
FOR FOUR MONTHS, I'VE BEEN DRAGGING EVERYONE DOWN WITH ME.
I CAN'T HOLD THEM BACK ANY LONGER.
IF YUZU ISN'T ABLE TO SING SOON...
...THEN WE WON'T HAVE MUCH TIME.

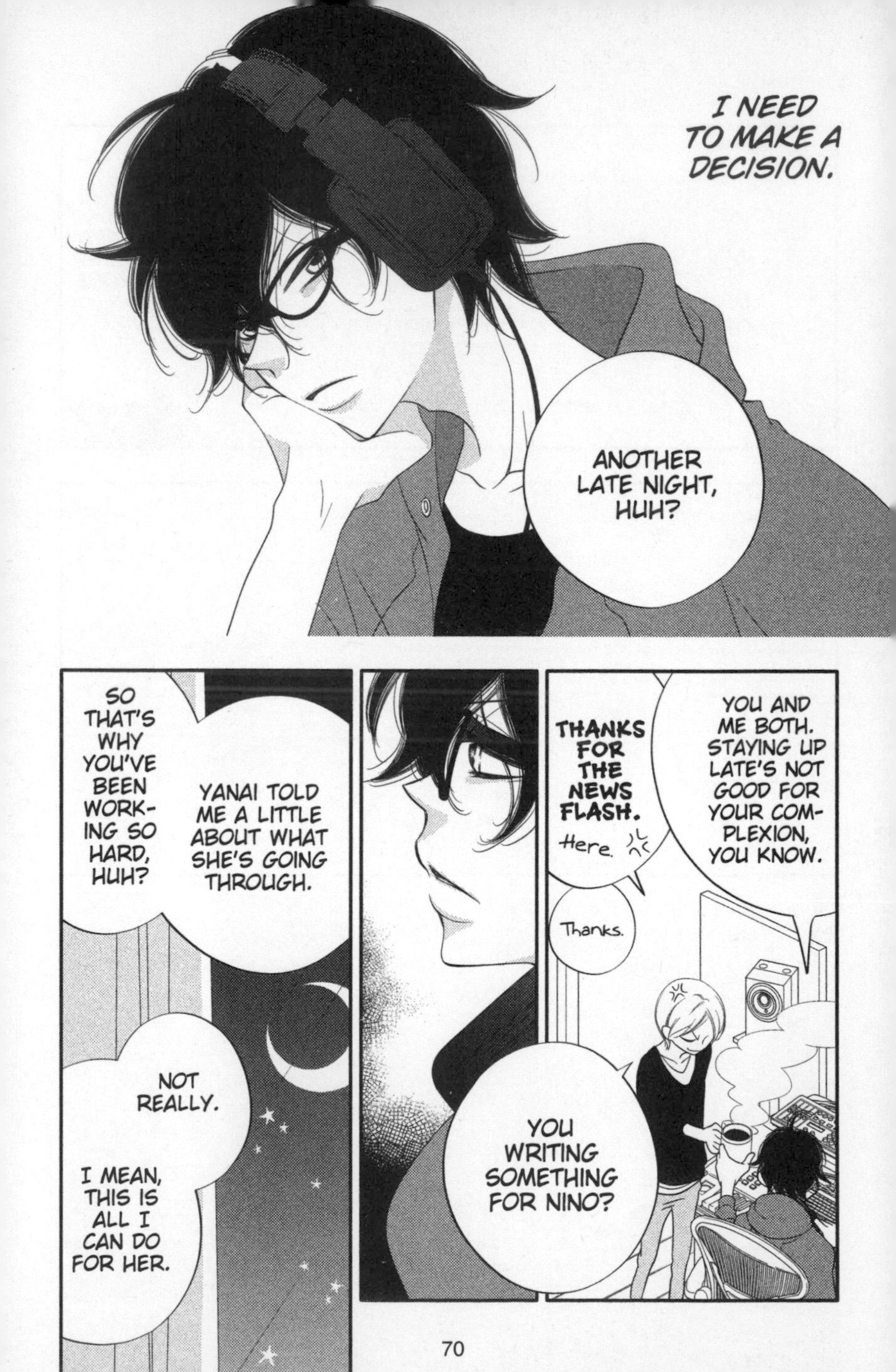
I NEED TO MAKE A DECISION.
ANOTHER LATE NIGHT, HUH?
YOU AND ME BOTH. STAYING UP LATE'S NOT GOOD FOR YOUR COMPLEXION, YOU KNOW.
THANKS FOR THE NEWS FLASH.
Here.
Thanks.
YOU WRITING SOMETHING FOR NINO?
YANAI TOLD ME A LITTLE ABOUT WHAT SHE'S GOING THROUGH.
SO THAT'S WHY YOU'VE BEEN WORKING SO HARD, HUH?
NOT REALLY.
I MEAN, THIS IS ALL I CAN DO FOR HER.

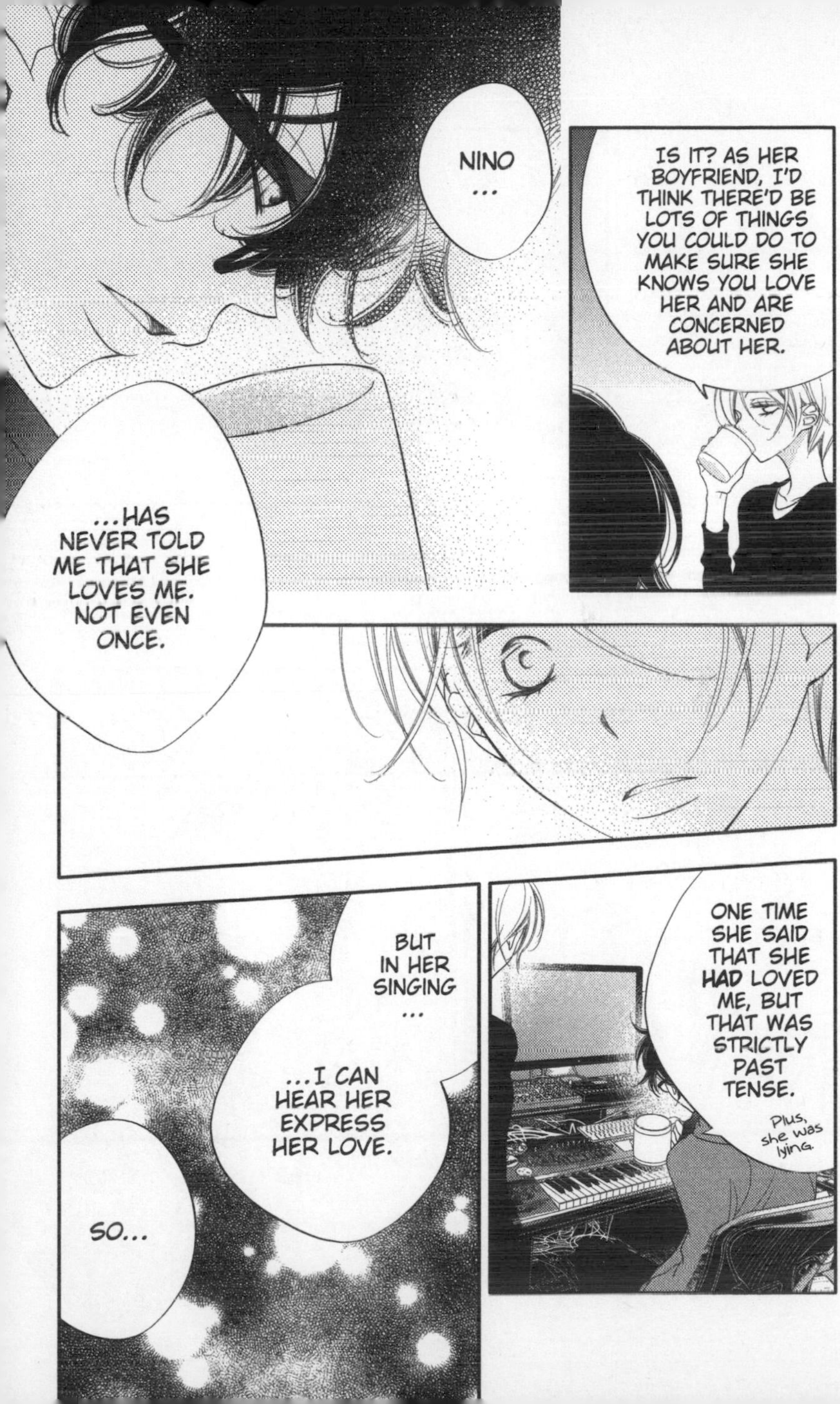
IS IT? AS HER BOYFRIEND, I'D THINK THERE'D BE LOTS OF THINGS YOU COULD DO TO MAKE SURE SHE KNOWS YOU LOVE HER AND ARE CONCERNED ABOUT HER.
NINO ...
...HAS NEVER TOLD ME THAT SHE LOVES ME. NOT EVEN ONCE.
ONE TIME SHE SAID THAT SHE **HAD** LOVED ME, BUT THAT WAS STRICTLY PAST TENSE.
Plus, she was lying.
BUT IN HER SINGING ...
...I CAN HEAR HER EXPRESS HER LOVE.
SO...

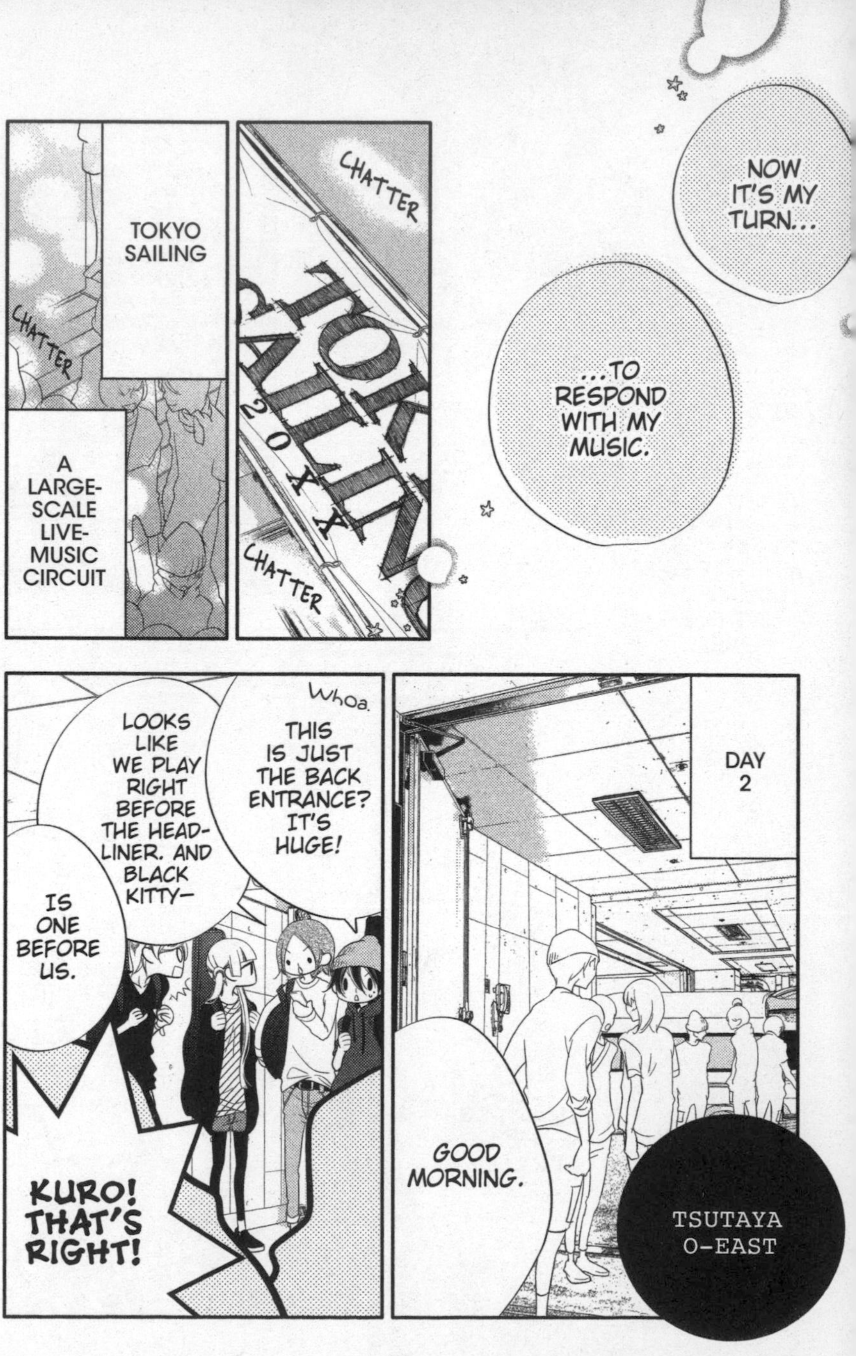
NOW IT'S MY TURN...
...TO RESPOND WITH MY MUSIC.
CHATTER
TOKYO SAILING 20XX
CHATTER
TOKYO SAILING
CHATTER
A LARGE-SCALE LIVE-MUSIC CIRCUIT
DAY 2
TSUTAYA O-EAST
GOOD MORNING.
Whoa.
THIS IS JUST THE BACK ENTRANCE? IT'S HUGE!
LOOKS LIKE WE PLAY RIGHT BEFORE THE HEAD-LINER. AND BLACK KITTY—
IS ONE BEFORE US.
KURO! THAT'S RIGHT!

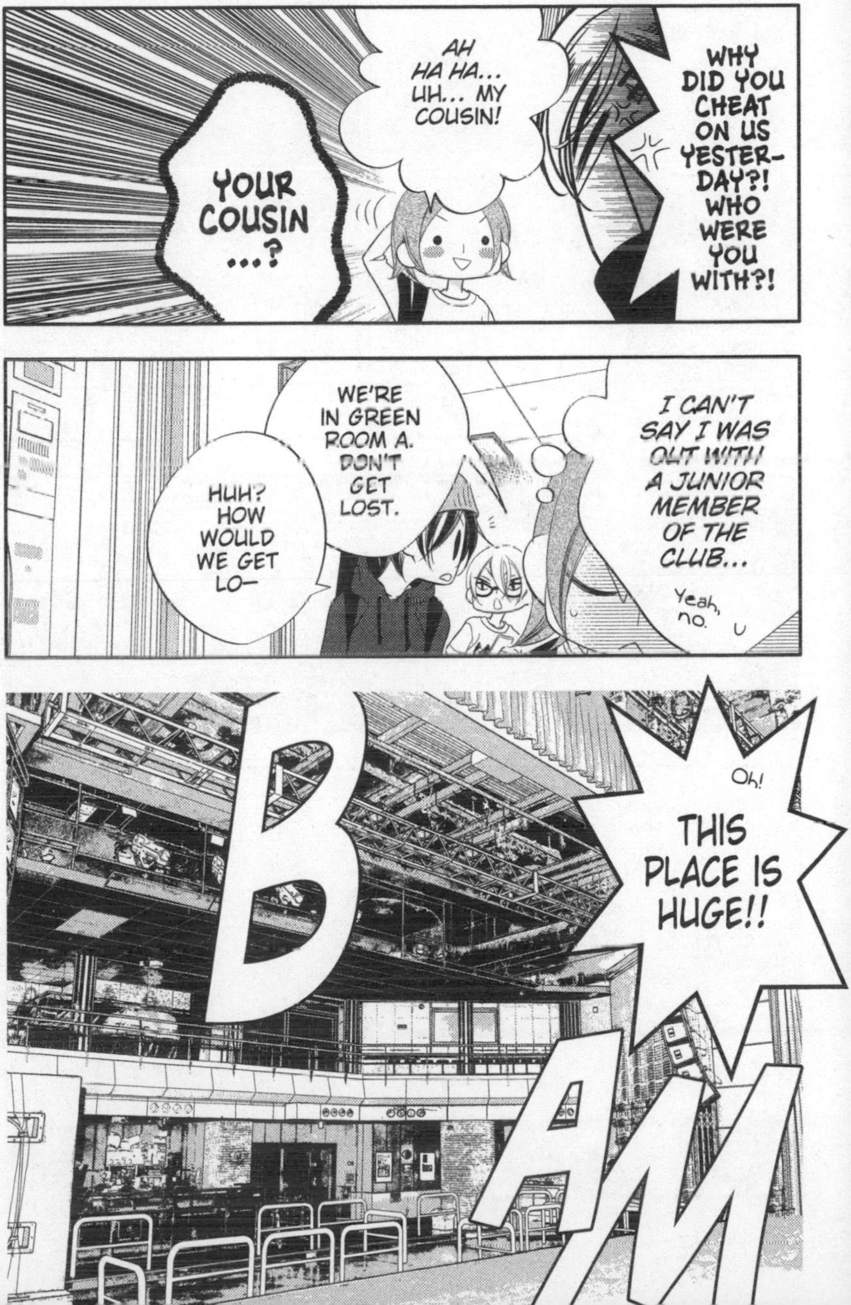
WHY DID YOU CHEAT ON US YESTER-DAY?! WHO WERE YOU WITH?!
AH HA HA... UH... MY COUSIN!
YOUR COUSIN ...?
I CAN'T SAY I WAS OUT WITH A JUNIOR MEMBER OF THE CLUB...
Yeah, no.
WE'RE IN GREEN ROOM A. DON'T GET LOST.
HUH? HOW WOULD WE GET LO—
Oh!
THIS PLACE IS HUGE!!
BAM

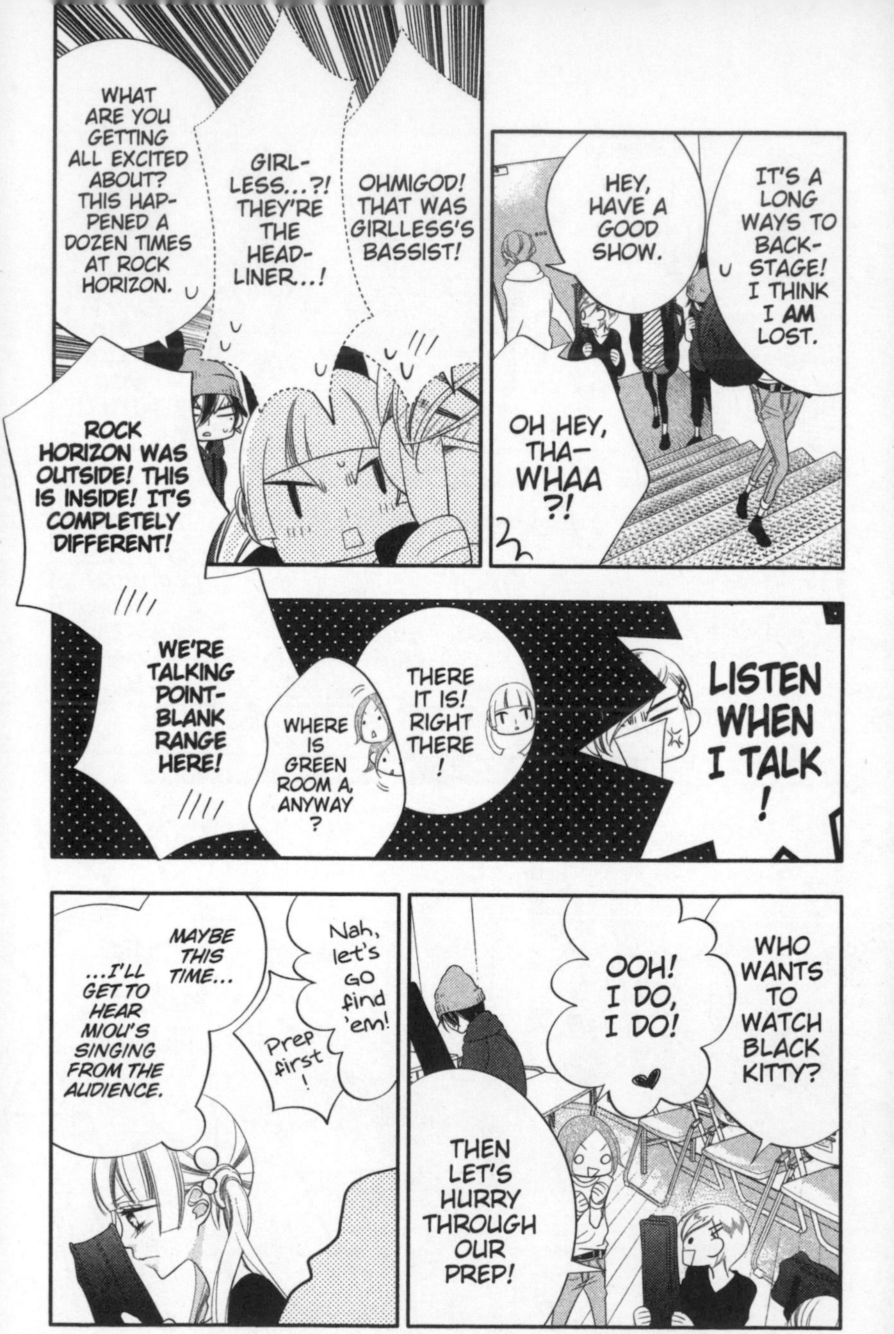
IT'S A LONG WAYS TO BACK-STAGE! I THINK I AM LOST.
HEY, HAVE A GOOD SHOW.
OH HEY, THA-WHAA?!
OHMIGOD! THAT WAS GIRLLESS'S BASSIST!
GIRL-LESS...?! THEY'RE THE HEAD-LINER...!
WHAT ARE YOU GETTING ALL EXCITED ABOUT? THIS HAP-PENED A DOZEN TIMES AT ROCK HORIZON.
ROCK HORIZON WAS OUTSIDE! THIS IS INSIDE! IT'S COMPLETELY DIFFERENT!
LISTEN WHEN I TALK!
THERE IT IS! RIGHT THERE!
WHERE IS GREEN ROOM A, ANYWAY?
WE'RE TALKING POINT-BLANK RANGE HERE!
WHO WANTS TO WATCH BLACK KITTY?
OOH! I DO, I DO!
THEN LET'S HURRY THROUGH OUR PREP!
Nah, let's go find 'em!
Prep first!
MAYBE THIS TIME...
...I'LL GET TO HEAR MIOU'S SINGING FROM THE AUDIENCE.

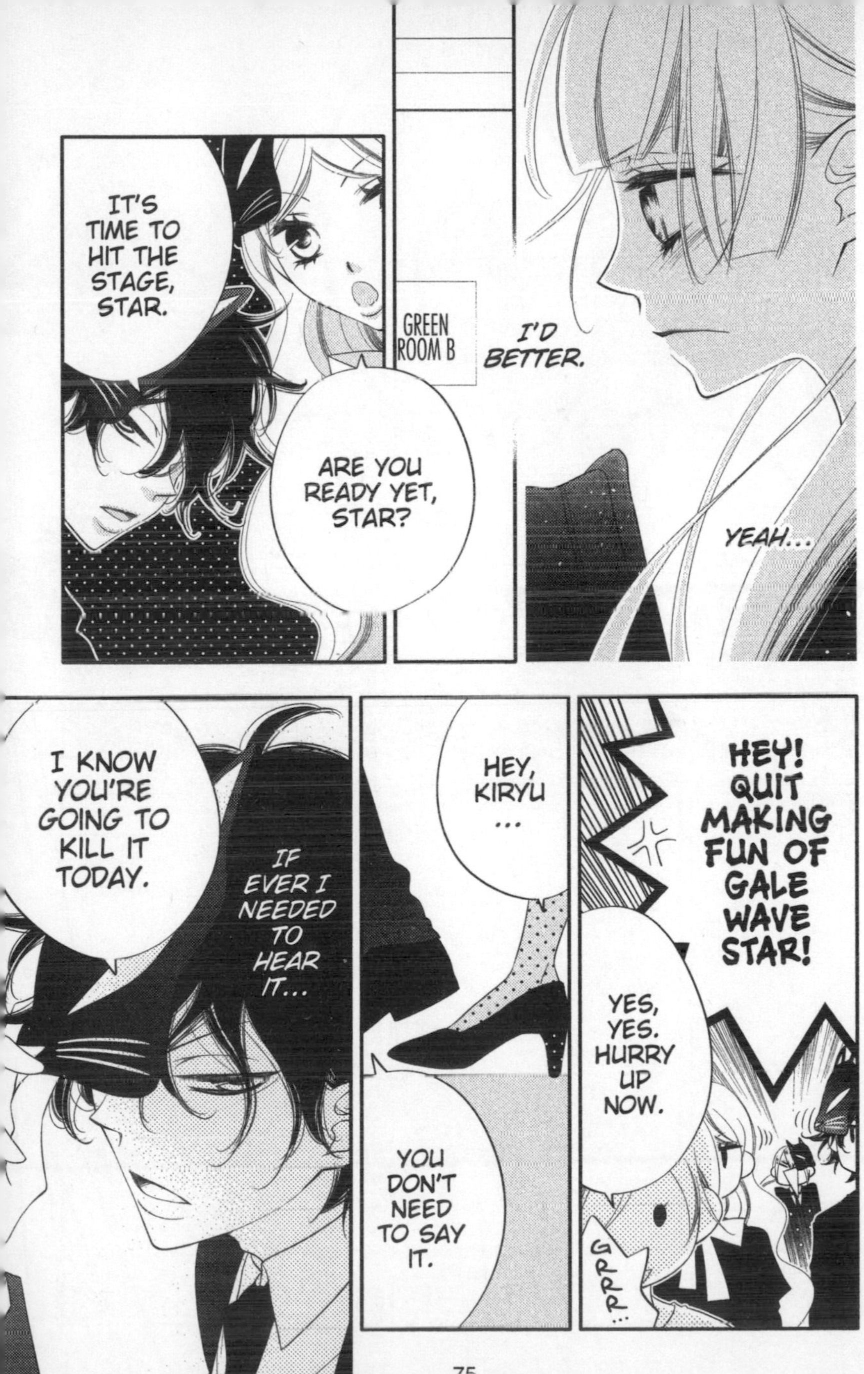
YEAH...
I'D BETTER.
GREEN ROOM B
ARE YOU READY YET, STAR?
IT'S TIME TO HIT THE STAGE, STAR.
HEY! QUIT MAKING FUN OF GALE WAVE STAR!
YES, YES. HURRY UP NOW.
GRRR...
HEY, KIRYU...
YOU DON'T NEED TO SAY IT.
I KNOW YOU'RE GOING TO KILL IT TODAY.
IF EVER I NEEDED TO HEAR IT...

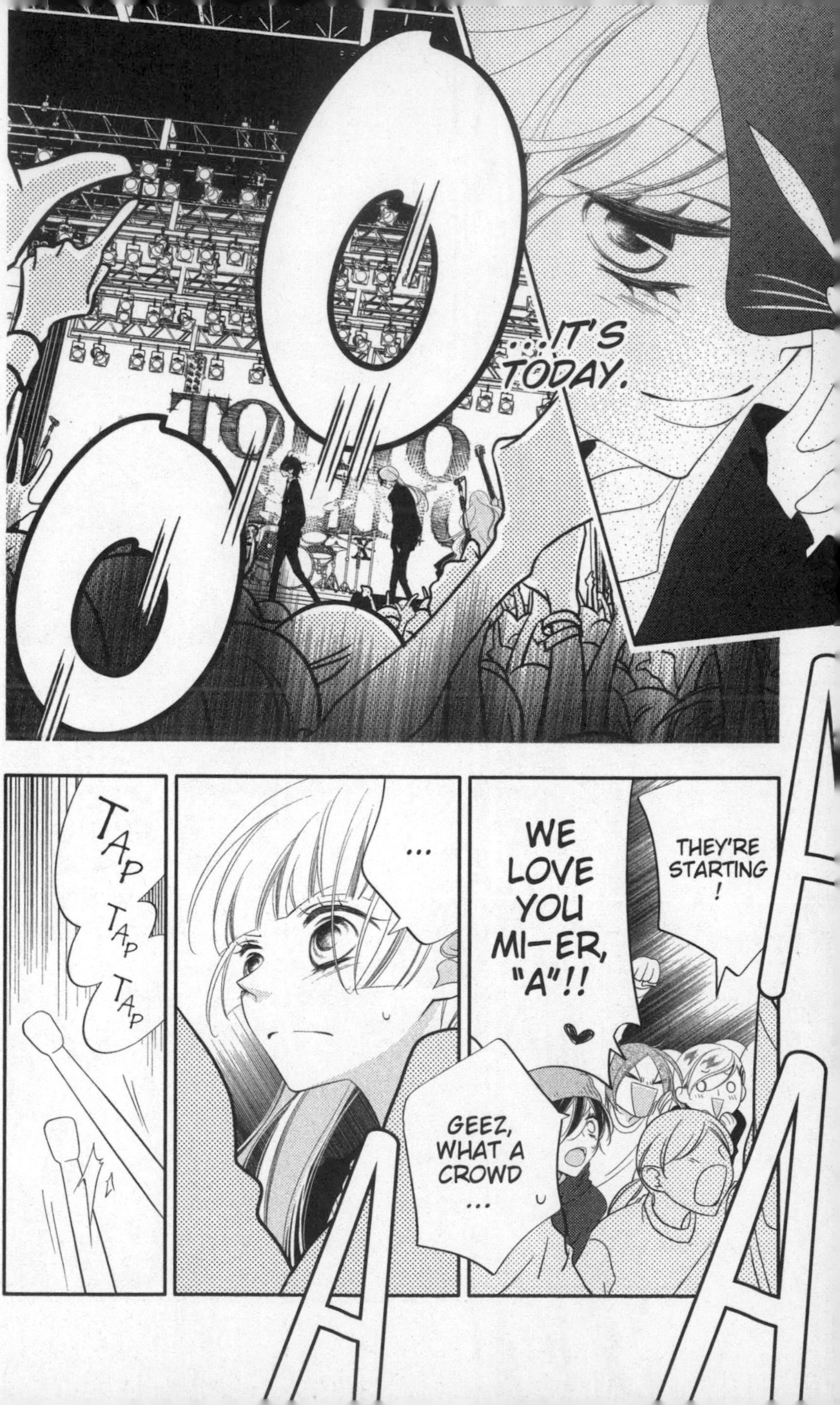
...IT'S TODAY.
OO
AA
THEY'RE STARTING!
WE LOVE YOU MI-ER, "A"!!
GEEZ, WHAT A CROWD...
...
TAP TAP TAP

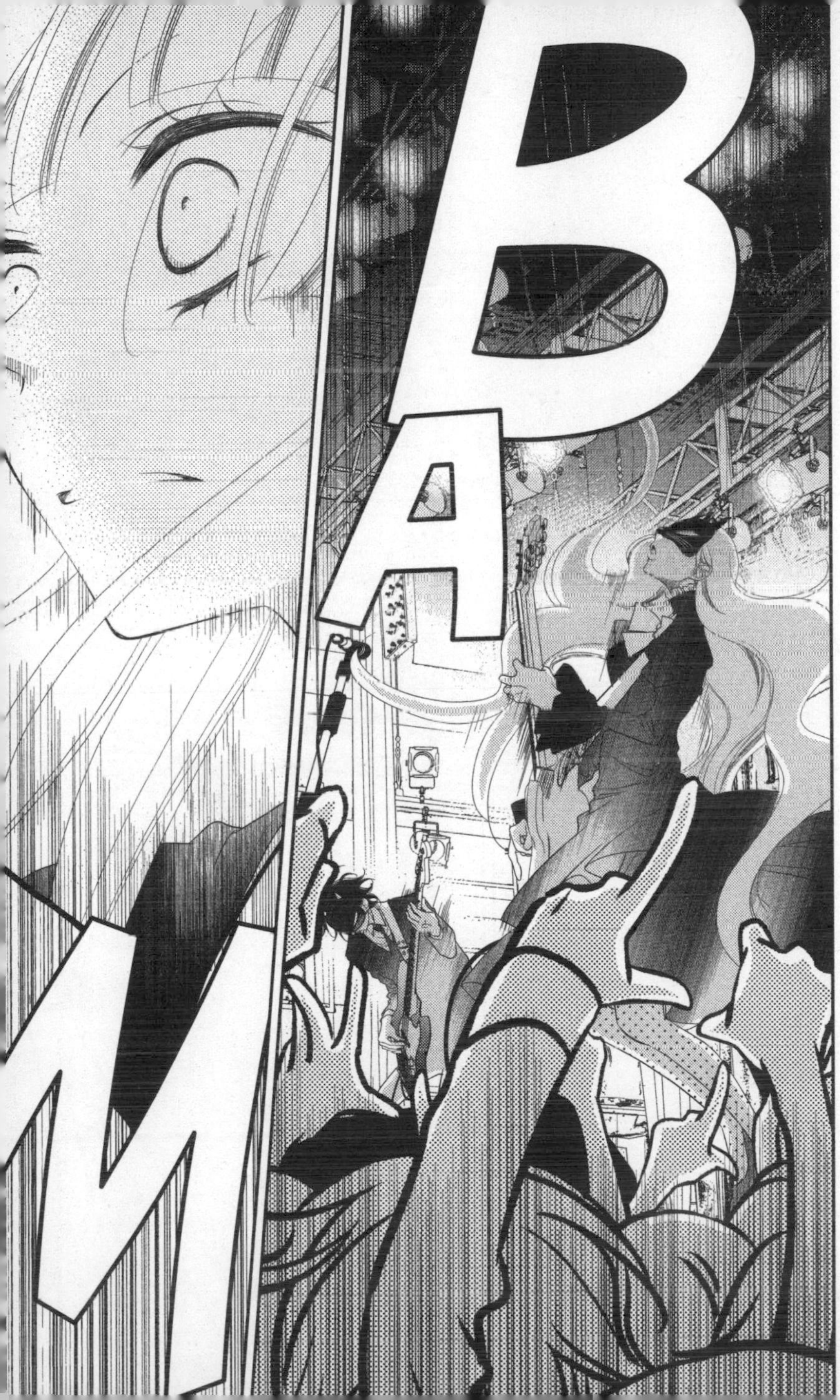
BAM

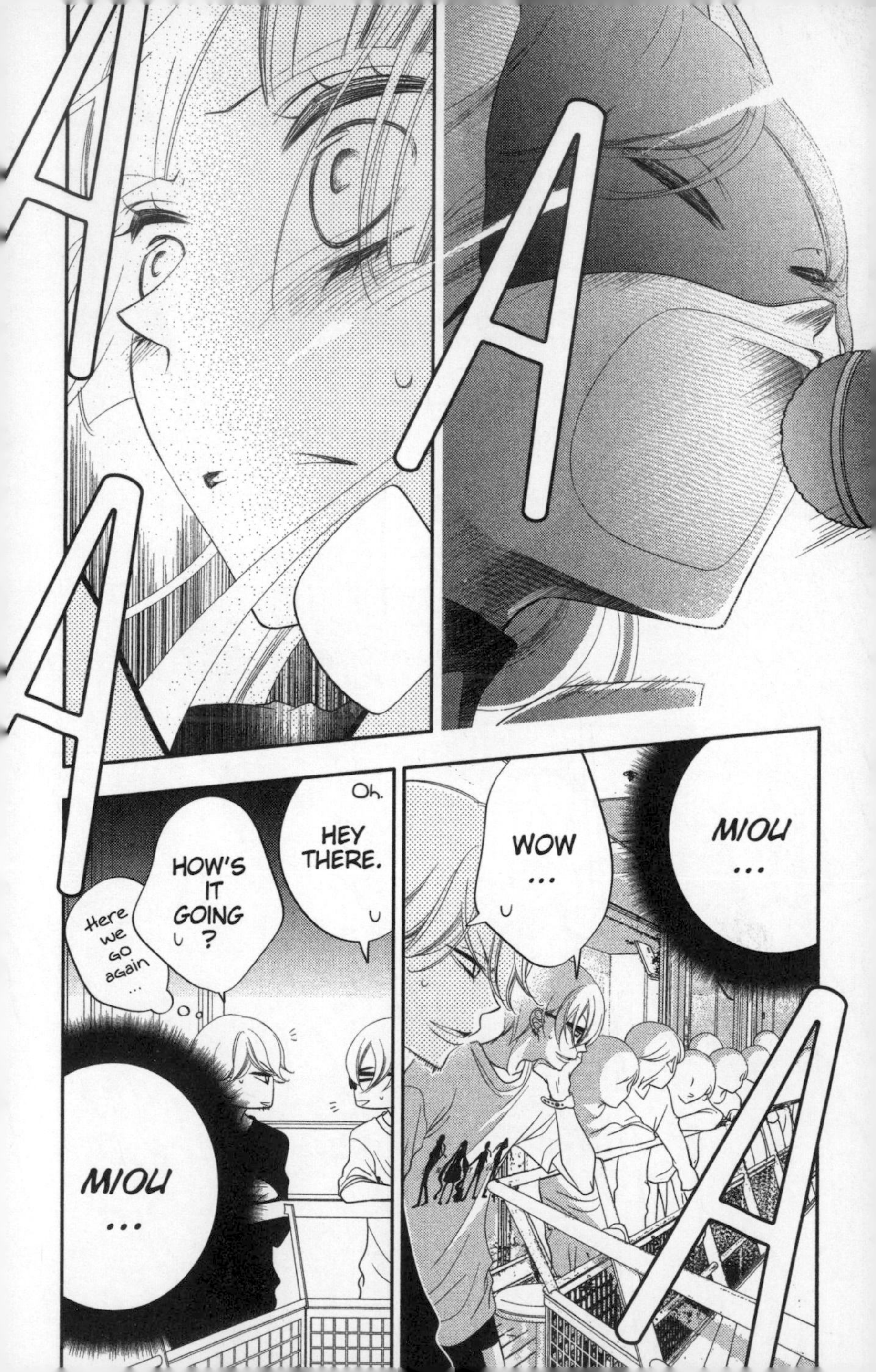

AAAA
AA
MIOU ...
WOW ...
Oh.
HEY THERE.
HOW'S IT GOING?
Here we go again ...
MIOU ...

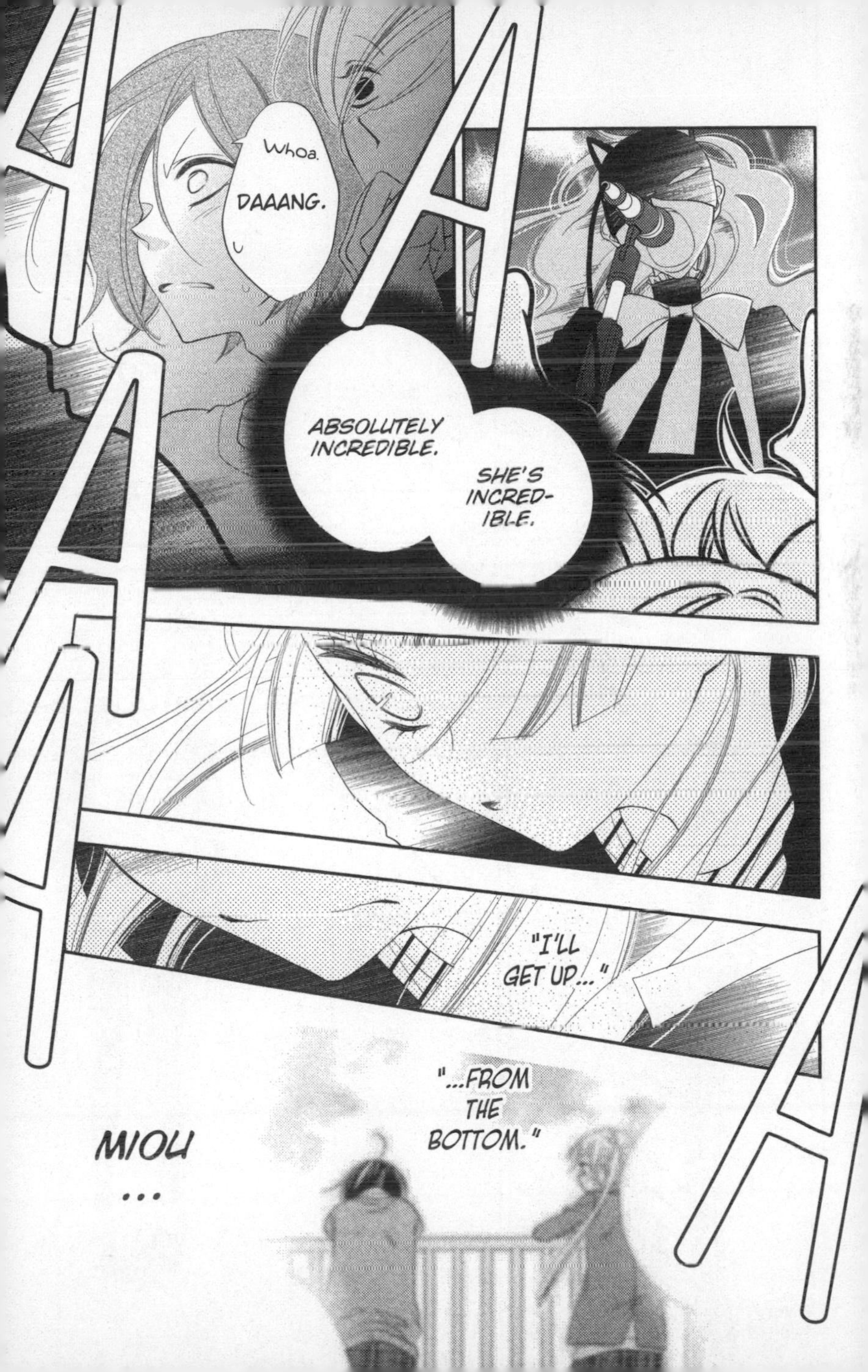
Whoa.
DAAANG.
SHE'S INCRED-IBLE.
ABSOLUTELY INCREDIBLE.
AAAAA
"I'LL GET UP..."
"...FROM THE BOTTOM."
MIOU ...

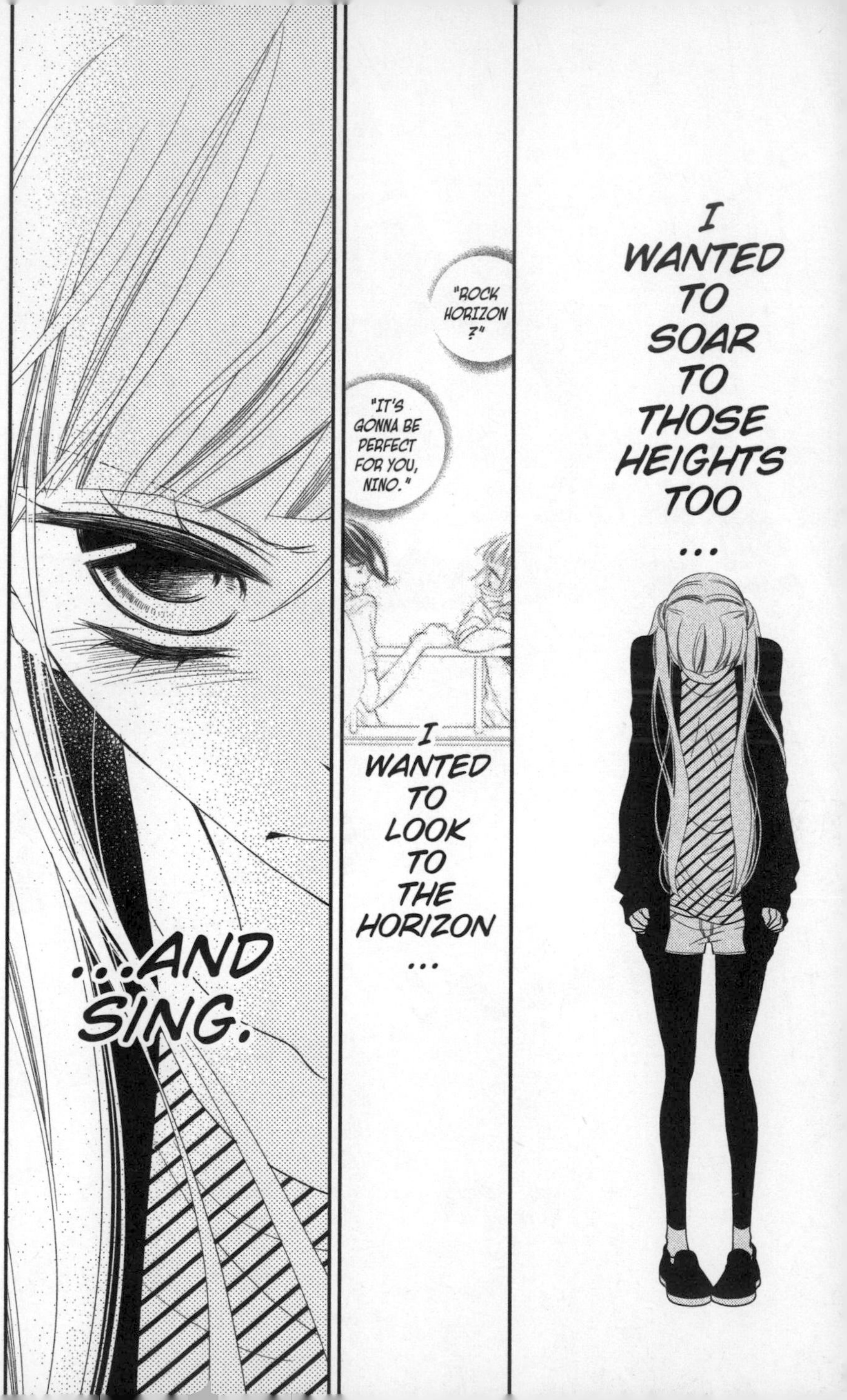
I WANTED TO SOAR TO THOSE HEIGHTS TOO ...
"ROCK HORIZON?"
"IT'S GONNA BE PERFECT FOR YOU, NINO."
I WANTED TO LOOK TO THE HORIZON ...
...AND SING.

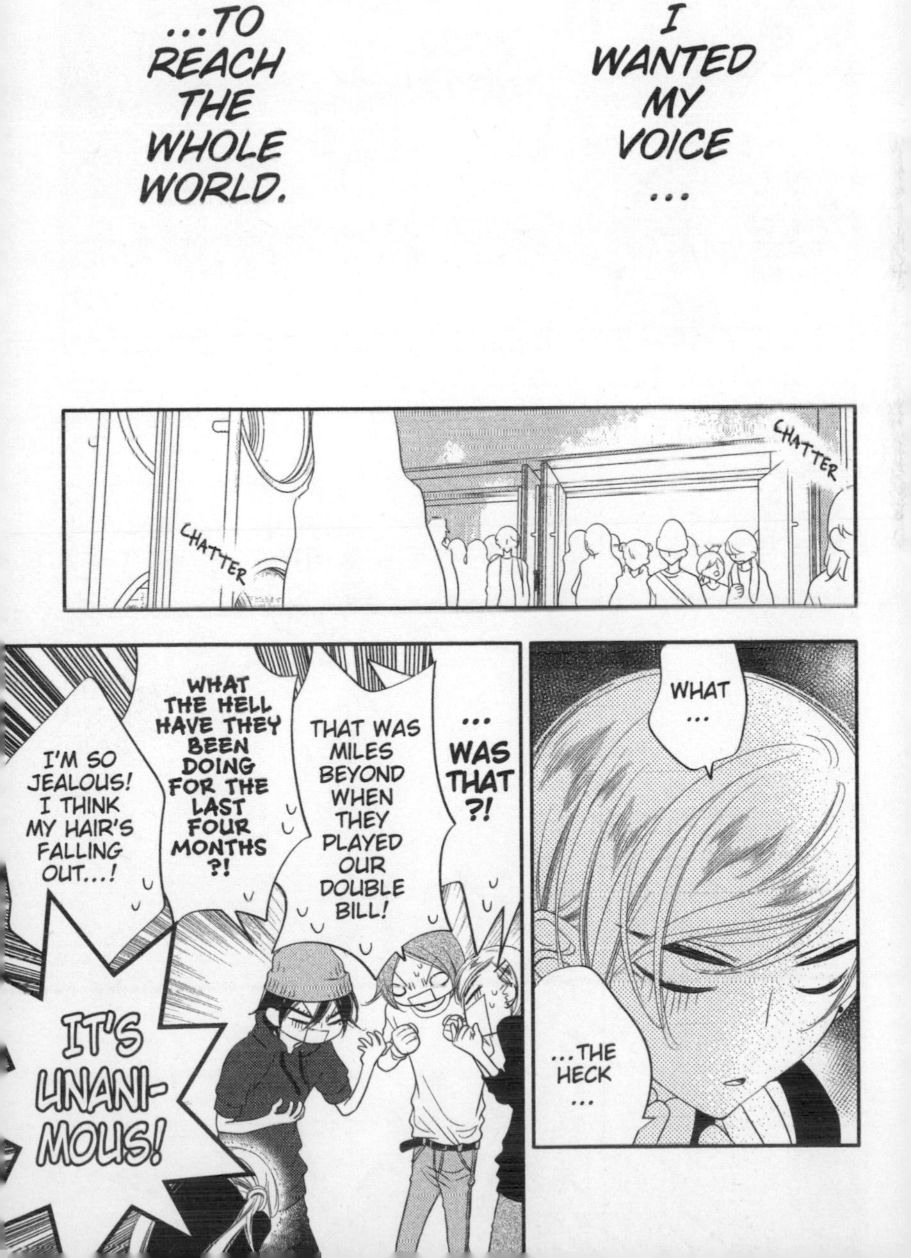
I WANTED MY VOICE ...
...TO REACH THE WHOLE WORLD.
CHATTER
CHATTER
WHAT ...
...THE HECK ...
... WAS THAT ?!
THAT WAS MILES BEYOND WHEN THEY PLAYED OUR DOUBLE BILL!
WHAT THE HELL HAVE THEY BEEN DOING FOR THE LAST FOUR MONTHS ?!
I'M SO JEALOUS! I THINK MY HAIR'S FALLING OUT...!
IT'S UNANIMOUS!

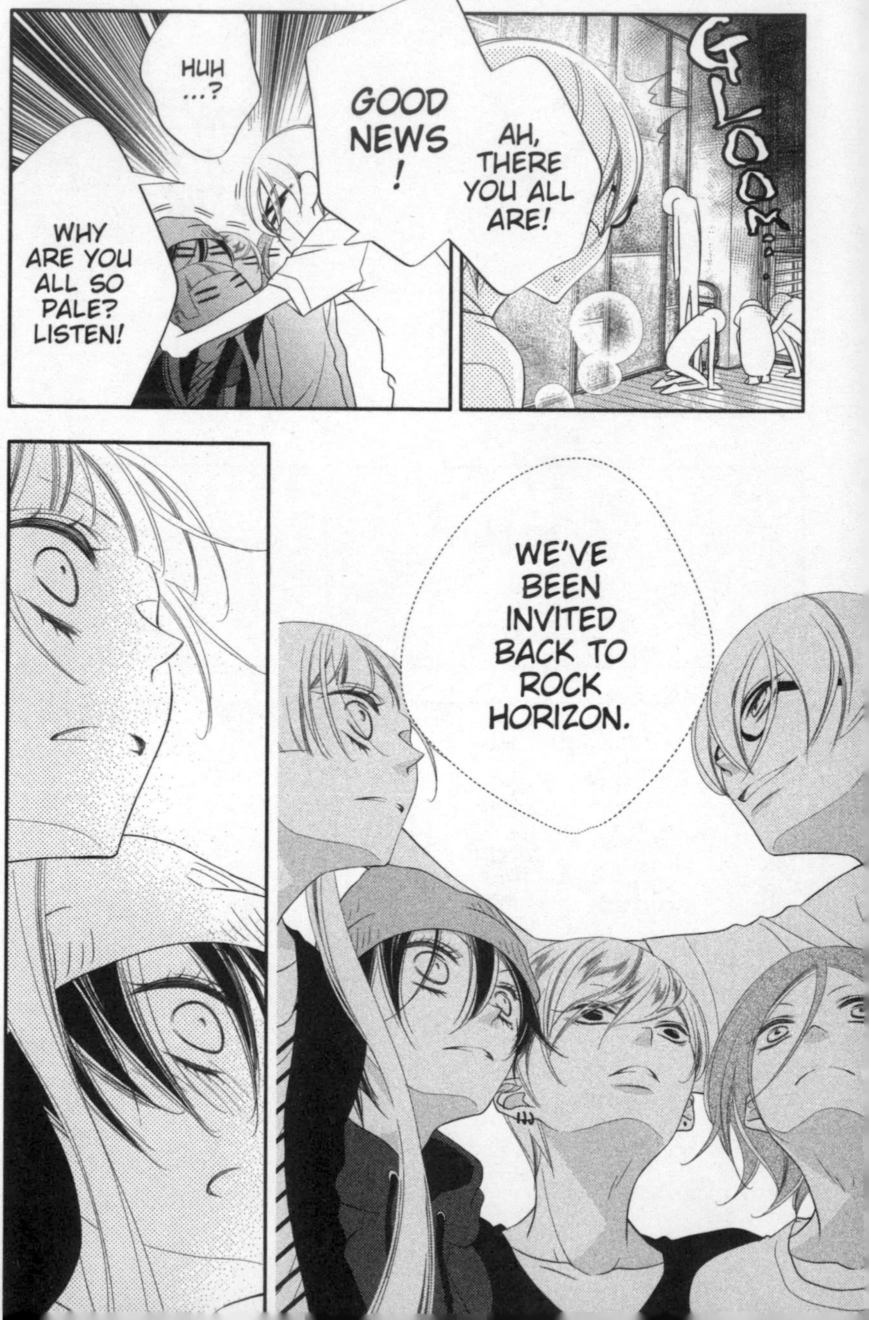
GLOOM...
AH, THERE YOU ALL ARE!
GOOD NEWS!
HUH...?
WHY ARE YOU ALL SO PALE? LISTEN!
WE'VE BEEN INVITED BACK TO ROCK HORIZON.

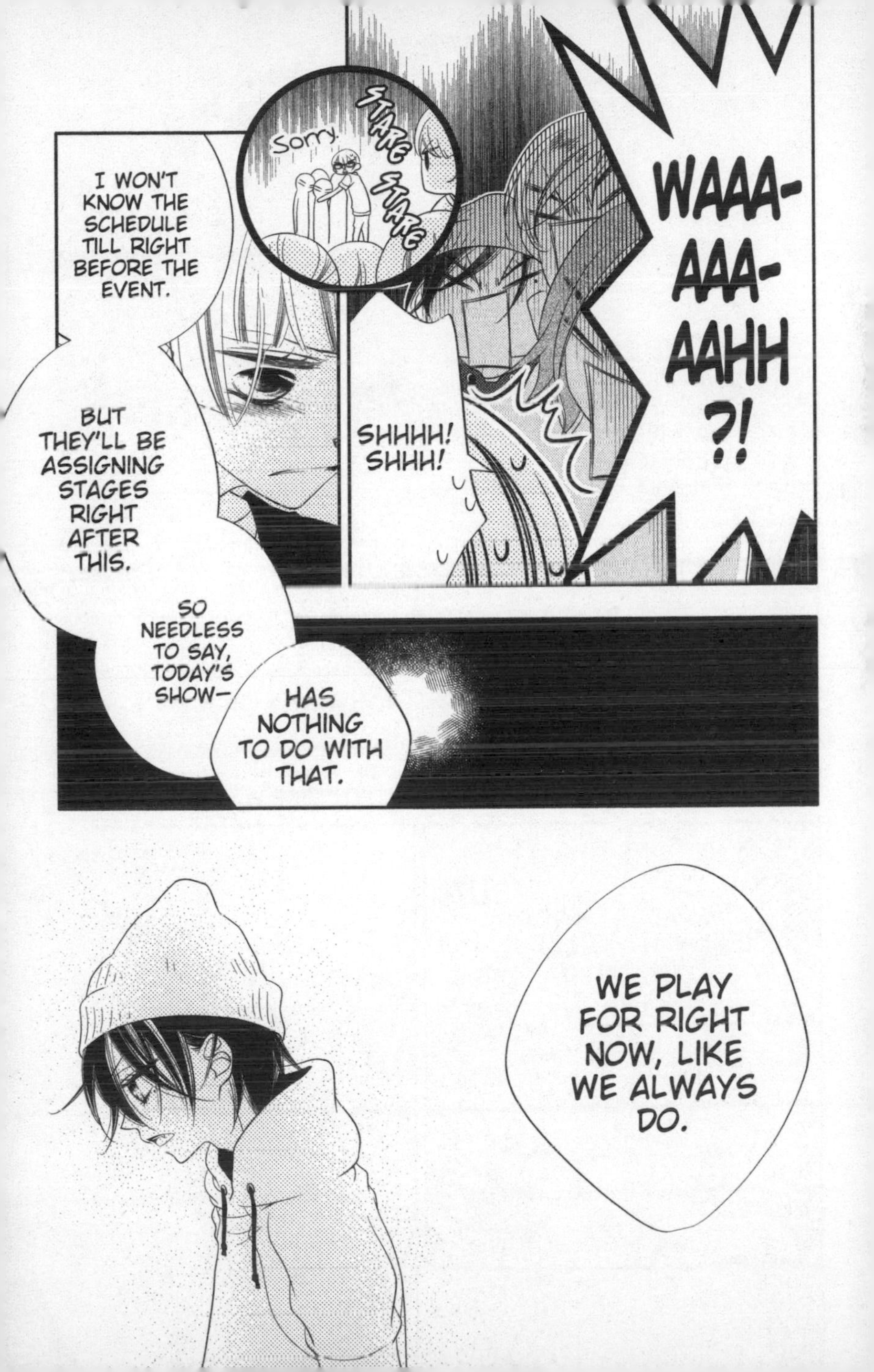
WAAAA-AAA-AAHH?!
STARE STARE
Sorry.
SHHHH! SHHH!
I WON'T KNOW THE SCHEDULE TILL RIGHT BEFORE THE EVENT.
BUT THEY'LL BE ASSIGNING STAGES RIGHT AFTER THIS.
SO NEEDLESS TO SAY, TODAY'S SHOW—
HAS NOTHING TO DO WITH THAT.
WE PLAY FOR RIGHT NOW, LIKE WE ALWAYS DO.

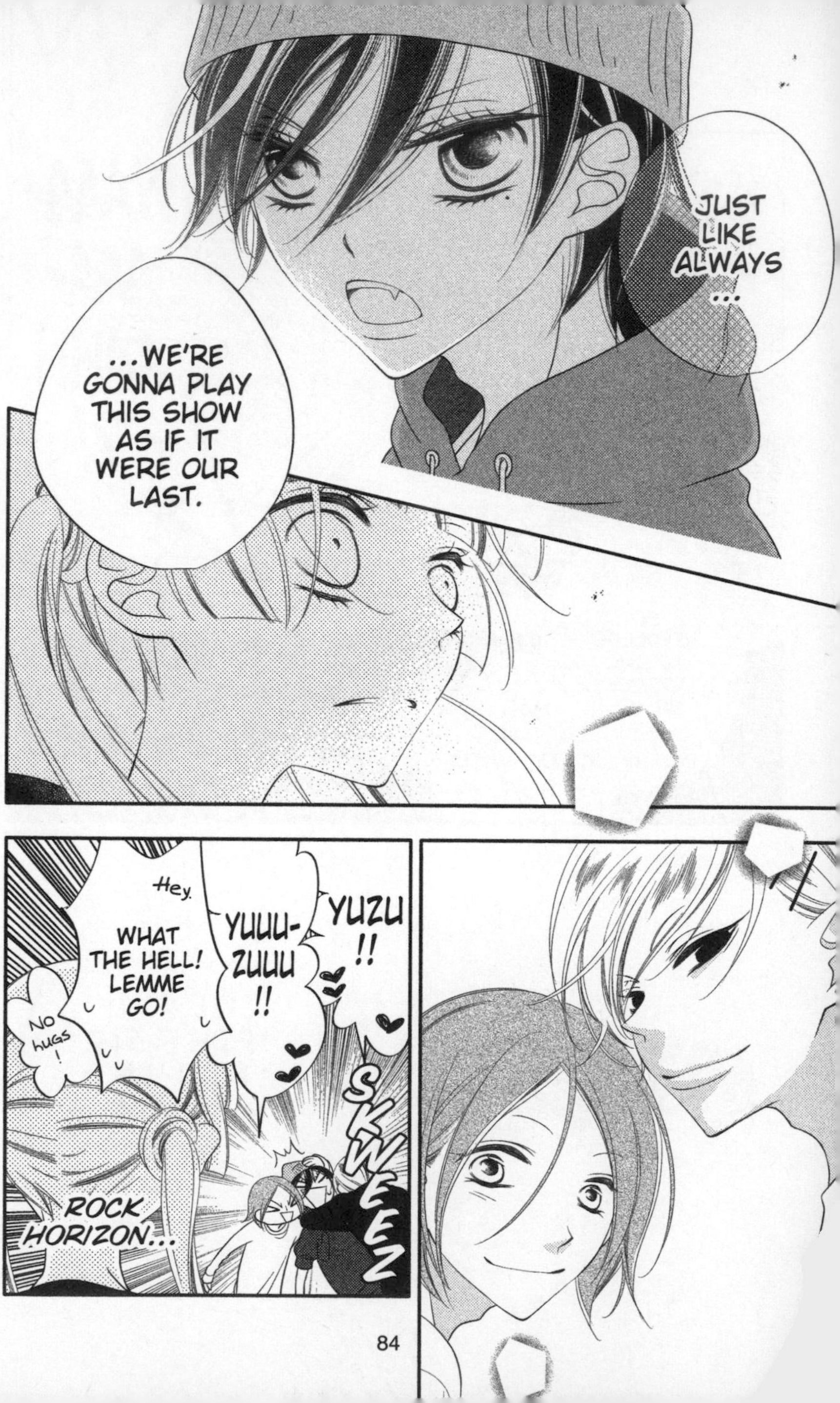
JUST LIKE ALWAYS ...
...WE'RE GONNA PLAY THIS SHOW AS IF IT WERE OUR LAST.
YUZU !!
YUUU-ZUUU !!
SKWEEZ
Hey.
WHAT THE HELL! LEMME GO!
No hugs!
ROCK HORIZON...

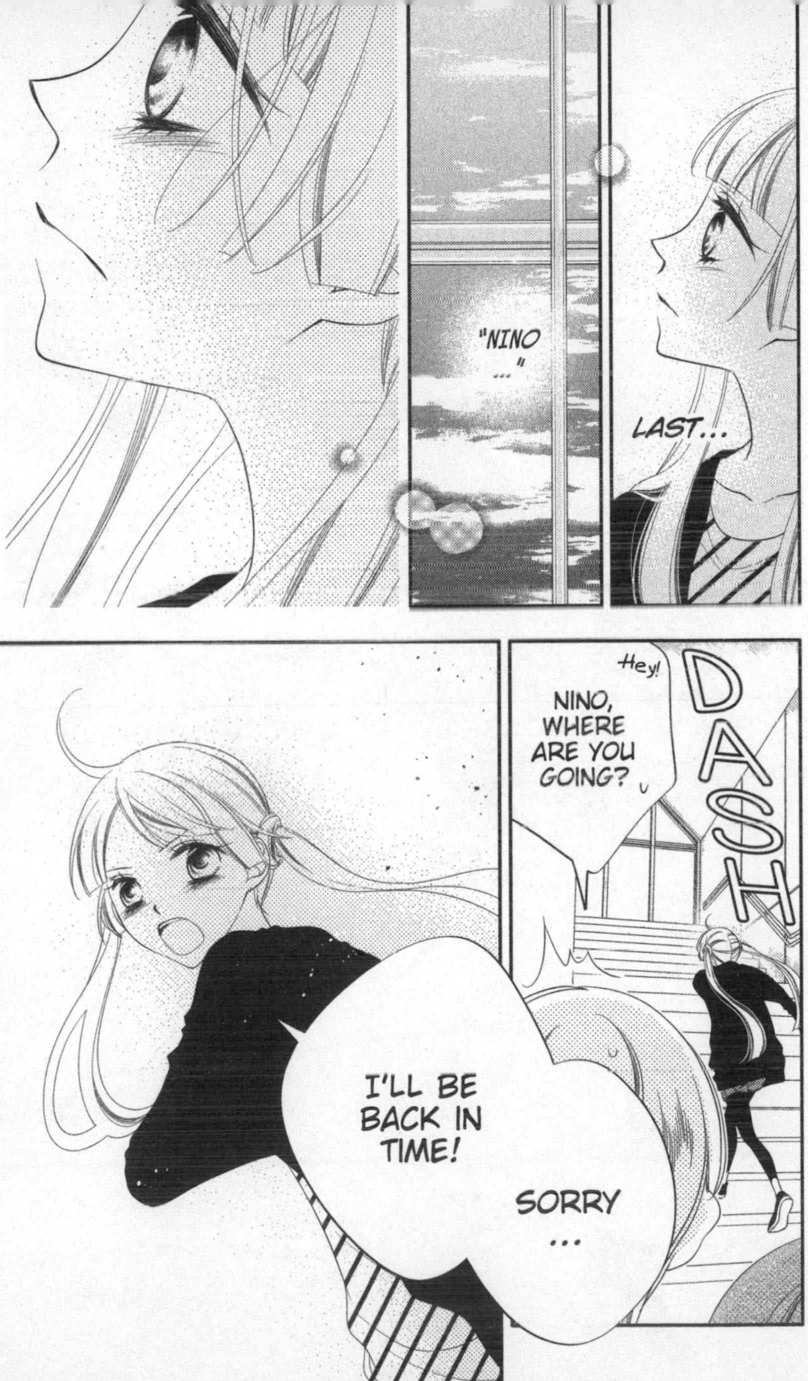
LAST...
"NINO..."
Hey!
NINO, WHERE ARE YOU GOING?
DASH
I'LL BE BACK IN TIME!
SORRY ...

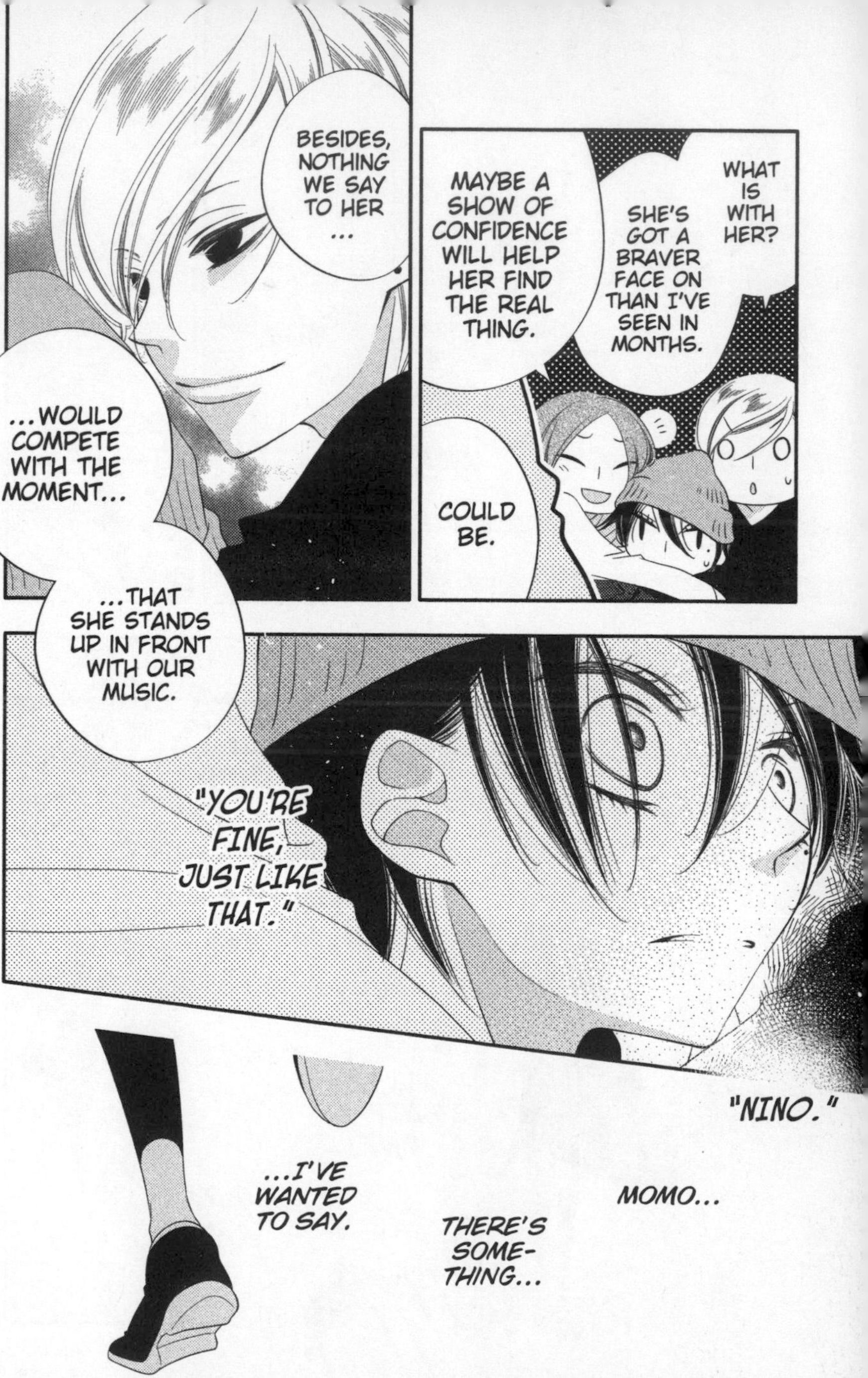
WHAT IS WITH HER?
SHE'S GOT A BRAVER FACE ON THAN I'VE SEEN IN MONTHS.
MAYBE A SHOW OF CONFIDENCE WILL HELP HER FIND THE REAL THING.
COULD BE.
BESIDES, NOTHING WE SAY TO HER ...
...WOULD COMPETE WITH THE MOMENT...
...THAT SHE STANDS UP IN FRONT WITH OUR MUSIC.
"YOU'RE FINE, JUST LIKE THAT."
"NINO."
MOMO...
THERE'S SOME-THING...
...I'VE WANTED TO SAY.

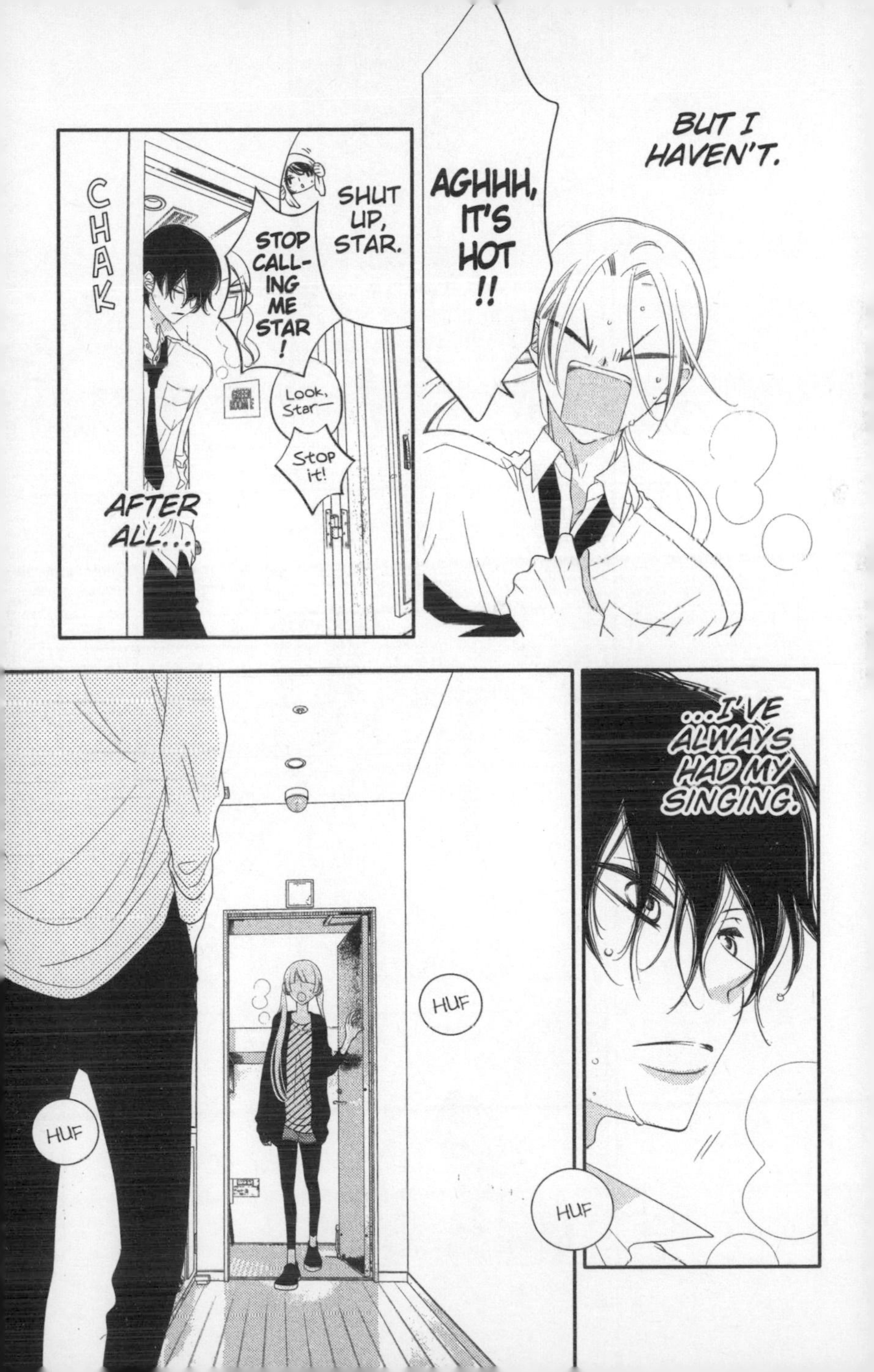
BUT I HAVEN'T.
AGHHH, IT'S HOT!!
SHUT UP, STAR.
STOP CALLING-ING ME STAR!
CHAK
Look, Star—
Stop it!
AFTER ALL...
...I'VE ALWAYS HAD MY SINGING.
HUF
HUF
HUF

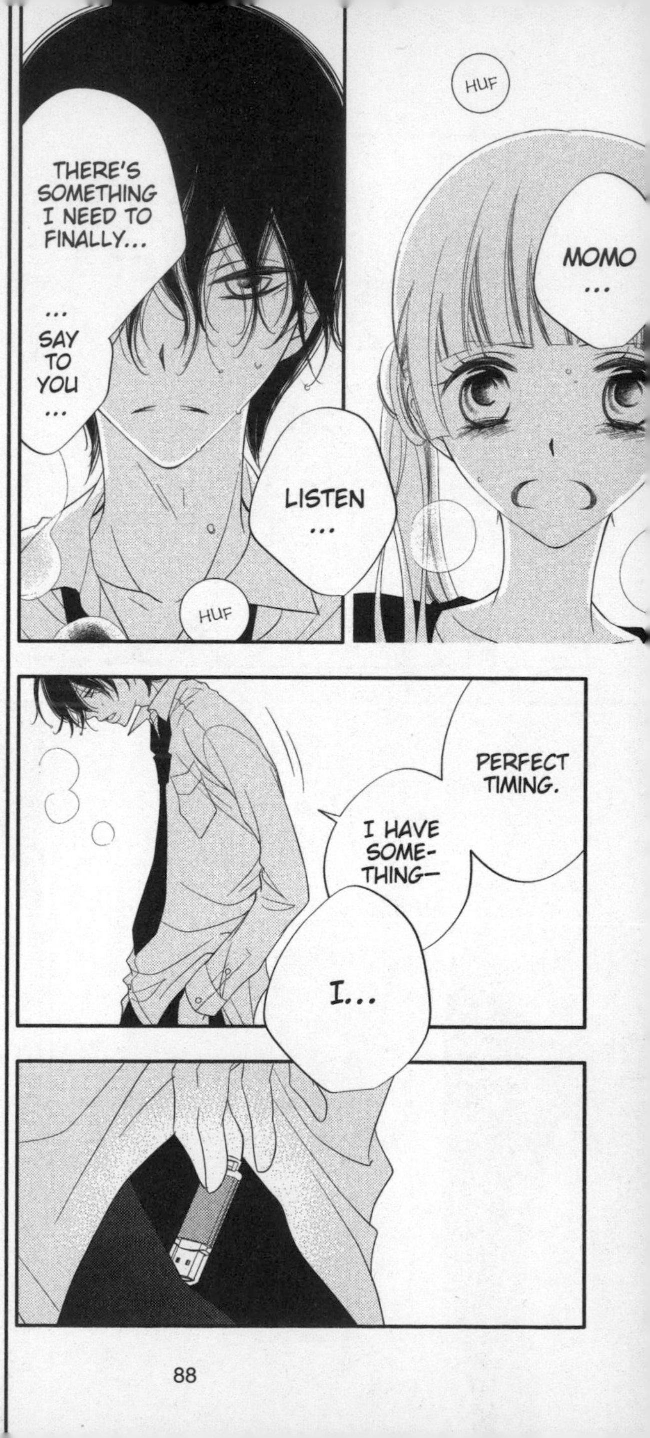
HUF
MOMO ...
LISTEN ...
THERE'S SOMETHING I NEED TO FINALLY...
... SAY TO YOU ...
HUF
PERFECT TIMING.
I HAVE SOME-THING—
I...

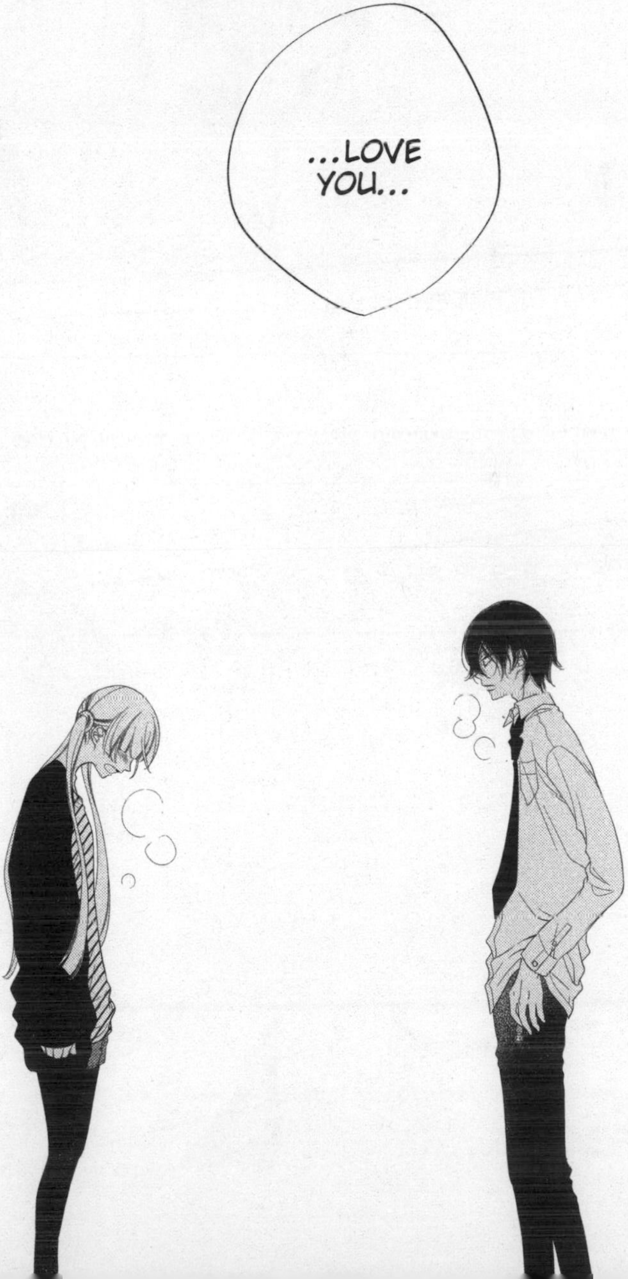
...LOVE YOU...

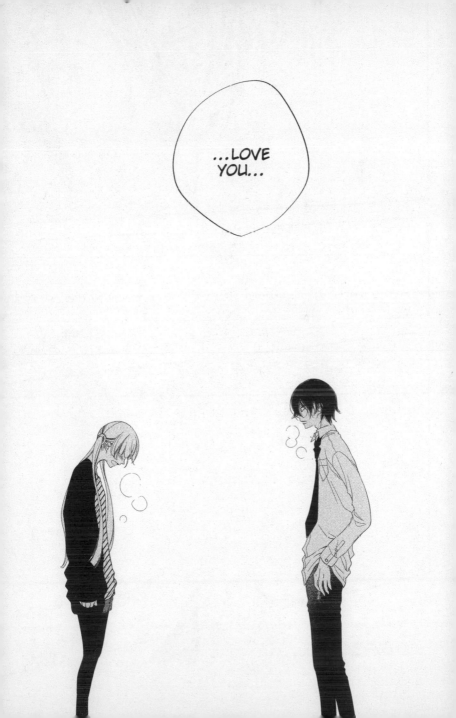

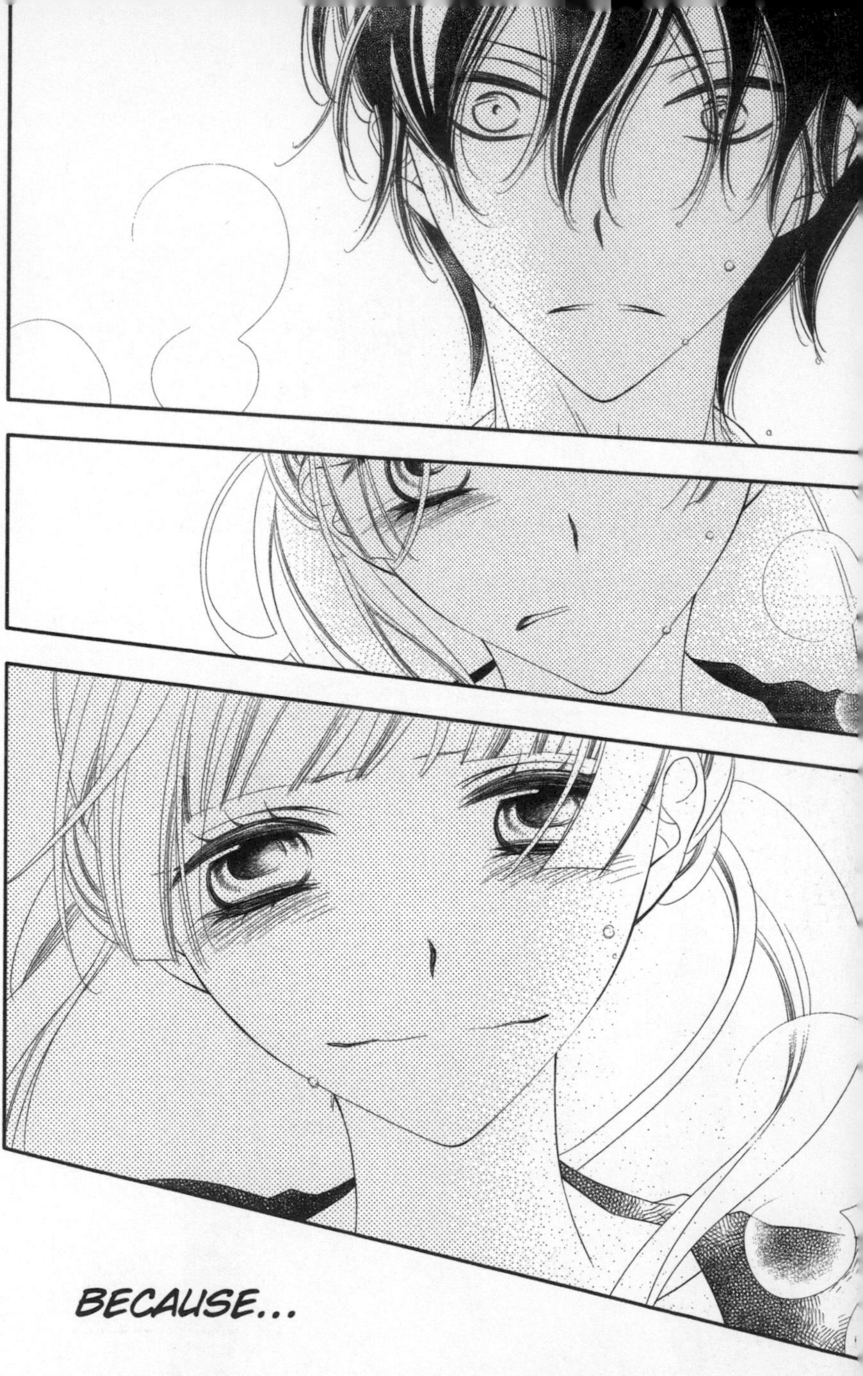
BECAUSE...

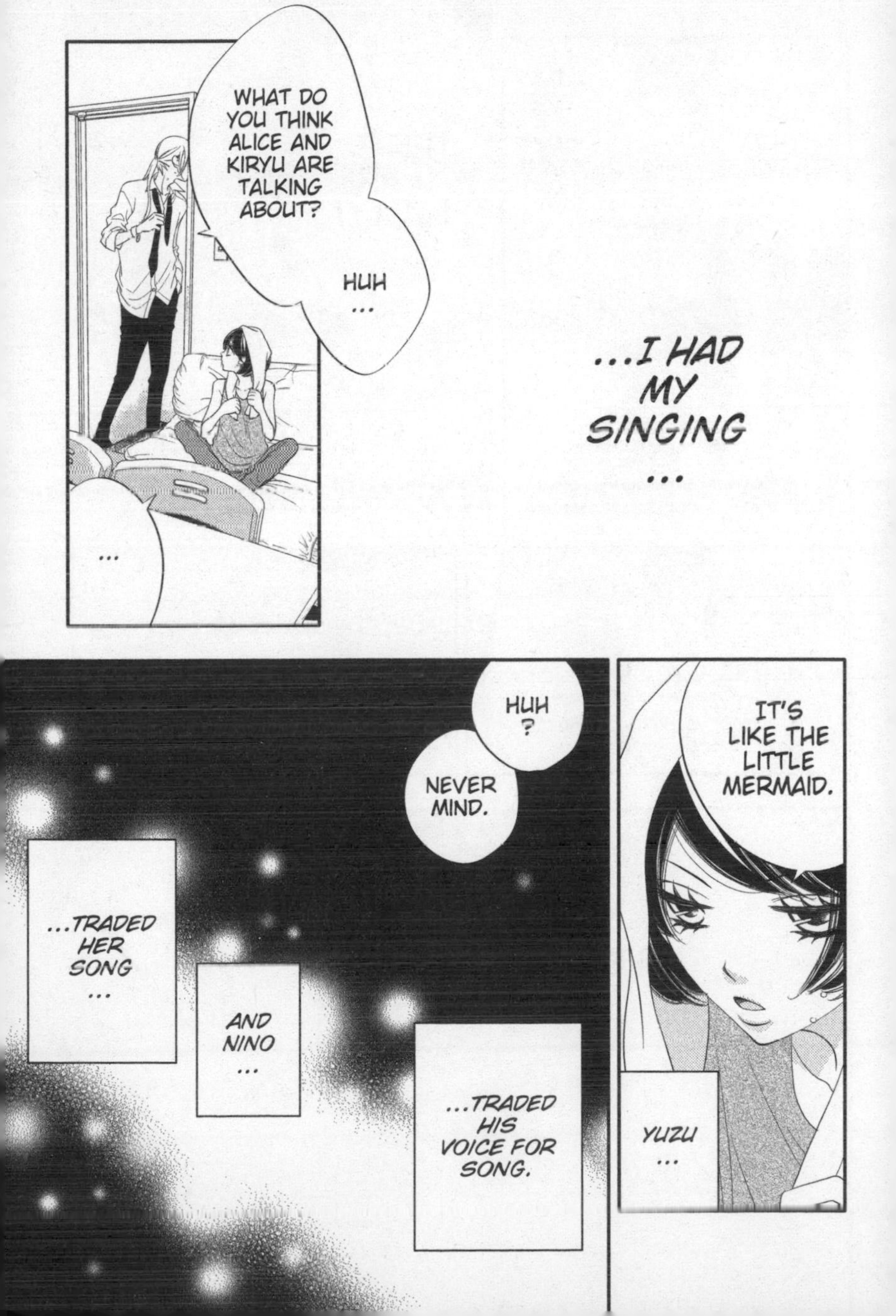
...I HAD MY SINGING...
WHAT DO YOU THINK ALICE AND KIRYU ARE TALKING ABOUT?
HUH...
...
IT'S LIKE THE LITTLE MERMAID.
YUZU...
HUH?
NEVER MIND.
...TRADED HER SONG...
AND NINO...
...TRADED HIS VOICE FOR SONG.

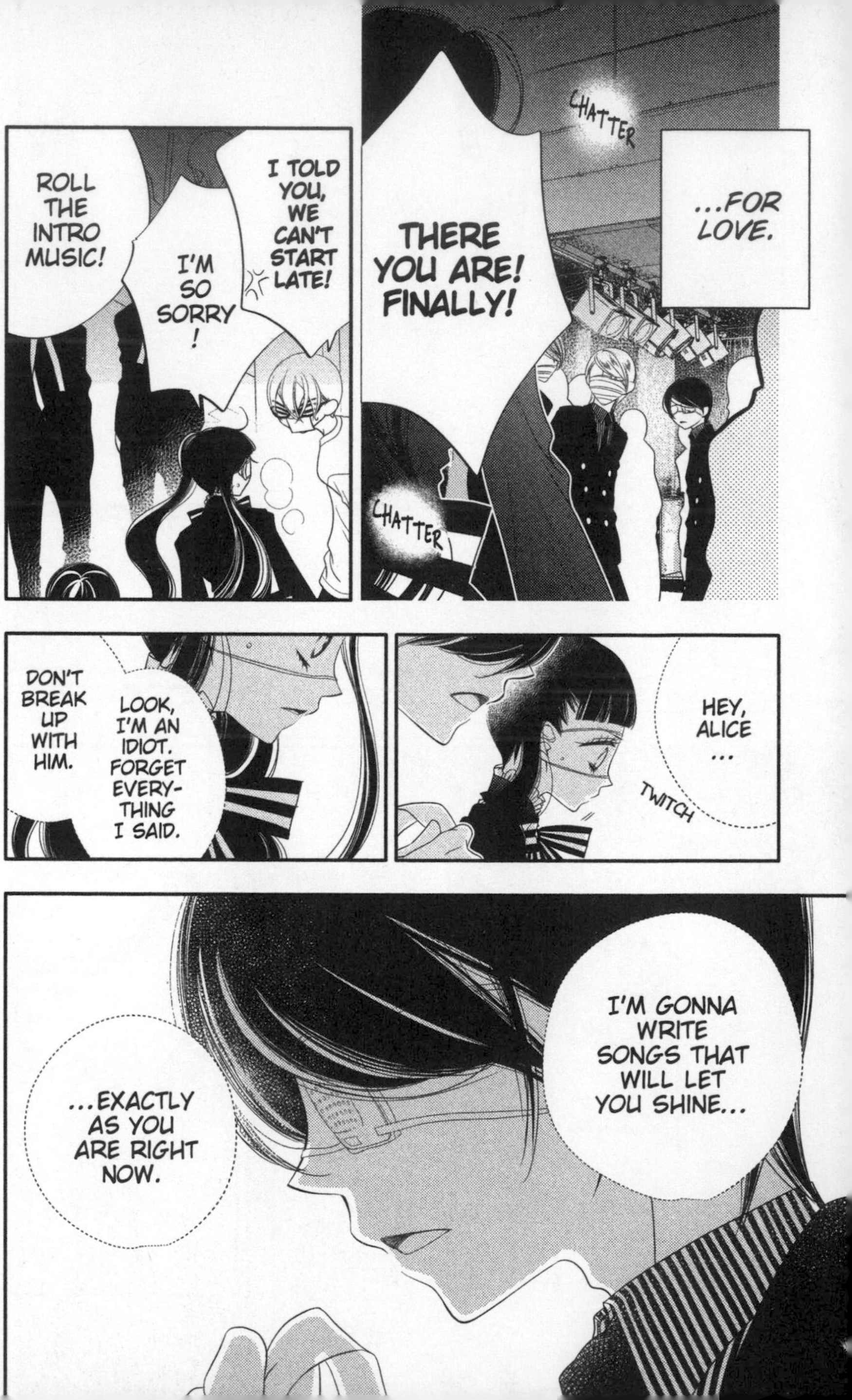
...FOR LOVE.
CHATTER
THERE YOU ARE! FINALLY!
CHATTER
I TOLD YOU, WE CAN'T START LATE!
I'M SO SORRY!
ROLL THE INTRO MUSIC!
HEY, ALICE...
TWITCH
LOOK, I'M AN IDIOT. FORGET EVERYTHING I SAID.
DON'T BREAK UP WITH HIM.
I'M GONNA WRITE SONGS THAT WILL LET YOU SHINE...
...EXACTLY AS YOU ARE RIGHT NOW.

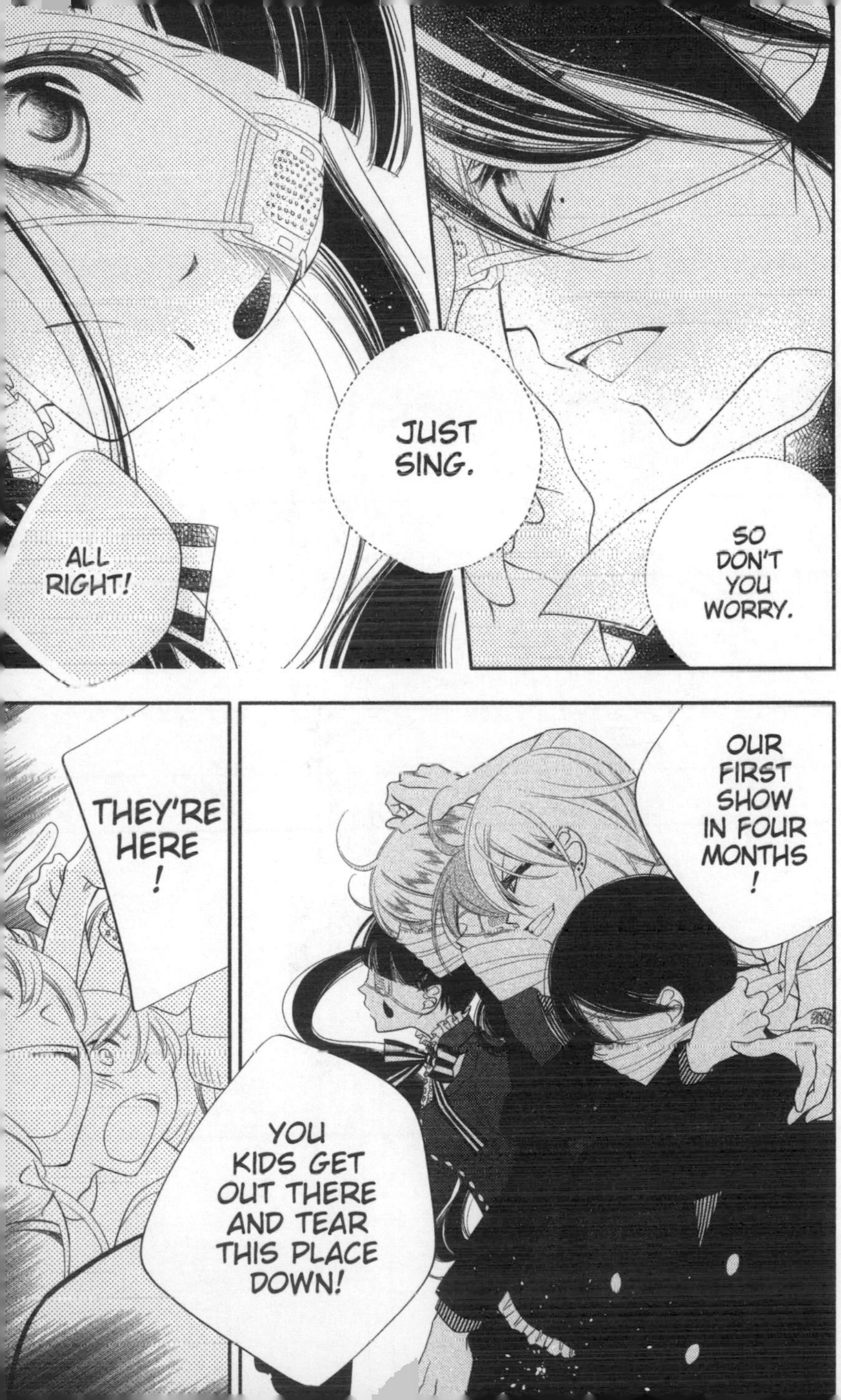
JUST SING.
SO DON'T YOU WORRY.
ALL RIGHT!
OUR FIRST SHOW IN FOUR MONTHS!
YOU KIDS GET OUT THERE AND TEAR THIS PLACE DOWN!
THEY'RE HERE!

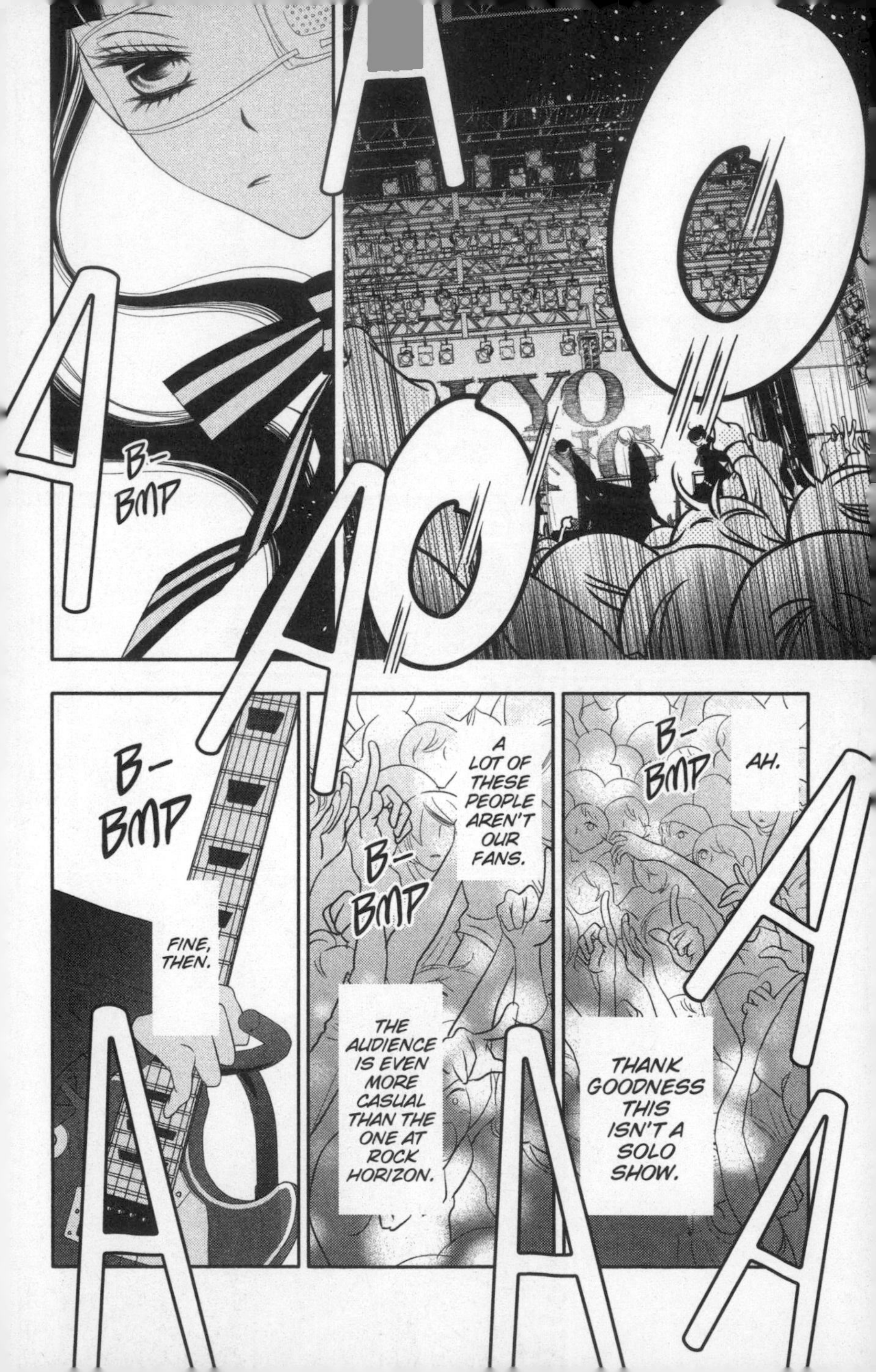
B-BMP
B-BMP
AH.
THANK GOODNESS THIS ISN'T A SOLO SHOW.
A LOT OF THESE PEOPLE AREN'T OUR FANS.
B-BMP
THE AUDIENCE IS EVEN MORE CASUAL THAN THE ONE AT ROCK HORIZON.
B-BMP
FINE, THEN.

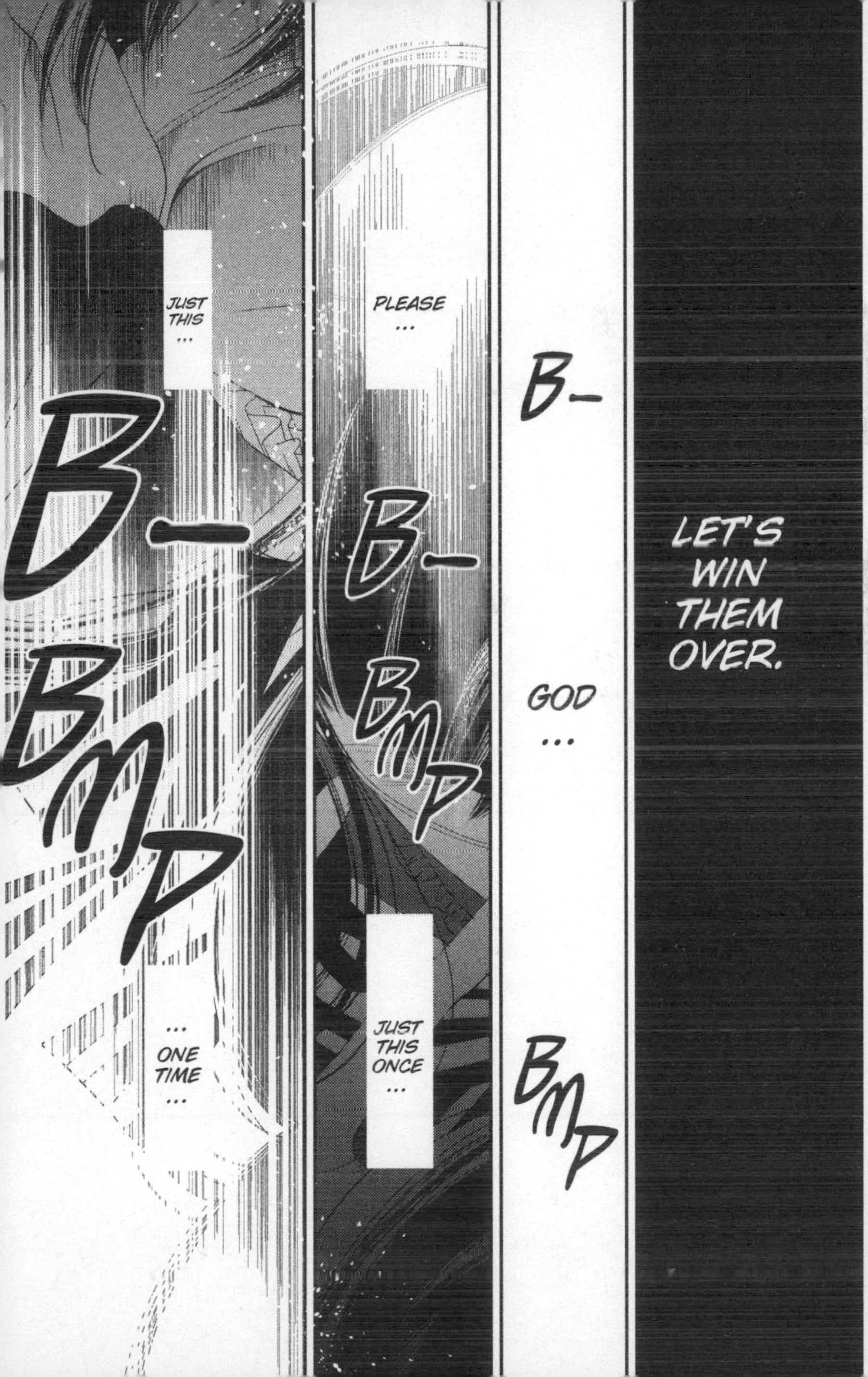
LET'S WIN THEM OVER.
B—
GOD ...
BMP
PLEASE ...
B—
BMP
JUST THIS ONCE ...
JUST THIS ...
B—
BMP
... ONE TIME ...

GIVE
ME
MY
VOICE.

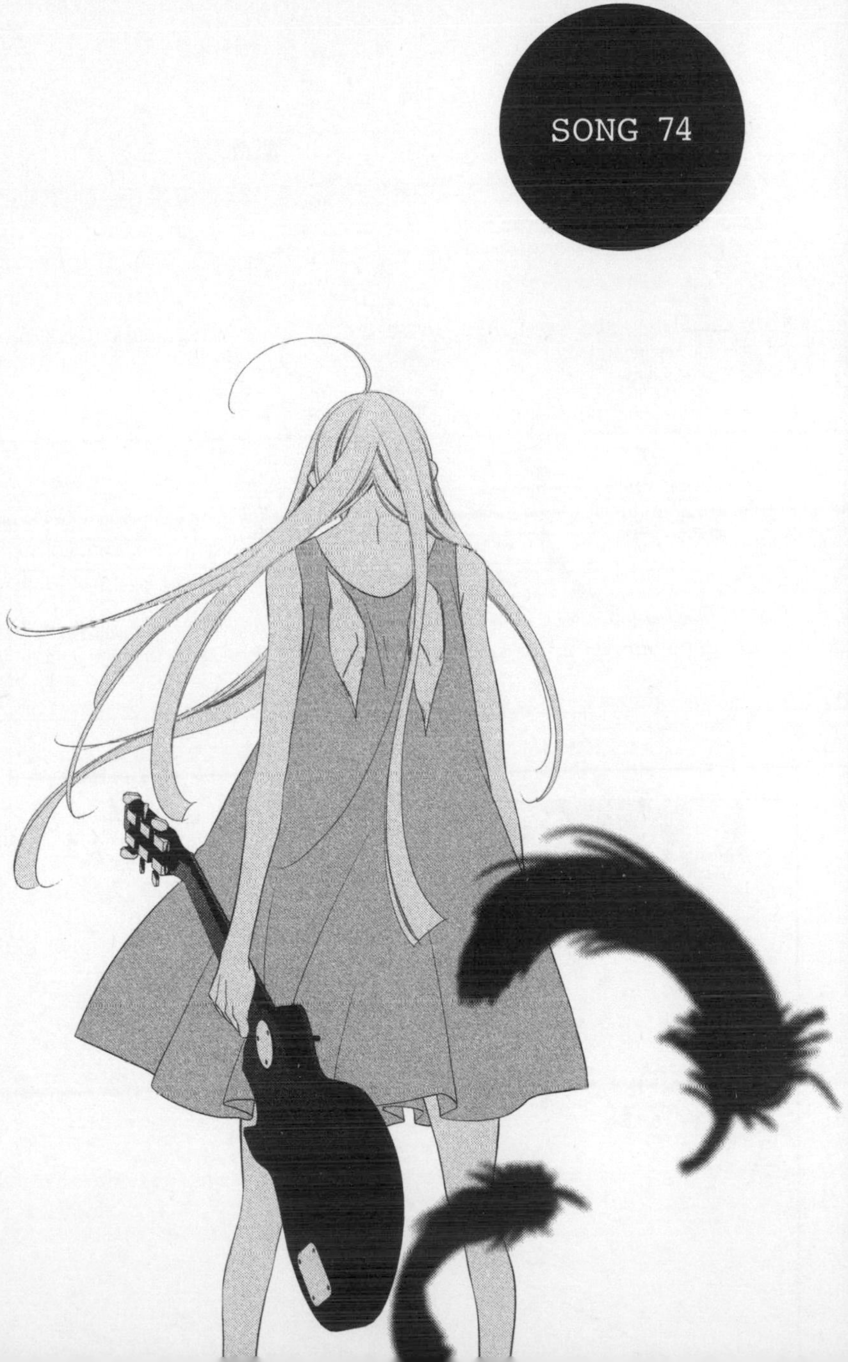
SONG 74

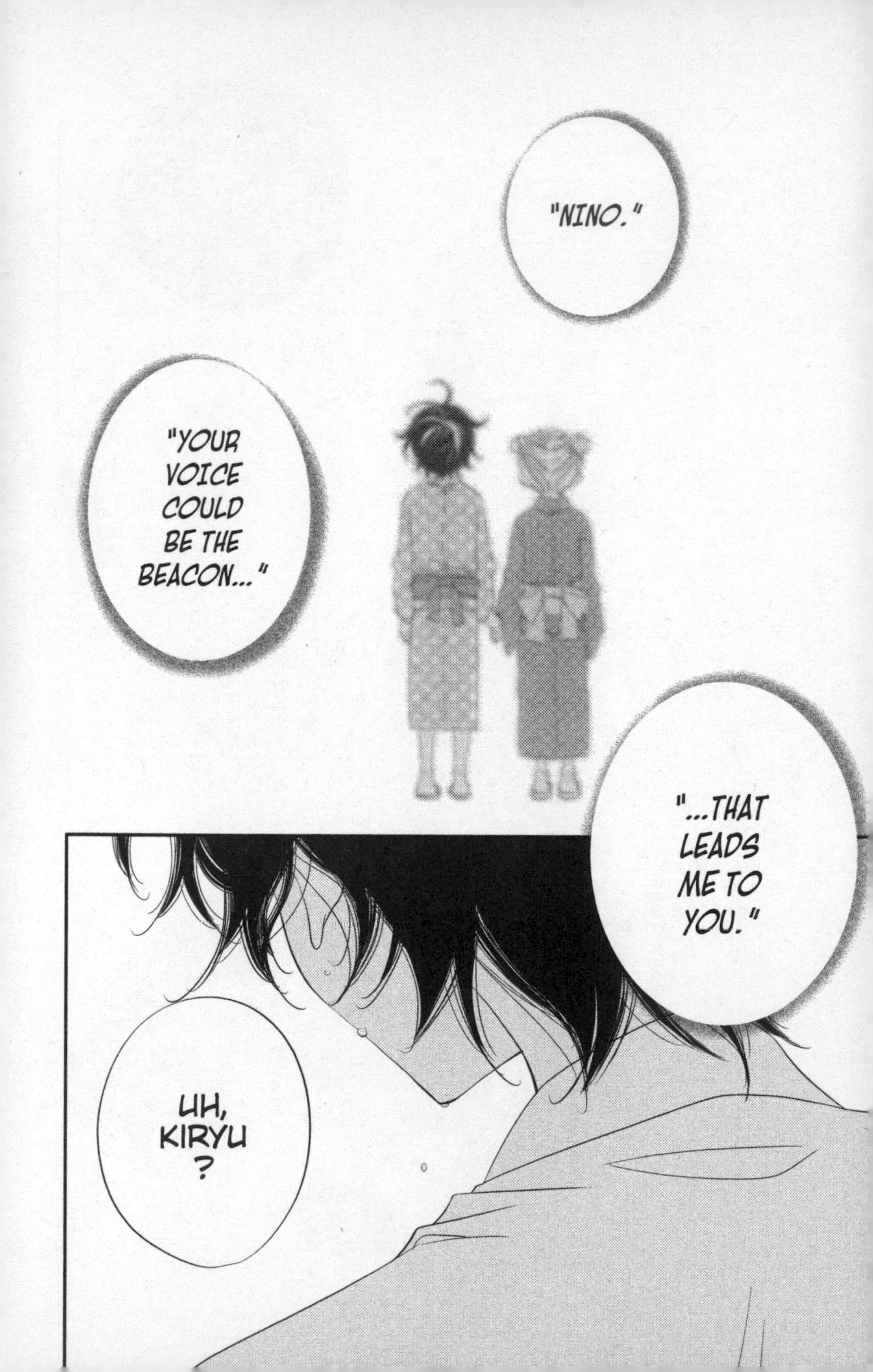
"NINO."
"YOUR VOICE COULD BE THE BEACON..."
"...THAT LEADS ME TO YOU."
UH, KIRYU?

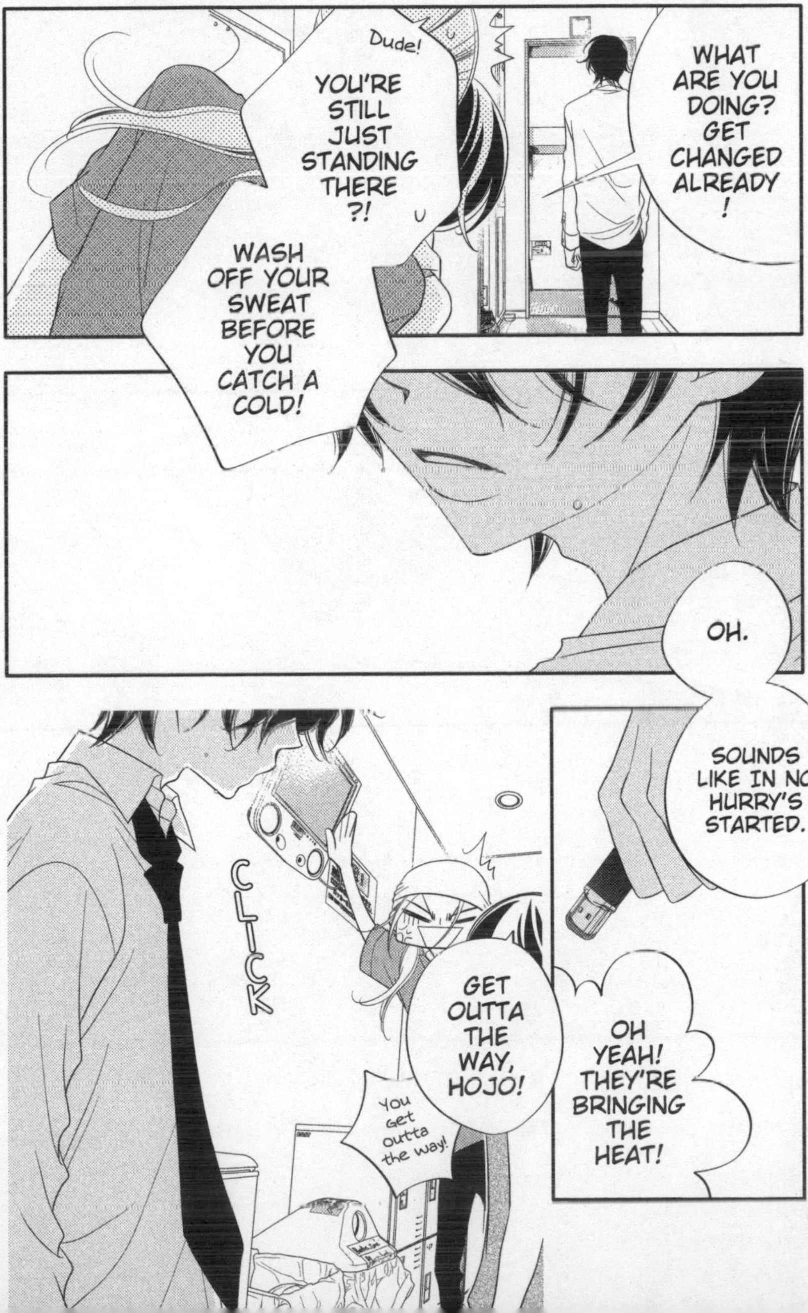
WHAT ARE YOU DOING? GET CHANGED ALREADY!
Dude!
YOU'RE STILL JUST STANDING THERE?!
WASH OFF YOUR SWEAT BEFORE YOU CATCH A COLD!
OH.
SOUNDS LIKE IN NO HURRY'S STARTED.
OH YEAH! THEY'RE BRINGING THE HEAT!
GET OUTTA THE WAY, HOJO!
You get outta the way!
CLICK

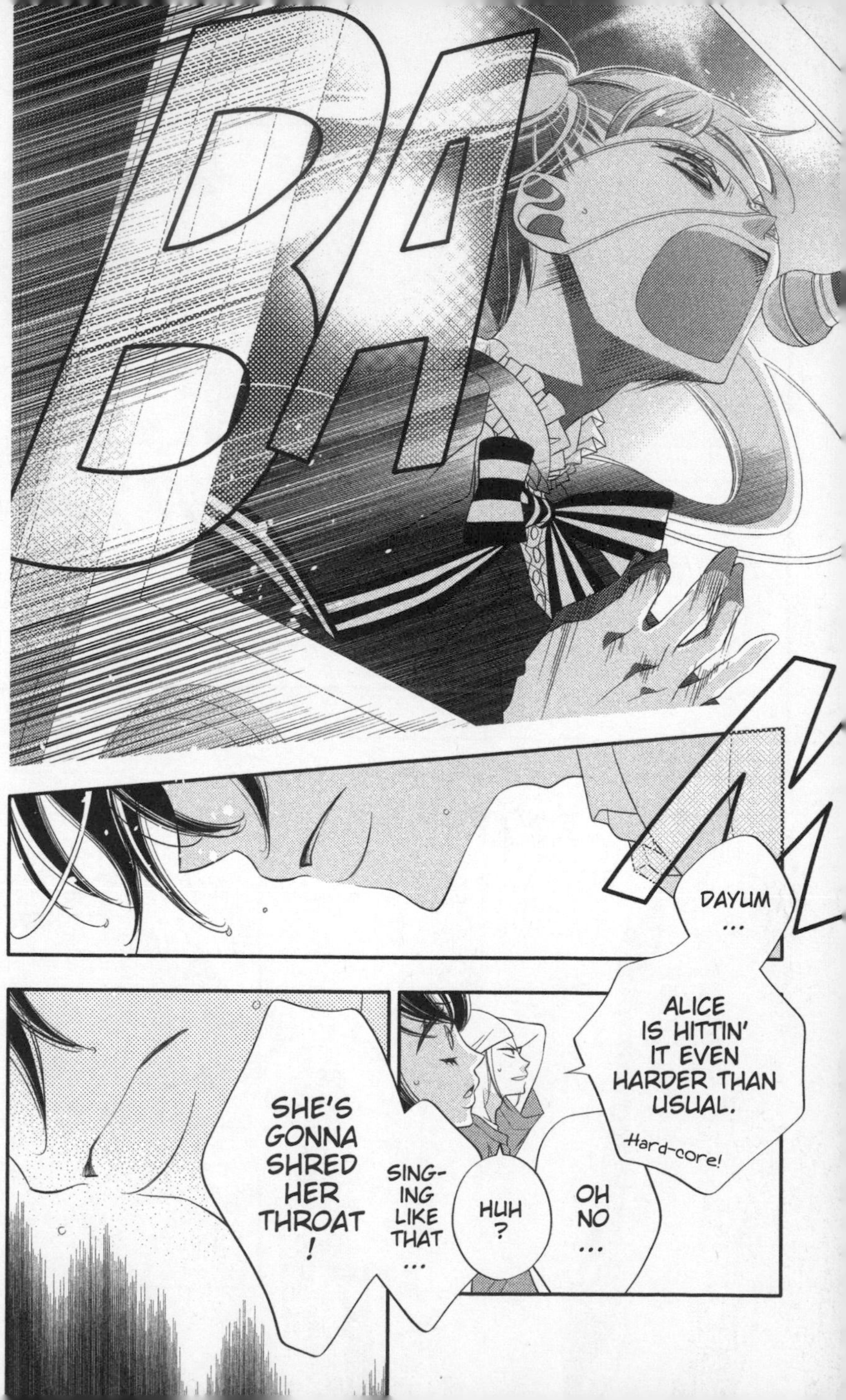
DAYUM …
ALICE IS HITTIN' IT EVEN HARDER THAN USUAL.
Hard-core!
OH NO …
HUH ?
SING-ING LIKE THAT …
SHE'S GONNA SHRED HER THROAT !

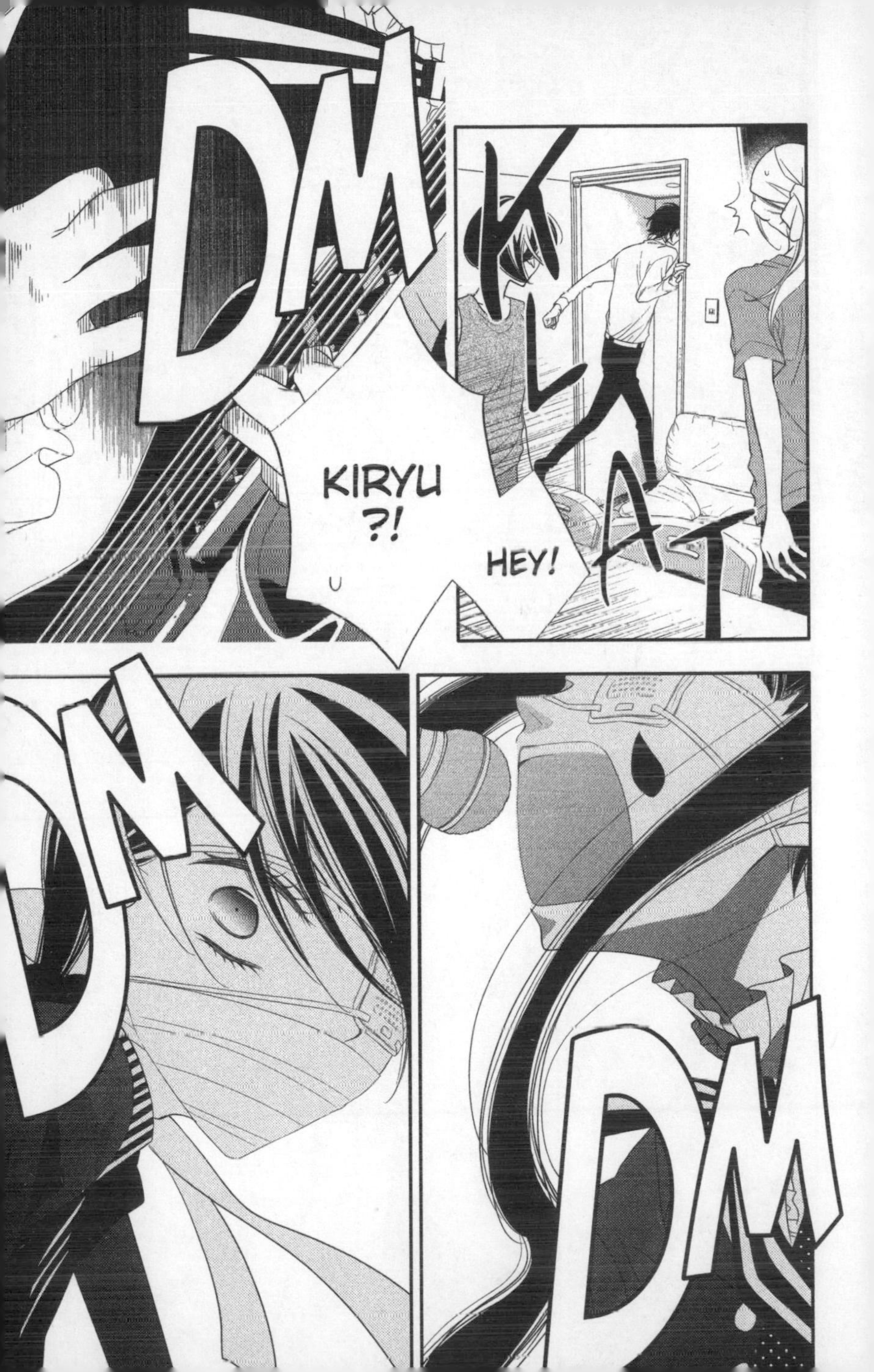
KLAT
HEY!
KIRYU ?!
DM
DM
DM

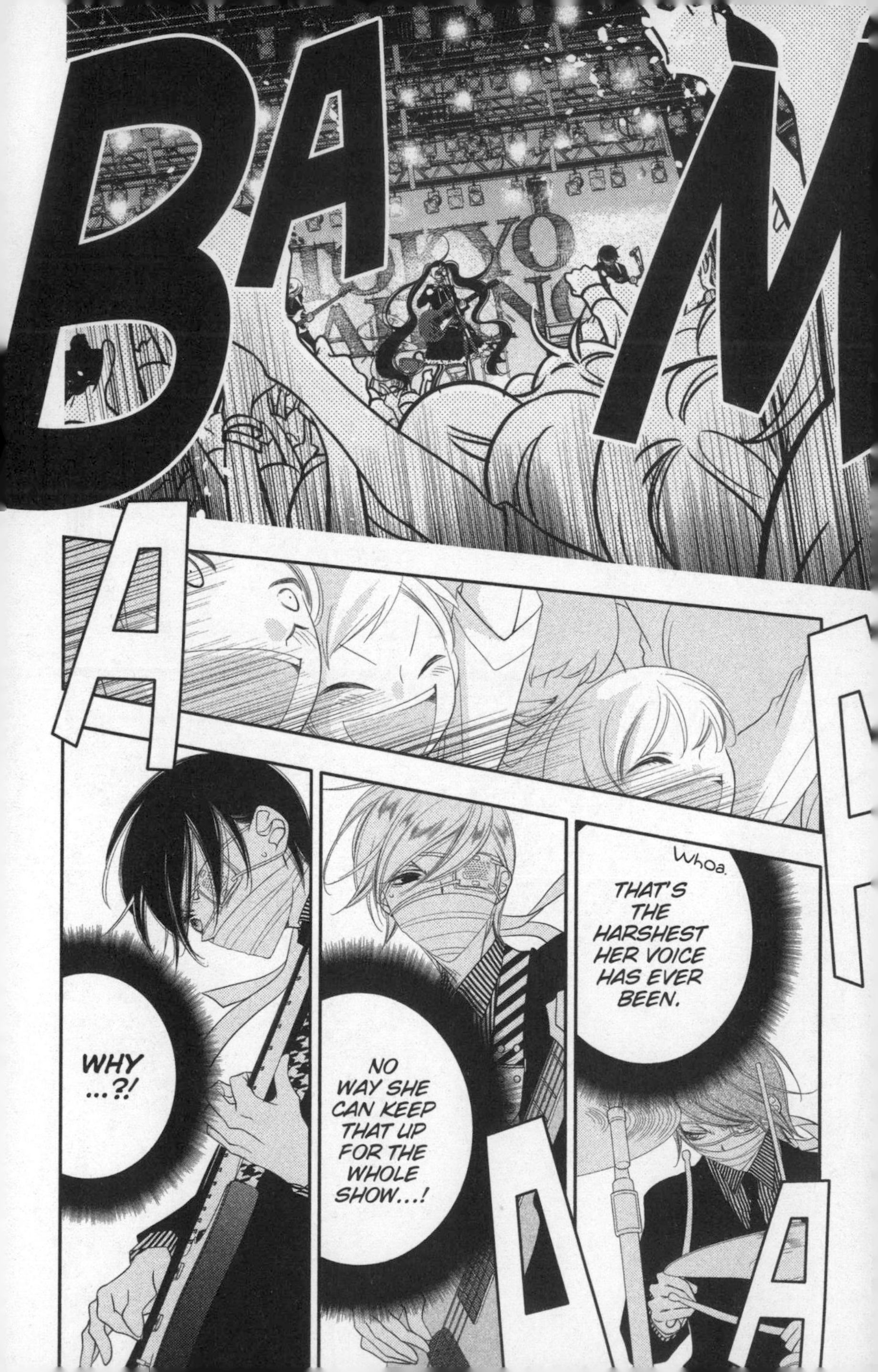
BAM
Whoa.
THAT'S THE HARSHEST HER VOICE HAS EVER BEEN.
NO WAY SHE CAN KEEP THAT UP FOR THE WHOLE SHOW...!
WHY ...?!

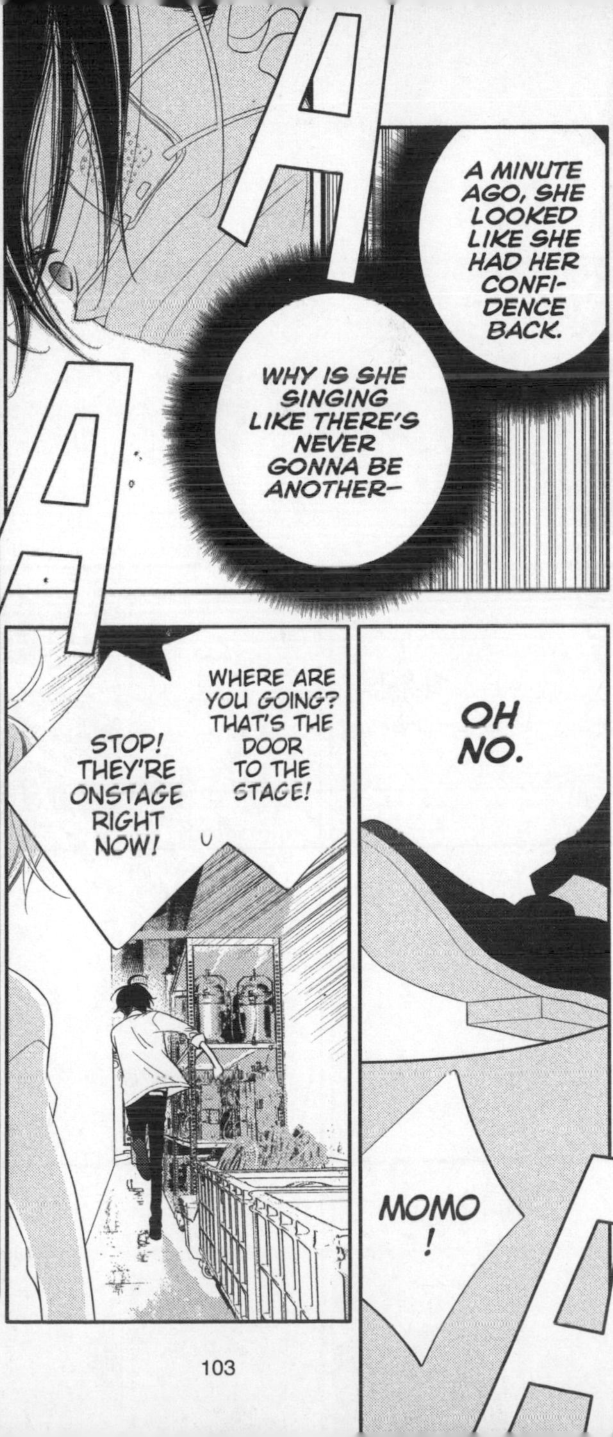
A MINUTE AGO, SHE LOOKED LIKE SHE HAD HER CONFIDENCE BACK.
WHY IS SHE SINGING LIKE THERE'S NEVER GONNA BE ANOTHER—
OH NO.
MOMO!
WHERE ARE YOU GOING? THAT'S THE DOOR TO THE STAGE!
STOP! THEY'RE ONSTAGE RIGHT NOW!

3

Oh, I almost forgot! We released a special edition of this volume in Japan with a drama CD included. It's our very first special edition! I'm so happy. In the special edition, the drama CD comes alongside the regular edition in a special box with new art and a script. As my regular readers know, I always want to do everything—ha! (By which I mean, I got to do all of the art.) Plus, the CD has new music on it, courtesy of NARASAKI (of course!), who composes the songs for the anime. It's the new song "Vanishing Sky," which Yuzu sends to Nino right before he disappears at the end of volume 11. NARASAKI composed it based on me saying that I "might" go with that title, and the song he came up with turned out to be a perfect fit.

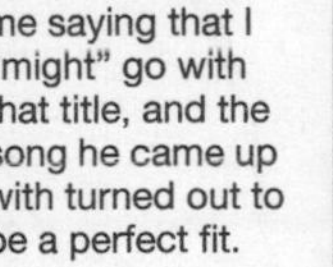
I LOVE THIS SONG!
WAAAH!

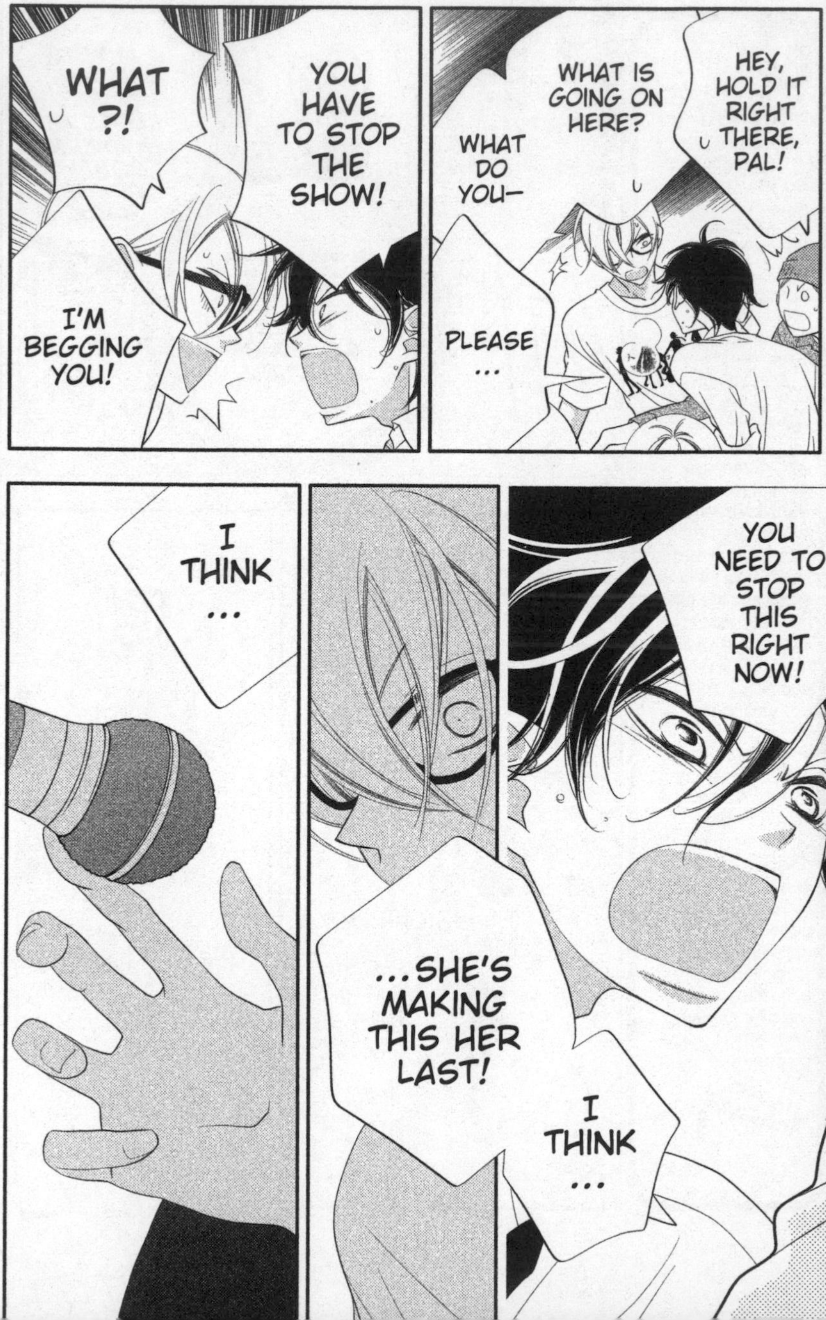
HEY, HOLD IT RIGHT THERE, PAL!
WHAT IS GOING ON HERE?
WHAT DO YOU—
PLEASE ...
YOU HAVE TO STOP THE SHOW!
WHAT ?!
I'M BEGGING YOU!
YOU NEED TO STOP THIS RIGHT NOW!
I THINK ...
...SHE'S MAKING THIS HER LAST!
I THINK ...

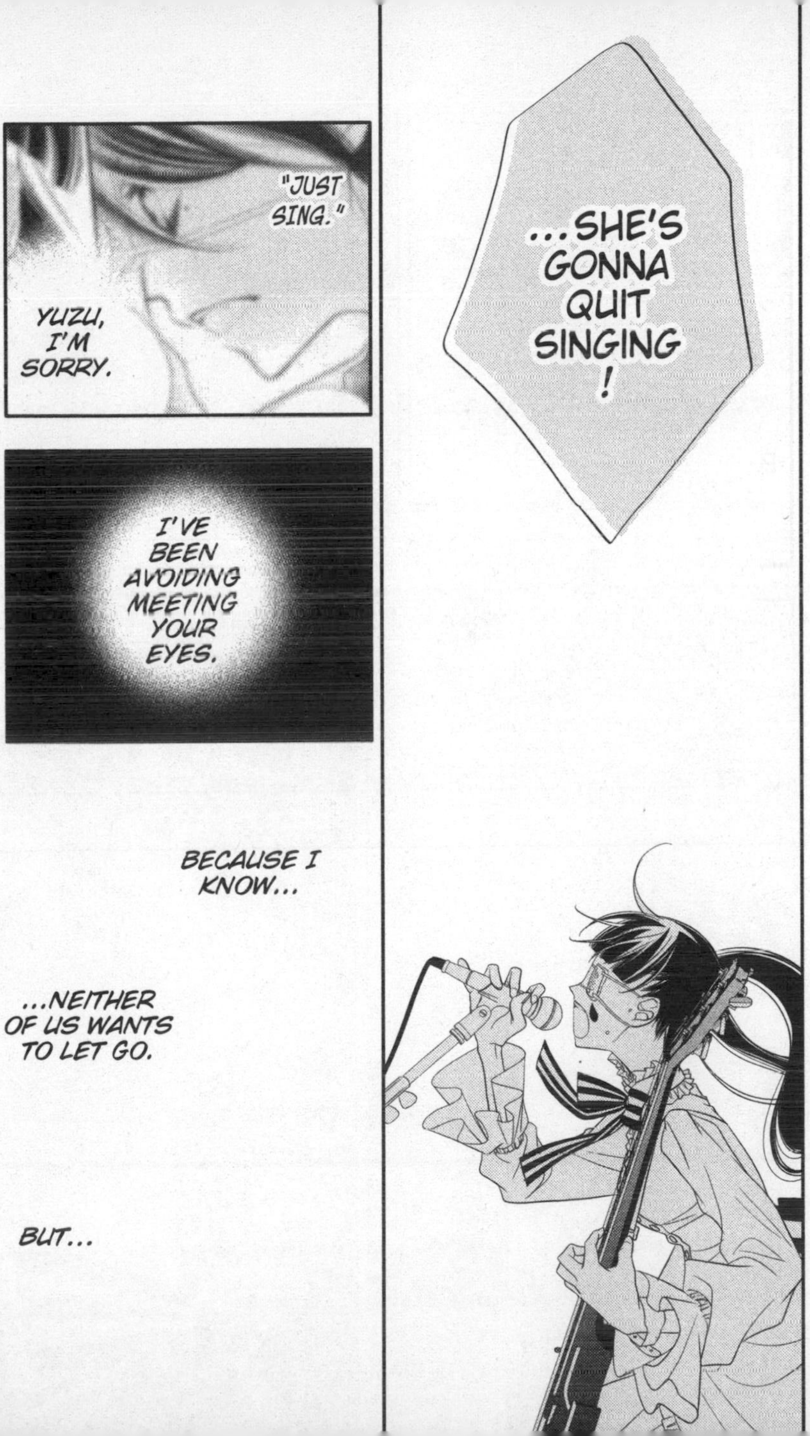
...SHE'S GONNA QUIT SINGING!
"JUST SING."
YUZU, I'M SORRY.
I'VE BEEN AVOIDING MEETING YOUR EYES.
BECAUSE I KNOW...
...NEITHER OF US WANTS TO LET GO.
BUT...

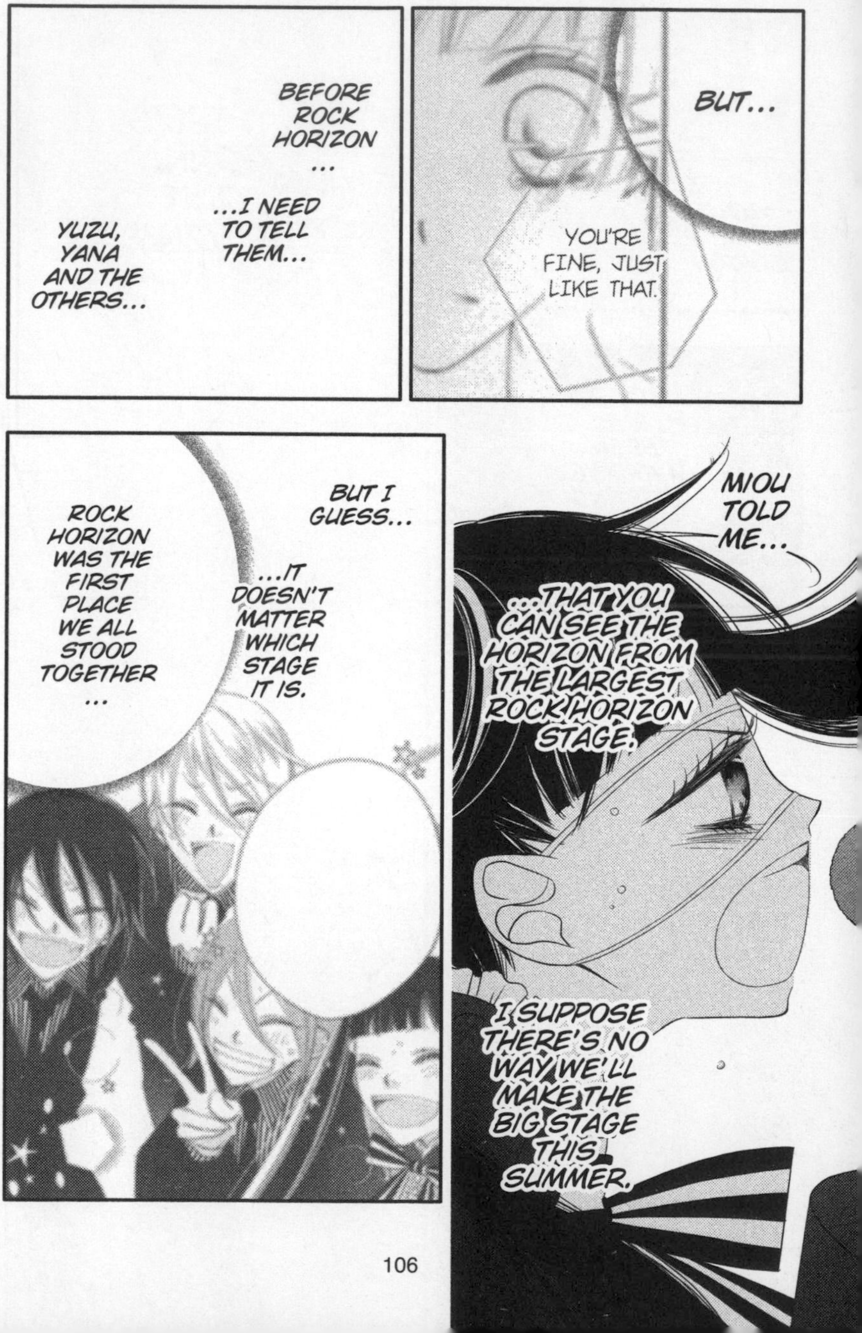
BUT...
YOU'RE FINE, JUST LIKE THAT.
BEFORE ROCK HORIZON...
...I NEED TO TELL THEM...
YUZU, YANA AND THE OTHERS...
MIOU TOLD ME...
...THAT YOU CAN SEE THE HORIZON FROM THE LARGEST ROCK HORIZON STAGE.
I SUPPOSE THERE'S NO WAY WE'LL MAKE THE BIG STAGE THIS SUMMER.
BUT I GUESS...
...IT DOESN'T MATTER WHICH STAGE IT IS.
ROCK HORIZON WAS THE FIRST PLACE WE ALL STOOD TOGETHER...

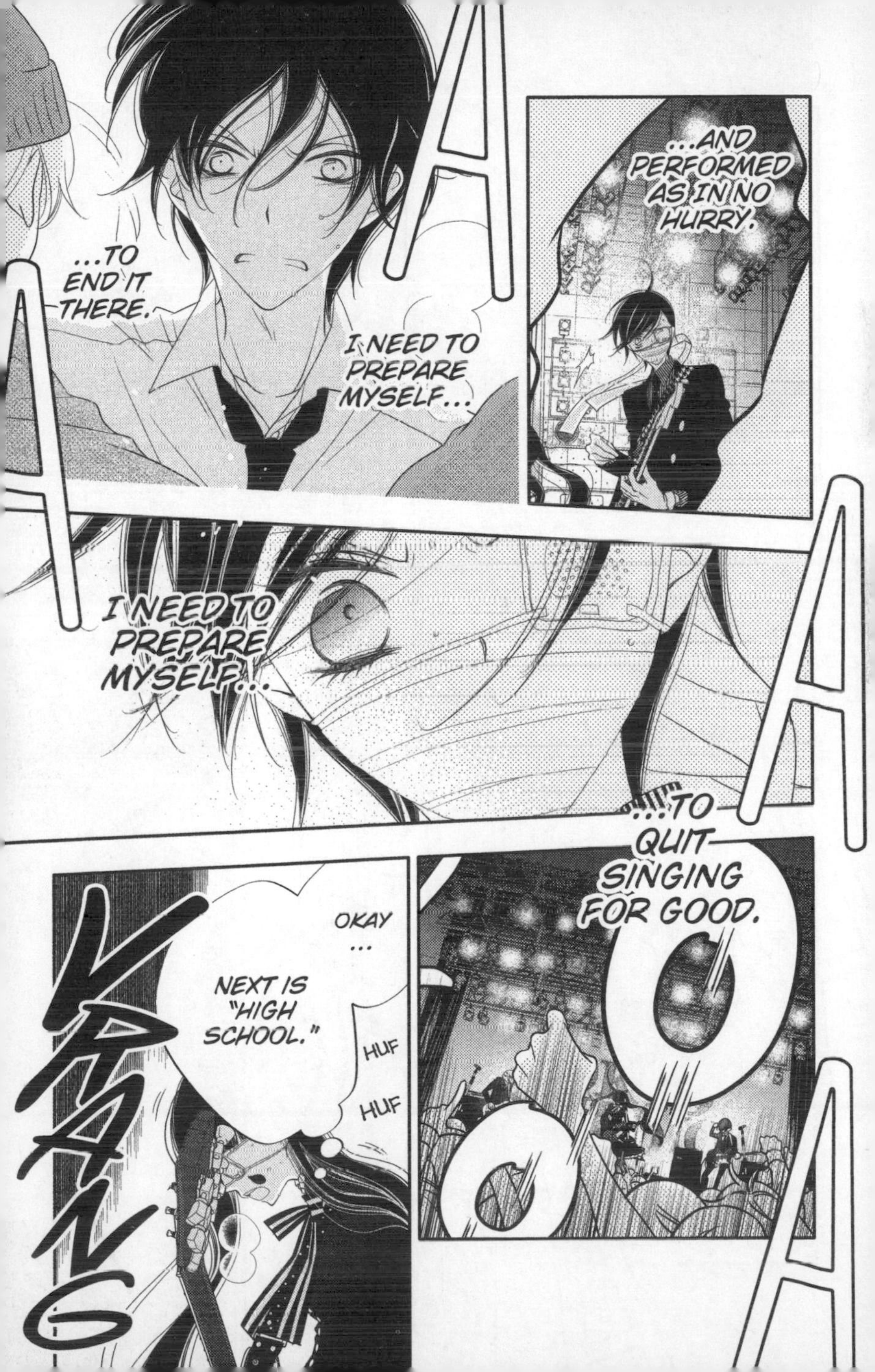

...AND PERFORMED AS IN NO HURRY.
...TO END IT THERE.
I NEED TO PREPARE MYSELF...
I NEED TO PREPARE MYSELF...
...TO QUIT SINGING FOR GOOD.
AAAOOA
OKAY ...
NEXT IS "HIGH SCHOOL."
HUF
HUF
VRANG

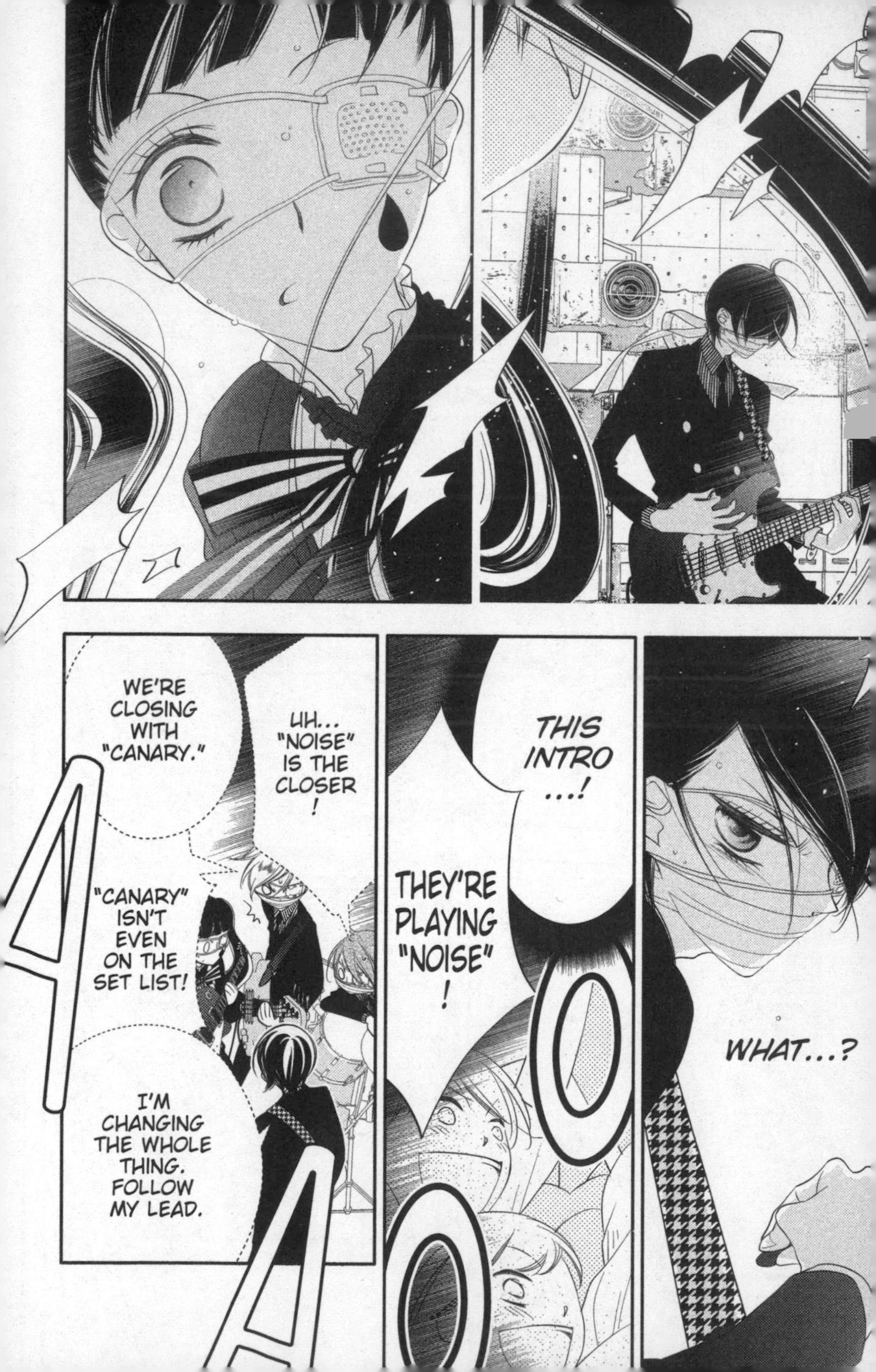
WHAT...?
THIS INTRO ...!
THEY'RE PLAYING "NOISE"!
WE'RE CLOSING WITH "CANARY."
UH... "NOISE" IS THE CLOSER!
"CANARY" ISN'T EVEN ON THE SET LIST!
I'M CHANGING THE WHOLE THING. FOLLOW MY LEAD.

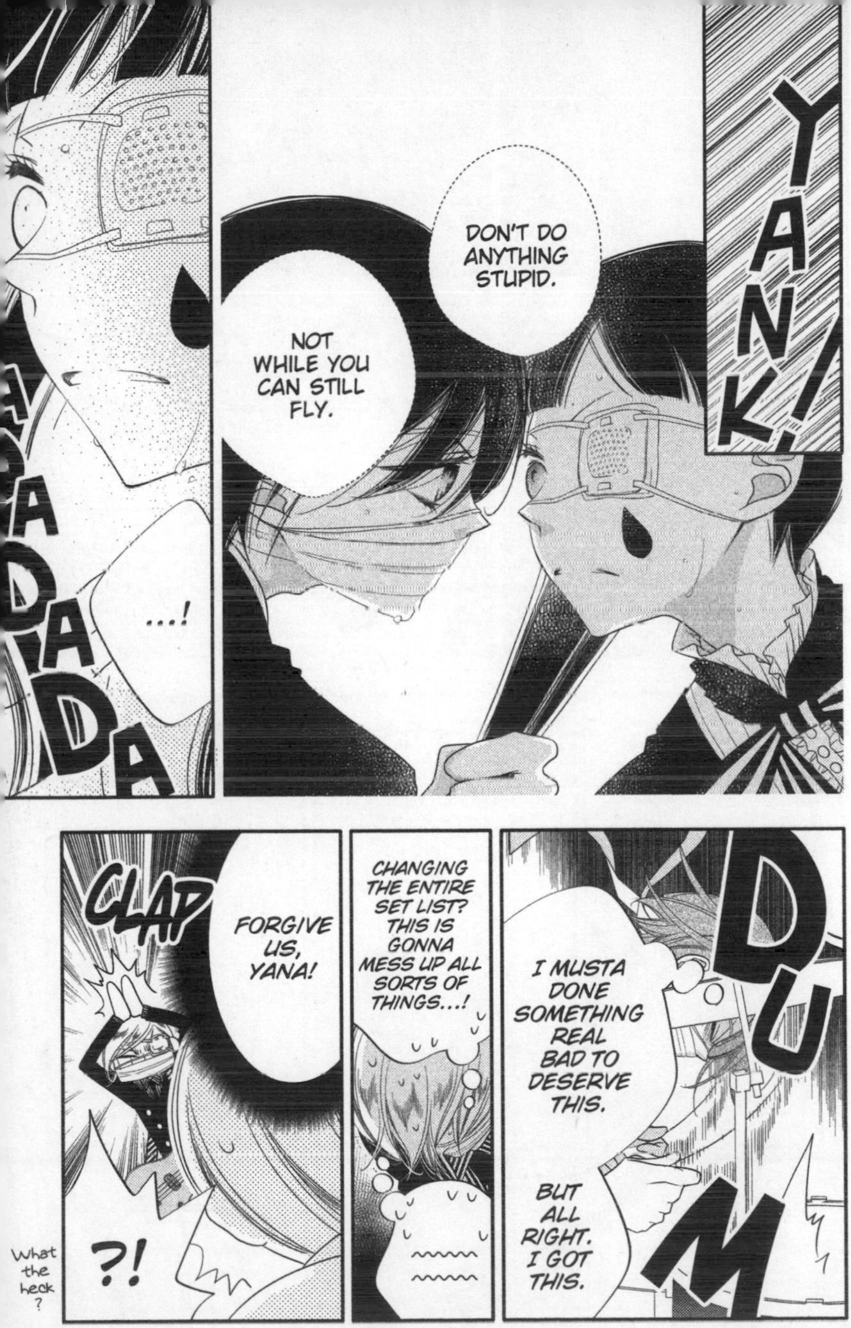
YANK!
DON'T DO ANYTHING STUPID.
NOT WHILE YOU CAN STILL FLY.
...!
DADADADA
DUM
I MUSTA DONE SOMETHING REAL BAD TO DESERVE THIS.
BUT ALL RIGHT. I GOT THIS.
CHANGING THE ENTIRE SET LIST? THIS IS GONNA MESS UP ALL SORTS OF THINGS...!
FORGIVE US, YANA!
CLAP
?!
What the heck?

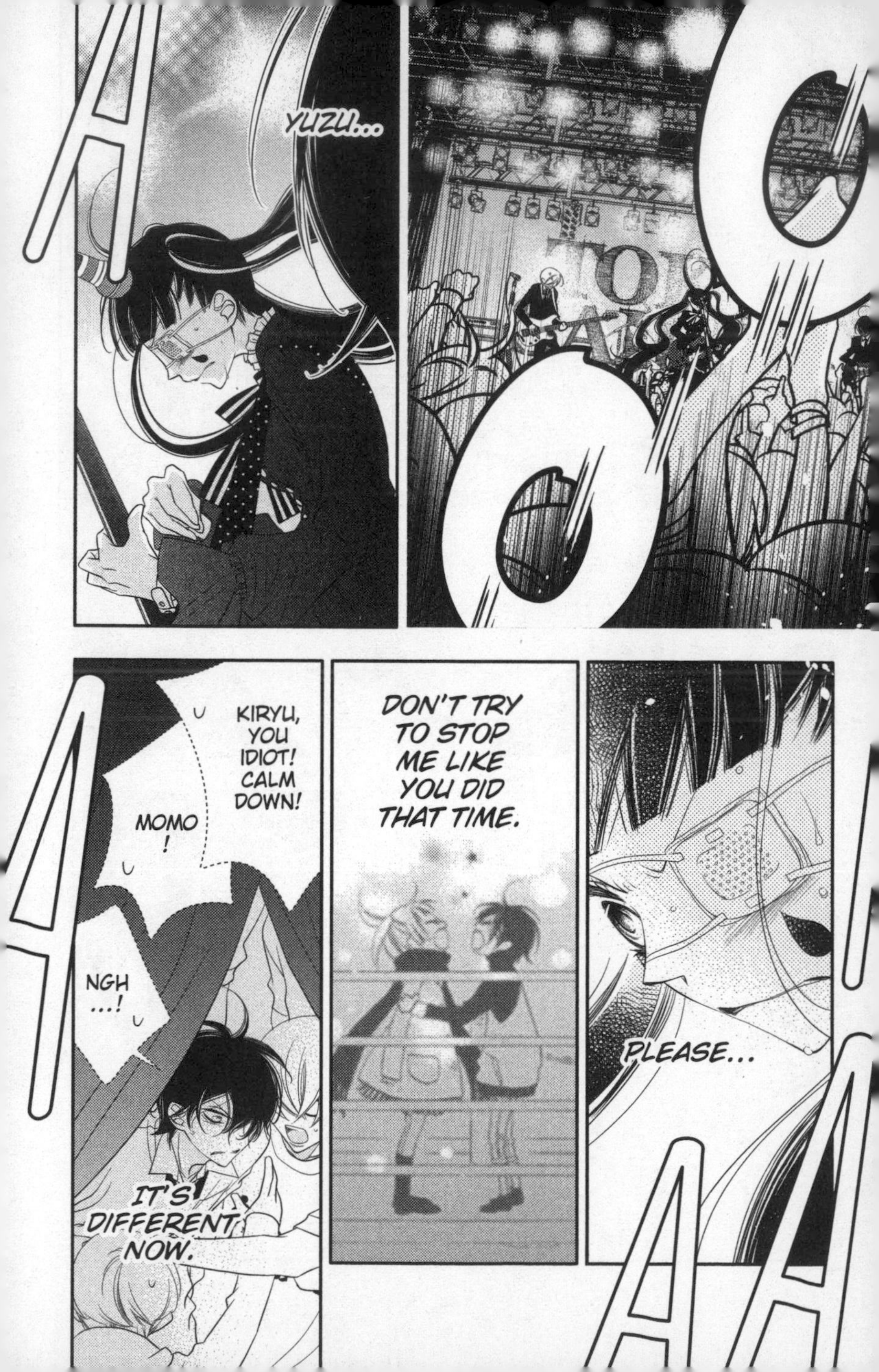
YUZU...
PLEASE...
DON'T TRY TO STOP ME LIKE YOU DID THAT TIME.
KIRYU, YOU IDIOT! CALM DOWN!
MOMO!
NGH...!
IT'S DIFFERENT NOW.

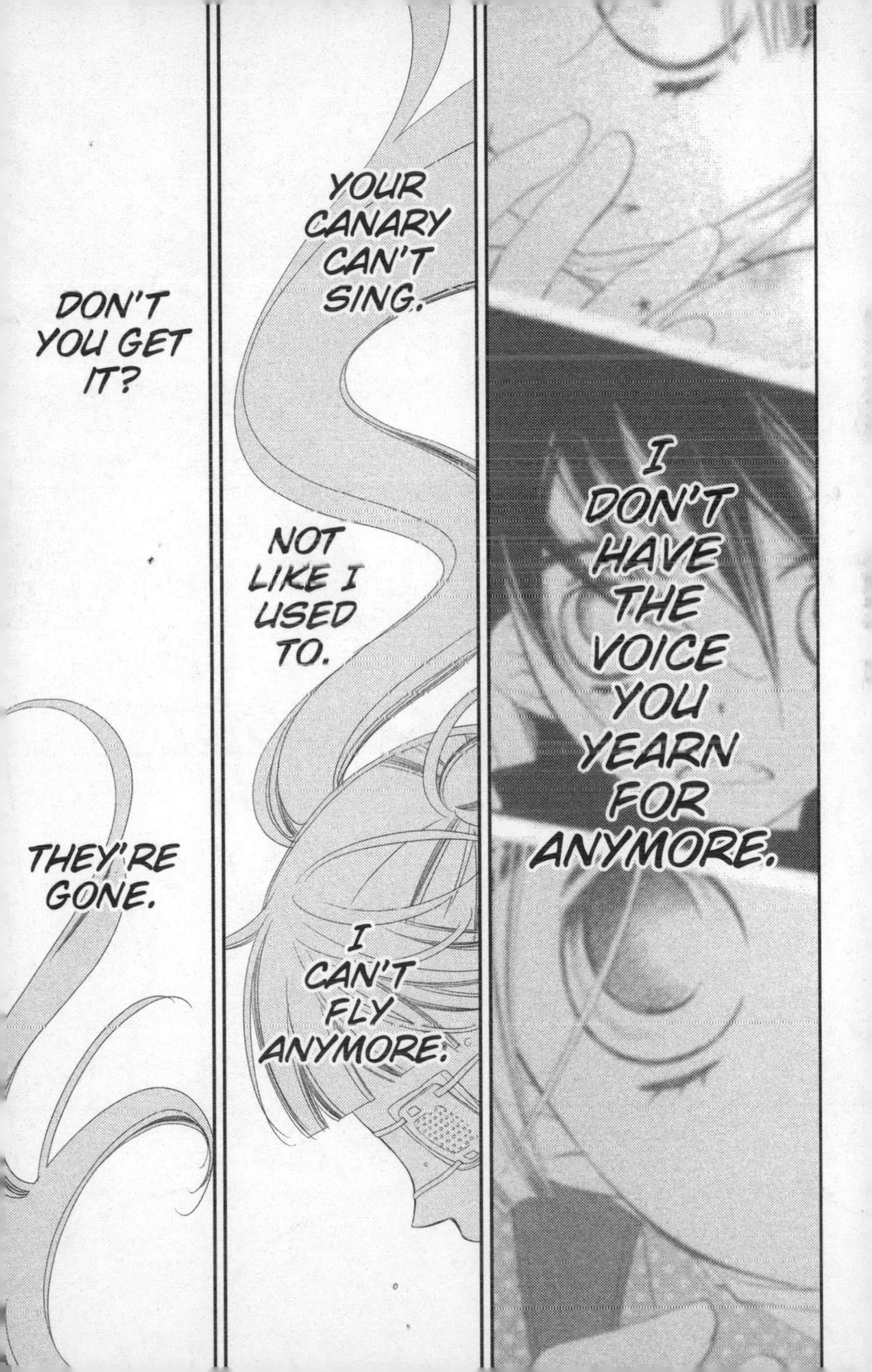
I DON'T HAVE THE VOICE YOU YEARN FOR ANYMORE.
YOUR CANARY CAN'T SING.
NOT LIKE I USED TO.
I CAN'T FLY ANYMORE.
DON'T YOU GET IT?
THEY'RE GONE.

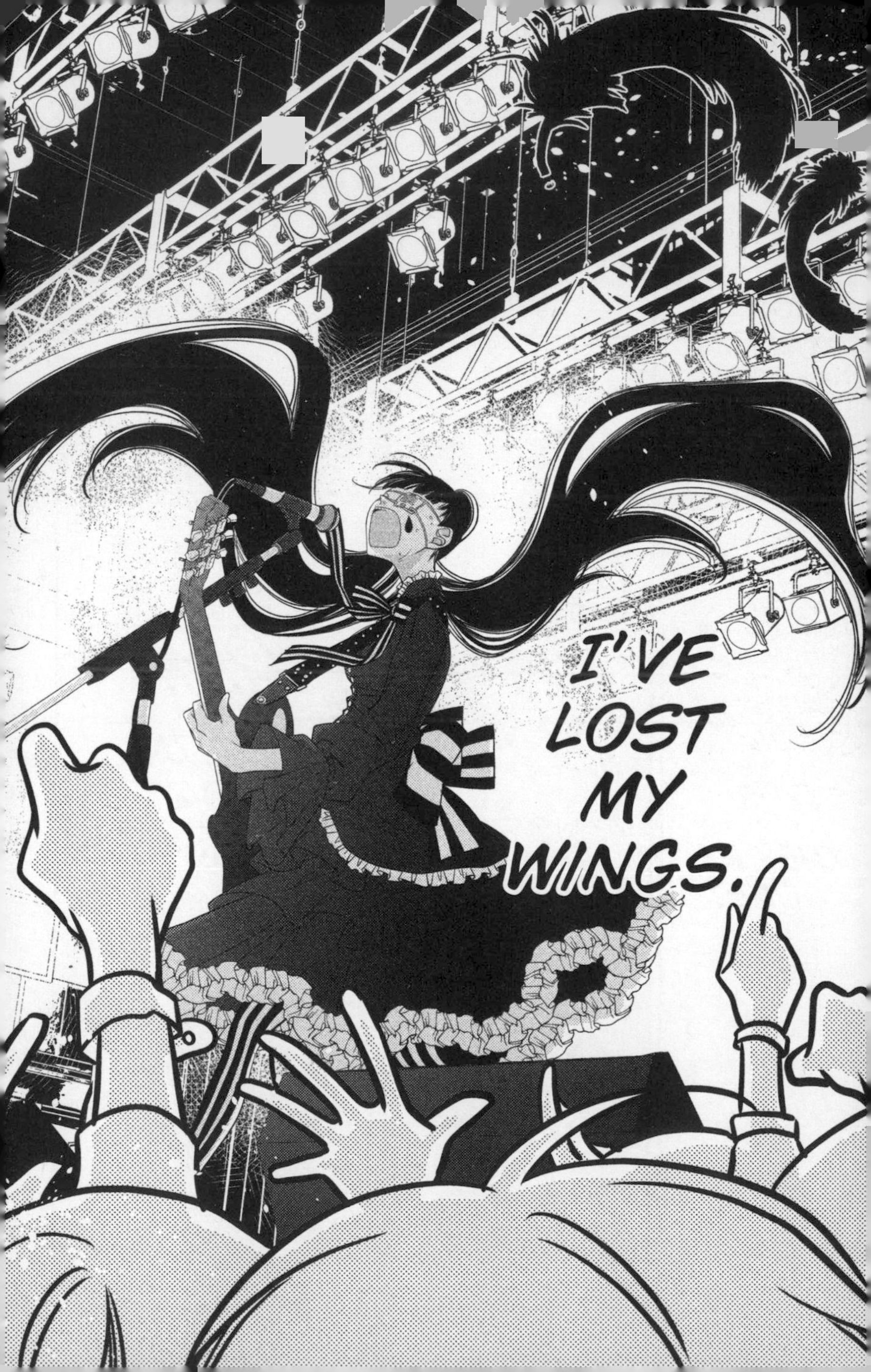
I'VE LOST MY WINGS.

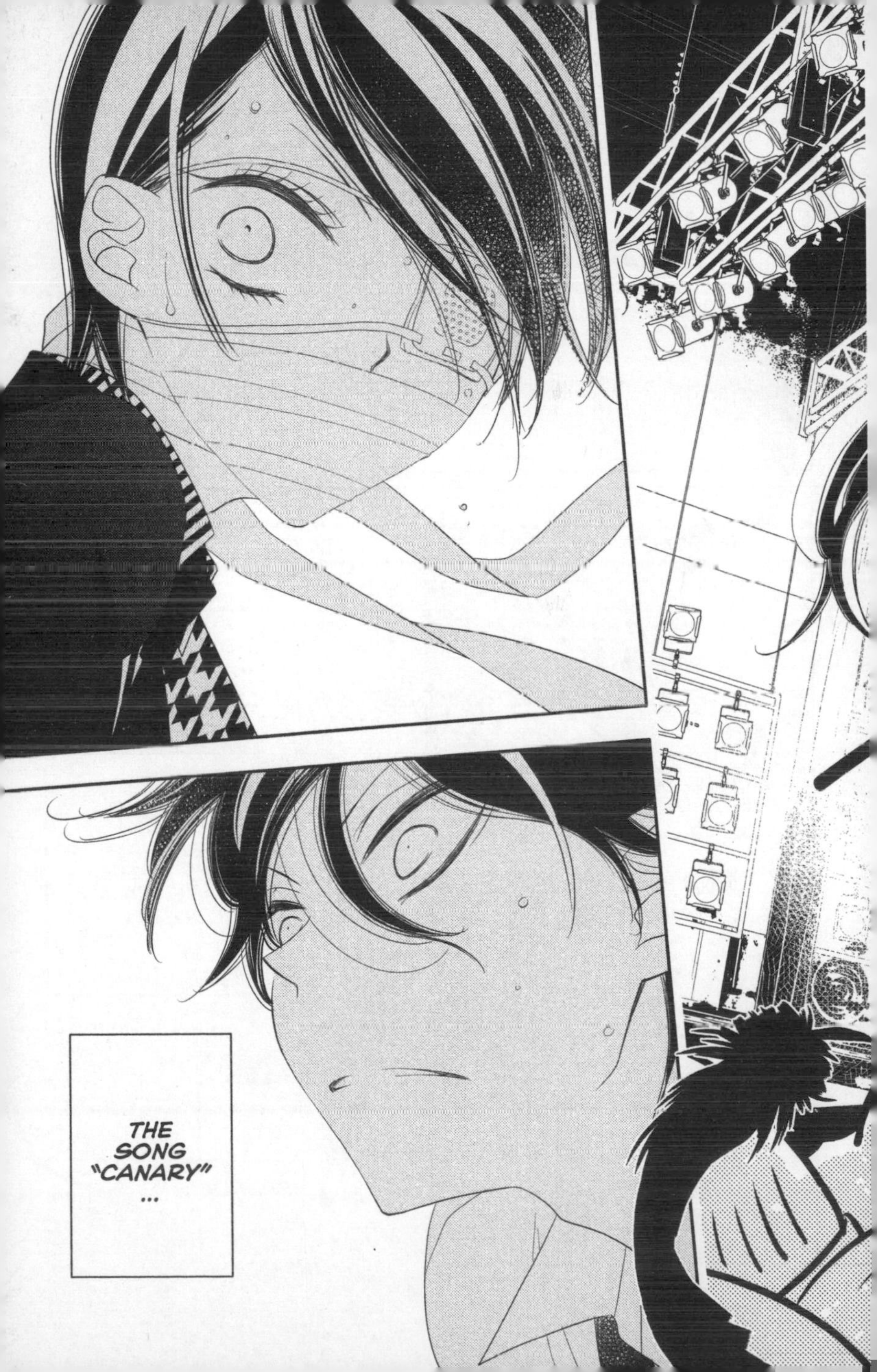
THE SONG "CANARY" ...

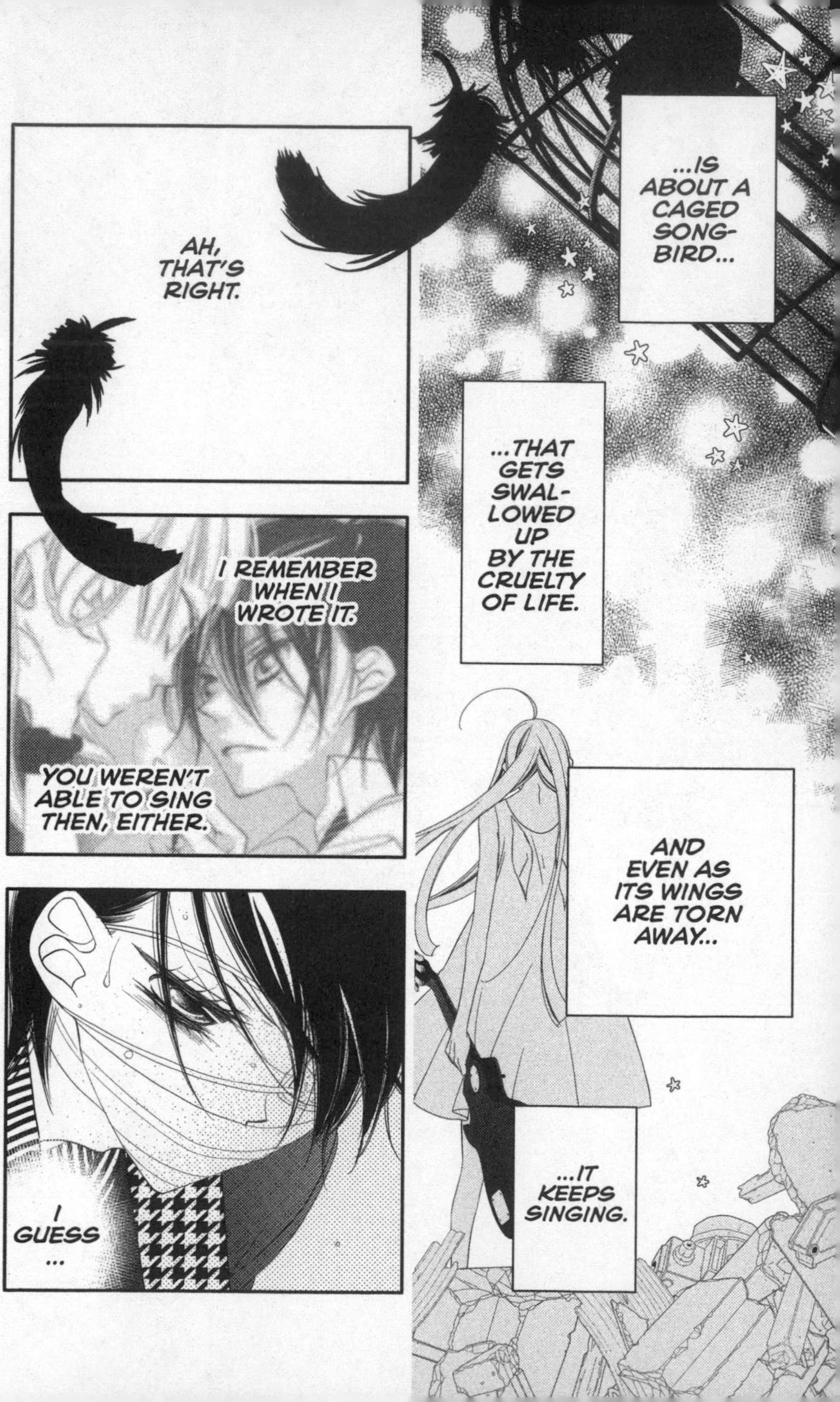
...IS ABOUT A CAGED SONG-BIRD...
...THAT GETS SWAL-LOWED UP BY THE CRUELTY OF LIFE.
AND EVEN AS ITS WINGS ARE TORN AWAY...
...IT KEEPS SINGING.
AH, THAT'S RIGHT.
I REMEMBER WHEN I WROTE IT.
YOU WEREN'T ABLE TO SING THEN, EITHER.
I GUESS ...

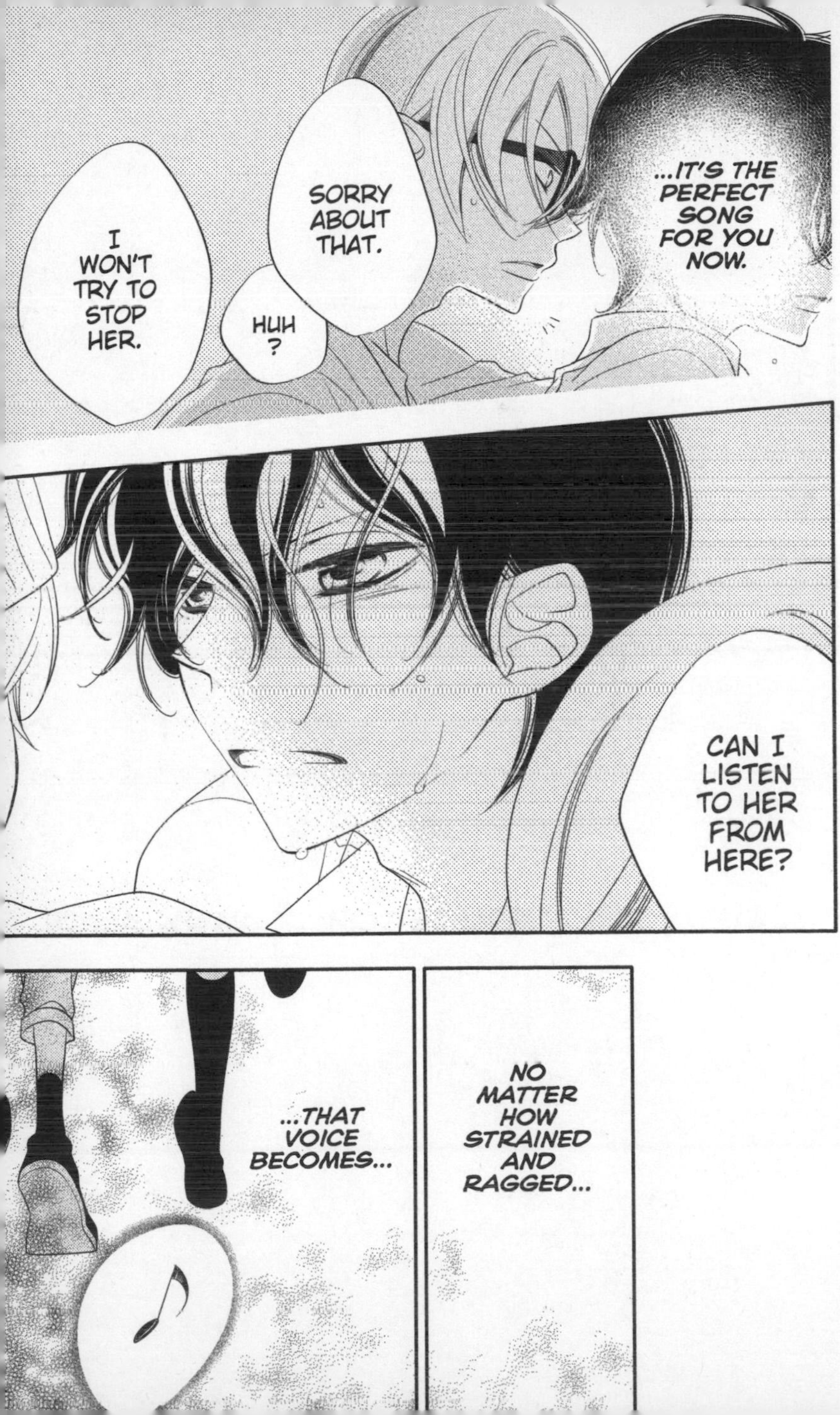
...IT'S THE PERFECT SONG FOR YOU NOW.
SORRY ABOUT THAT.
HUH?
I WON'T TRY TO STOP HER.
CAN I LISTEN TO HER FROM HERE?
NO MATTER HOW STRAINED AND RAGGED...
...THAT VOICE BECOMES...

...I WON'T LET YOU THROW IT AWAY, ALICE.

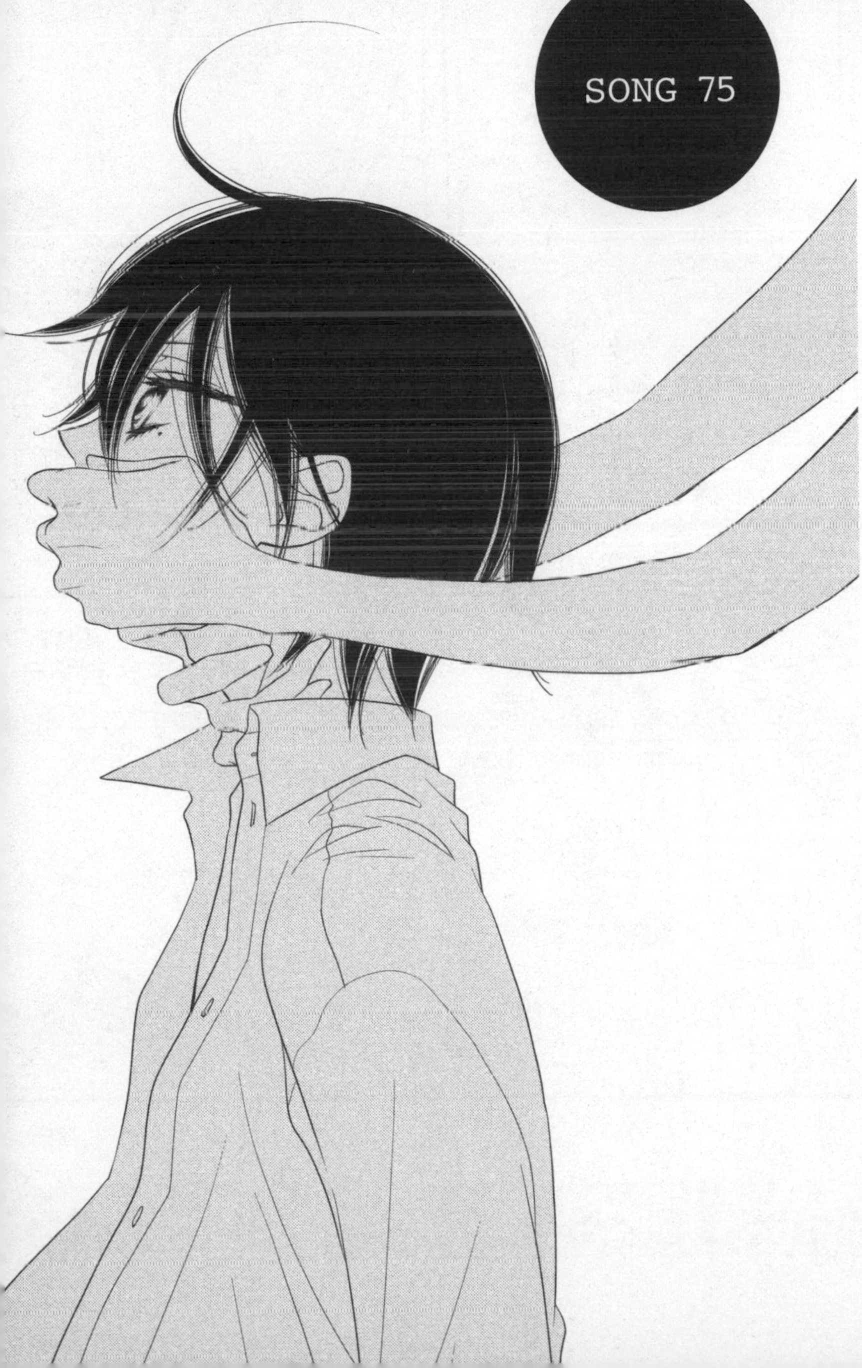
SONG 75

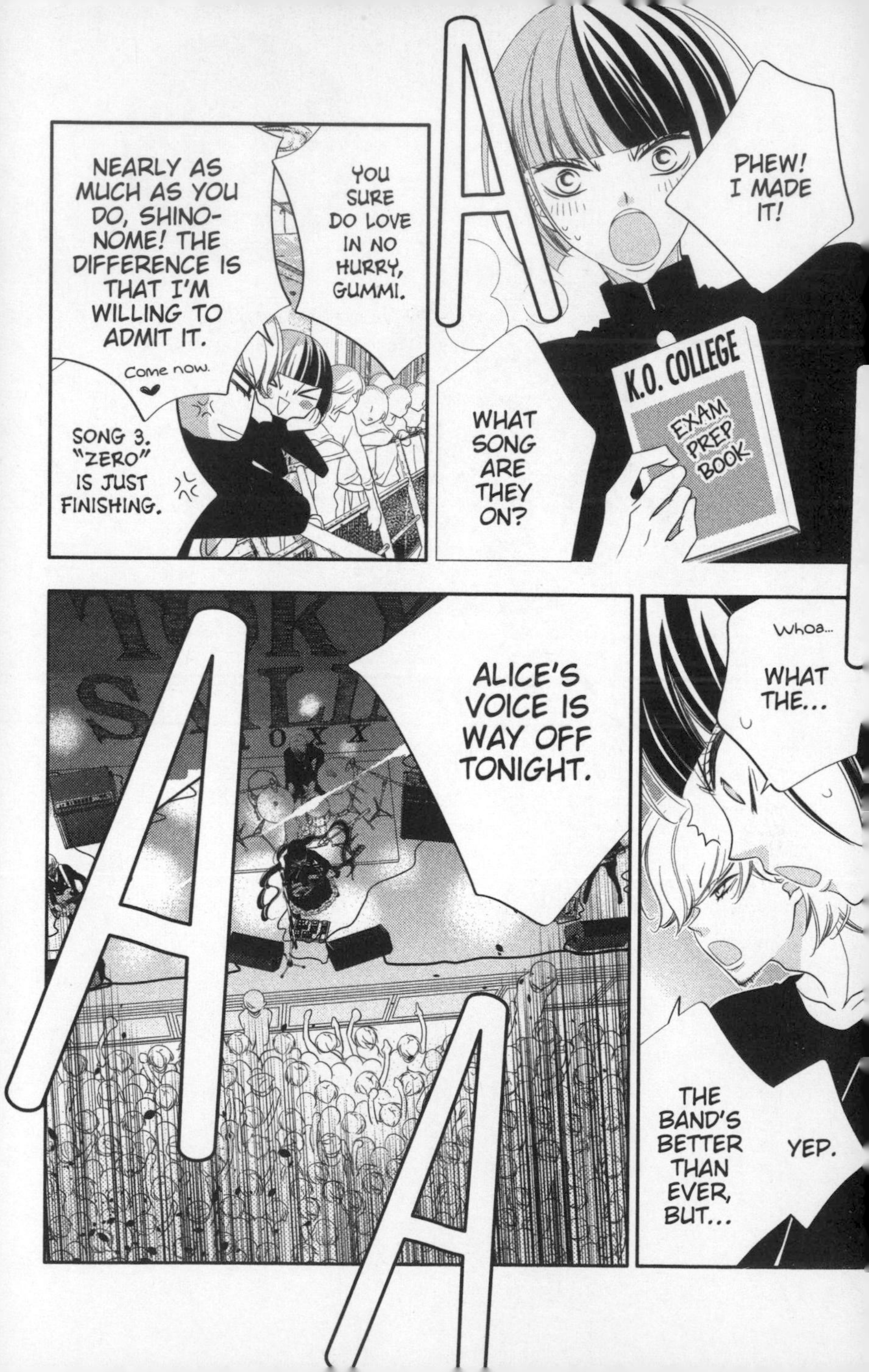
A
PHEW! I MADE IT!
WHAT SONG ARE THEY ON?
K.O. COLLEGE EXAM PREP BOOK
YOU SURE DO LOVE IN NO HURRY, GUMMI.
NEARLY AS MUCH AS YOU DO, SHINO-NOME! THE DIFFERENCE IS THAT I'M WILLING TO ADMIT IT.
Come now.
SONG 3. "ZERO" IS JUST FINISHING.
Whoa...
WHAT THE...
THE BAND'S BETTER THAN EVER, BUT...
YEP.
ALICE'S VOICE IS WAY OFF TONIGHT.
A
A

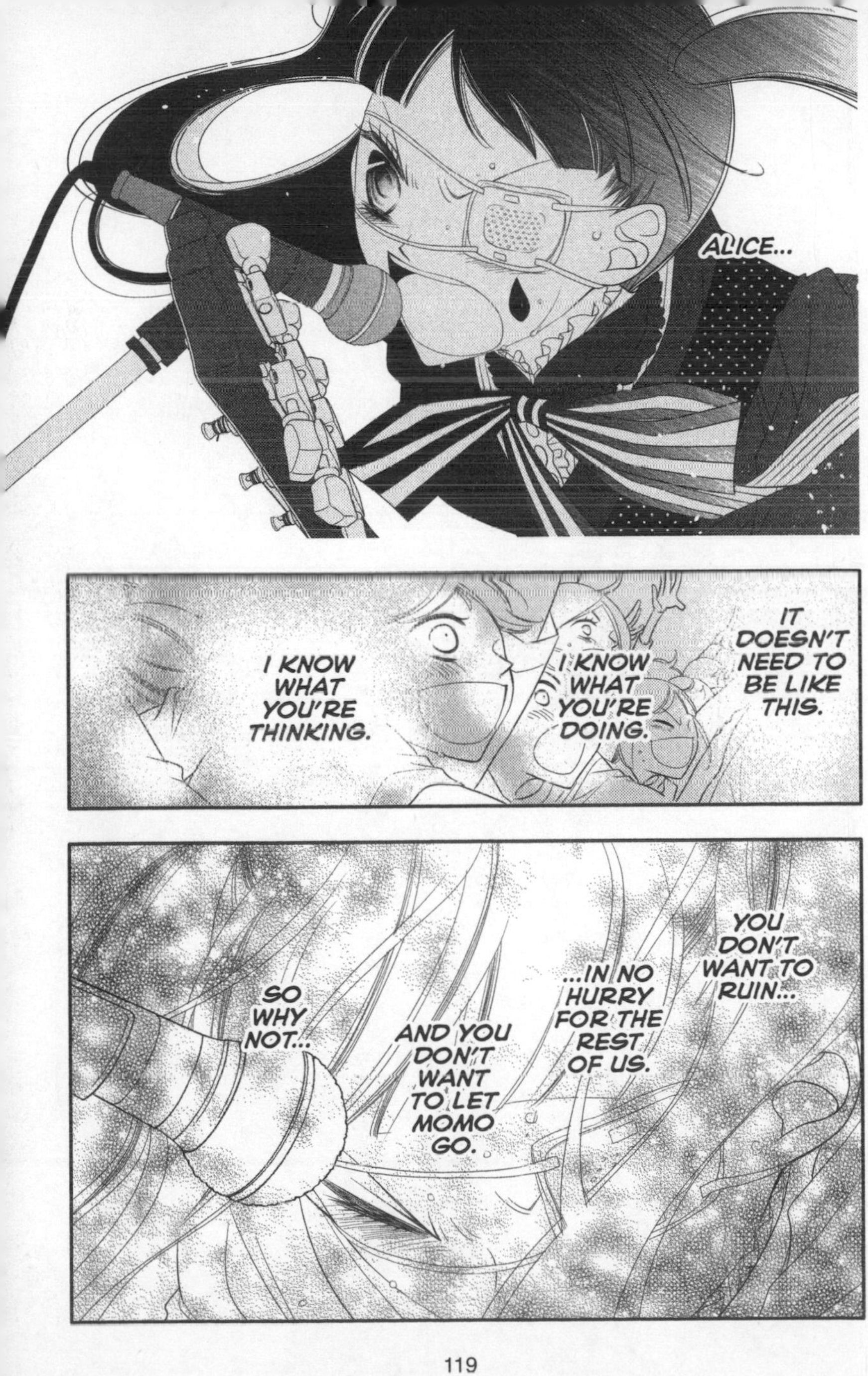
ALICE...
IT DOESN'T NEED TO BE LIKE THIS.
I KNOW WHAT YOU'RE DOING.
I KNOW WHAT YOU'RE THINKING.
YOU DON'T WANT TO RUIN...
...IN NO HURRY FOR THE REST OF US.
AND YOU DON'T WANT TO LET MOMO GO.
SO WHY NOT...

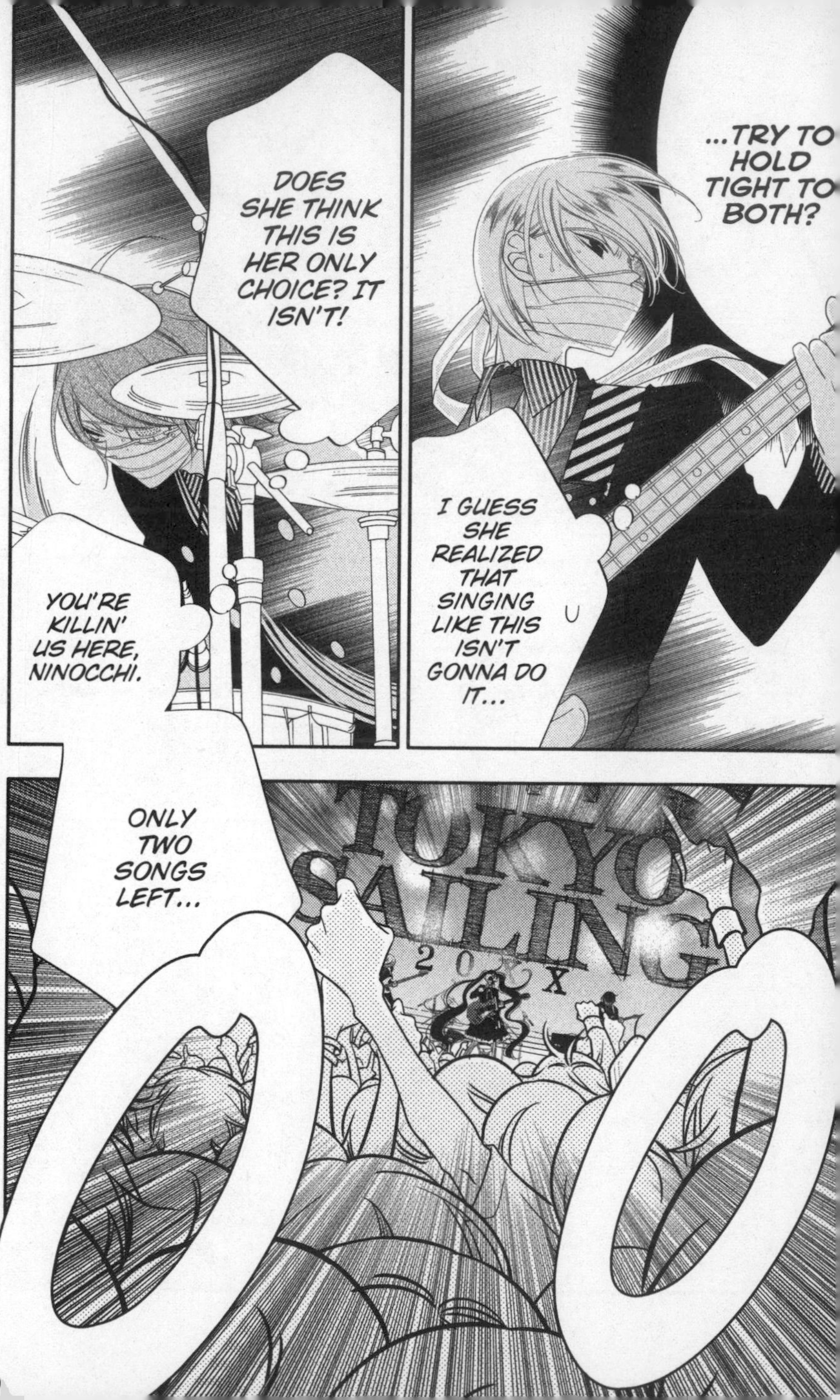
...TRY TO HOLD TIGHT TO BOTH?
I GUESS SHE REALIZED THAT SINGING LIKE THIS ISN'T GONNA DO IT...
DOES SHE THINK THIS IS HER ONLY CHOICE? IT ISN'T!
YOU'RE KILLIN' US HERE, NINOCCHI.
ONLY TWO SONGS LEFT...
TOKYO SAILING
20XX

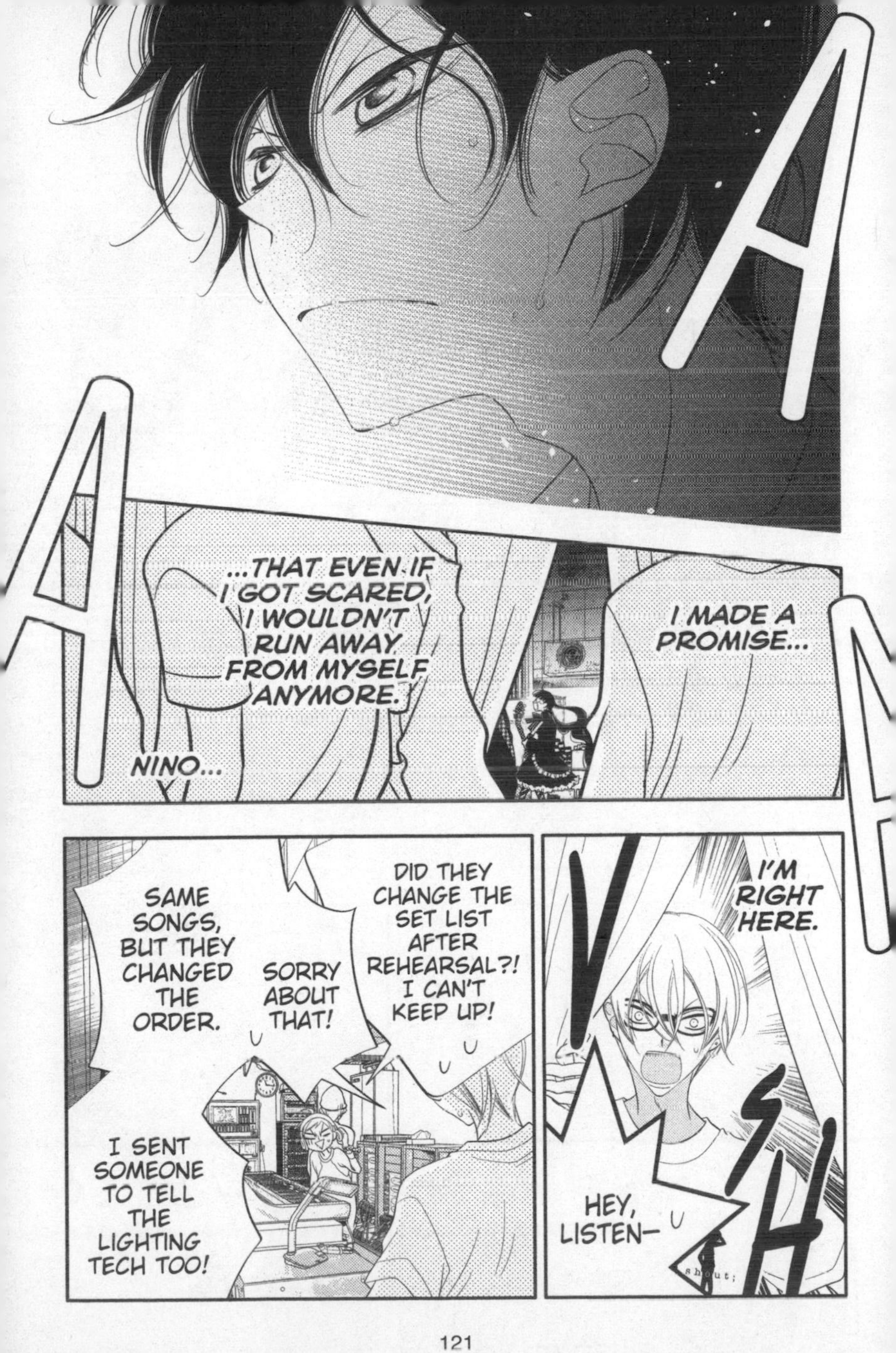
I MADE A PROMISE...
...THAT EVEN IF I GOT SCARED, I WOULDN'T RUN AWAY FROM MYSELF ANYMORE.
NINO...
I'M RIGHT HERE.
HEY, LISTEN—
shout;
DID THEY CHANGE THE SET LIST AFTER REHEARSAL?! I CAN'T KEEP UP!
SORRY ABOUT THAT!
SAME SONGS, BUT THEY CHANGED THE ORDER.
I SENT SOMEONE TO TELL THE LIGHTING TECH TOO!

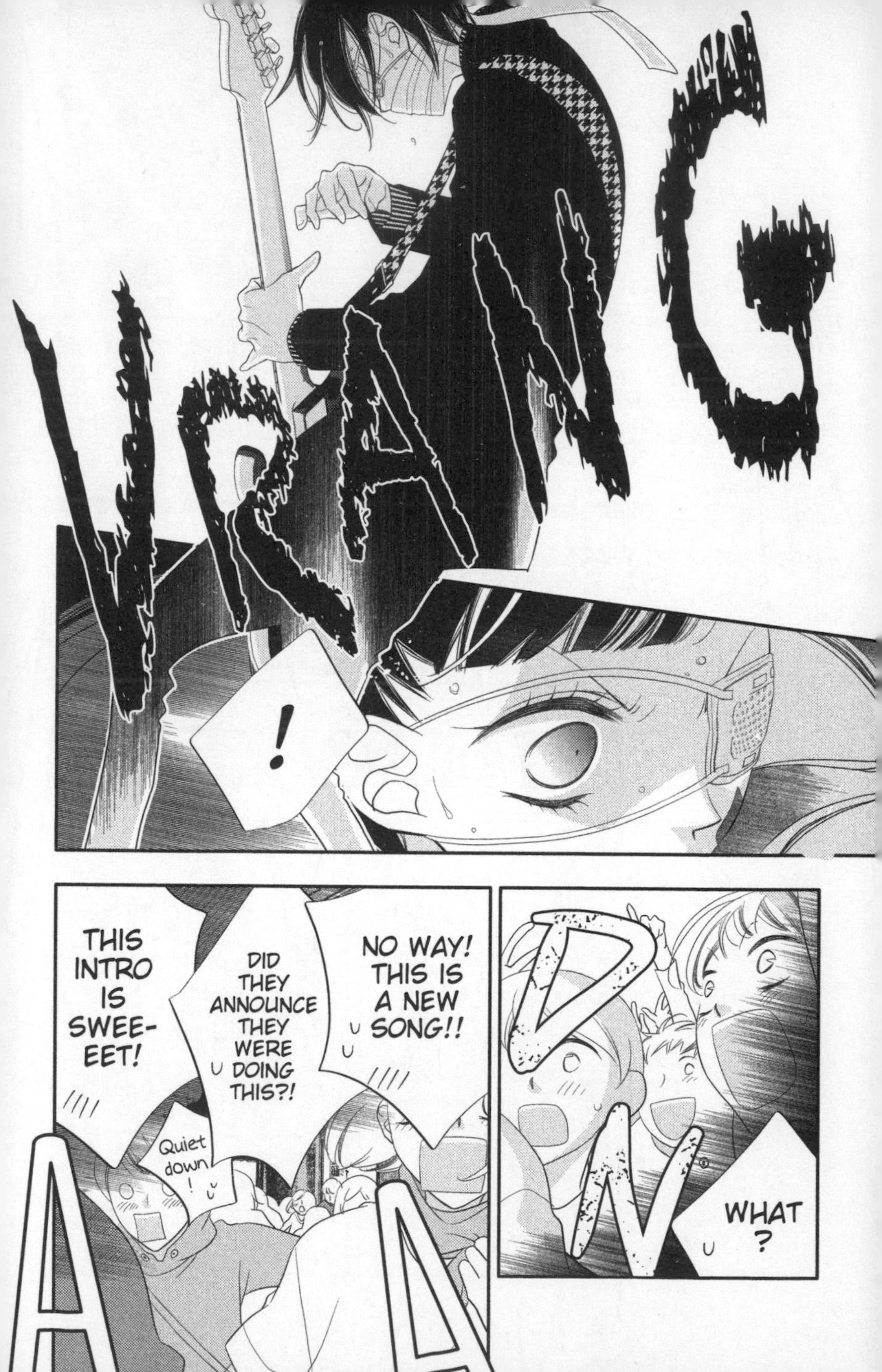
WRANG
!
WHAT?
NO WAY! THIS IS A NEW SONG!!
DID THEY ANNOUNCE THEY WERE DOING THIS?!
THIS INTRO IS SWEEE-EET!
Quiet down!

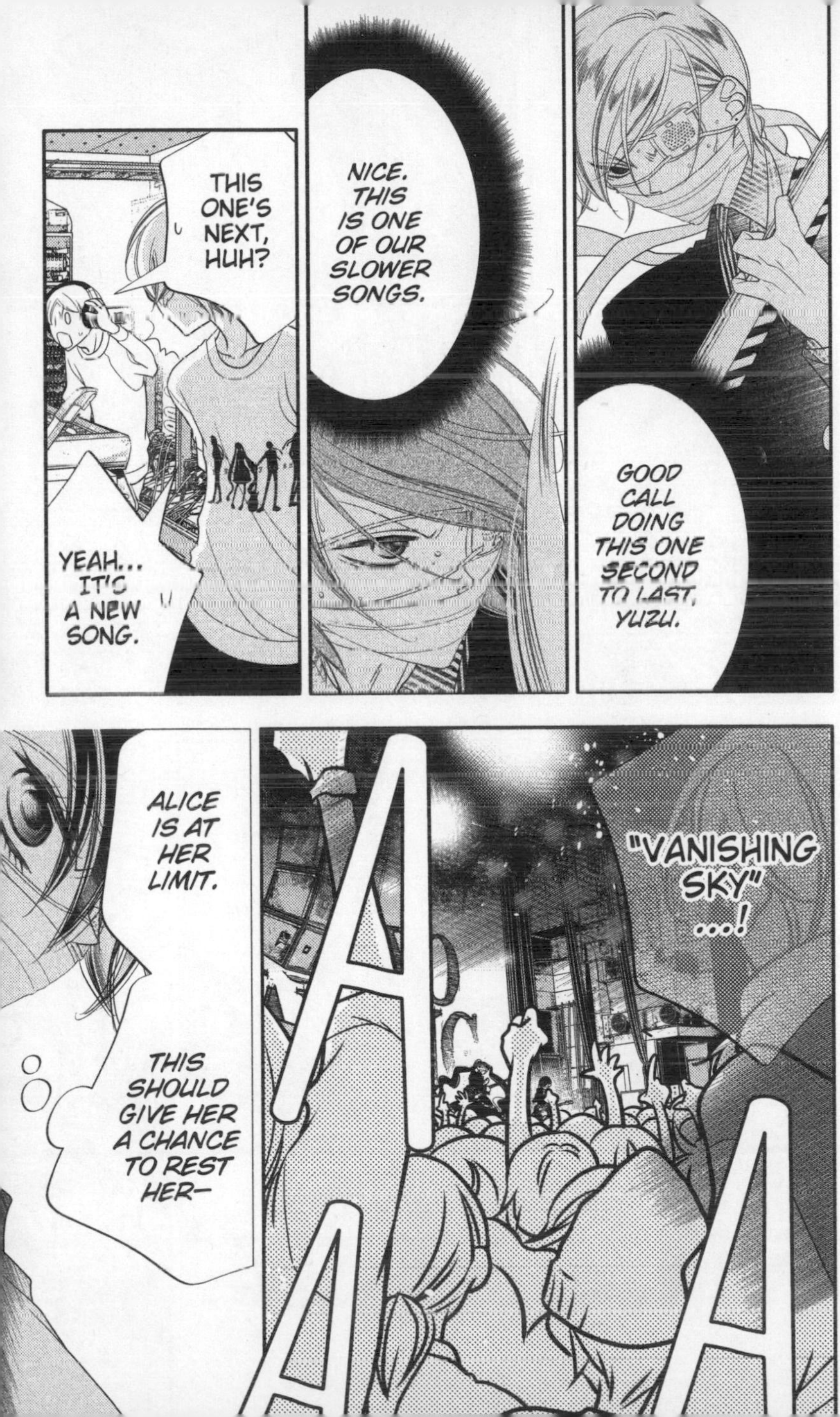
GOOD CALL DOING THIS ONE SECOND TO LAST, YUZU.
NICE. THIS IS ONE OF OUR SLOWER SONGS.
THIS ONE'S NEXT, HUH?
YEAH... IT'S A NEW SONG.
"VANISHING SKY" ...!
ALICE IS AT HER LIMIT.
THIS SHOULD GIVE HER A CHANCE TO REST HER—

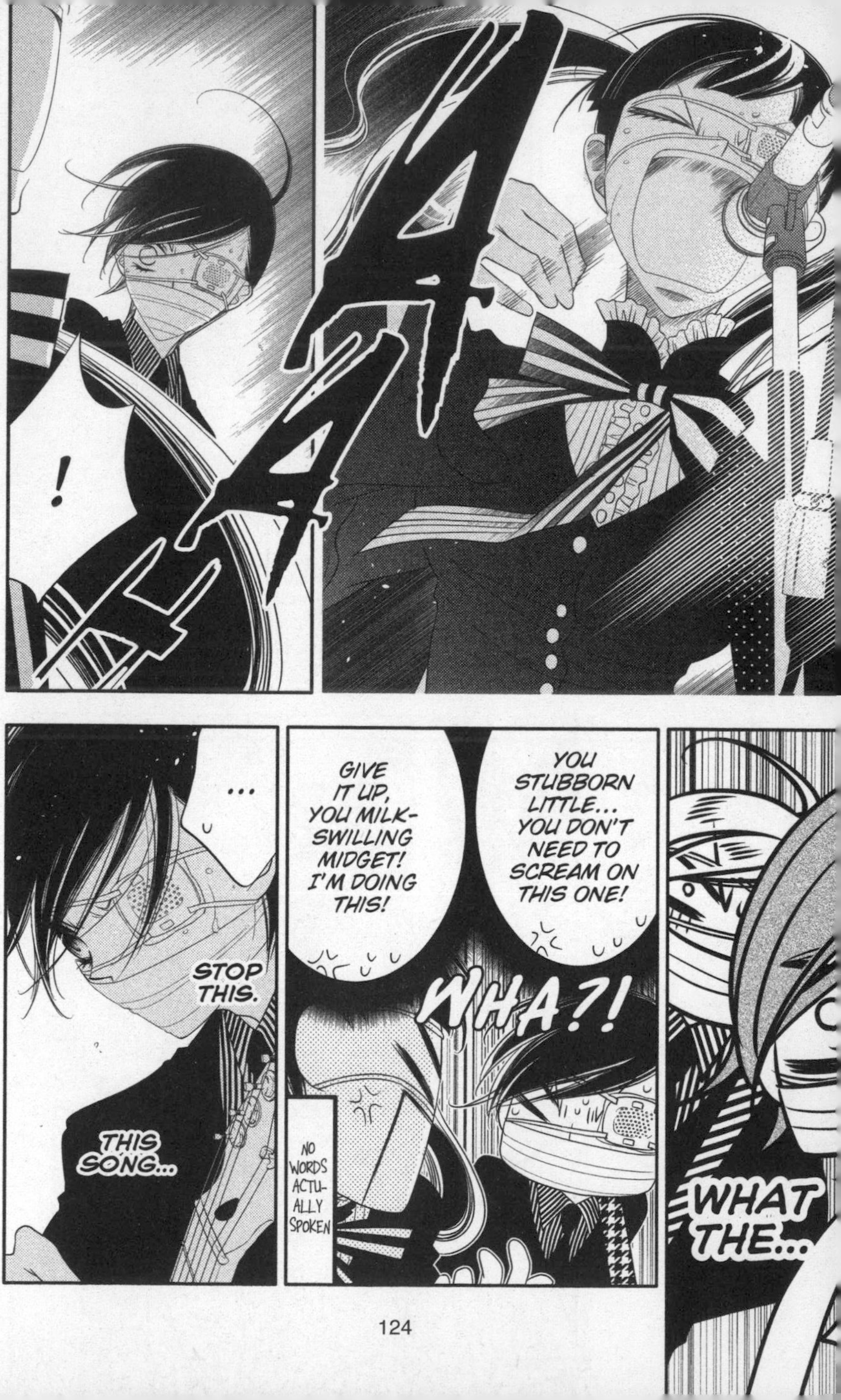
!
WHAT THE...
YOU STUBBORN LITTLE... YOU DON'T NEED TO SCREAM ON THIS ONE!
GIVE IT UP, YOU MILK-SWILLING MIDGET! I'M DOING THIS!
WHA?!
NO WORDS ACTU-ALLY SPOKEN
...
STOP THIS.
THIS SONG...

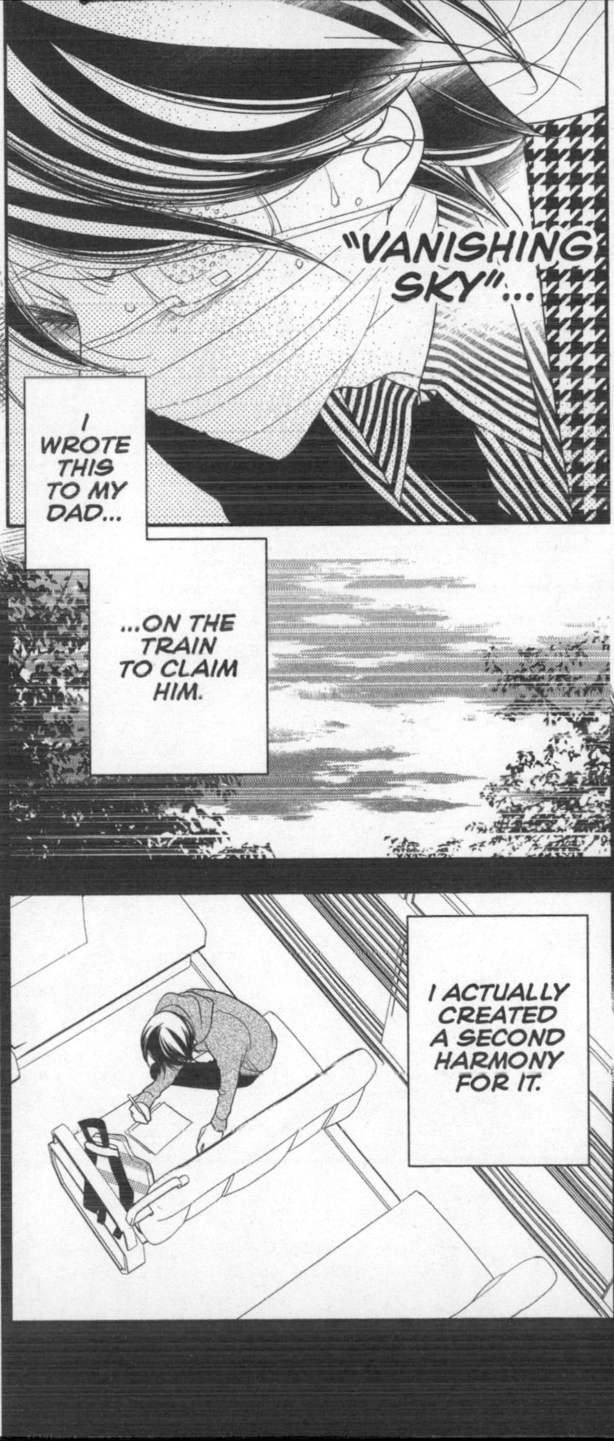
"VANISHING SKY"...
I WROTE THIS TO MY DAD...
...ON THE TRAIN TO CLAIM HIM.
I ACTUALLY CREATED A SECOND HARMONY FOR IT.

4

I like to be involved with the music that appears in *Anonymous Noise*, so once again I asked if I could write the lyrics to "Vanishing Sky." Since I hadn't yet figured out what sort of role the song would play in the manga, all I had to go off of was the title and the music. But this time, I thought about what Yuzu had experienced, and the words flowed right out of me. It was one of the easiest things I've ever written. Even when it doesn't go that smoothly, writing lyrics is a lot of fun. There's a strong puzzle element to it that you don't get when just writing titles, and the opportunities for wordplay delight me to no end. And it certainly helps that I really appreciate the music NARASAKI composes. It's truly a joy to write words you love for music you love. I'm so grateful that I had this opportunity.

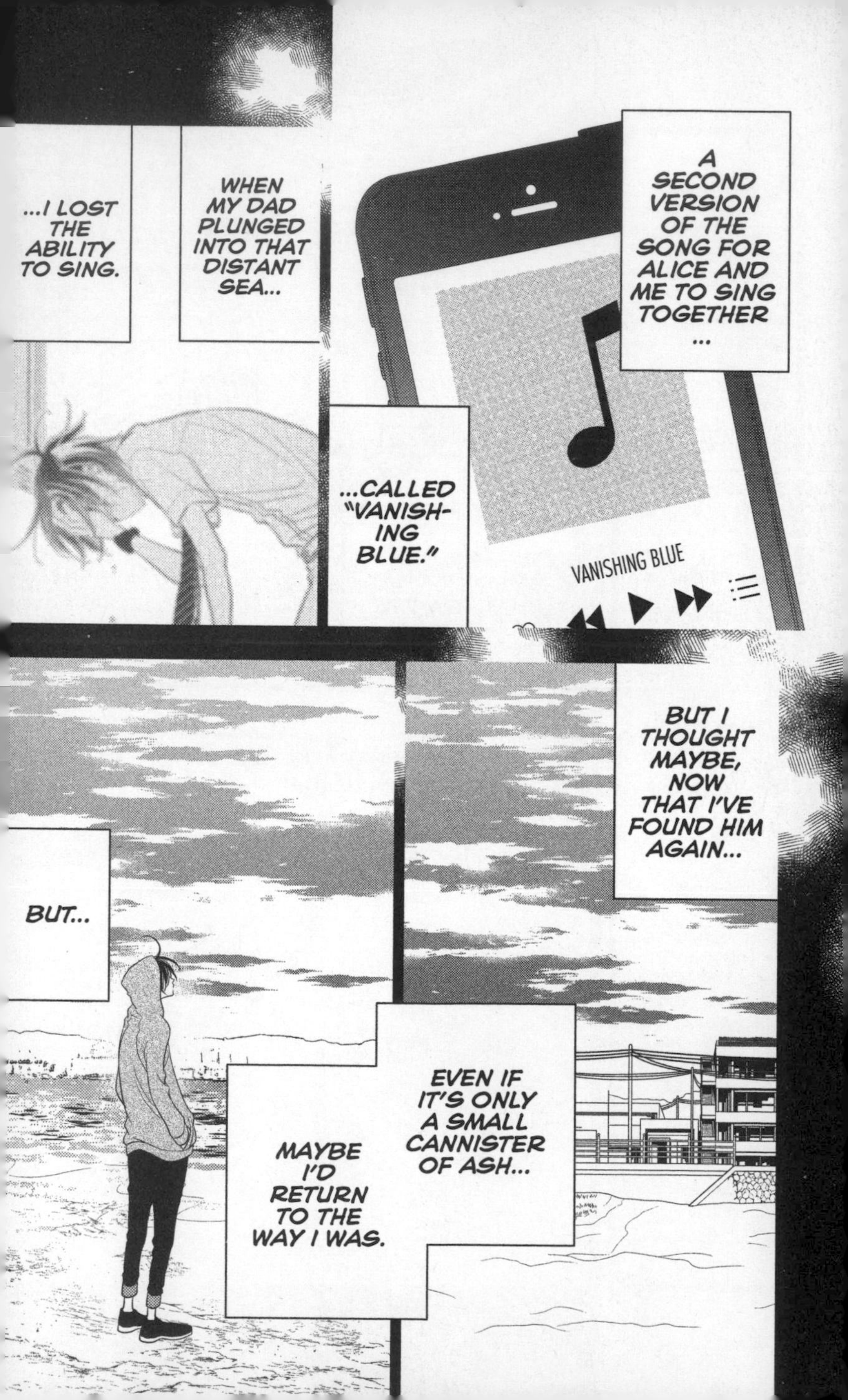
A SECOND VERSION OF THE SONG FOR ALICE AND ME TO SING TOGETHER...
VANISHING BLUE
...CALLED "VANISHING BLUE."
WHEN MY DAD PLUNGED INTO THAT DISTANT SEA...
...I LOST THE ABILITY TO SING.
BUT I THOUGHT MAYBE, NOW THAT I'VE FOUND HIM AGAIN...
BUT...
EVEN IF IT'S ONLY A SMALL CANNISTER OF ASH...
MAYBE I'D RETURN TO THE WAY I WAS.

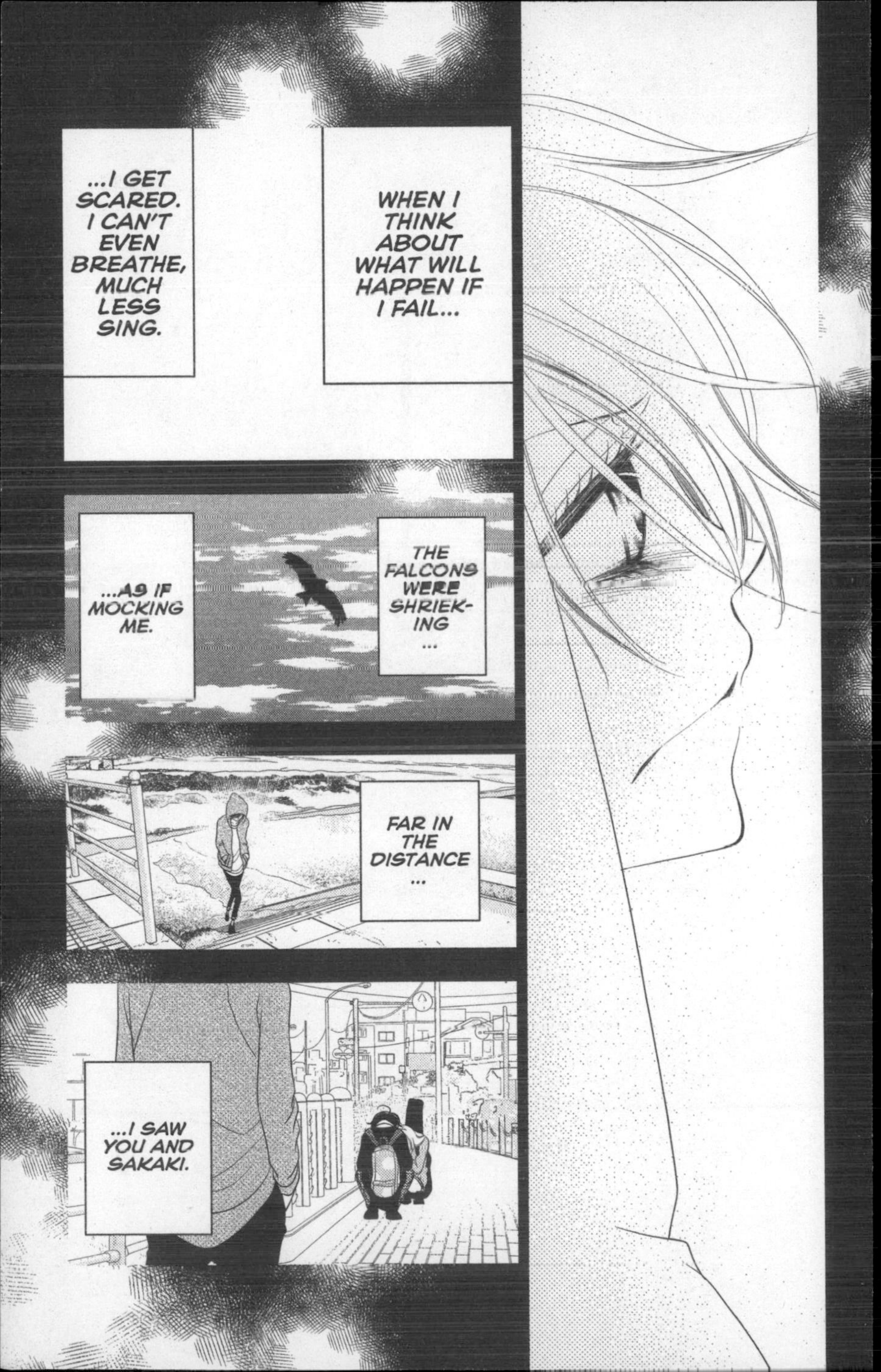
WHEN I THINK ABOUT WHAT WILL HAPPEN IF I FAIL...
...I GET SCARED. I CAN'T EVEN BREATHE, MUCH LESS SING.
THE FALCONS WERE SHRIEK-ING...
...AS IF MOCKING ME.
FAR IN THE DISTANCE...
...I SAW YOU AND SAKAKI.

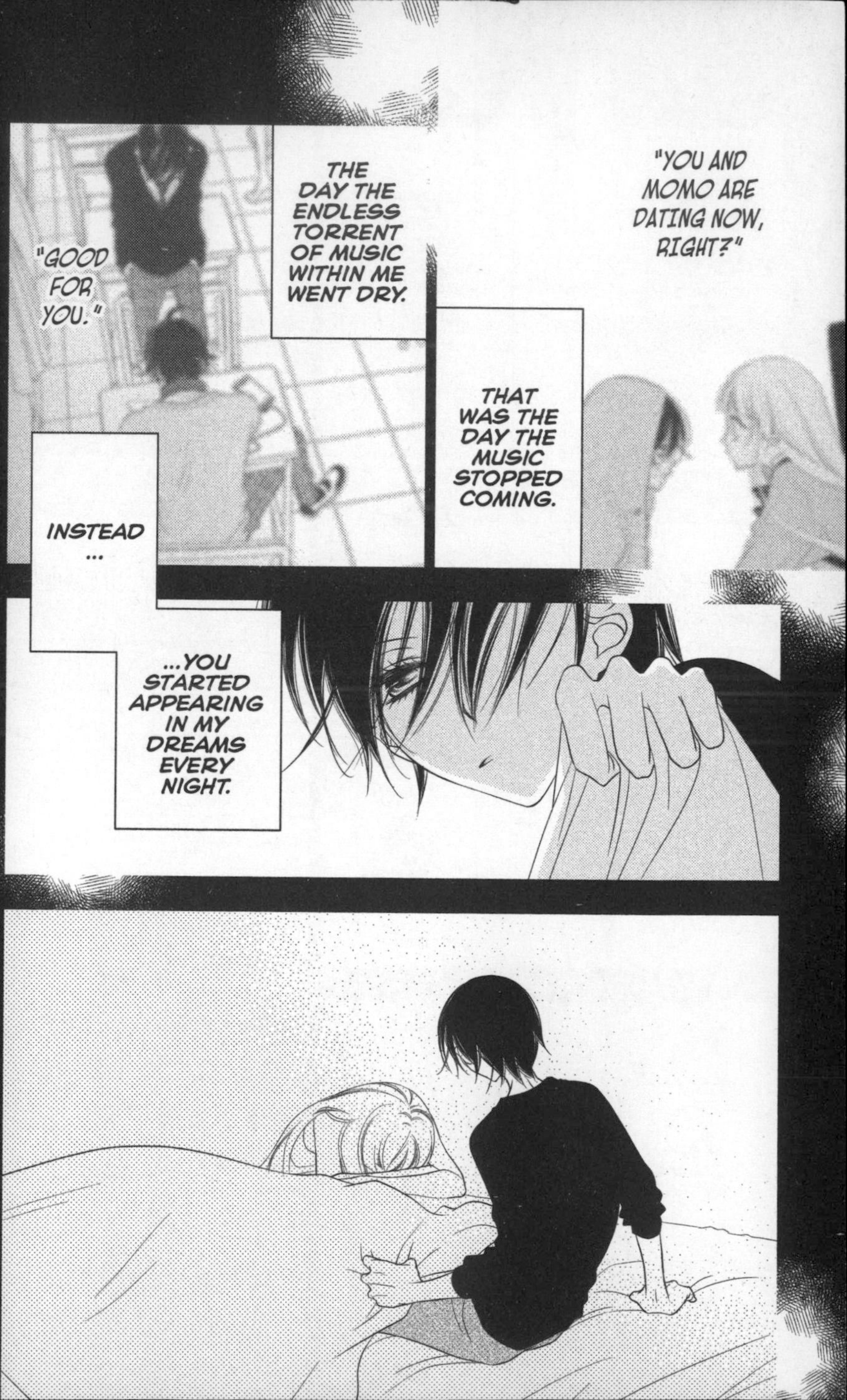

"YOU AND MOMO ARE DATING NOW, RIGHT?"
THAT WAS THE DAY THE MUSIC STOPPED COMING.
THE DAY THE ENDLESS TORRENT OF MUSIC WITHIN ME WENT DRY.
"GOOD FOR YOU."
INSTEAD...
...YOU STARTED APPEARING IN MY DREAMS EVERY NIGHT.

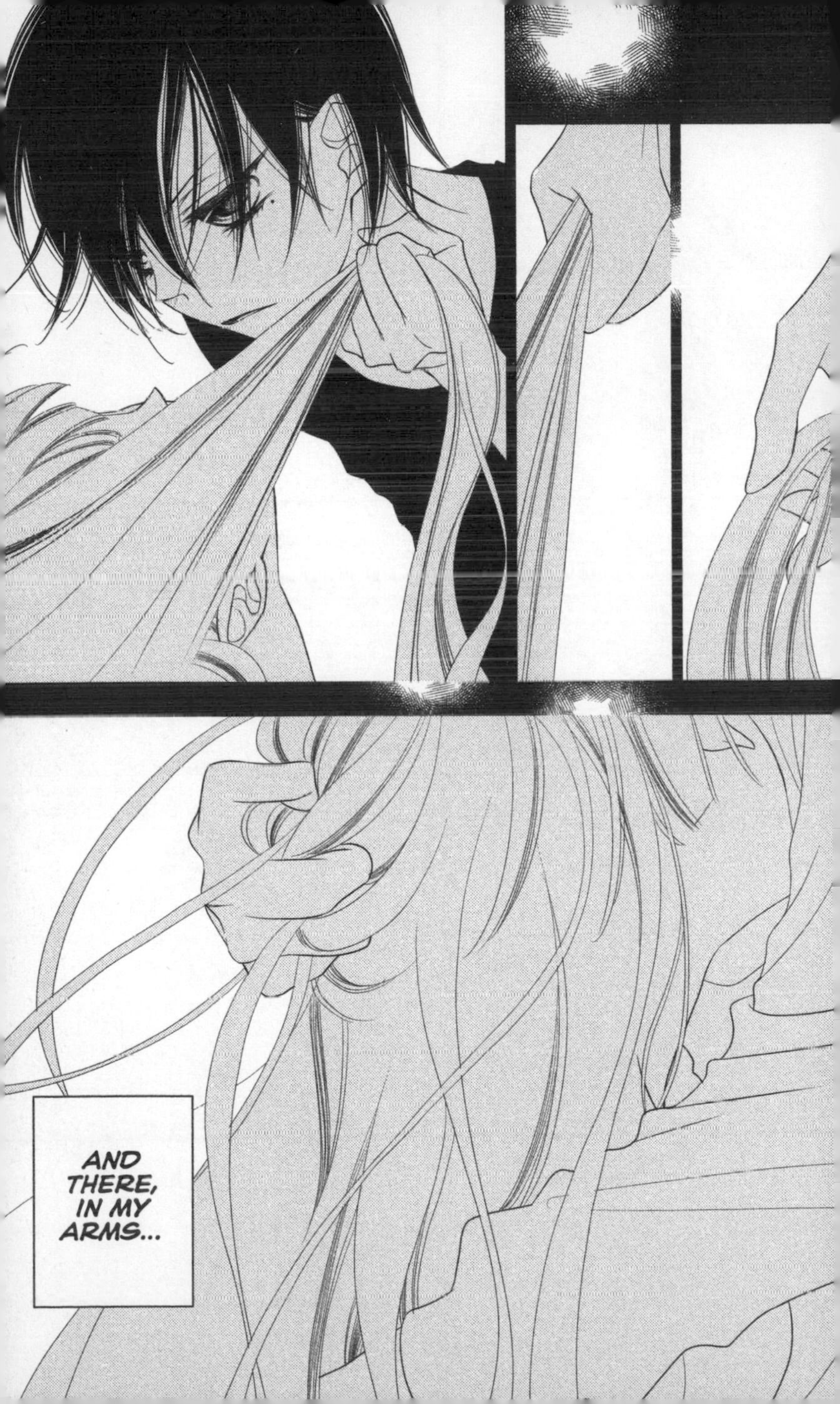
AND THERE, IN MY ARMS...

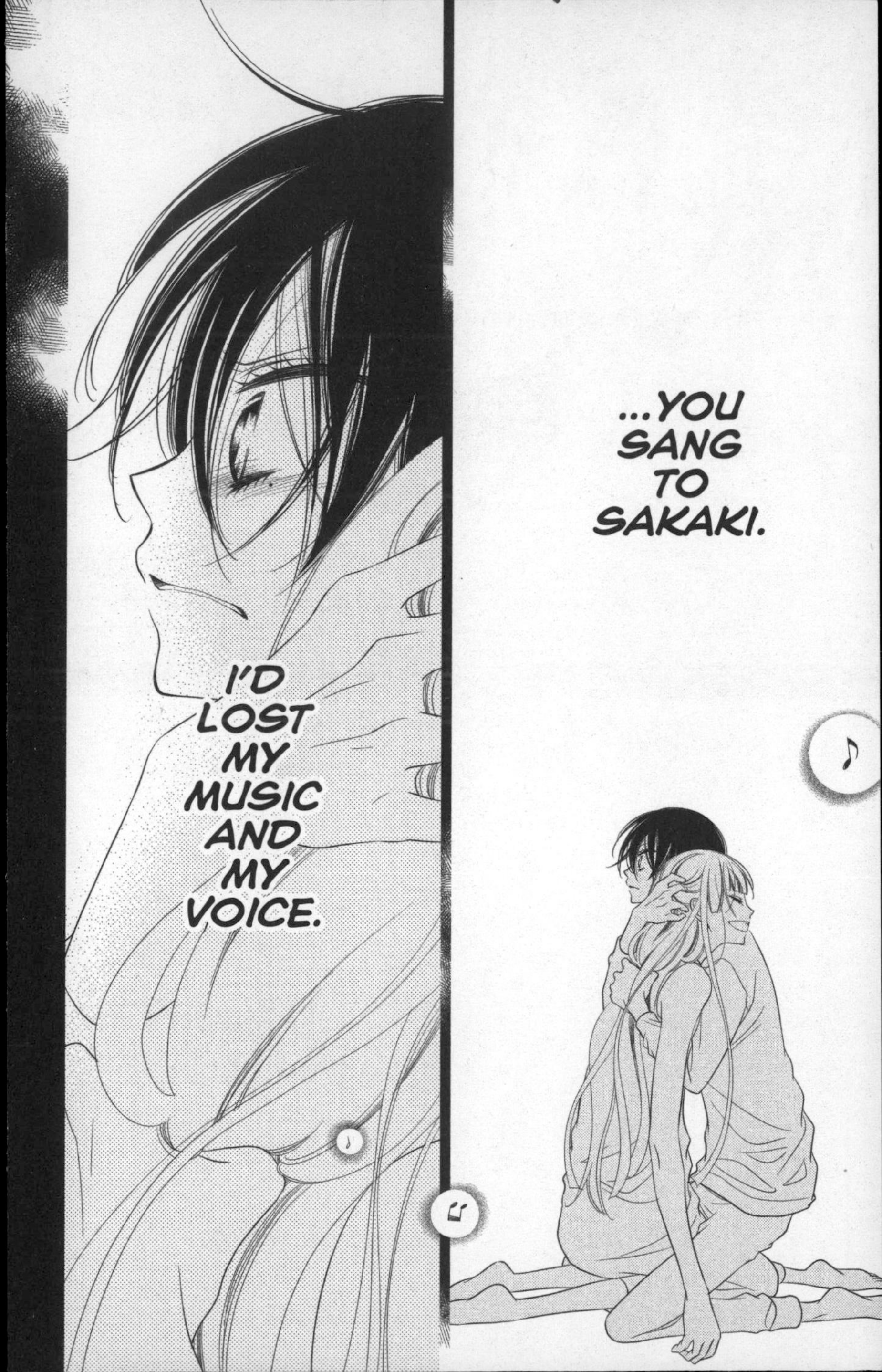
...YOU SANG TO SAKAKI.
I'D LOST MY MUSIC AND MY VOICE.

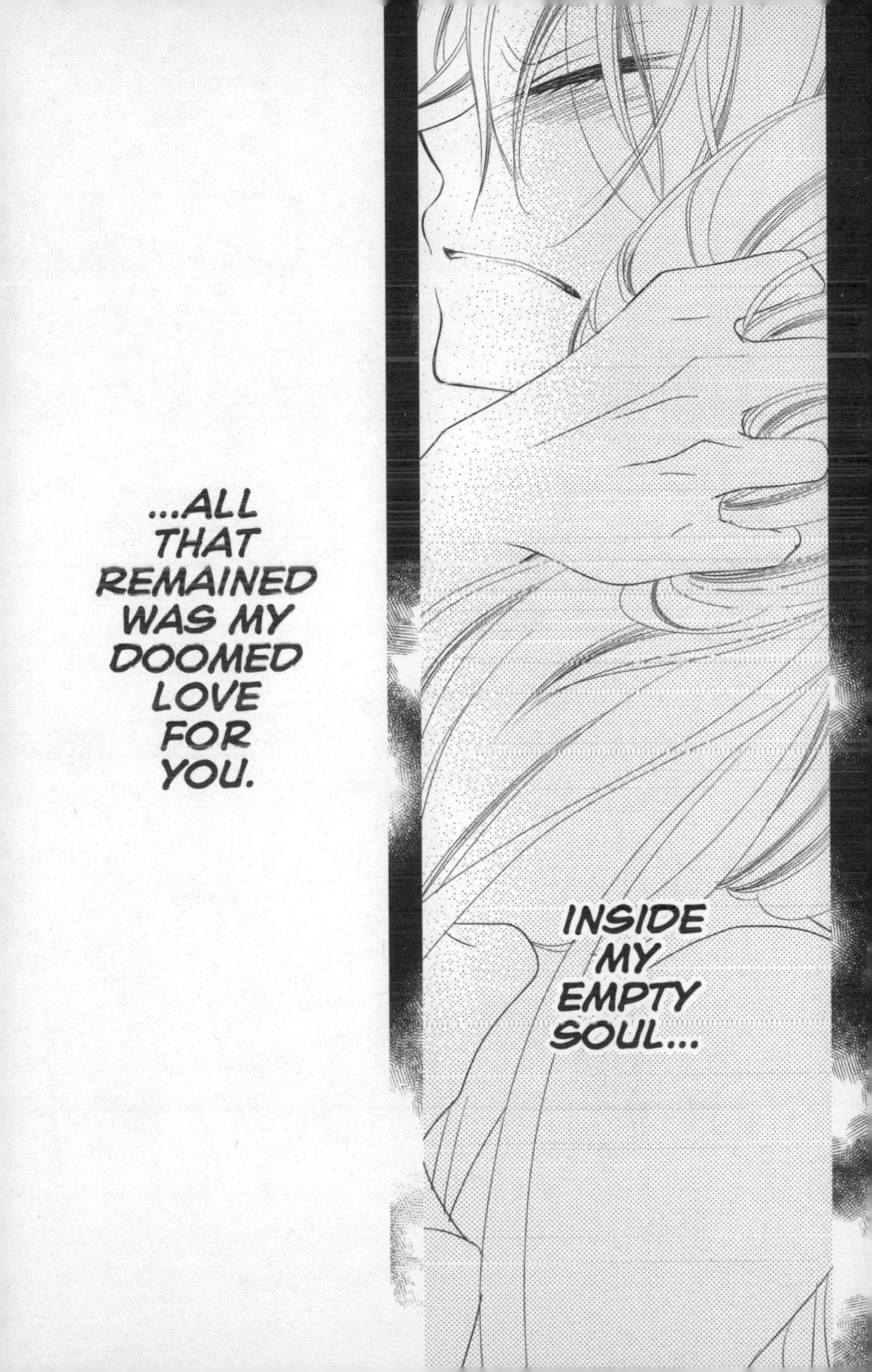
INSIDE MY EMPTY SOUL...
...ALL THAT REMAINED WAS MY DOOMED LOVE FOR YOU.

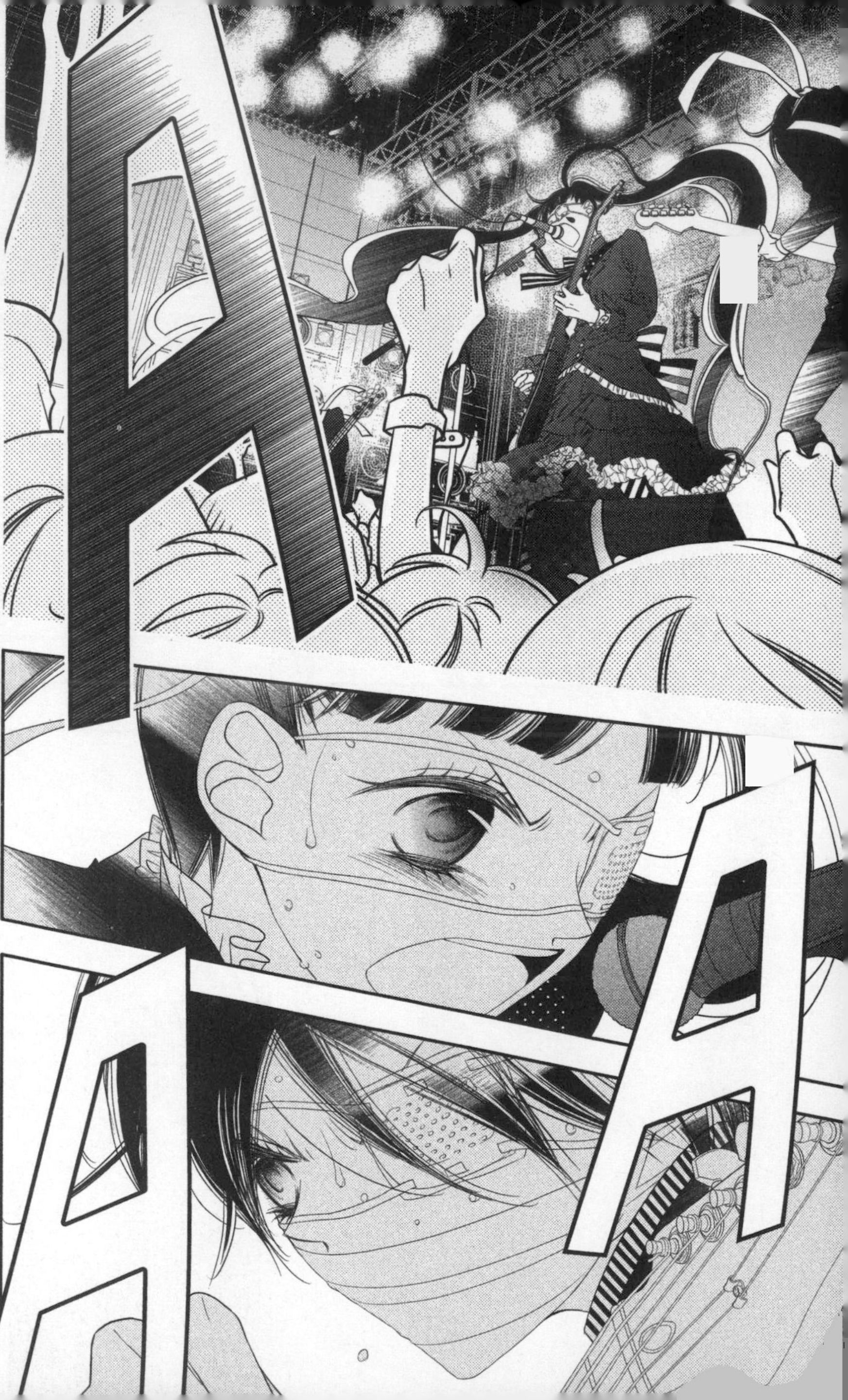
AAA

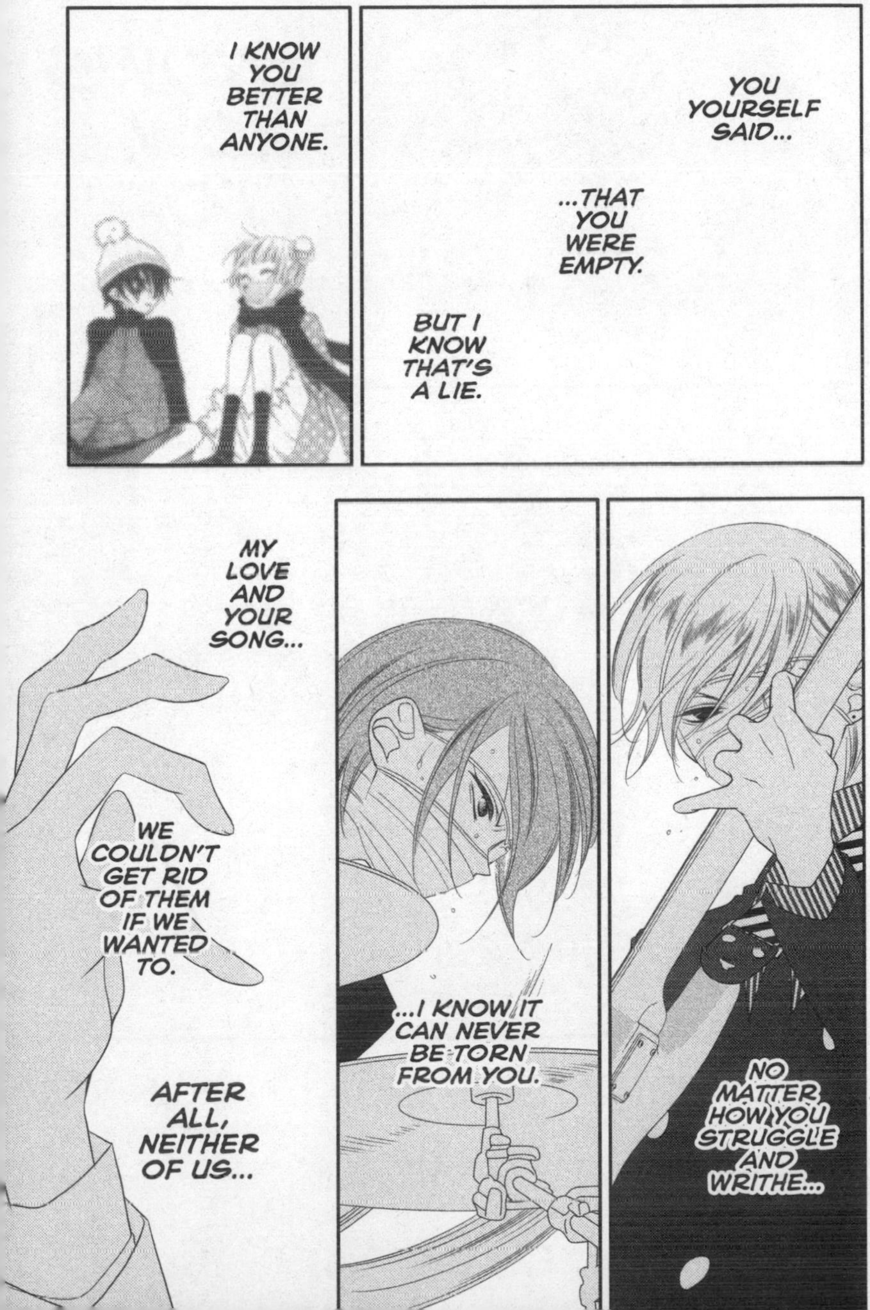
YOU YOURSELF SAID...
...THAT YOU WERE EMPTY.
BUT I KNOW THAT'S A LIE.
I KNOW YOU BETTER THAN ANYONE.
NO MATTER HOW YOU STRUGGLE AND WRITHE...
...I KNOW IT CAN NEVER BE TORN FROM YOU.
MY LOVE AND YOUR SONG...
WE COULDN'T GET RID OF THEM IF WE WANTED TO.
AFTER ALL, NEITHER OF US...

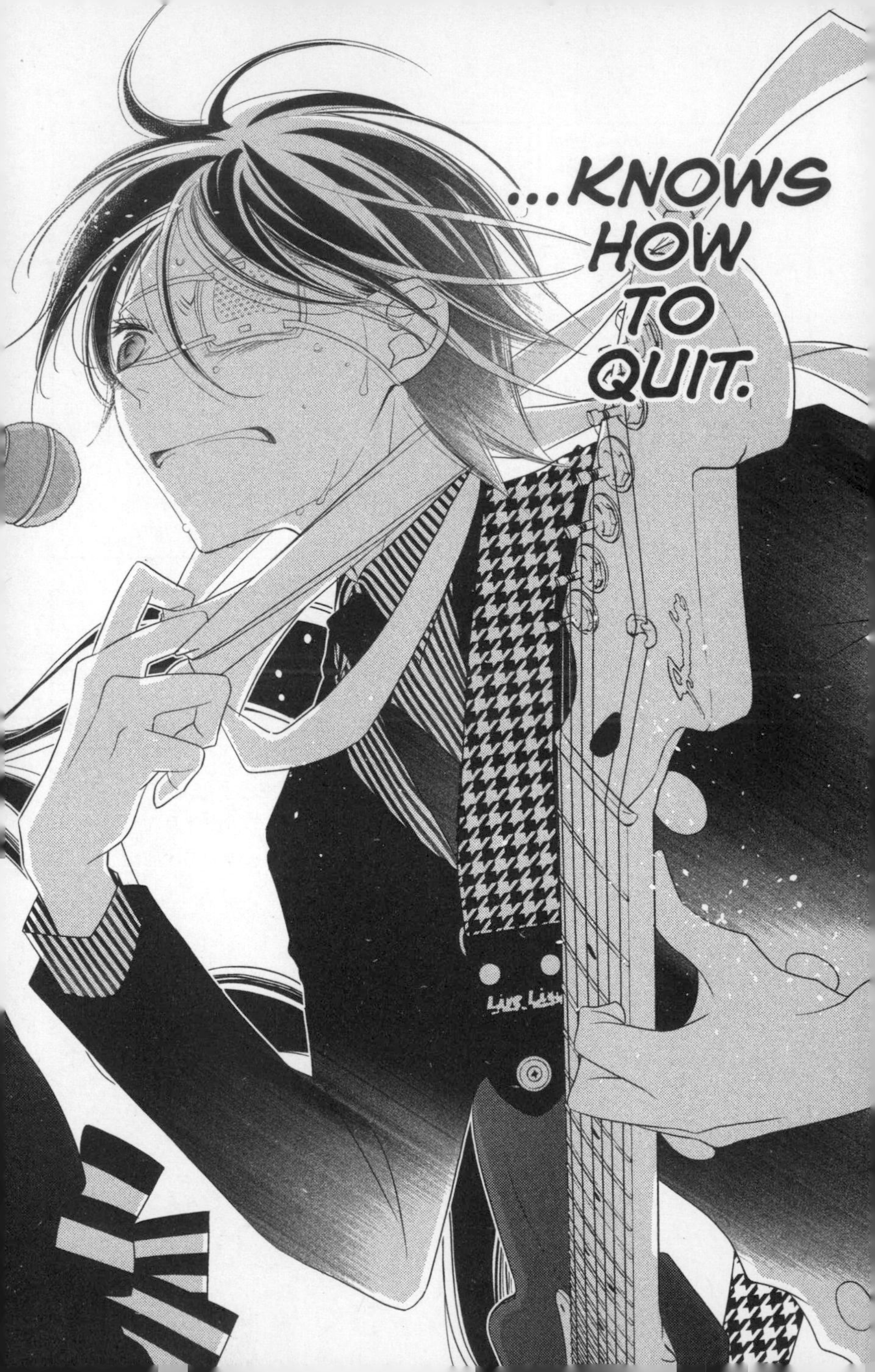
...KNOWS HOW TO QUIT.

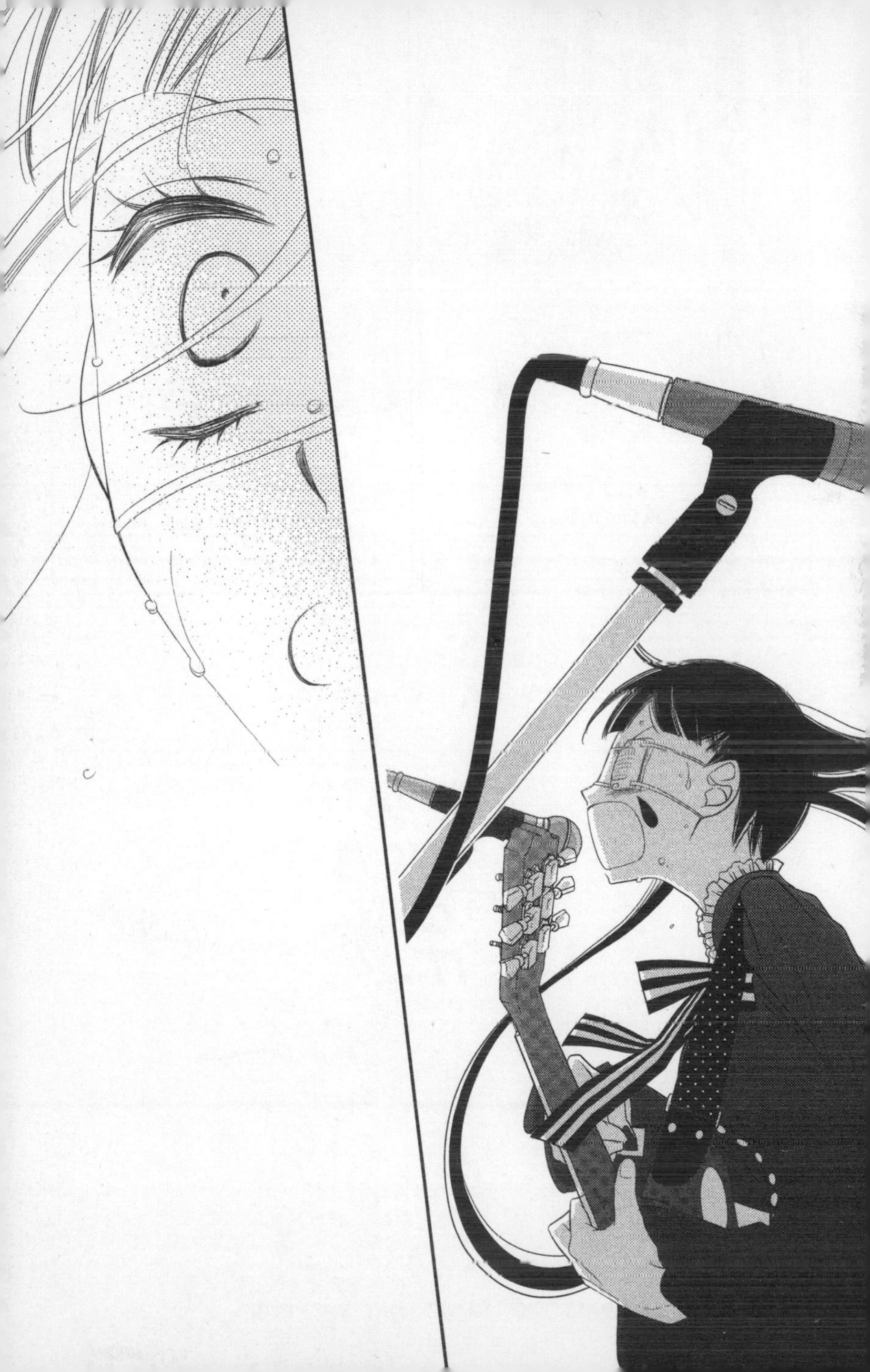

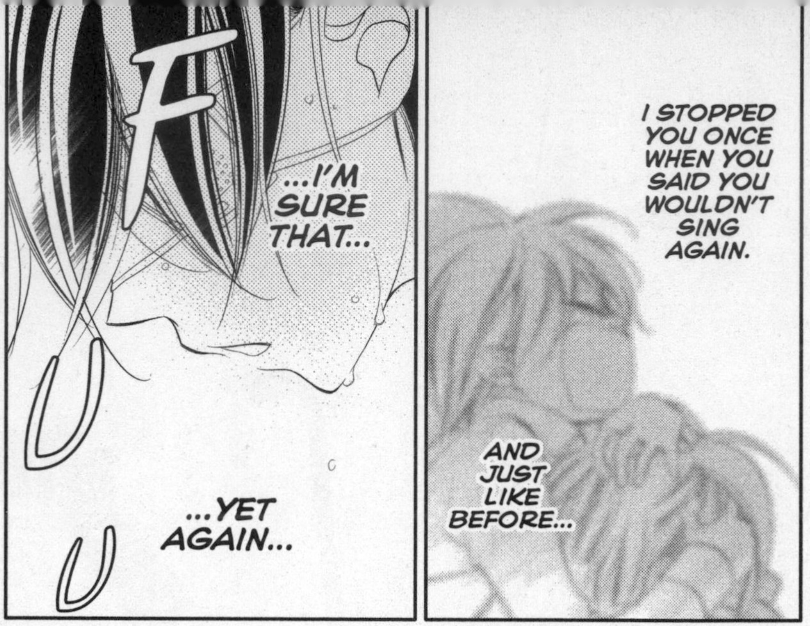
I STOPPED YOU ONCE WHEN YOU SAID YOU WOULDN'T SING AGAIN.
AND JUST LIKE BEFORE...
...I'M SURE THAT...
FUU
...YET AGAIN...

I'M SURE OF IT...!

ANONYMOUS NOISE ⑬ / THE END

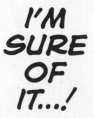

TO BE CONTINUED IN ANONYMOUS NOISE 14

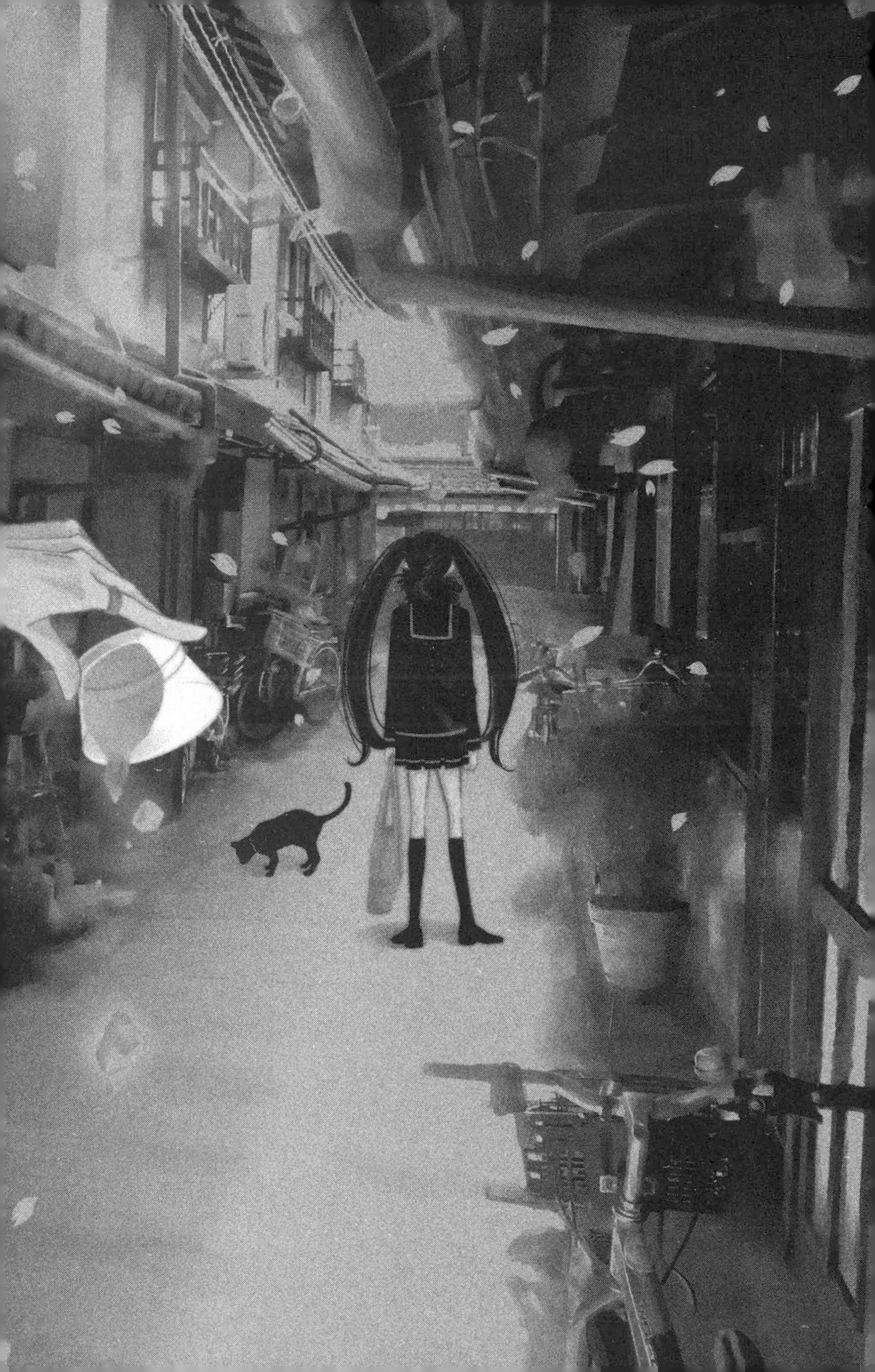

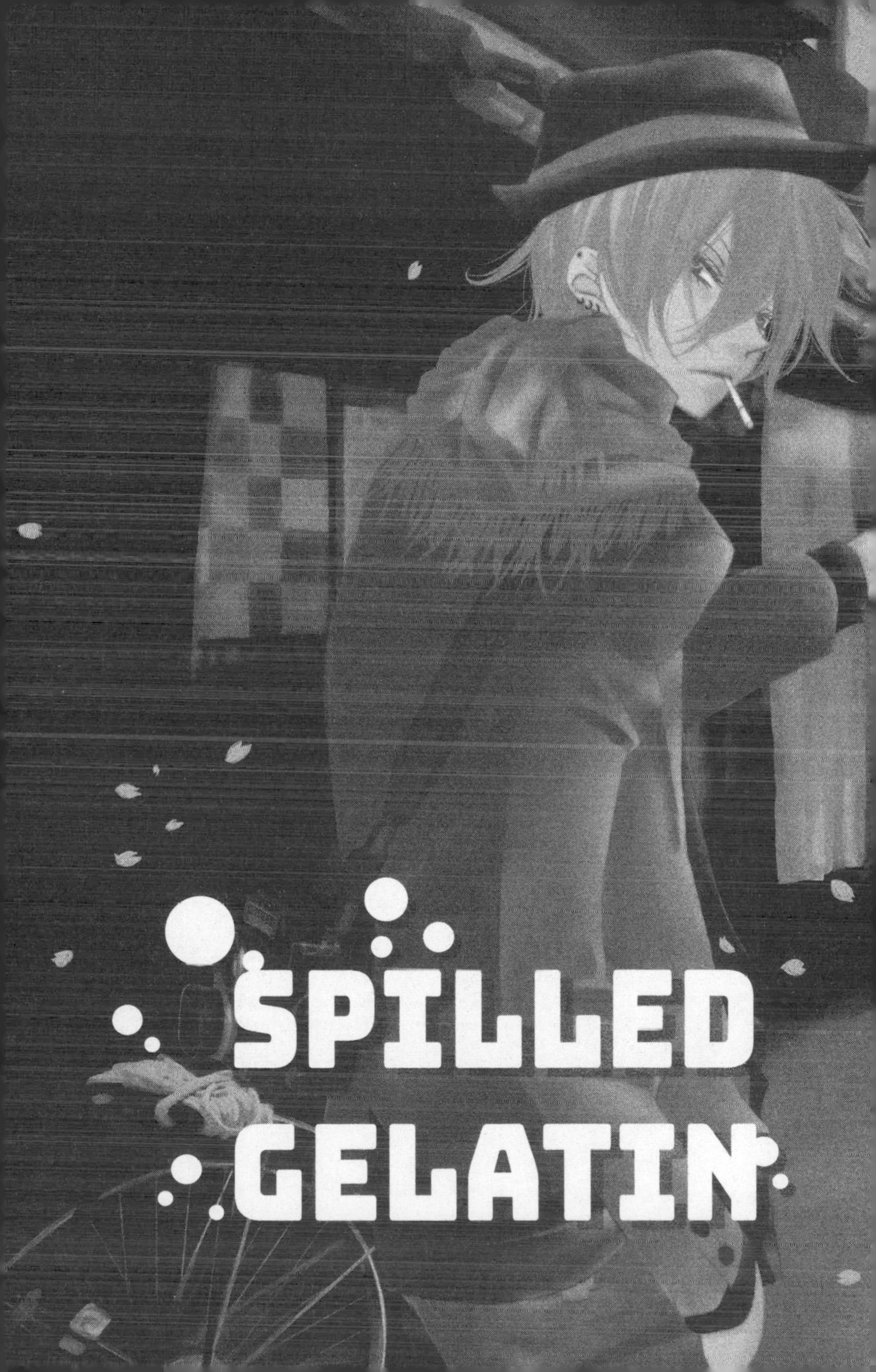
SPILLED
GELATIN

I'm running a one-shot comic for the first time in…
I don't even know how long! It's called "Spilled Gelatin."

I'm going to spoil some of the story here, so don't read this until after
you've finished it! I wrote this a very long time ago and have been looking for a
place to publish it ever since. It got close to getting printed a number of times but always
ended up being too long to fit. I wrote it around the time that I was wrapping up my
previous manga, *Monochrome Kids*. At the time, I was really getting into film cameras,
and I wanted to write something to put my newfound love to paper. Back then, manga
hadn't gone digital yet, so depicting a classic camera wasn't easy! I know my poor
assistants had a really tough time dealing with all the screentone!

The twin-lens Rolleiflex that Kuroe uses in the manga is actually
one of my most prized possessions. Back when I was getting started with manga,
I loved playing with my toy Lomo film camera, but when I encountered the Rolleiflex,
I fell in love. Since then, a wide variety of film and digital cameras have crossed my path,
but I always come back to that Rollei. If I was forced to pick one camera to use for
the rest of my life, I have no doubt that would be the one.

For one thing, it's a beautiful object from any angle. I love the sensation of looking down
through the viewfinder, and no camera is as much fun to focus. But more importantly, it
takes some beautiful pictures. Really, I don't understand how anyone could not fall in love
with the Rolleiflex! It's—no, wait. Now that I've started talking about it, I'm having trouble
keeping my love for it in check, and it's starting to get weird.

Let's get back to the manga. In the story, Kuroe gets the Rollei from his grandfather, and
the first one I ever touched belonged to my grandfather too. But that one now belongs to
my father, so I had to buy one of my own. My father's Rollei has some mold on the lens,
so its pictures always come out hazy, as if taken through a soft-focus lens.
I actually kind of like that about it. The scene where Kuroe plays with the Rollei on
his grandfather's lap is something of a dream of mine—or rather, a regret.
Sadly, I had no interest whatsoever in photography while my grandfather
was still alive. But my father is a camera aficionado, and he and I have
lots of lively discussions about photography now.

Wow, reading back on what I've written, I realize I've just been rambling
without saying much of anything about the manga itself!
Please forgive me! I do hope you'll enjoy
"Spilled Gelatin" all the same.

The gelatin
dances in the cup.
A piece breaks away

jiggling as it falls

and then

comes the crash.

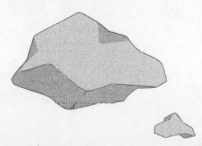

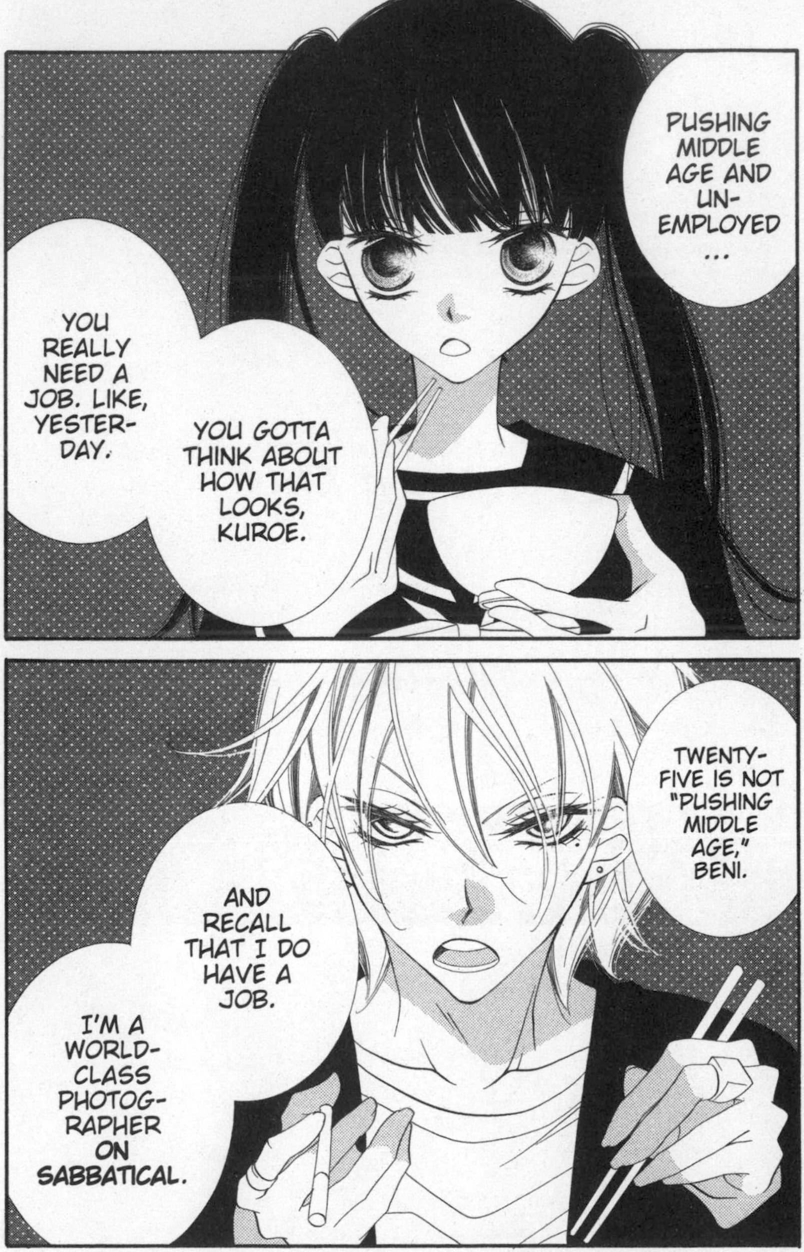
PUSHING MIDDLE AGE AND UN-EMPLOYED...
YOU GOTTA THINK ABOUT HOW THAT LOOKS, KUROE.
YOU REALLY NEED A JOB. LIKE, YESTERDAY.
TWENTY-FIVE IS NOT "PUSHING MIDDLE AGE," BENI.
AND RECALL THAT I DO HAVE A JOB.
I'M A WORLD-CLASS PHOTOGRAPHER ON SABBATICAL.

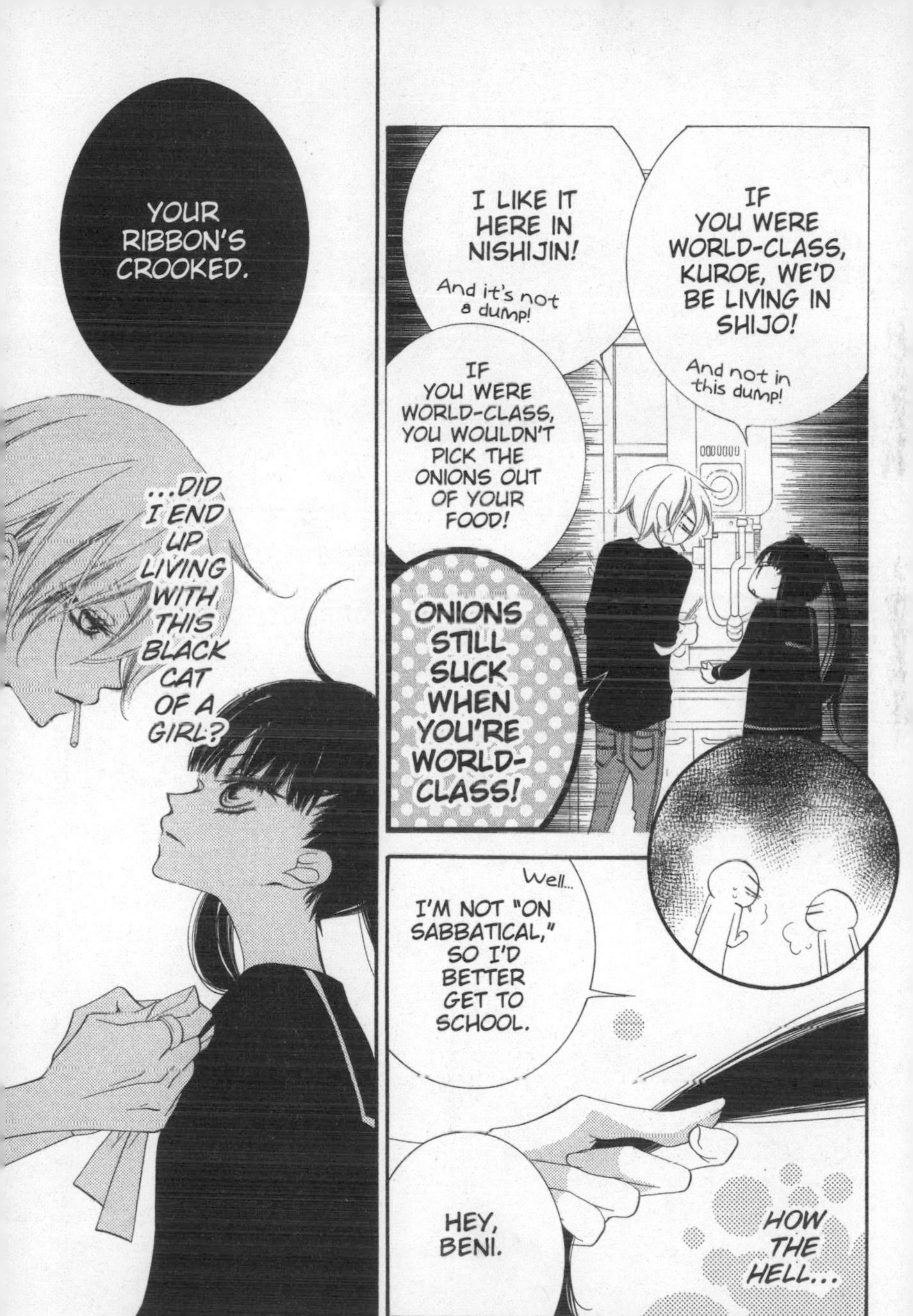

IF YOU WERE WORLD-CLASS, KUROE, WE'D BE LIVING IN SHIJO!
And not in this dump!
I LIKE IT HERE IN NISHIJIN!
And it's not a dump!
IF YOU WERE WORLD-CLASS, YOU WOULDN'T PICK THE ONIONS OUT OF YOUR FOOD!
ONIONS STILL SUCK WHEN YOU'RE WORLD-CLASS!
Well...
I'M NOT "ON SABBATICAL," SO I'D BETTER GET TO SCHOOL.
HOW THE HELL...
HEY, BENI.
YOUR RIBBON'S CROOKED.
...DID I END UP LIVING WITH THIS BLACK CAT OF A GIRL?

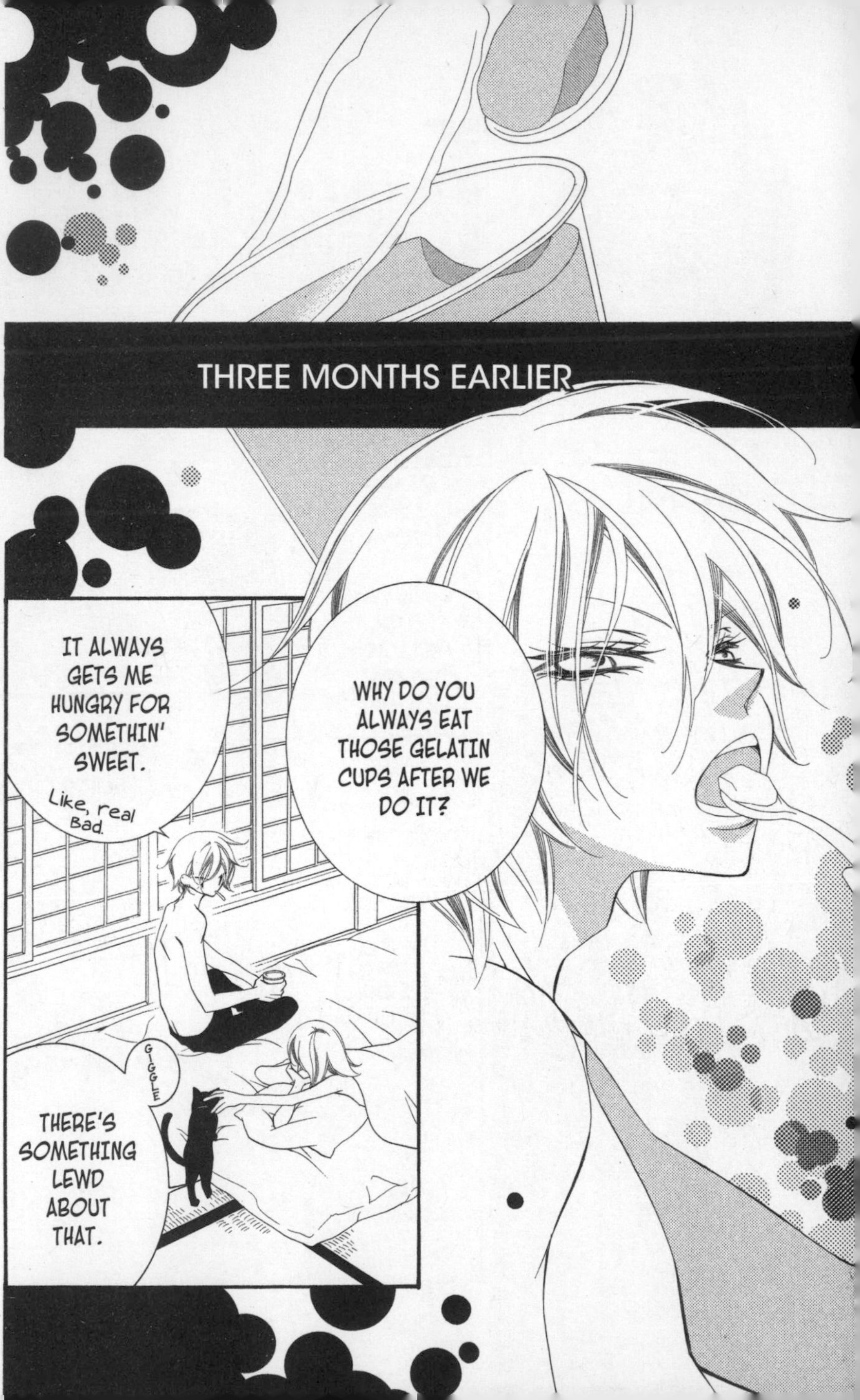
THREE MONTHS EARLIER
WHY DO YOU ALWAYS EAT THOSE GELATIN CUPS AFTER WE DO IT?
IT ALWAYS GETS ME HUNGRY FOR SOMETHIN' SWEET.
Like, real Bad.
GIGGLE
THERE'S SOMETHING LEWD ABOUT THAT.

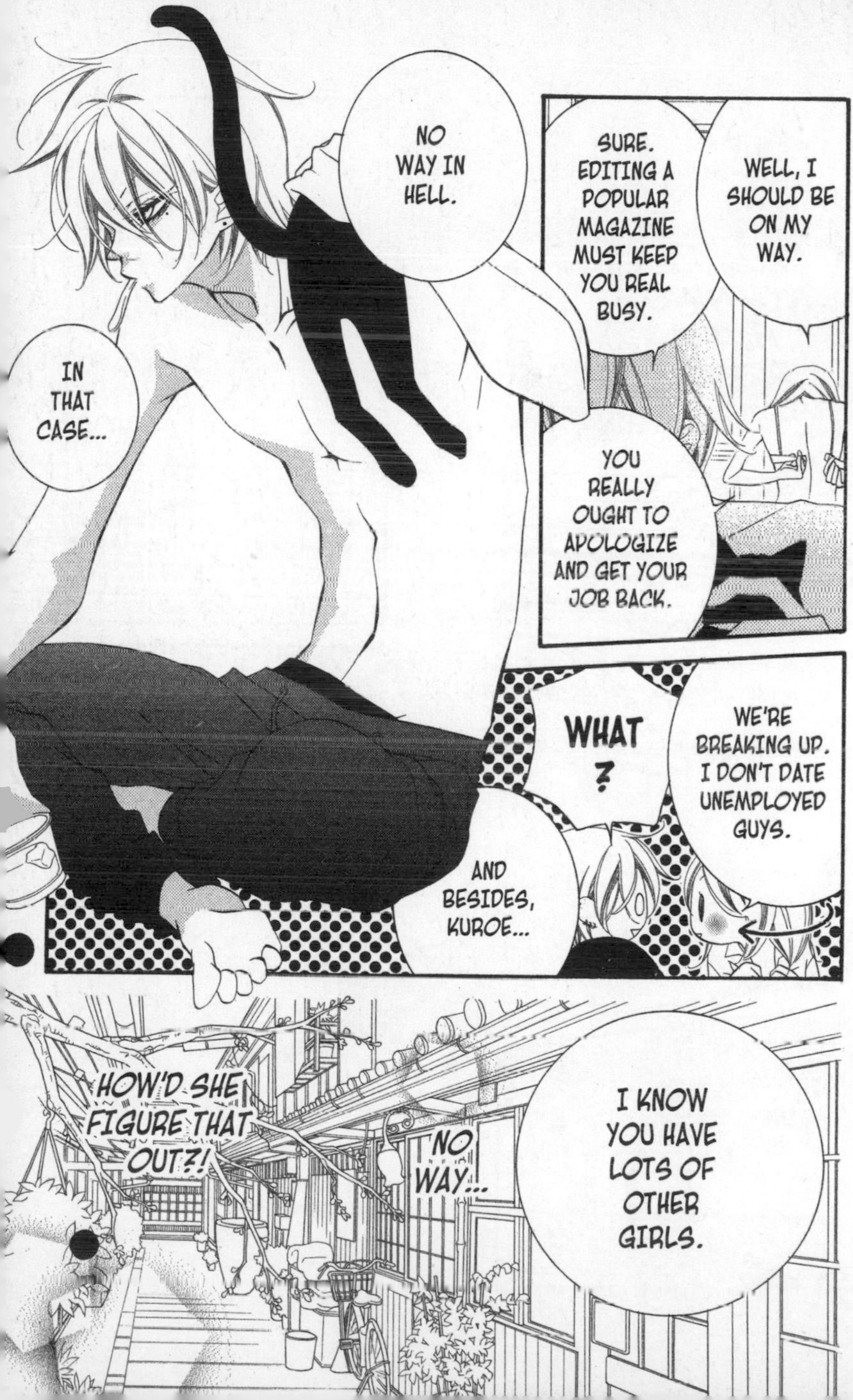
WELL, I SHOULD BE ON MY WAY.
SURE. EDITING A POPULAR MAGAZINE MUST KEEP YOU REAL BUSY.
YOU REALLY OUGHT TO APOLOGIZE AND GET YOUR JOB BACK.
WE'RE BREAKING UP. I DON'T DATE UNEMPLOYED GUYS.
WHAT?
AND BESIDES, KUROE...
NO WAY IN HELL.
IN THAT CASE...
I KNOW YOU HAVE LOTS OF OTHER GIRLS.
NO WAY...
HOW'D SHE FIGURE THAT OUT?!

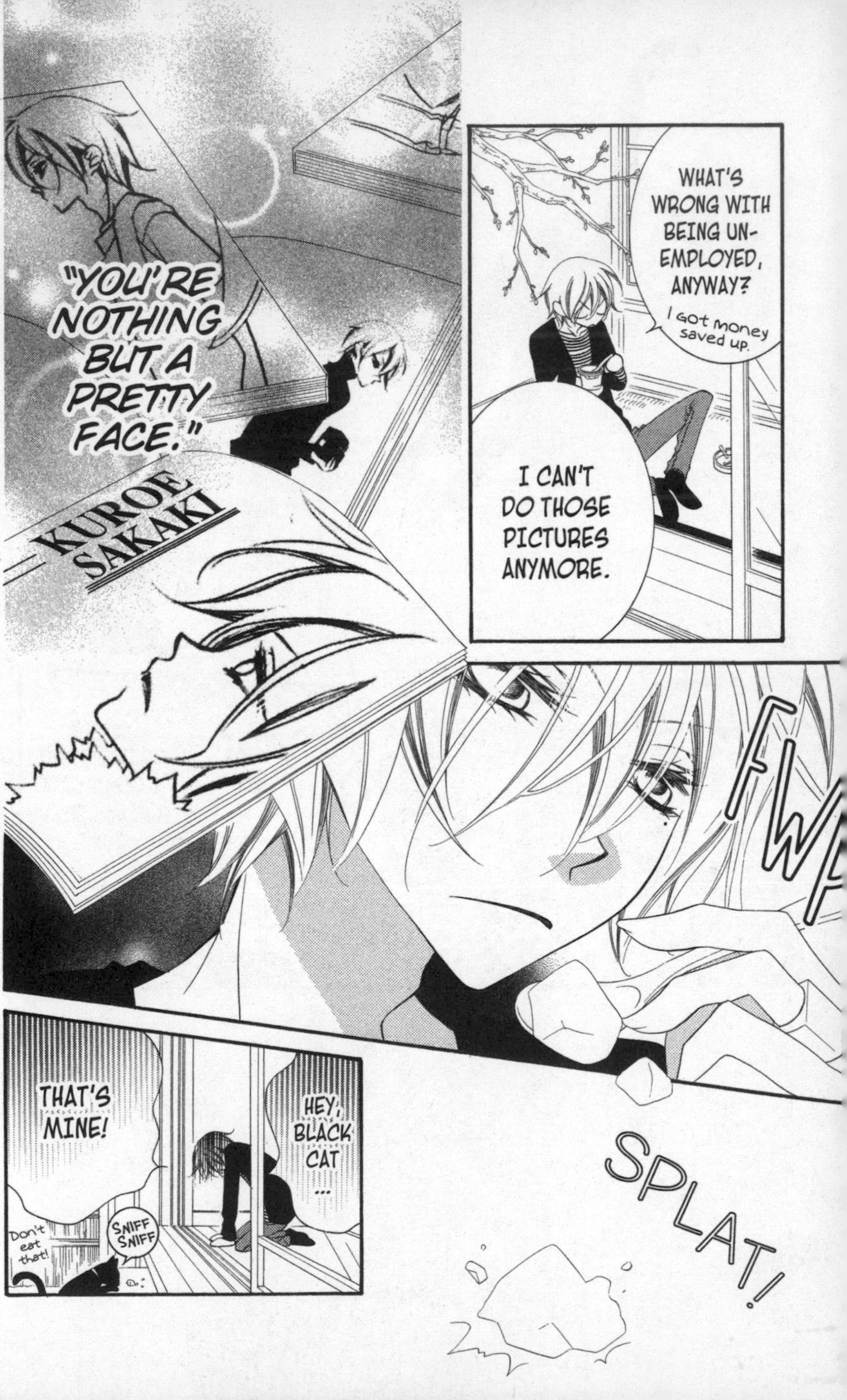

WHAT'S WRONG WITH BEING UN-EMPLOYED, ANYWAY?
I got money saved up.
I CAN'T DO THOSE PICTURES ANYMORE.
"YOU'RE NOTHING BUT A PRETTY FACE."
KUROE SAKAKI
FWP
SPLAT!
HEY, BLACK CAT...
THAT'S MINE!
SNIFF SNIFF
Don't eat that!

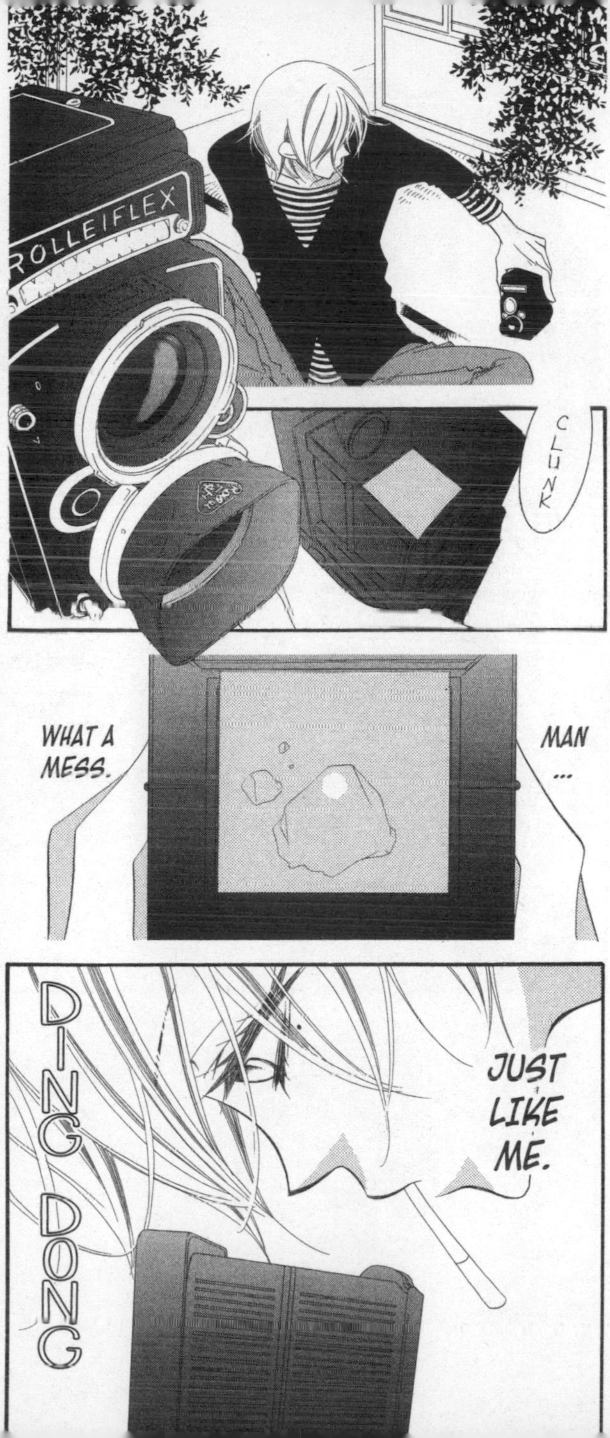
CLUNK
MAN ...
WHAT A MESS.
JUST LIKE ME.
DING DONG

5

I certainly hope you've enjoyed volume 13 of *Anonymous Noise*! Oh, I totally forgot to write about the contents of the drama CD. *Ha ha*. Well, if you got a copy, I hope you'll give it a listen. I'm actually planning to write a continuation of it tomorrow, and I promise to give it my all. I do hope to see you again in volume 14, where I'll be welcoming you back to my author's note column with my chicken-scratch handwriting!

Ryoko Fukuyama
6/20/2017
YEAH!

[SPECIAL THANKS]
MOSAGE
TAKAYUKI NAGASHIMA
KENJU NORO
MY FAMILY
MY FRIENDS
AND YOU!!

Ryoko Fukuyama
c/o Anonymous Noise Editor
VIZ Media
P.O. Box 77010
San Francisco, CA 94107

HP http://ryoconet/
@ryocoryocoryoco
http://facebook.com/ryocoryocoryoco/

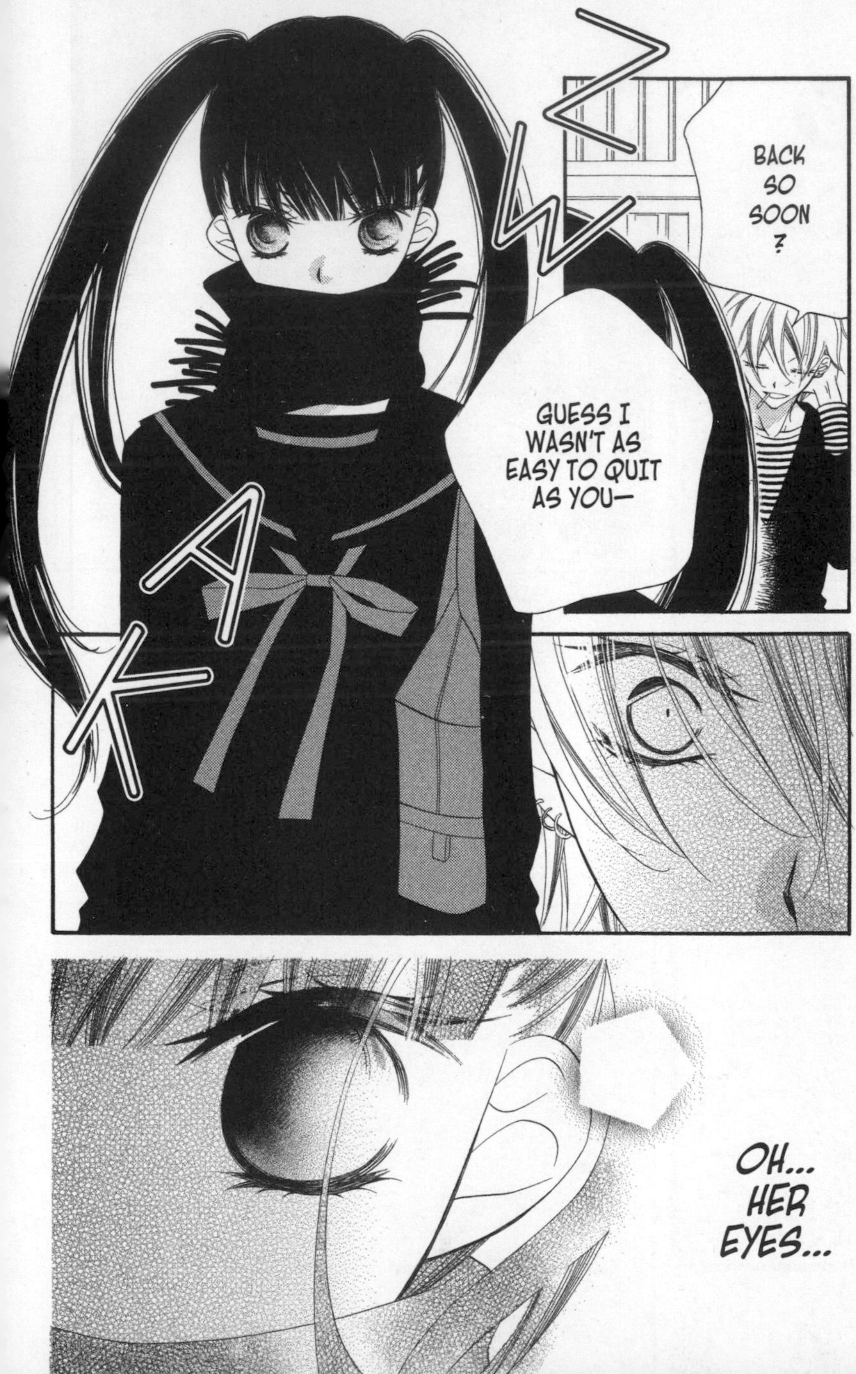
BACK SO SOON?
GUESS I WASN'T AS EASY TO QUIT AS YOU—
ZWAK
OH... HER EYES...

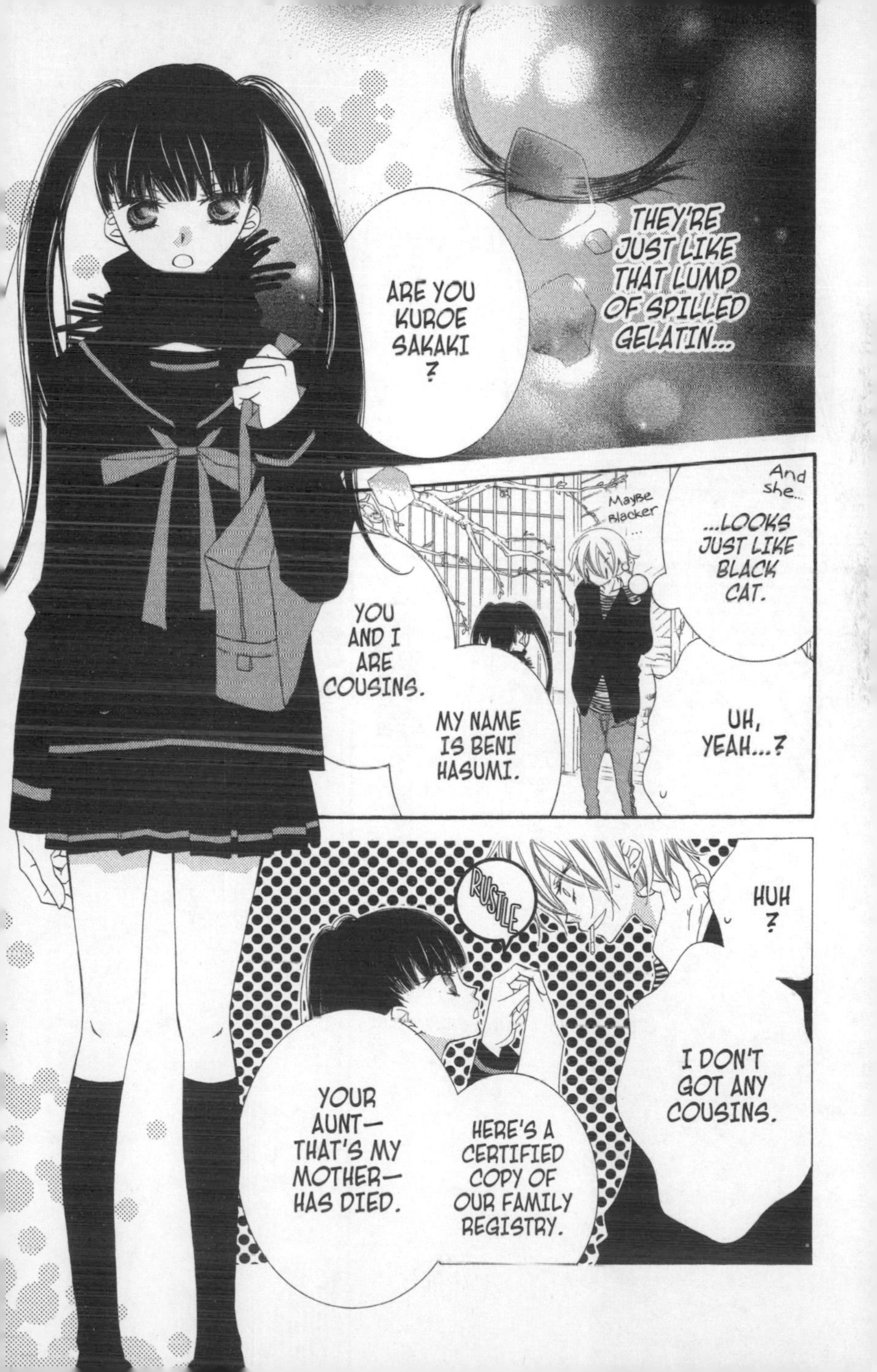
THEY'RE JUST LIKE THAT LUMP OF SPILLED GELATIN...
ARE YOU KUROE SAKAKI?
And she...
...LOOKS JUST LIKE BLACK CAT.
Maybe Blacker...
UH, YEAH...?
YOU AND I ARE COUSINS.
MY NAME IS BENI HASUMI.
HUH?
RUSTLE
I DON'T GOT ANY COUSINS.
HERE'S A CERTIFIED COPY OF OUR FAMILY REGISTRY.
YOUR AUNT—THAT'S MY MOTHER—HAS DIED.

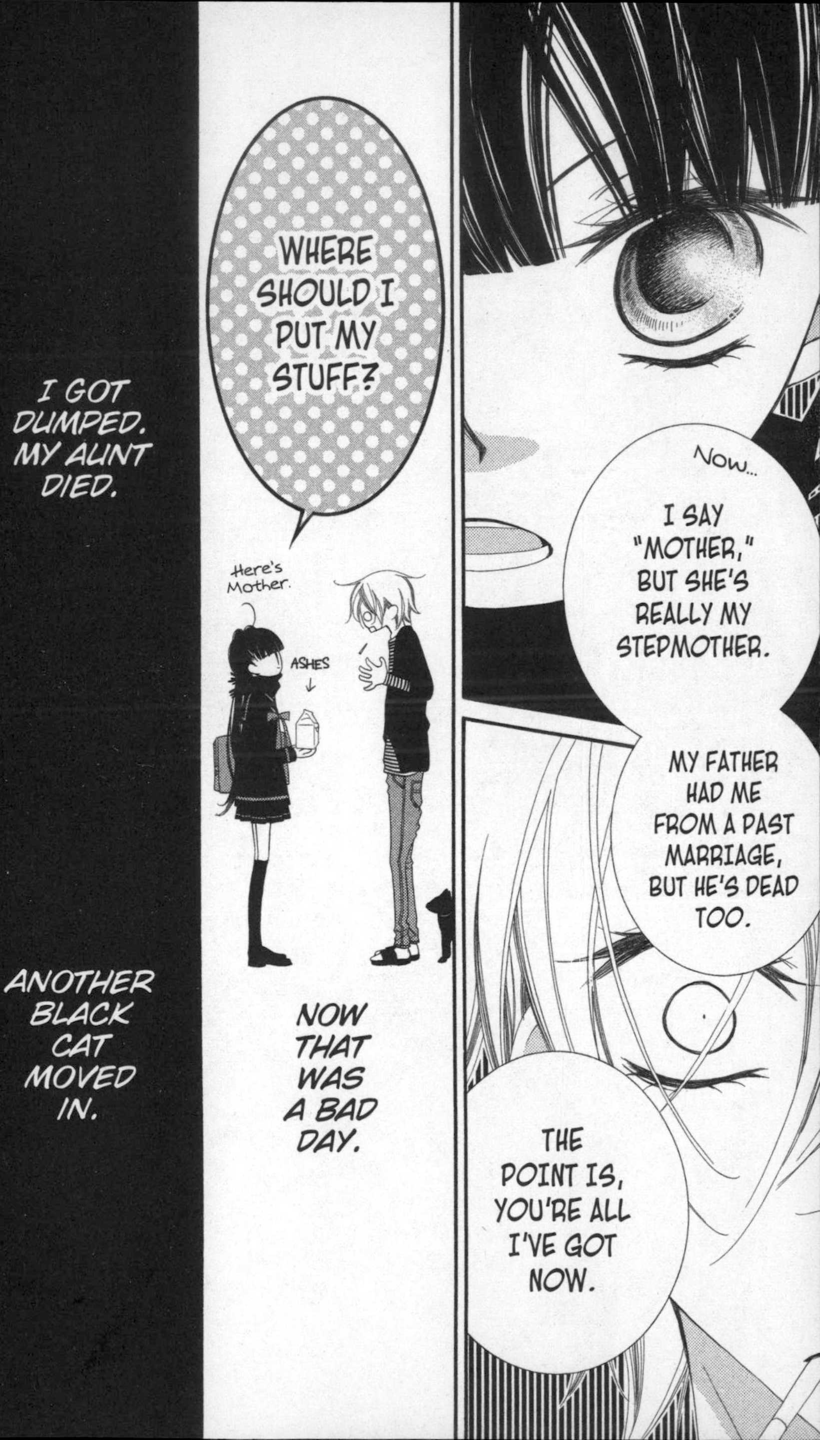
Now...
I SAY "MOTHER," BUT SHE'S REALLY MY STEPMOTHER.
MY FATHER HAD ME FROM A PAST MARRIAGE, BUT HE'S DEAD TOO.
THE POINT IS, YOU'RE ALL I'VE GOT NOW.
WHERE SHOULD I PUT MY STUFF?
Here's Mother.
ASHES
NOW THAT WAS A BAD DAY.
I GOT DUMPED. MY AUNT DIED.
ANOTHER BLACK CAT MOVED IN.

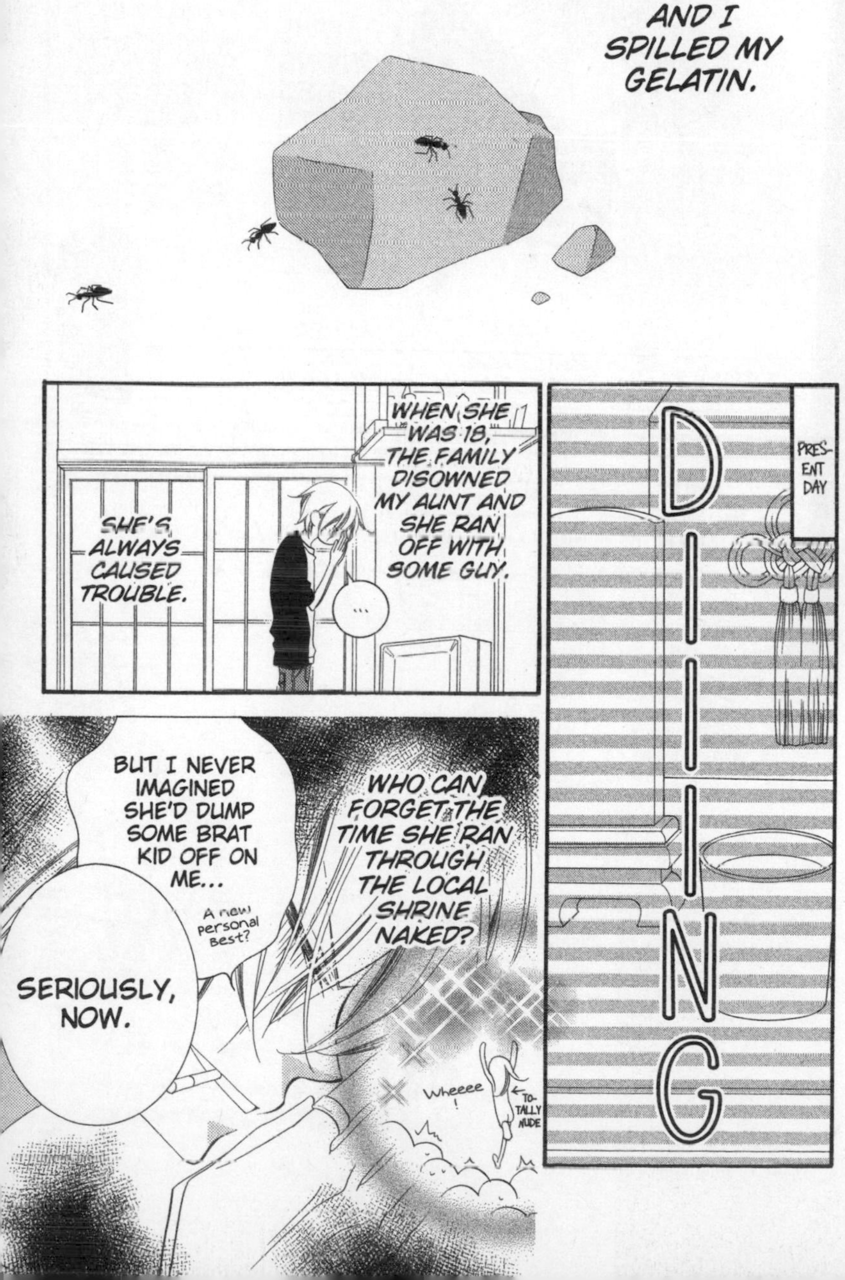
AND I SPILLED MY GELATIN.
PRES-ENT DAY
DIIING
WHEN SHE WAS 18, THE FAMILY DISOWNED MY AUNT AND SHE RAN OFF WITH SOME GUY.
SHE'S ALWAYS CAUSED TROUBLE.
...
WHO CAN FORGET THE TIME SHE RAN THROUGH THE LOCAL SHRINE NAKED?
TO-TALLY NUDE
Wheeee!
BUT I NEVER IMAGINED SHE'D DUMP SOME BRAT KID OFF ON ME...
A new personal Best?
SERIOUSLY, NOW.

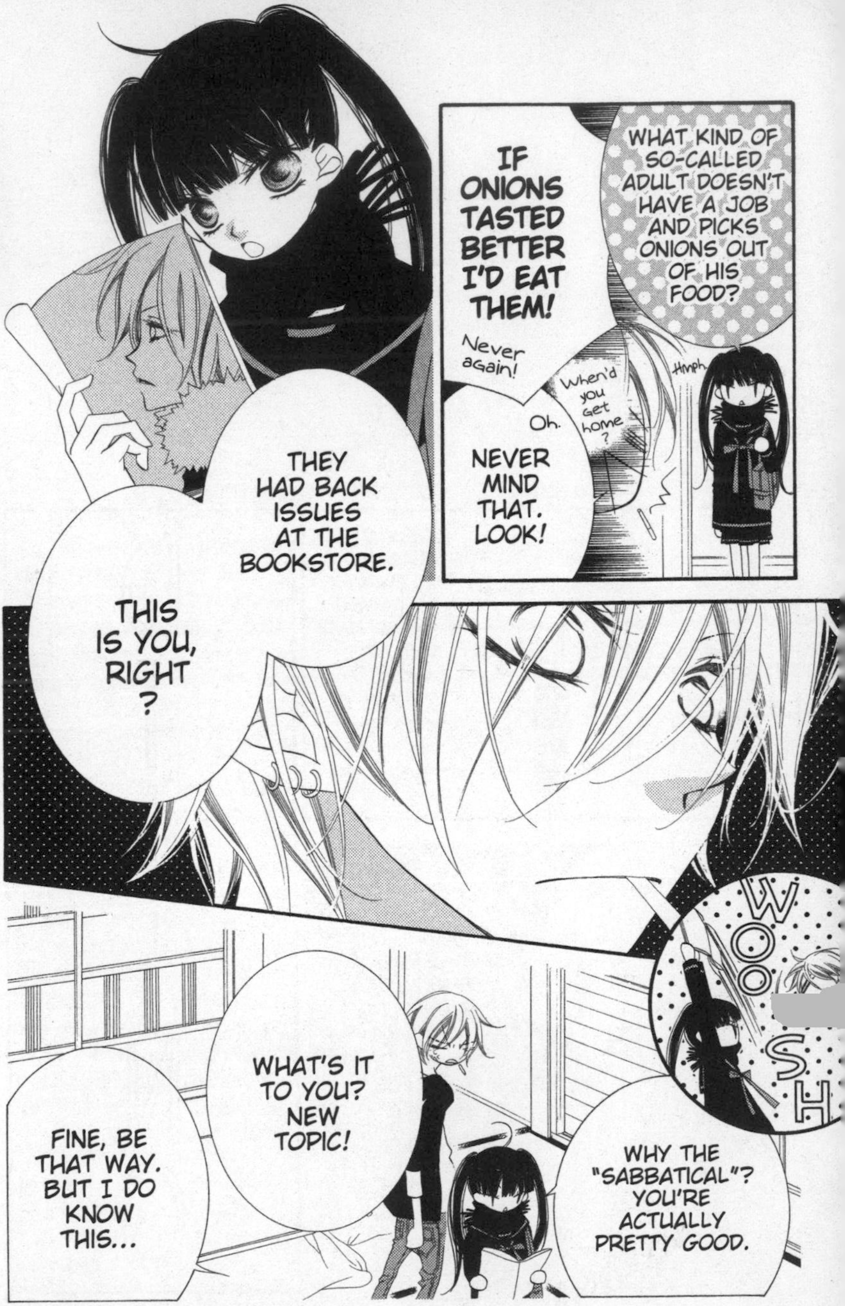
WHAT KIND OF SO-CALLED ADULT DOESN'T HAVE A JOB AND PICKS ONIONS OUT OF HIS FOOD?
Hmph.
IF ONIONS TASTED BETTER I'D EAT THEM!
Never again!
When'd you get home?
Oh.
NEVER MIND THAT. LOOK!
THEY HAD BACK ISSUES AT THE BOOKSTORE.
THIS IS YOU, RIGHT?
WOOSH
WHY THE "SABBATICAL"? YOU'RE ACTUALLY PRETTY GOOD.
WHAT'S IT TO YOU? NEW TOPIC!
FINE, BE THAT WAY. BUT I DO KNOW THIS...

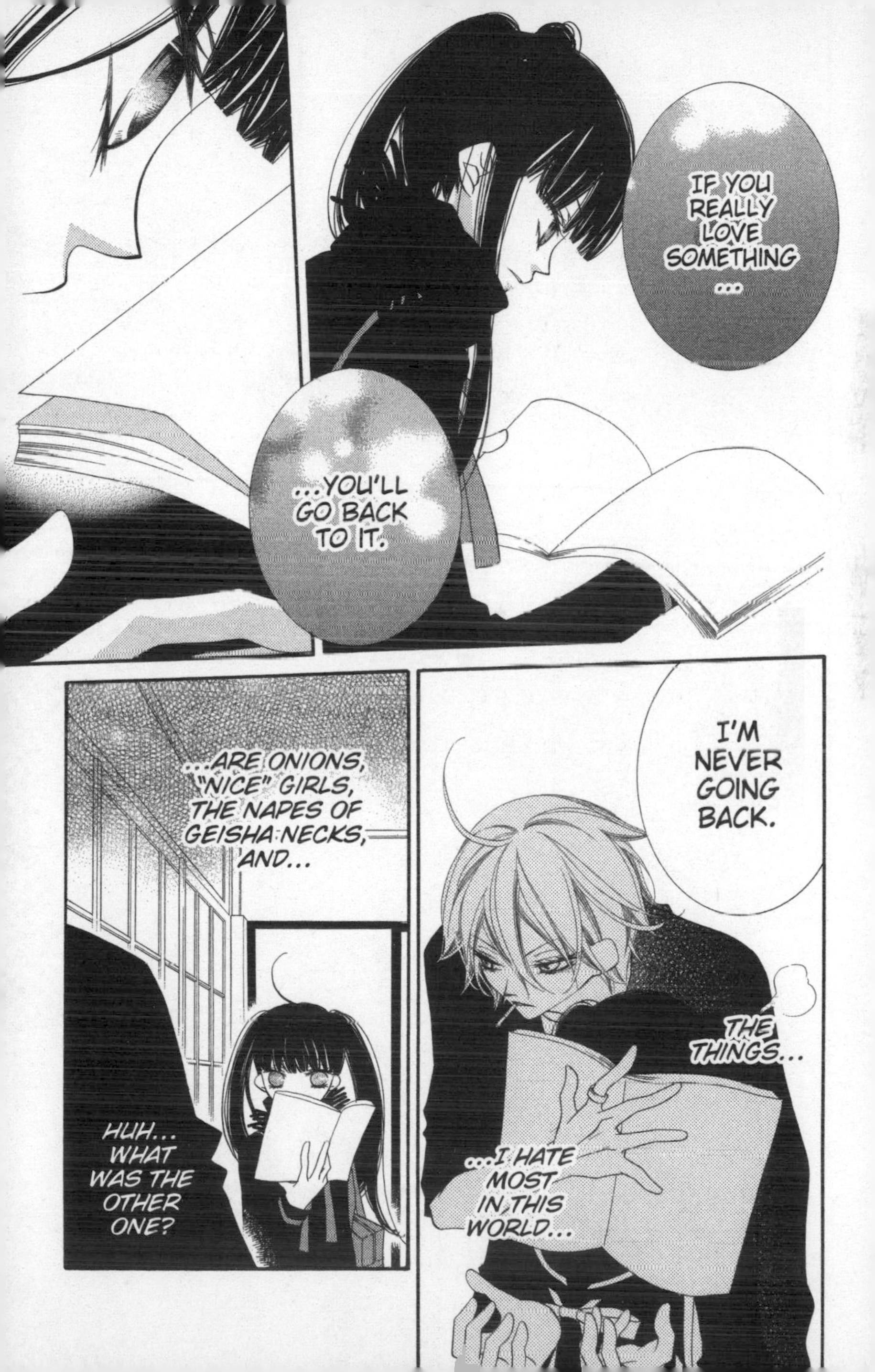
IF YOU REALLY LOVE SOMETHING ...
...YOU'LL GO BACK TO IT.
I'M NEVER GOING BACK.
THE THINGS...
...I HATE MOST IN THIS WORLD...
...ARE ONIONS, "NICE" GIRLS, THE NAPES OF GEISHA NECKS, AND...
HUH... WHAT WAS THE OTHER ONE?

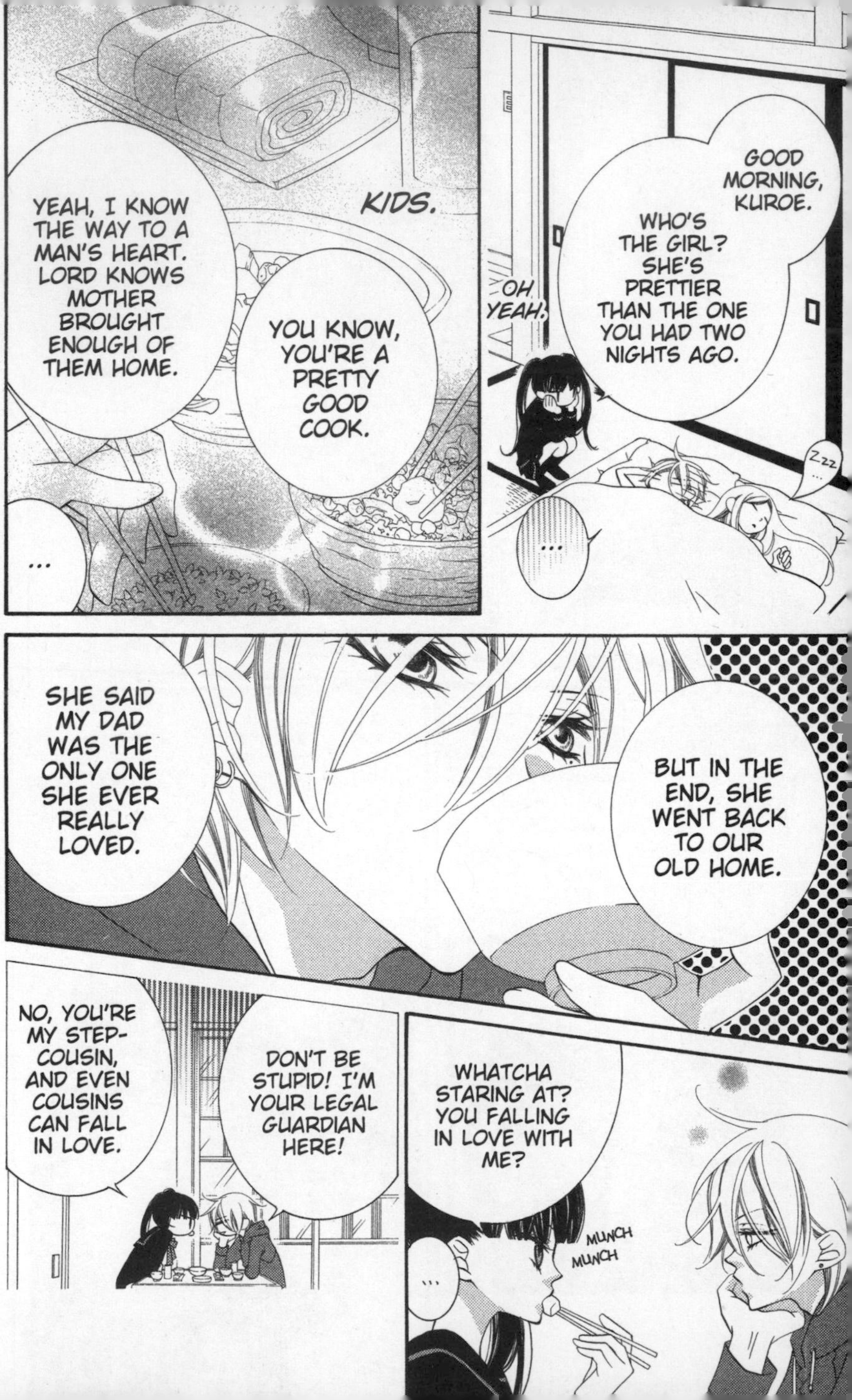

GOOD MORNING, KUROE.
WHO'S THE GIRL? SHE'S PRETTIER THAN THE ONE YOU HAD TWO NIGHTS AGO.
OH YEAH.
Zzz...
...
KIDS.
YOU KNOW, YOU'RE A PRETTY GOOD COOK.
YEAH, I KNOW THE WAY TO A MAN'S HEART. LORD KNOWS MOTHER BROUGHT ENOUGH OF THEM HOME.
...
BUT IN THE END, SHE WENT BACK TO OUR OLD HOME.
SHE SAID MY DAD WAS THE ONLY ONE SHE EVER REALLY LOVED.
WHATCHA STARING AT? YOU FALLING IN LOVE WITH ME?
MUNCH MUNCH
...
DON'T BE STUPID! I'M YOUR LEGAL GUARDIAN HERE!
NO, YOU'RE MY STEP-COUSIN, AND EVEN COUSINS CAN FALL IN LOVE.

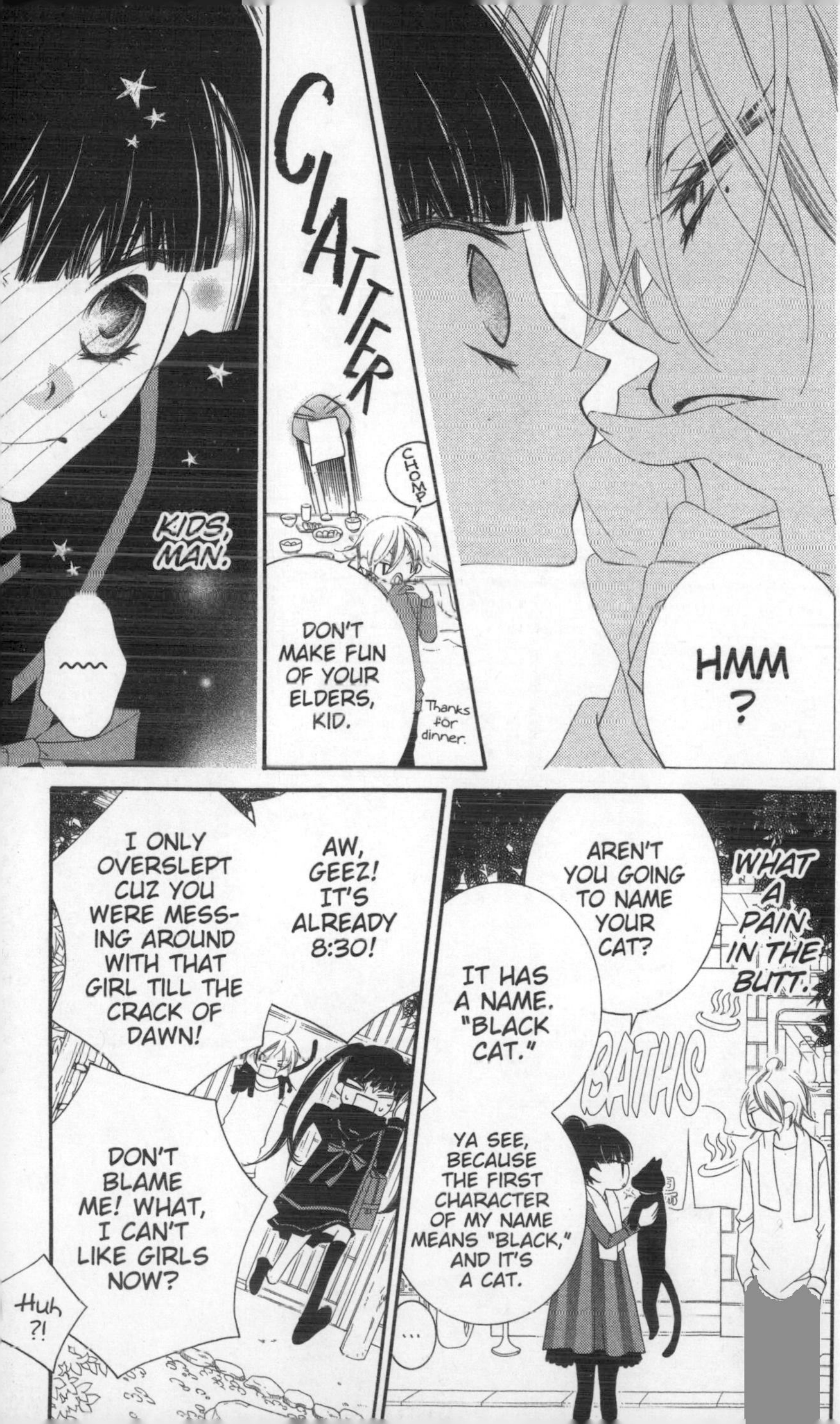
HMM ?
CLATTER
CHOMP
DON'T MAKE FUN OF YOUR ELDERS, KID.
Thanks for dinner.
KIDS, MAN.
~~~
WHAT A PAIN IN THE BUTT.
AREN'T YOU GOING TO NAME YOUR CAT?
IT HAS A NAME. "BLACK CAT."
BATHS
YA SEE, BECAUSE THE FIRST CHARACTER OF MY NAME MEANS "BLACK," AND IT'S A CAT.
...
AW, GEEZ! IT'S ALREADY 8:30!
I ONLY OVERSLEPT CUZ YOU WERE MESS-ING AROUND WITH THAT GIRL TILL THE CRACK OF DAWN!
DON'T BLAME ME! WHAT, I CAN'T LIKE GIRLS NOW?
Huh ?!
~~~

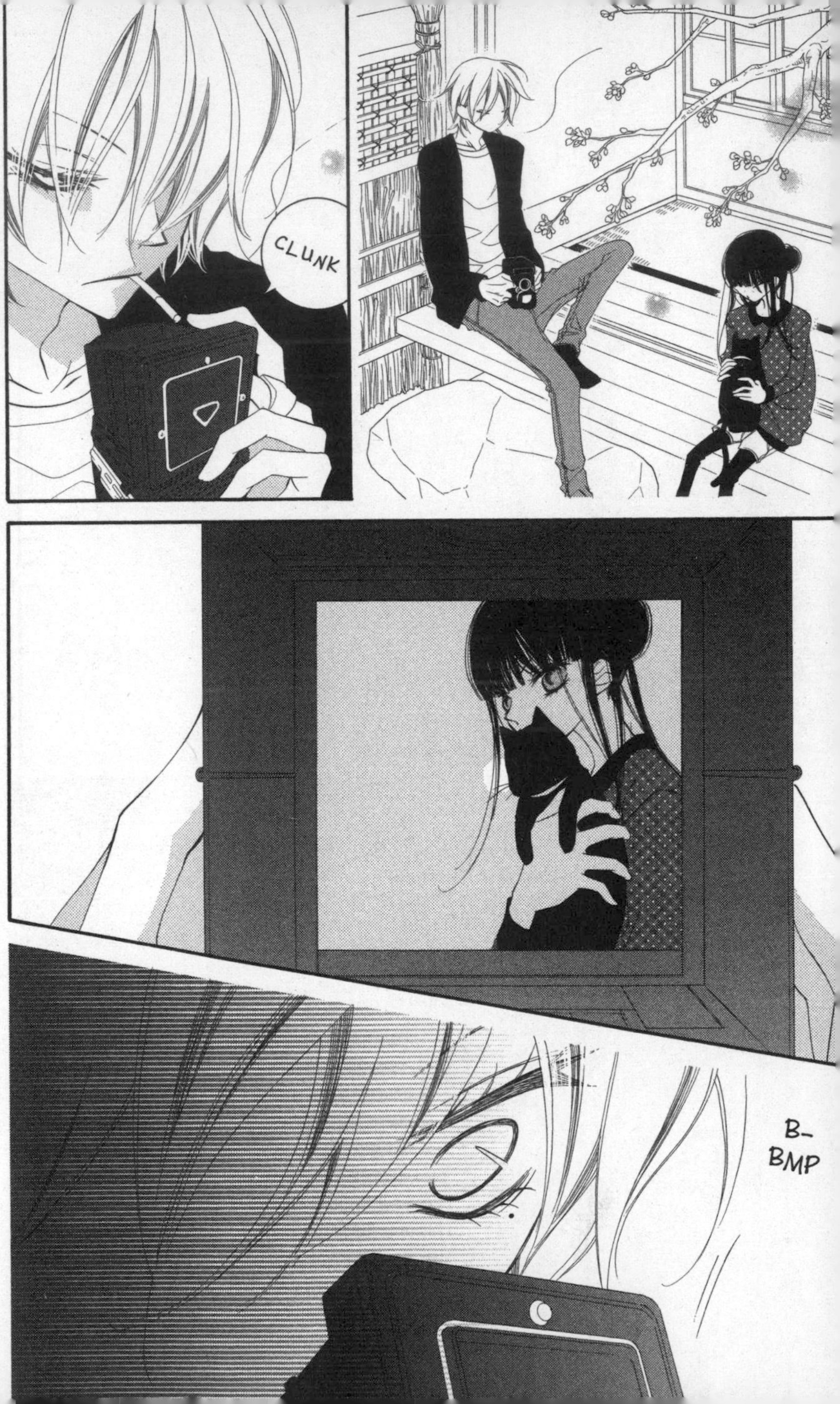
CLUNK
B-
BMP

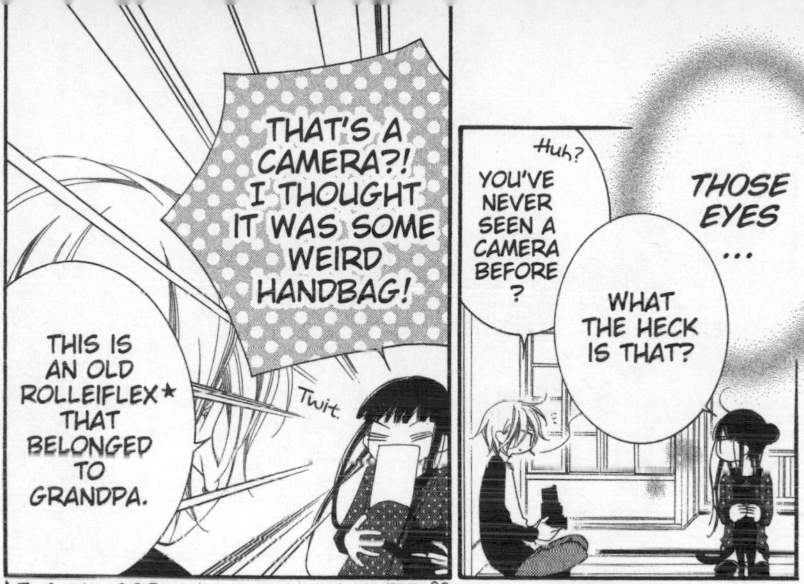
THOSE EYES...
WHAT THE HECK IS THAT?
Huh?
YOU'VE NEVER SEEN A CAMERA BEFORE?
THAT'S A CAMERA?! I THOUGHT IT WAS SOME WEIRD HANDBAG!
Twit.
THIS IS AN OLD ROLLEIFLEX★ THAT BELONGED TO GRANDPA.

★The Rolleiflex 2.8 F, a twin-lens camera sold in the 1960s

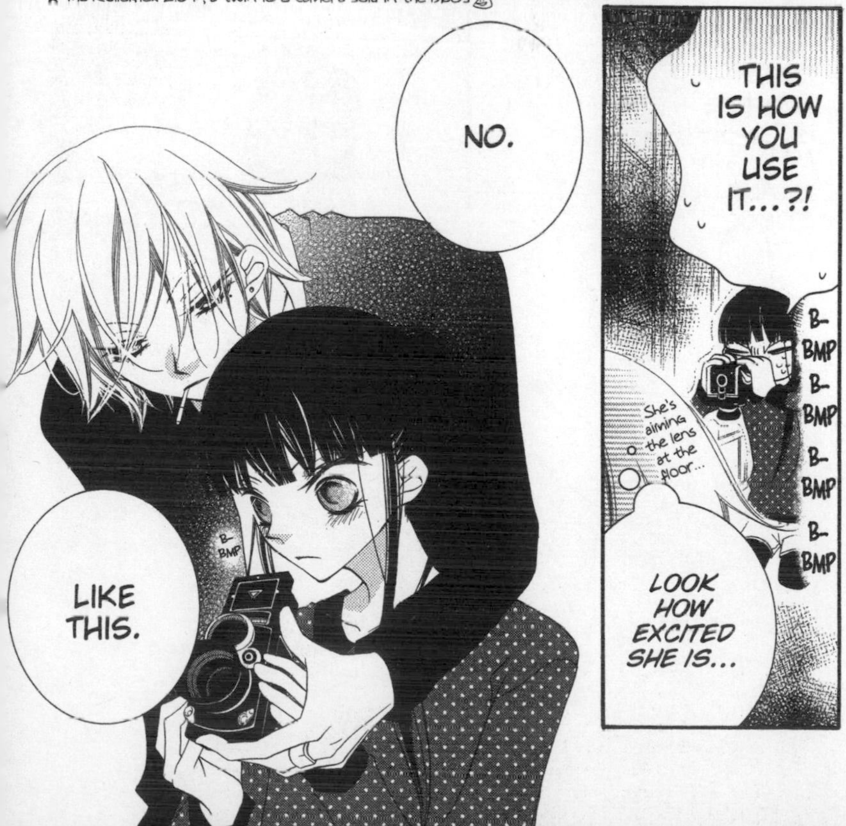
THIS IS HOW YOU USE IT...?!
B-BMP B-BMP B-BMP B-BMP
She's aiming the lens at the floor...
LOOK HOW EXCITED SHE IS...
NO.
B-BMP
LIKE THIS.

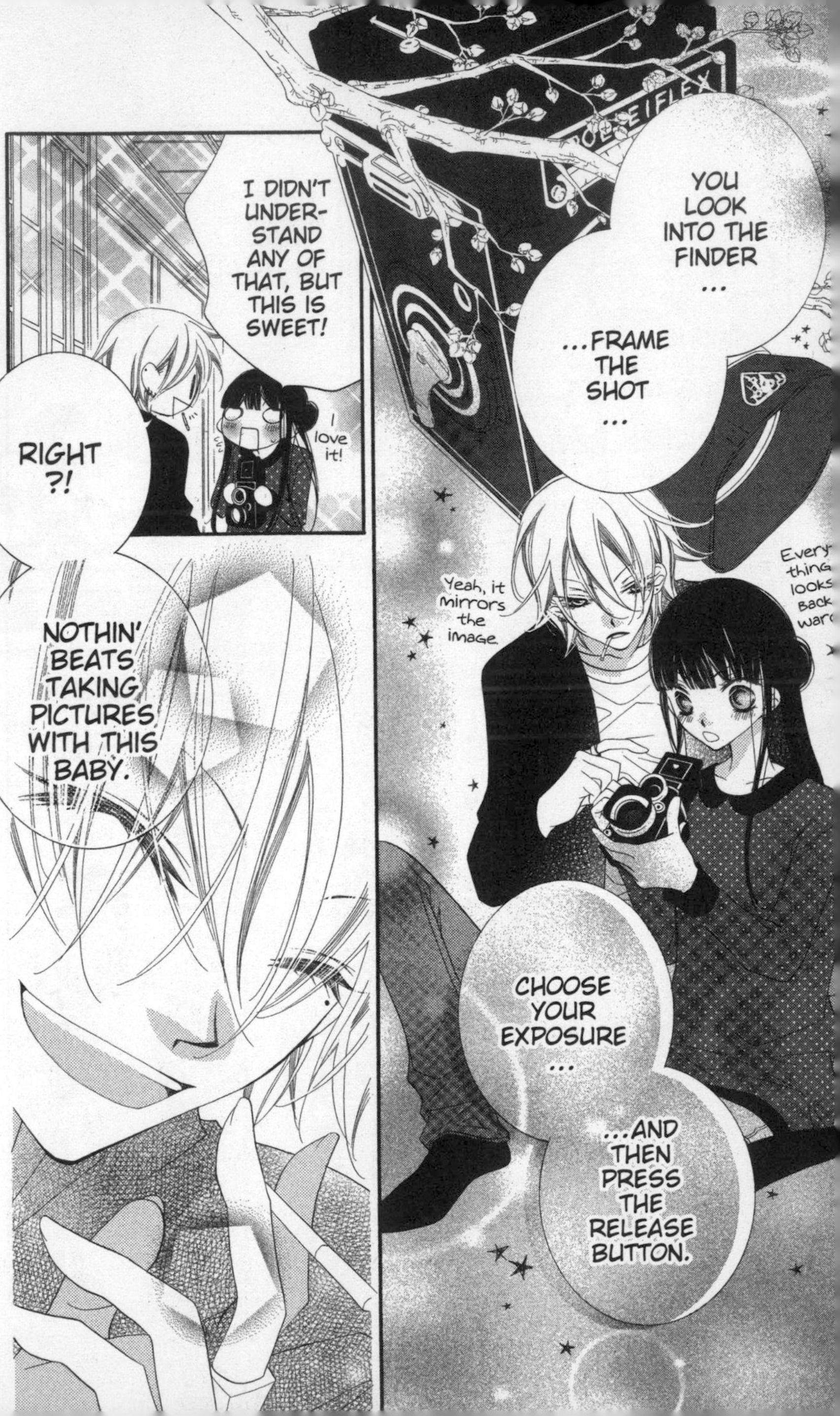
YOU LOOK INTO THE FINDER...
...FRAME THE SHOT...
Every-thing looks Back war
Yeah, it mirrors the image.
CHOOSE YOUR EXPOSURE...
...AND THEN PRESS THE RELEASE BUTTON.
I DIDN'T UNDER-STAND ANY OF THAT, BUT THIS IS SWEET!
I love it!
RIGHT?!
NOTHIN' BEATS TAKING PICTURES WITH THIS BABY.

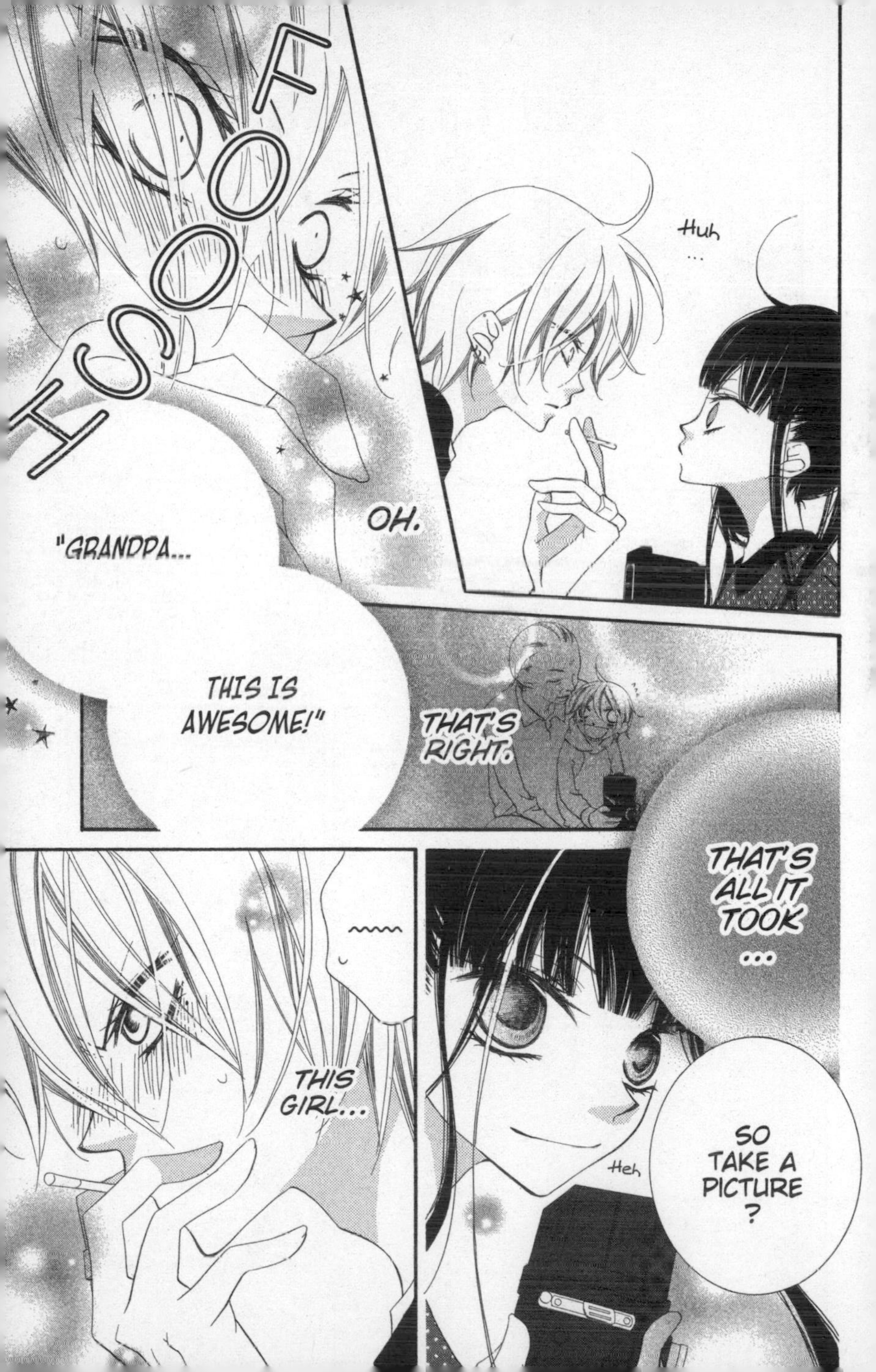
Huh...
SHOOOF
OH.
"GRANDPA...
THIS IS AWESOME!"
THAT'S RIGHT.
THAT'S ALL IT TOOK...
Heh
SO TAKE A PICTURE?
THIS GIRL...

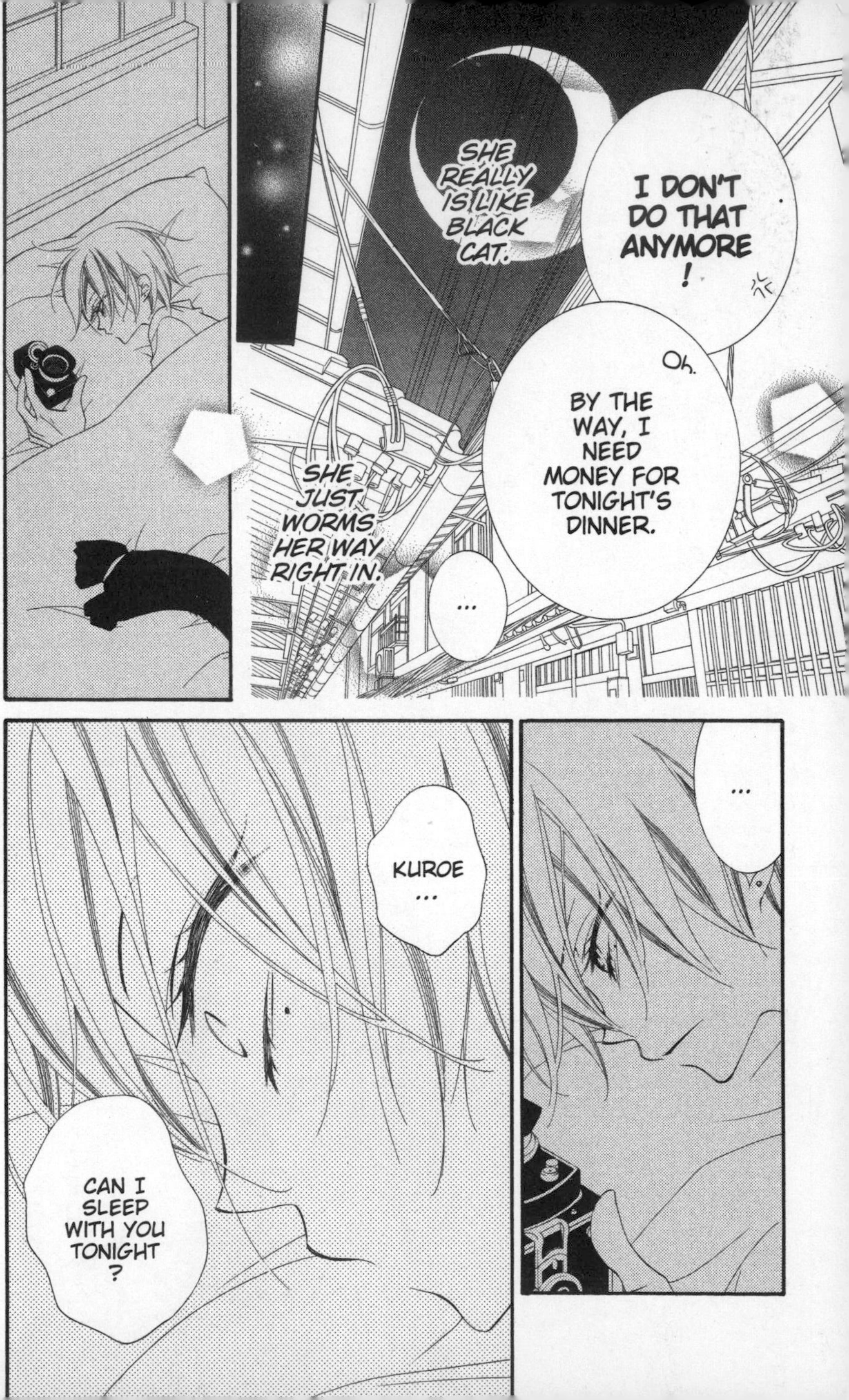
I DON'T DO THAT ANYMORE!
SHE REALLY IS LIKE BLACK CAT.
Oh.
BY THE WAY, I NEED MONEY FOR TONIGHT'S DINNER.
...
SHE JUST WORMS HER WAY RIGHT IN.
...
KUROE ...
CAN I SLEEP WITH YOU TONIGHT?

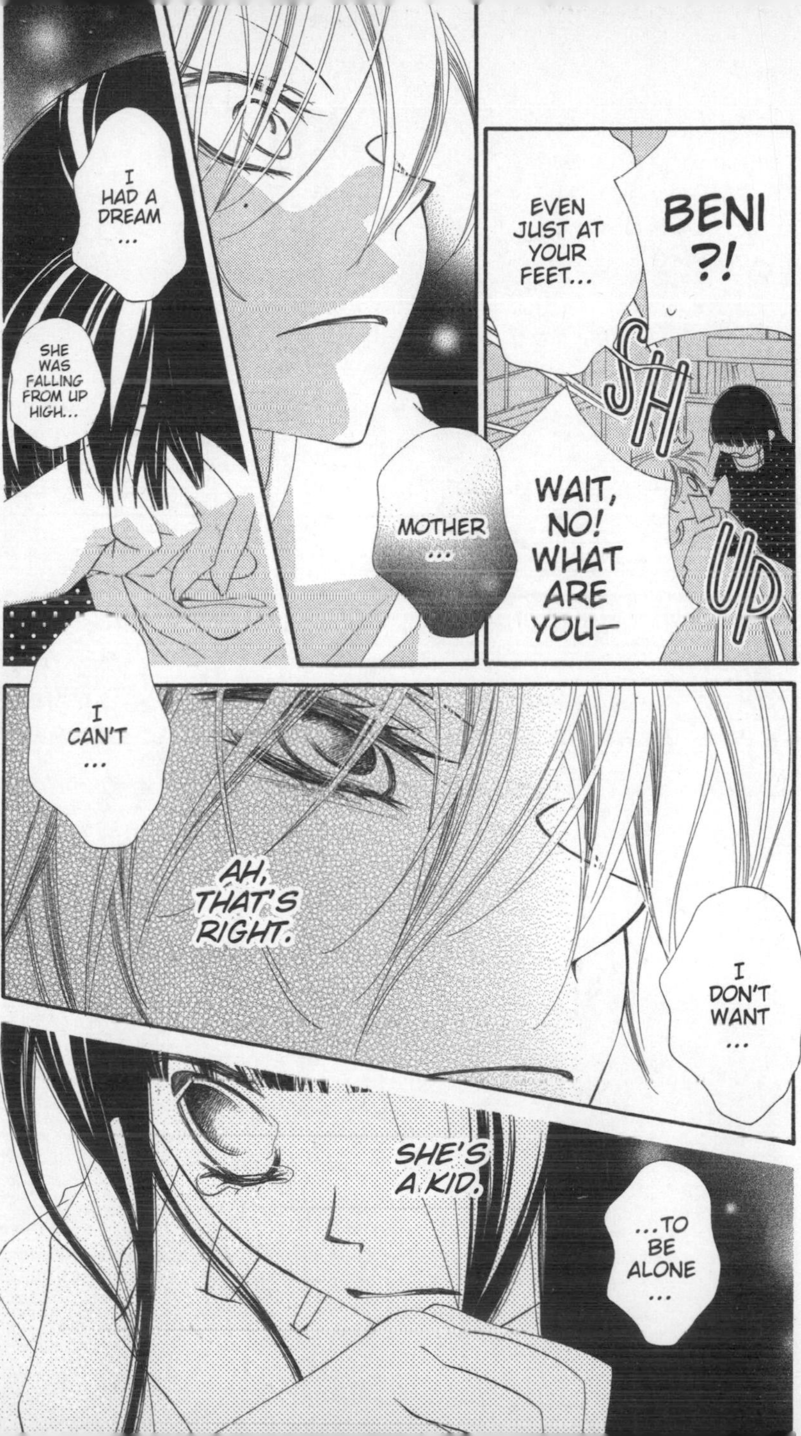
BENI ?!
EVEN JUST AT YOUR FEET...
SH UP
WAIT, NO! WHAT ARE YOU—
MOTHER ...
I HAD A DREAM ...
SHE WAS FALLING FROM UP HIGH...
I DON'T WANT ...
AH, THAT'S RIGHT.
I CAN'T ...
...TO BE ALONE ...
SHE'S A KID.

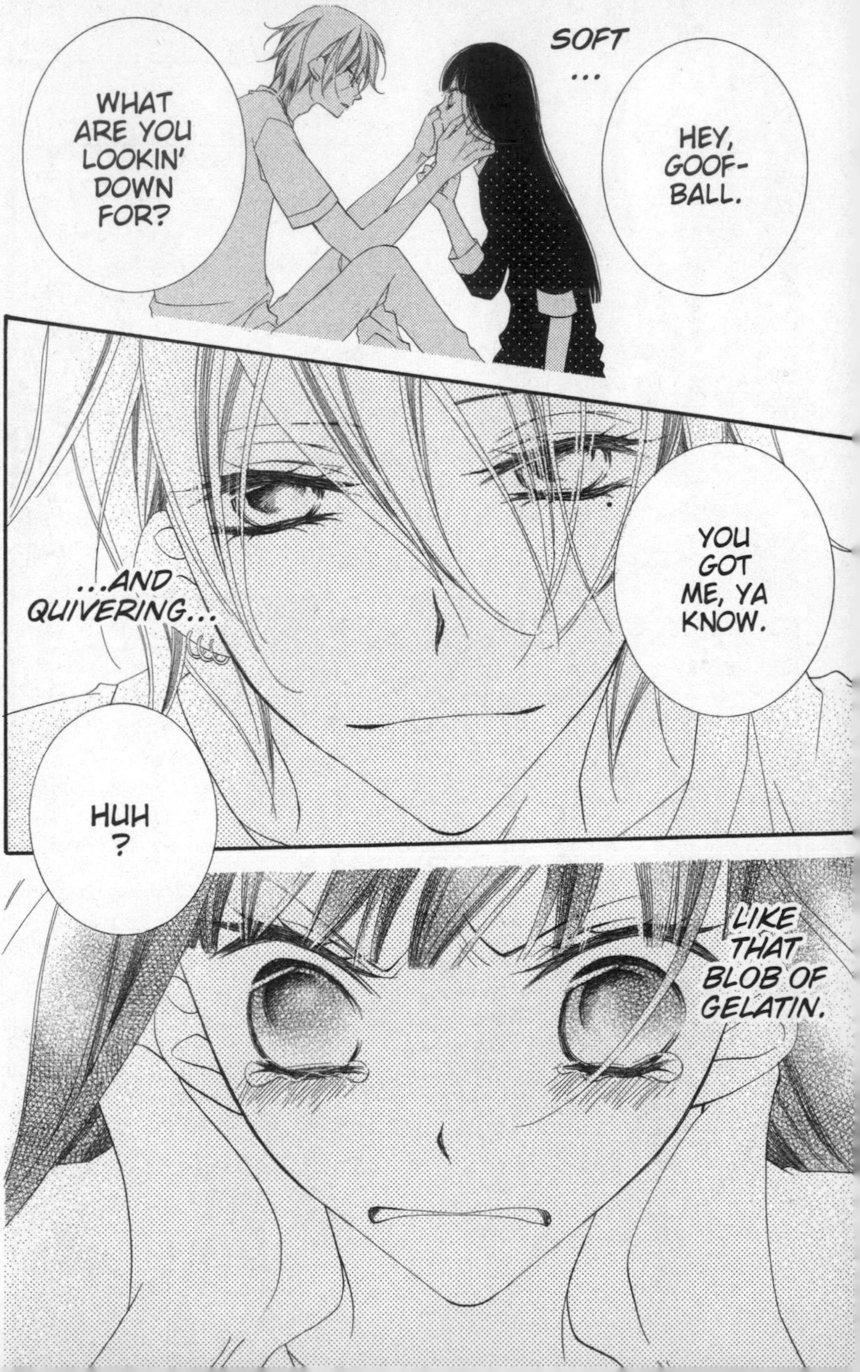
SOFT ...
HEY, GOOF-BALL.
WHAT ARE YOU LOOKIN' DOWN FOR?
YOU GOT ME, YA KNOW.
...AND QUIVERING...
HUH?
LIKE THAT BLOB OF GELATIN.

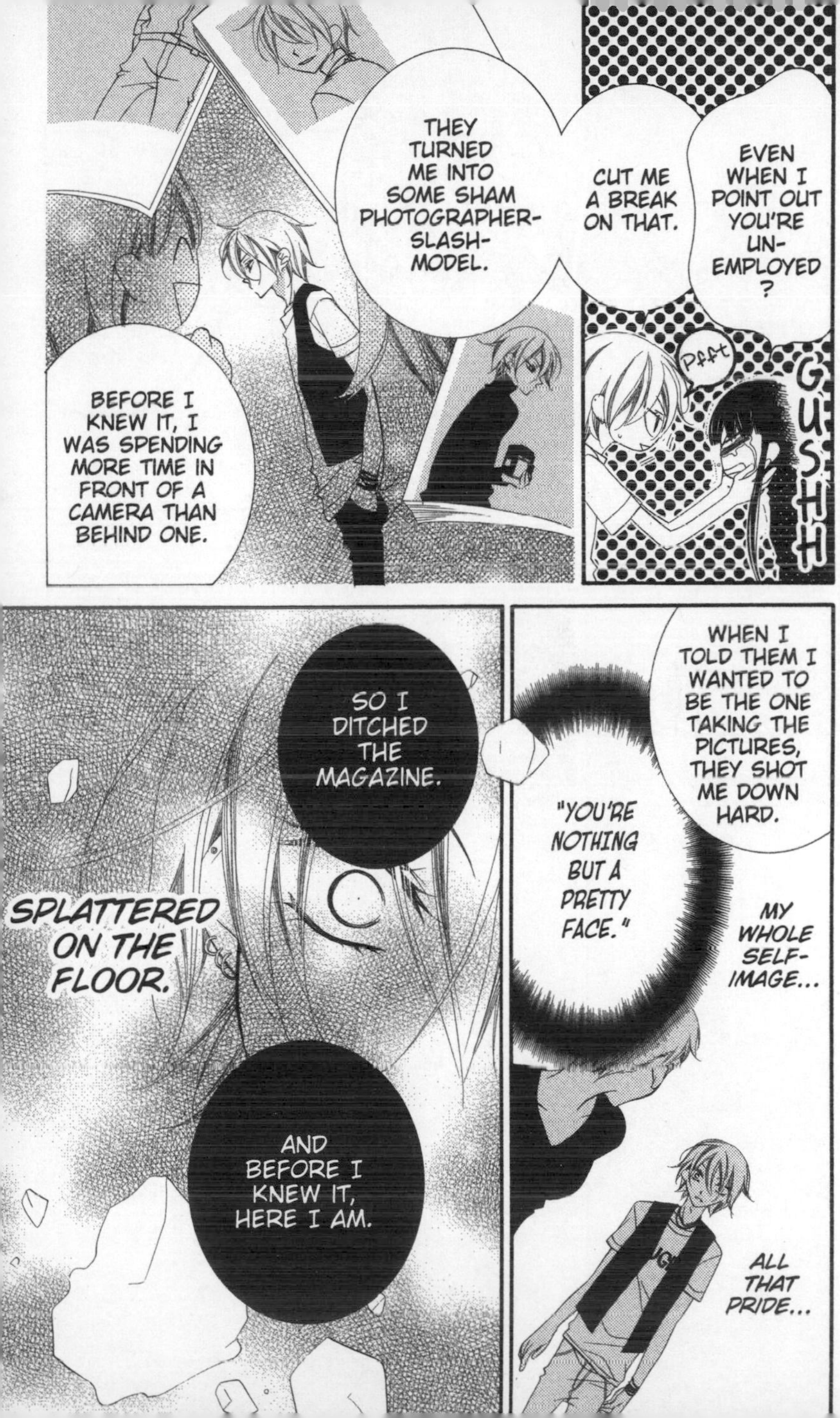
EVEN WHEN I POINT OUT YOU'RE UN-EMPLOYED?
CUT ME A BREAK ON THAT.
Pfft
GUSHH
THEY TURNED ME INTO SOME SHAM PHOTOGRAPHER-SLASH-MODEL.
BEFORE I KNEW IT, I WAS SPENDING MORE TIME IN FRONT OF A CAMERA THAN BEHIND ONE.
WHEN I TOLD THEM I WANTED TO BE THE ONE TAKING THE PICTURES, THEY SHOT ME DOWN HARD.
"YOU'RE NOTHING BUT A PRETTY FACE."
MY WHOLE SELF-IMAGE...
ALL THAT PRIDE...
SO I DITCHED THE MAGAZINE.
SPLATTERED ON THE FLOOR.
AND BEFORE I KNEW IT, HERE I AM.

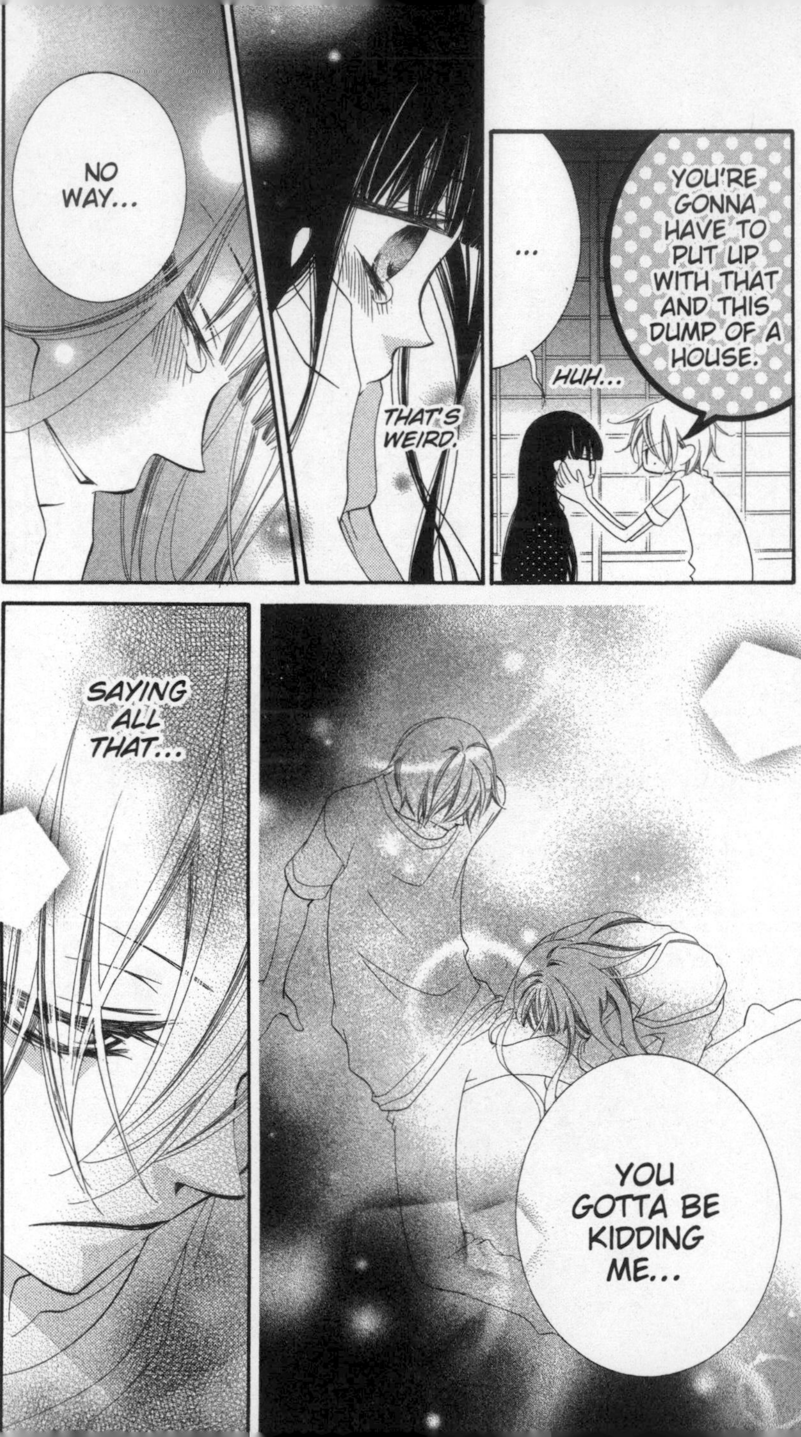
YOU'RE GONNA HAVE TO PUT UP WITH THAT AND THIS DUMP OF A HOUSE.
...
HUH...
THAT'S WEIRD.
NO WAY...
YOU GOTTA BE KIDDING ME...
SAYING ALL THAT...

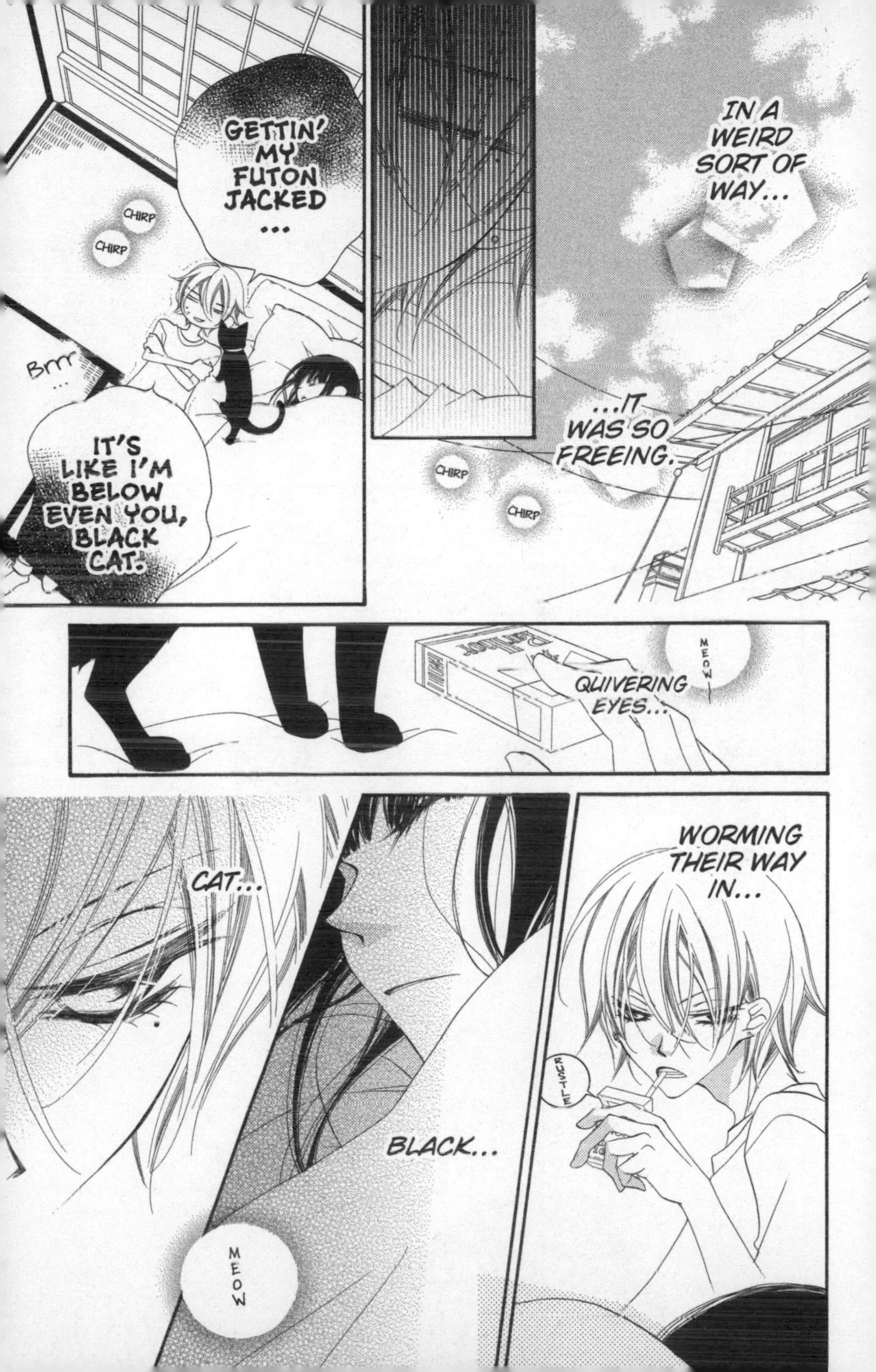
IN A WEIRD SORT OF WAY...
...IT WAS SO FREEING.
CHIRP
CHIRP
GETTIN' MY FUTON JACKED...
CHIRP
CHIRP
Brrr...
IT'S LIKE I'M BELOW EVEN YOU, BLACK CAT.
MEOW
QUIVERING EYES...
WORMING THEIR WAY IN...
RUSTLE
CAT...
BLACK...
MEOW

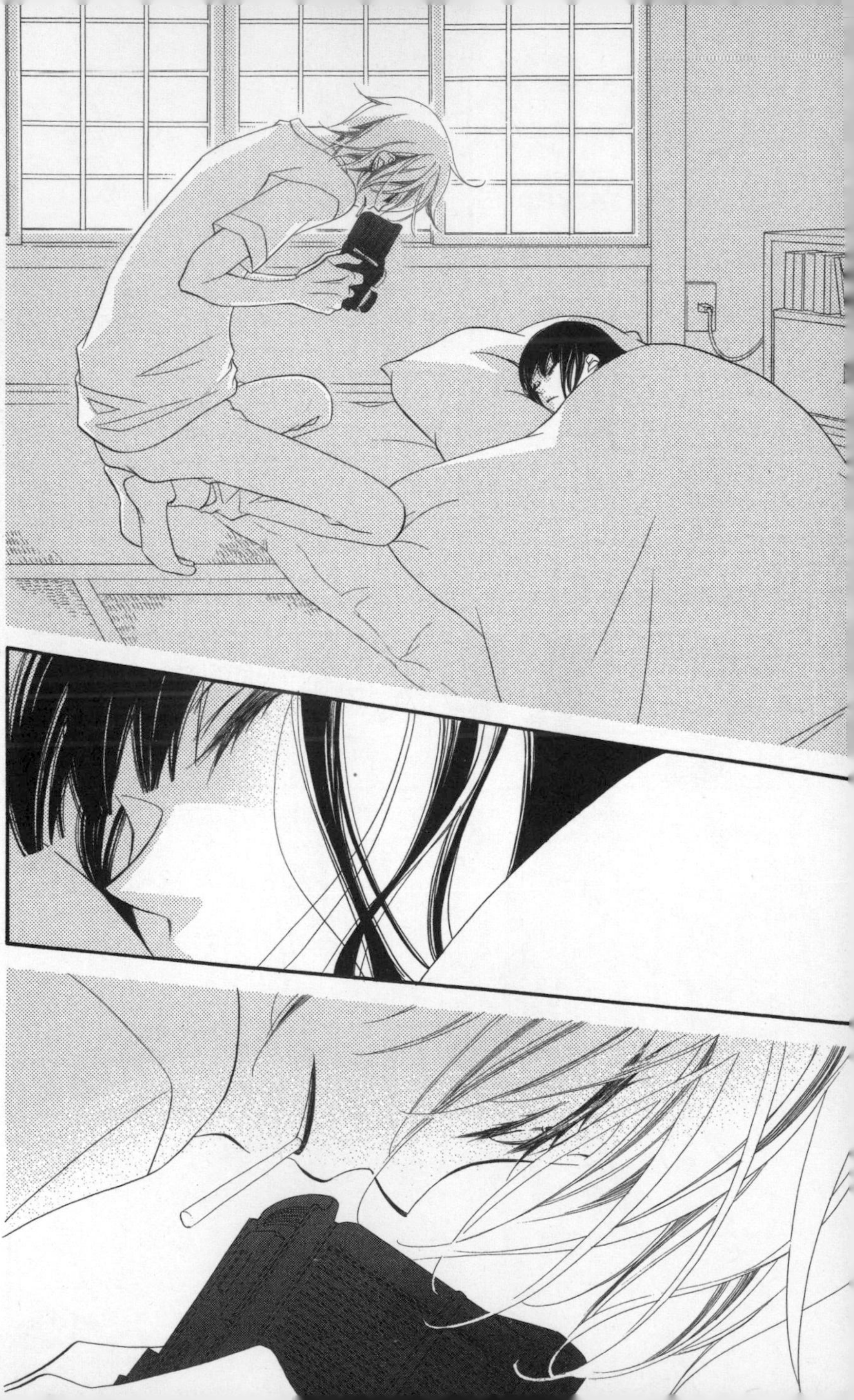

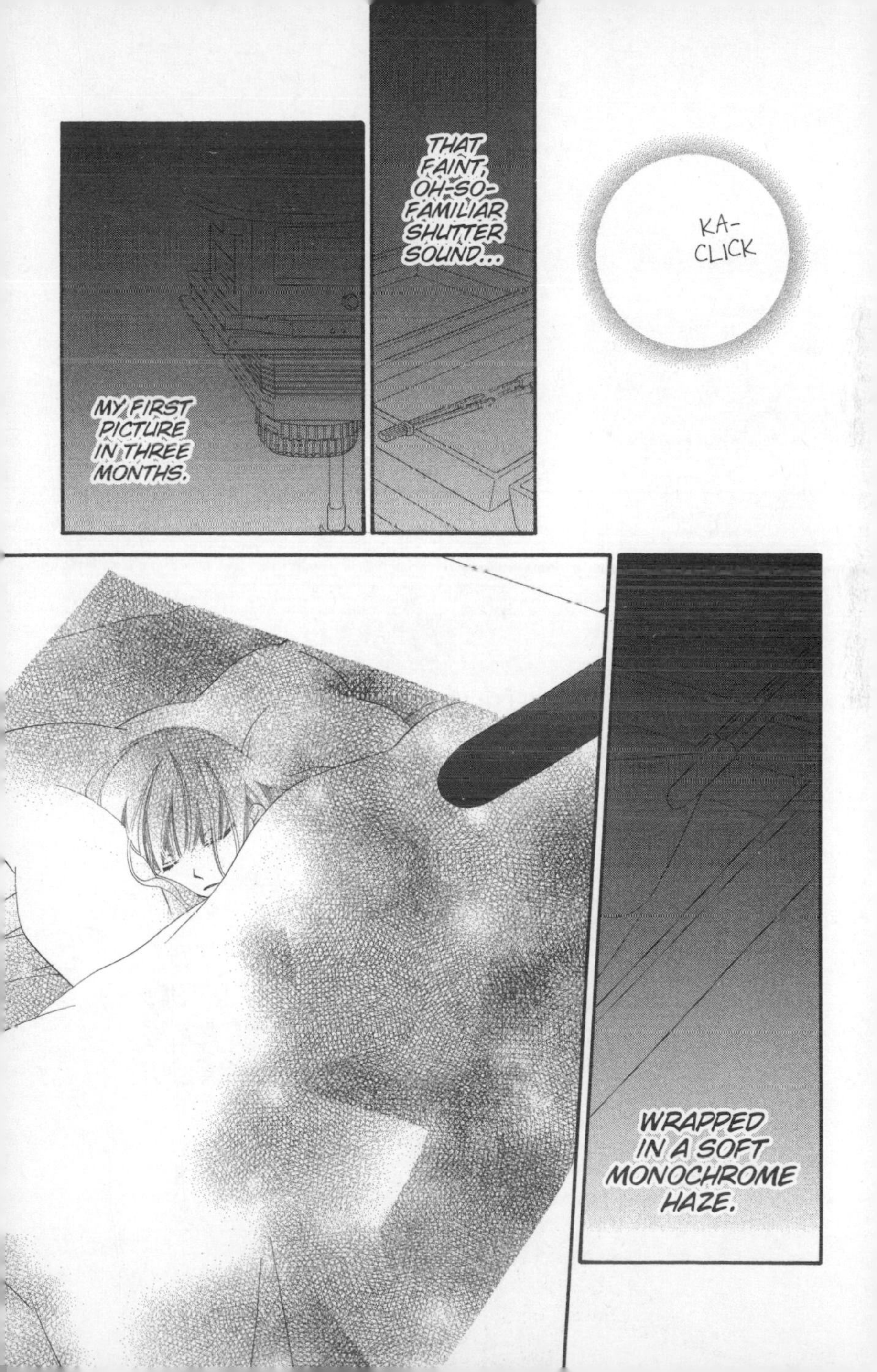
KA-CLICK
THAT FAINT, OH-SO-FAMILIAR SHUTTER SOUND...
MY FIRST PICTURE IN THREE MONTHS.
WRAPPED IN A SOFT MONOCHROME HAZE.

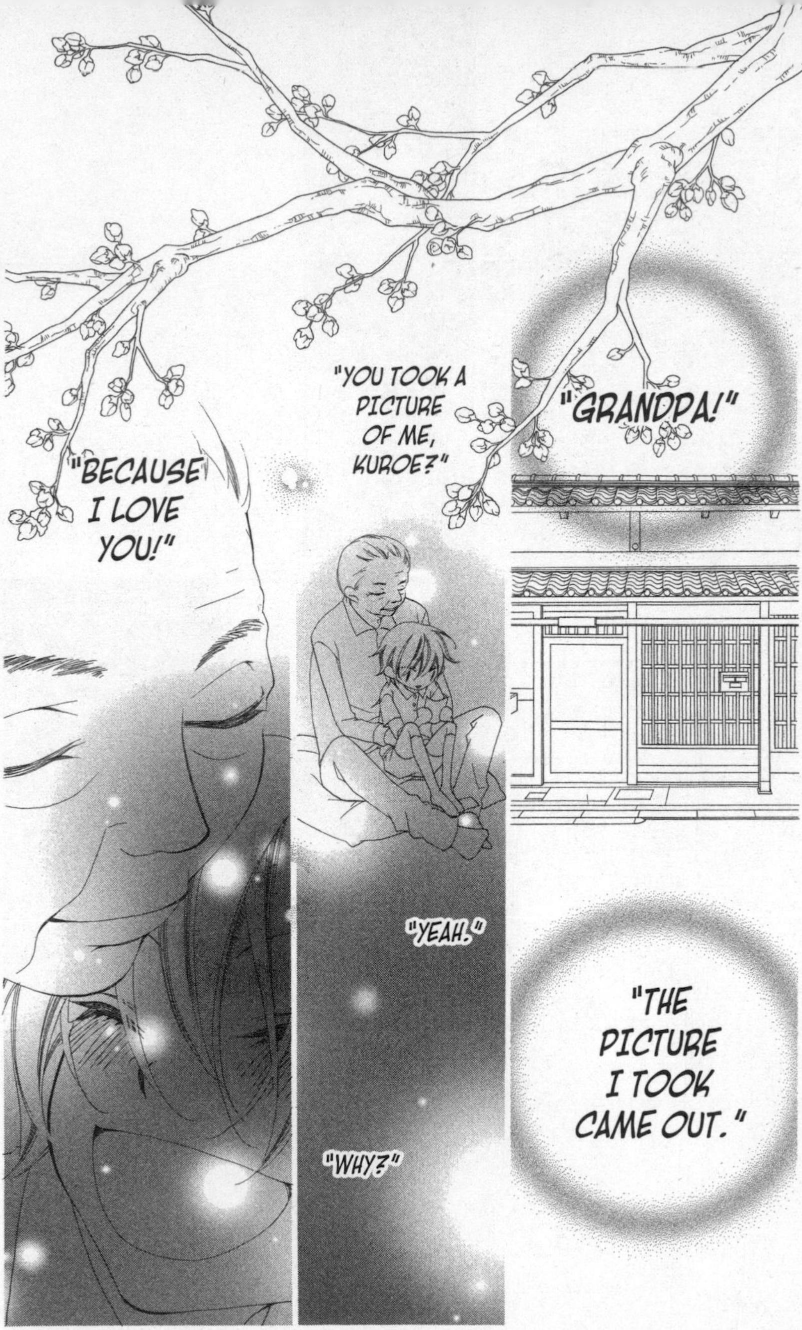
"GRANDPA!"
"THE PICTURE I TOOK CAME OUT."
"YOU TOOK A PICTURE OF ME, KUROE?"
"YEAH."
"WHY?"
"BECAUSE I LOVE YOU!"

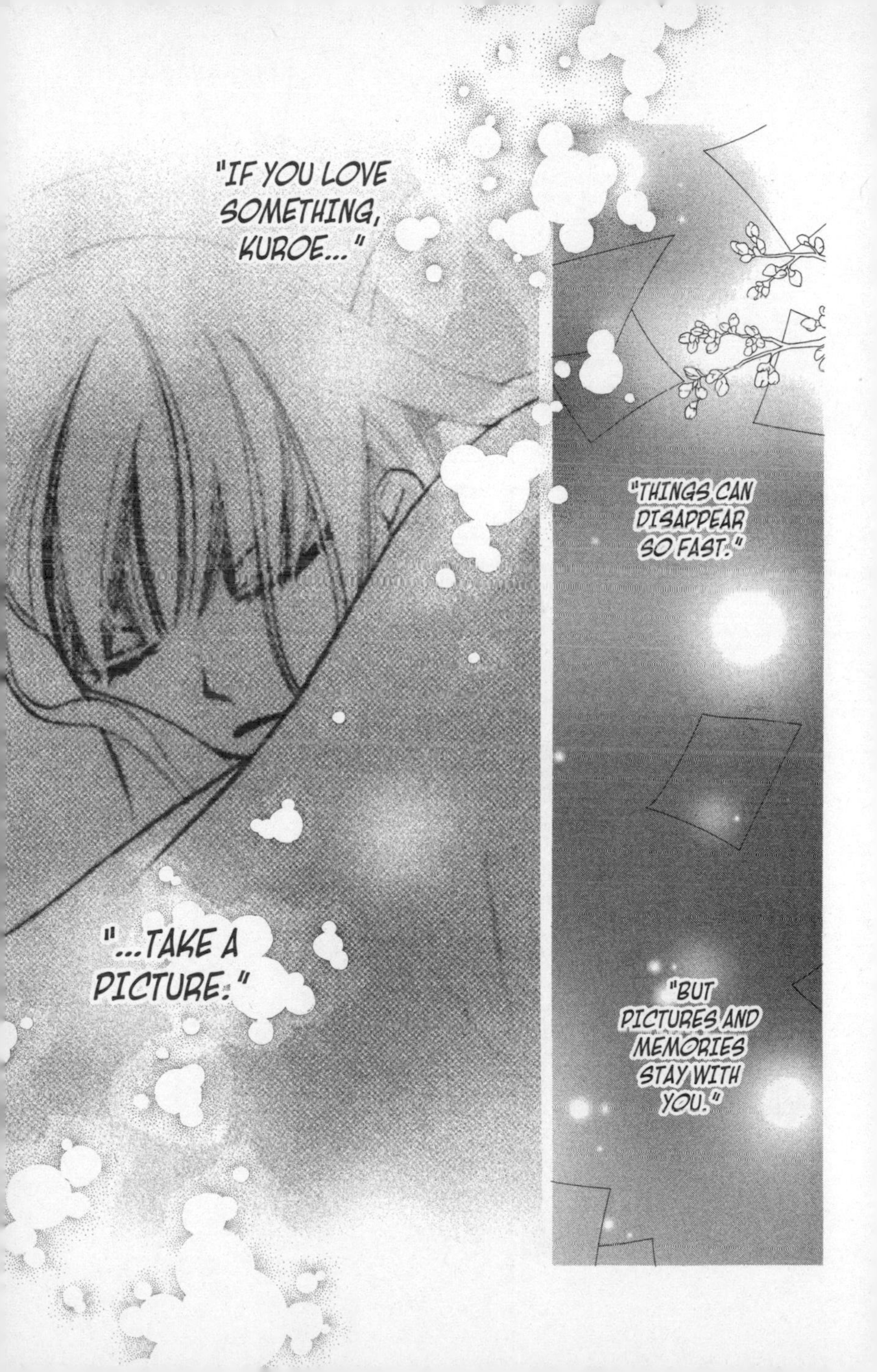
"THINGS CAN DISAPPEAR SO FAST."
"BUT PICTURES AND MEMORIES STAY WITH YOU."
"IF YOU LOVE SOMETHING, KUROE..."
"...TAKE A PICTURE."

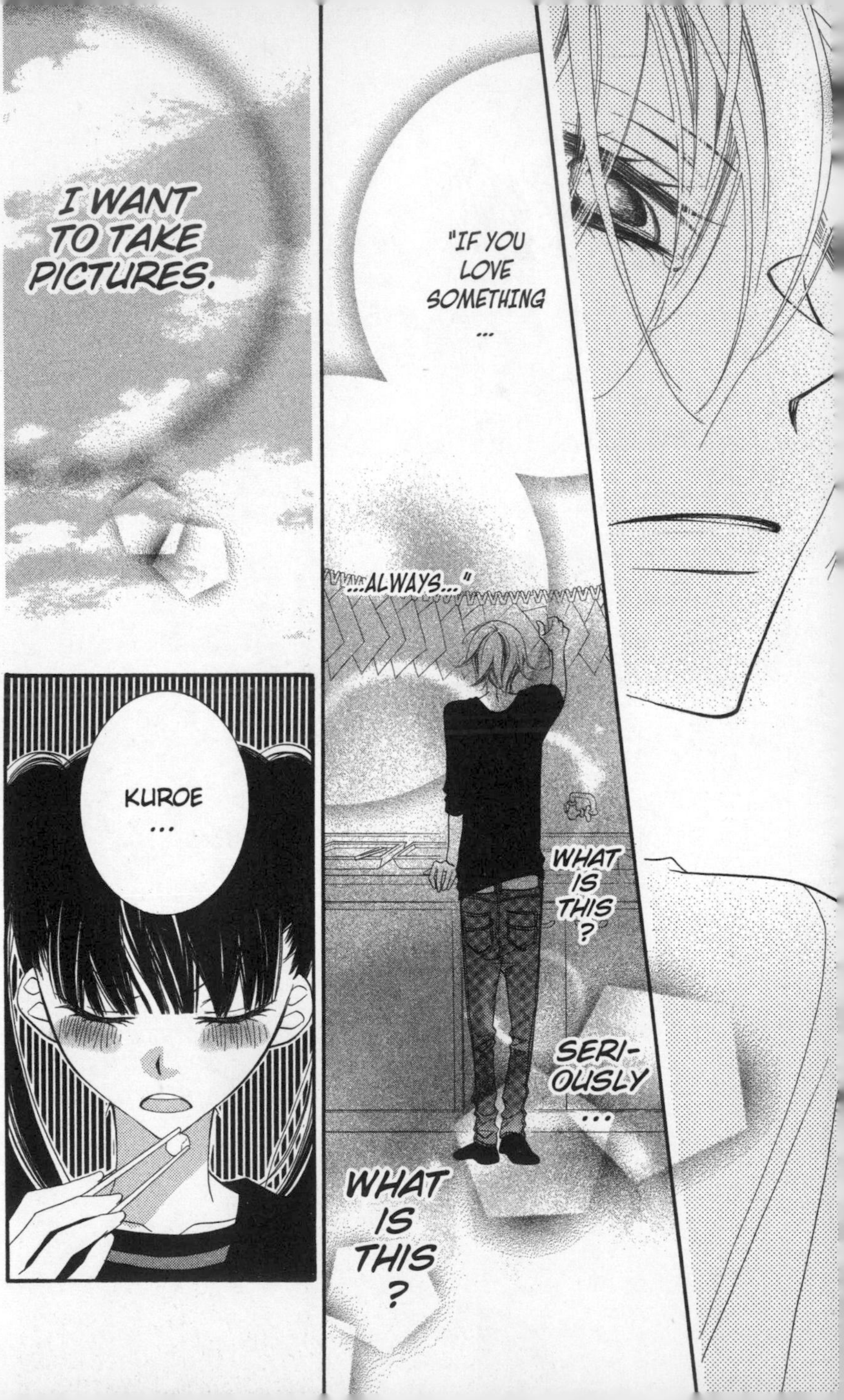
"IF YOU LOVE SOMETHING ...
...ALWAYS..."
WHAT IS THIS?
SERI-OUSLY ...
WHAT IS THIS?
I WANT TO TAKE PICTURES.
KUROE ...

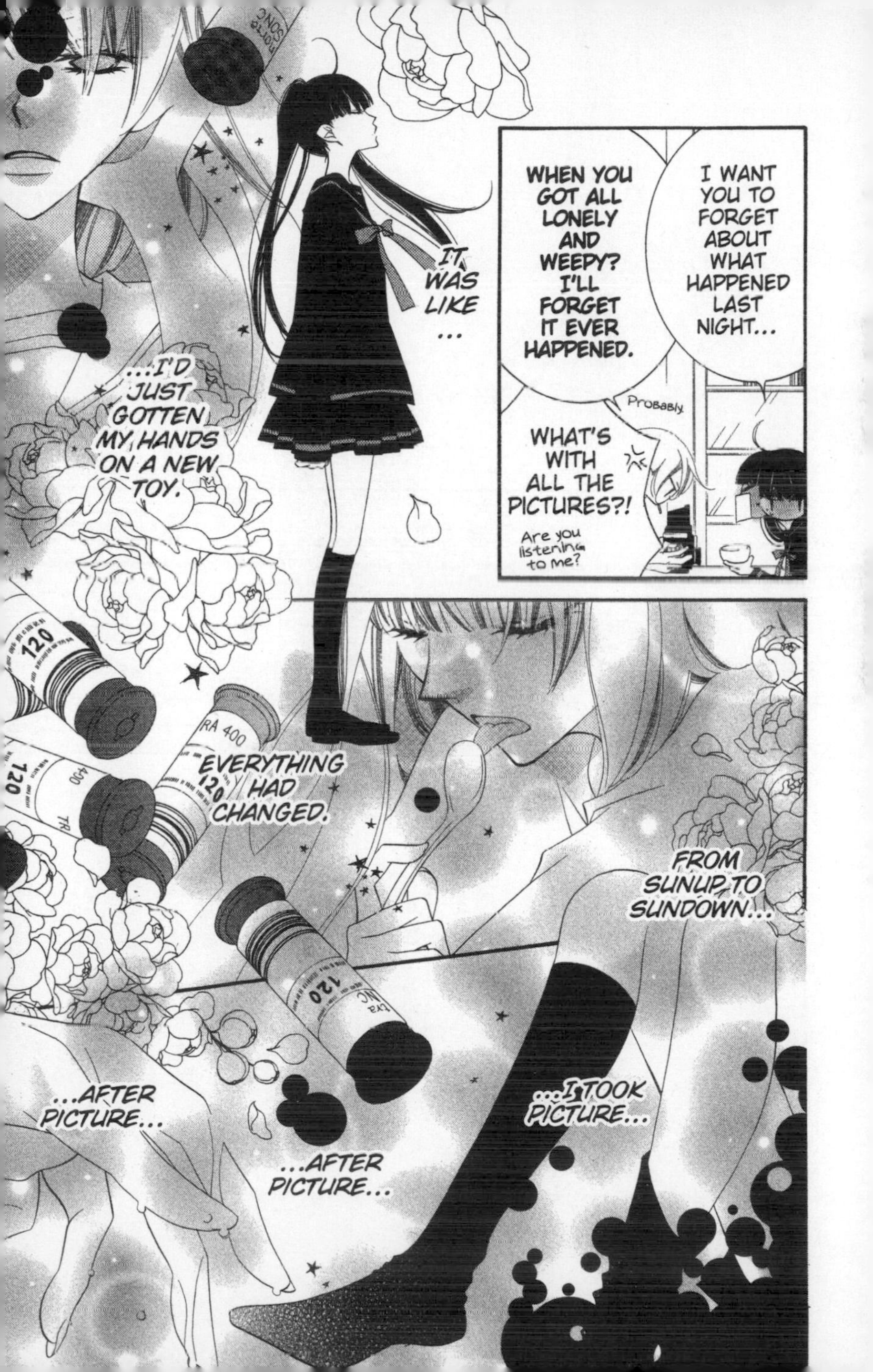
I WANT YOU TO FORGET ABOUT WHAT HAPPENED LAST NIGHT...
WHEN YOU GOT ALL LONELY AND WEEPY? I'LL FORGET IT EVER HAPPENED.
Probably.
WHAT'S WITH ALL THE PICTURES?!
Are you listening to me?
IT WAS LIKE...
...I'D JUST GOTTEN MY HANDS ON A NEW TOY.
EVERYTHING HAD CHANGED.
FROM SUNUP TO SUNDOWN...
...I TOOK PICTURE...
...AFTER PICTURE...
...AFTER PICTURE...

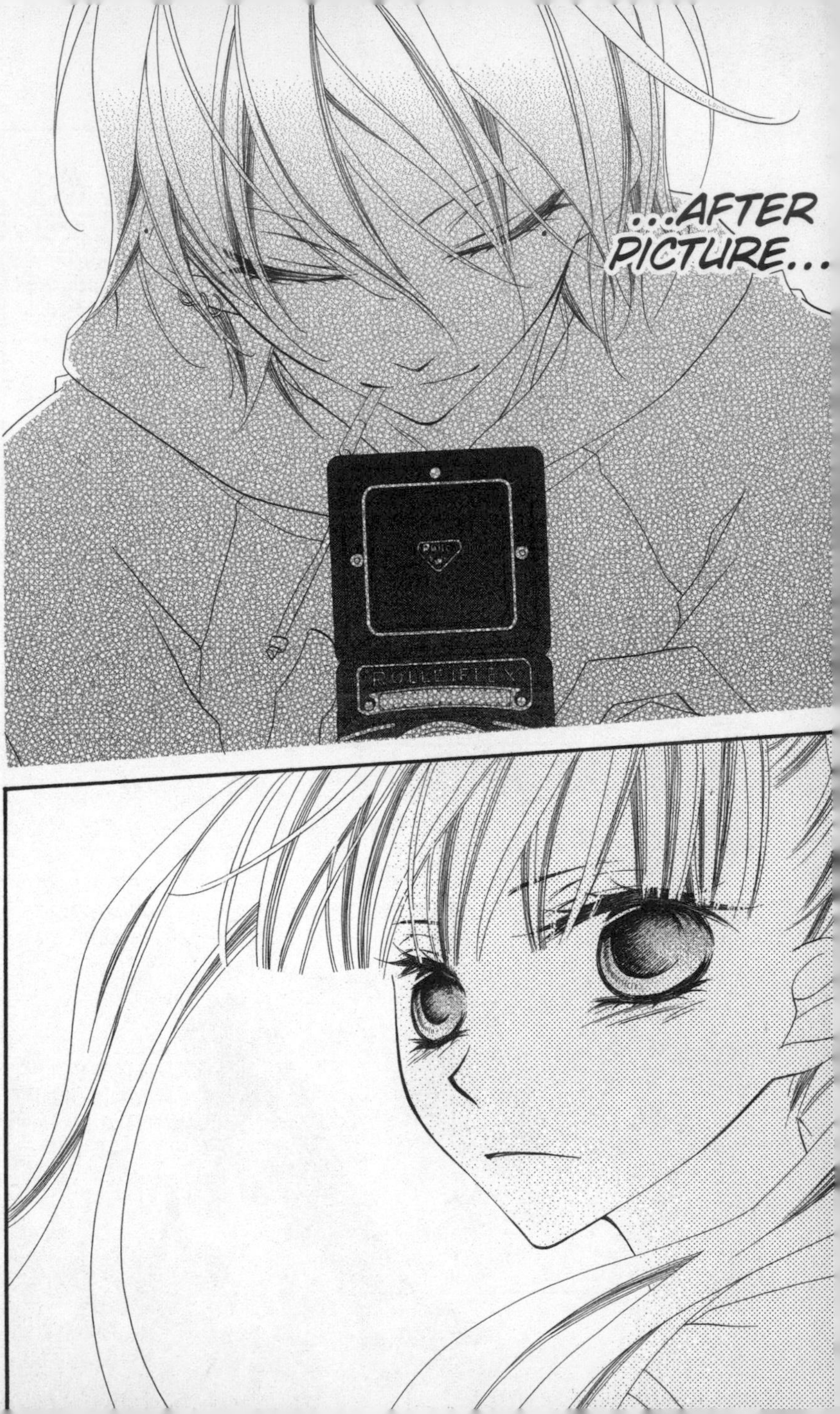
...AFTER PICTURE...
ROLLEIFLEX

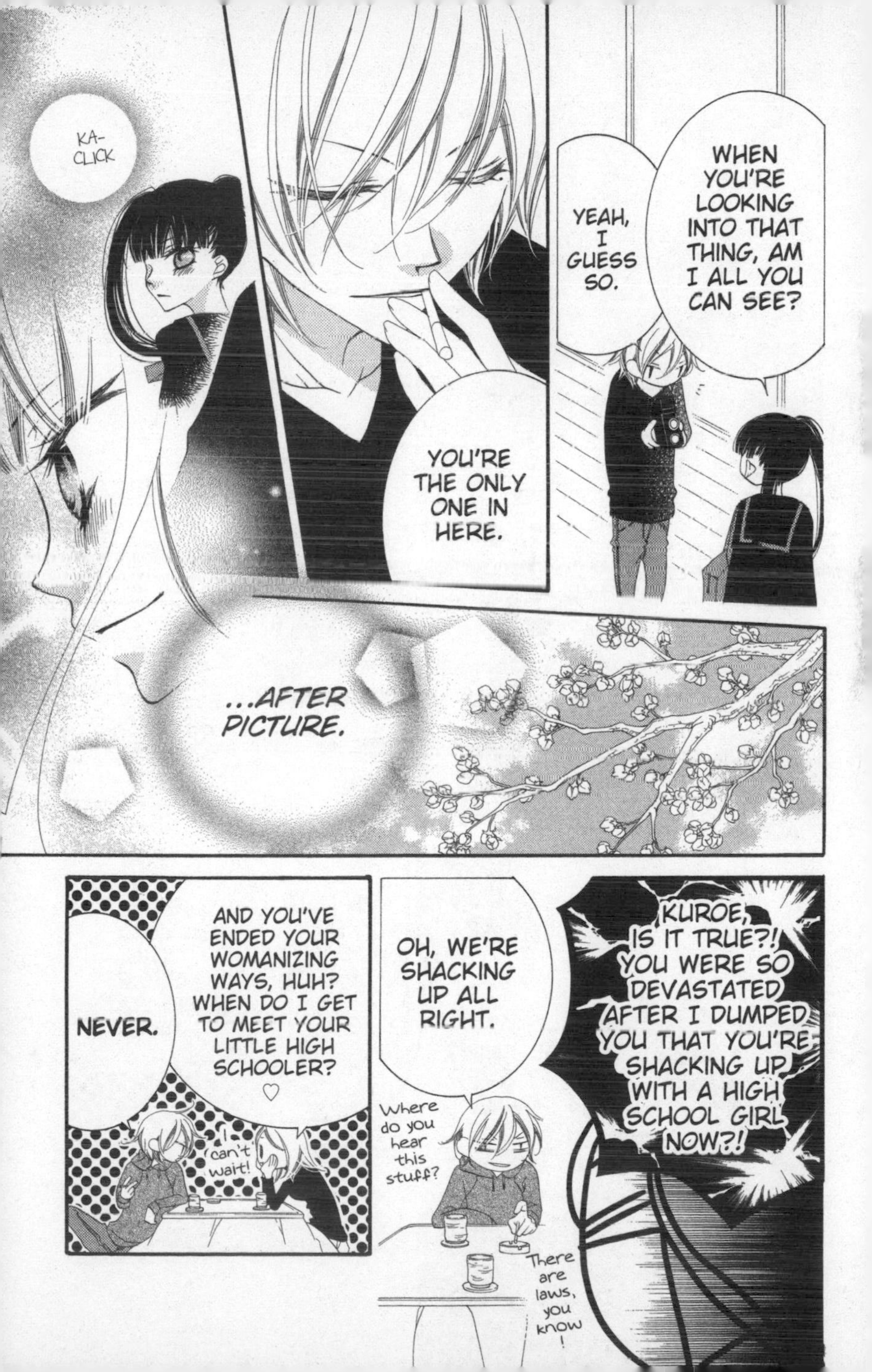
WHEN YOU'RE LOOKING INTO THAT THING, AM I ALL YOU CAN SEE?
YEAH, I GUESS SO.
YOU'RE THE ONLY ONE IN HERE.
KA-CLICK
...AFTER PICTURE.
KUROE, IS IT TRUE?! YOU WERE SO DEVASTATED AFTER I DUMPED YOU THAT YOU'RE SHACKING UP WITH A HIGH SCHOOL GIRL NOW?!
OH, WE'RE SHACKING UP ALL RIGHT.
Where do you hear this stuff?
There are laws, you know!
AND YOU'VE ENDED YOUR WOMANIZING WAYS, HUH? WHEN DO I GET TO MEET YOUR LITTLE HIGH SCHOOLER? ♡
NEVER.
I can't wait!

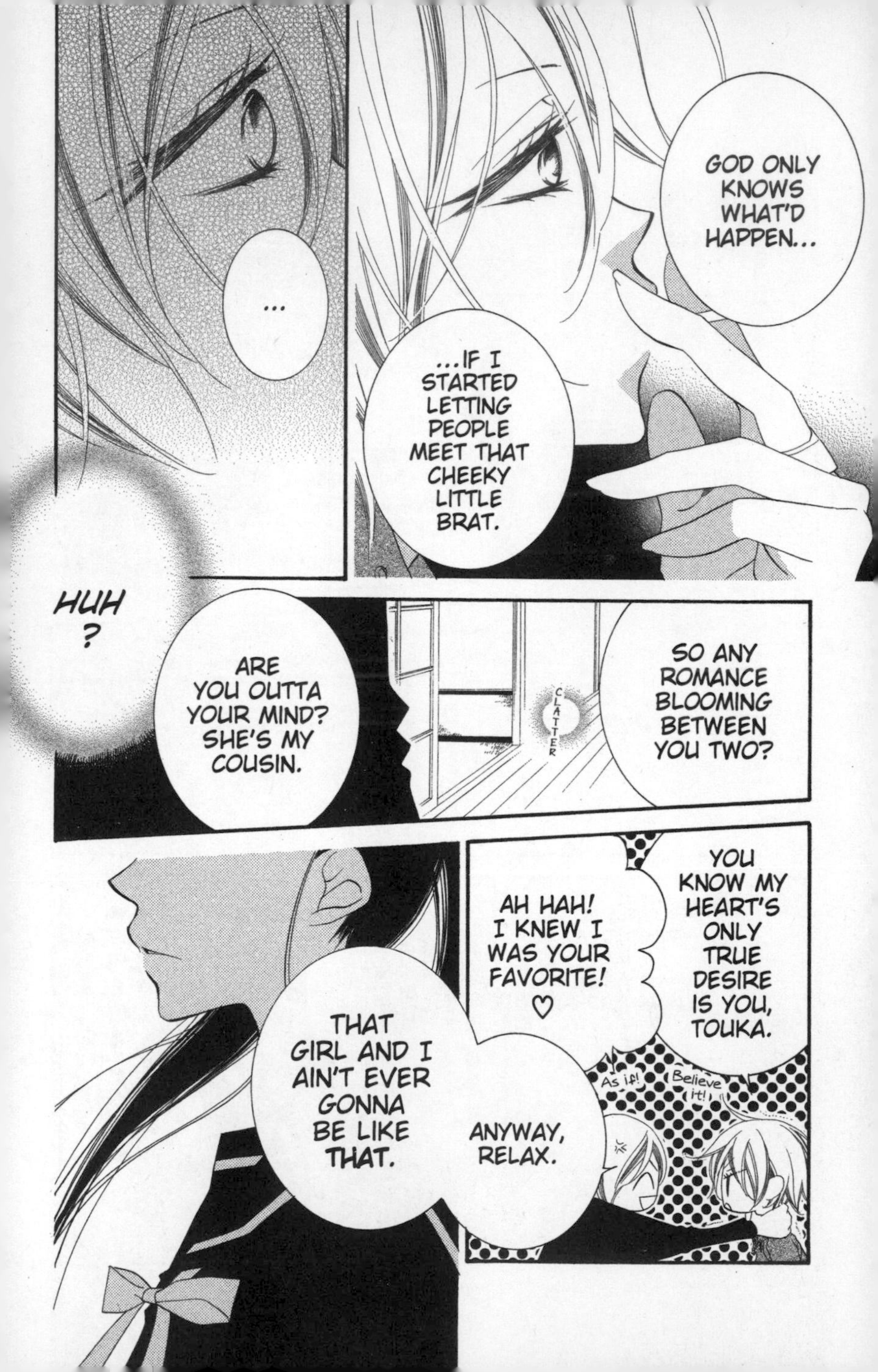
GOD ONLY KNOWS WHAT'D HAPPEN...
...IF I STARTED LETTING PEOPLE MEET THAT CHEEKY LITTLE BRAT.
...
SO ANY ROMANCE BLOOMING BETWEEN YOU TWO?
CLATTER
ARE YOU OUTTA YOUR MIND? SHE'S MY COUSIN.
HUH?
YOU KNOW MY HEART'S ONLY TRUE DESIRE IS YOU, TOUKA.
AH HAH! I KNEW I WAS YOUR FAVORITE! ♡
Believe it!
As if!
ANYWAY, RELAX.
THAT GIRL AND I AIN'T EVER GONNA BE LIKE THAT.

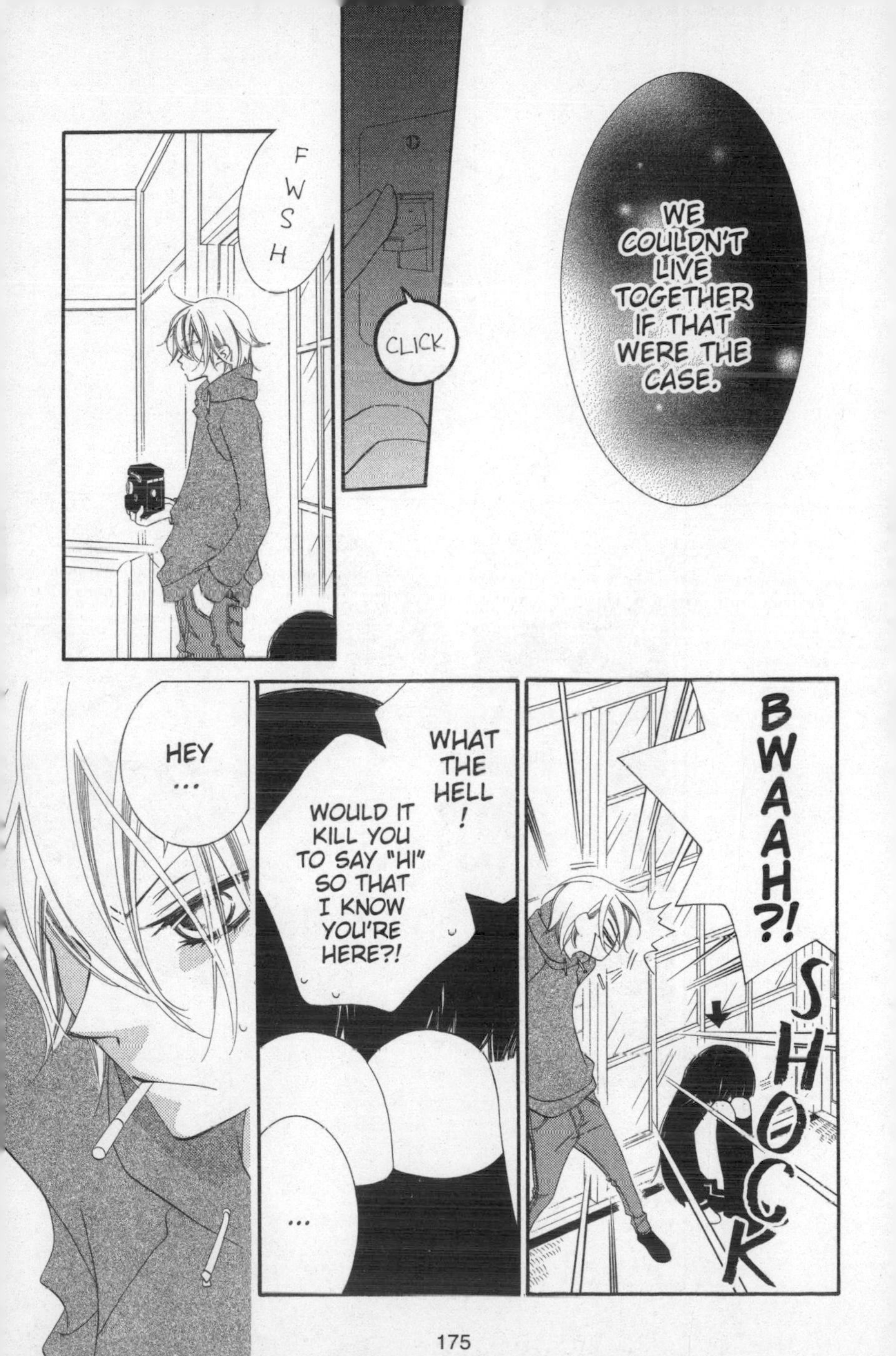
WE COULDN'T LIVE TOGETHER IF THAT WERE THE CASE.
CLICK
FWSH
BWAAAH?!
SHOCK
WHAT THE HELL!
WOULD IT KILL YOU TO SAY "HI" SO THAT I KNOW YOU'RE HERE?!
...
HEY...

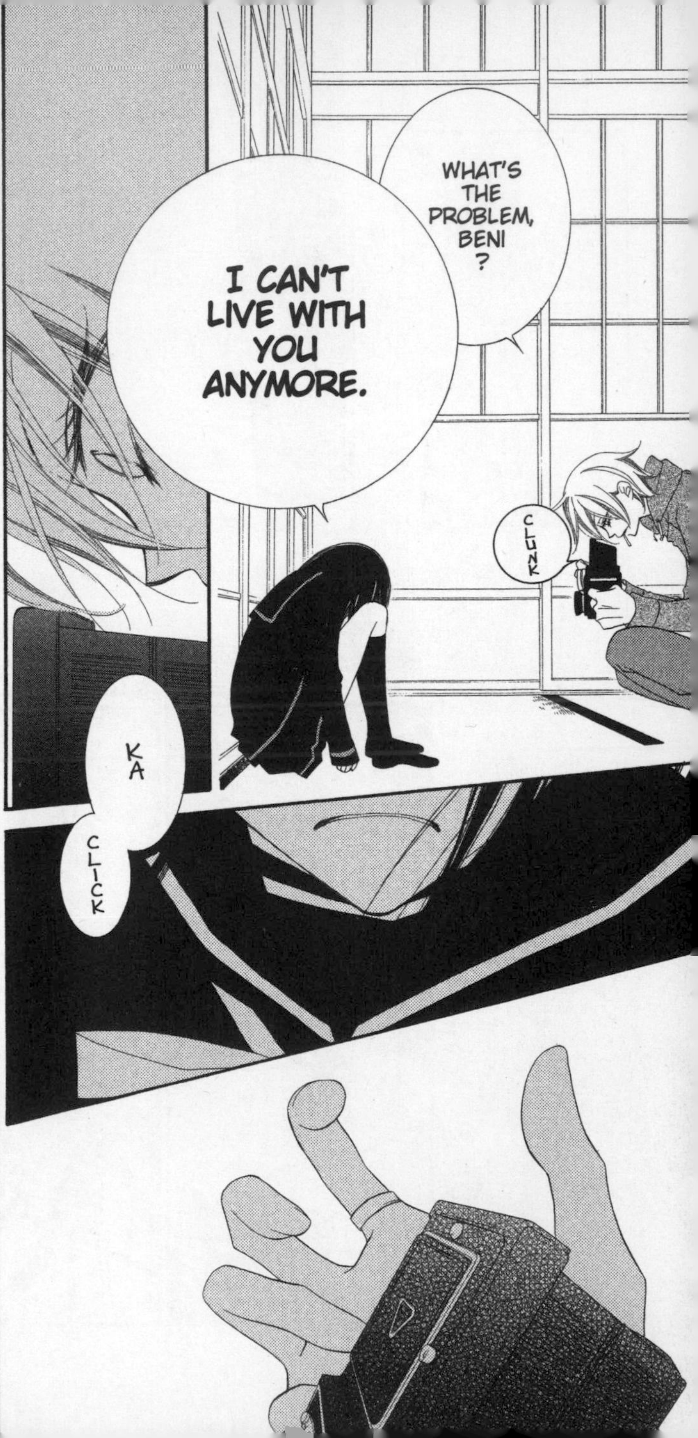
WHAT'S THE PROBLEM, BENI?
I CAN'T LIVE WITH YOU ANYMORE.
CLUNK
KA
CLICK

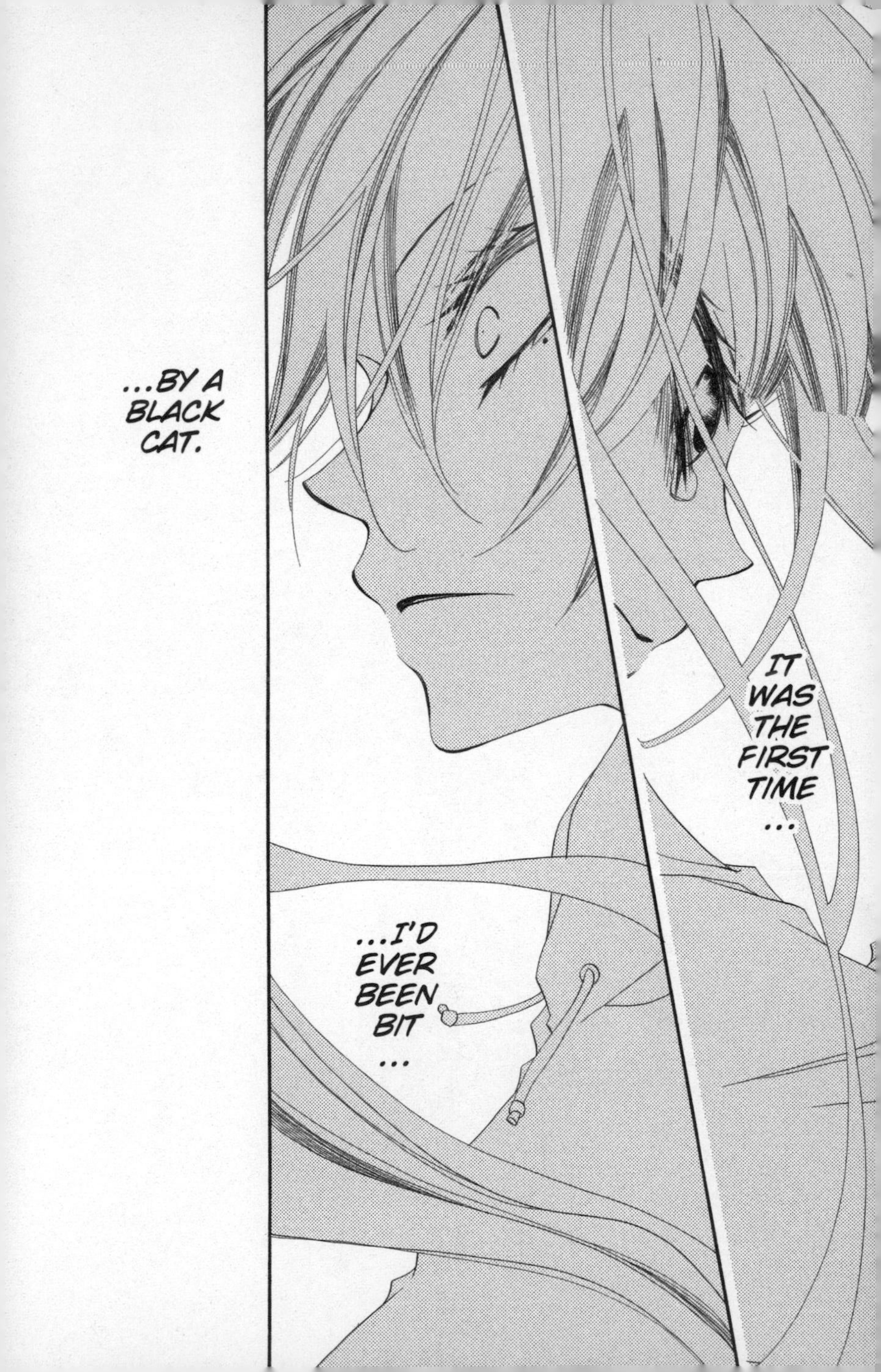
IT WAS THE FIRST TIME...
...I'D EVER BEEN BIT...
...BY A BLACK CAT.

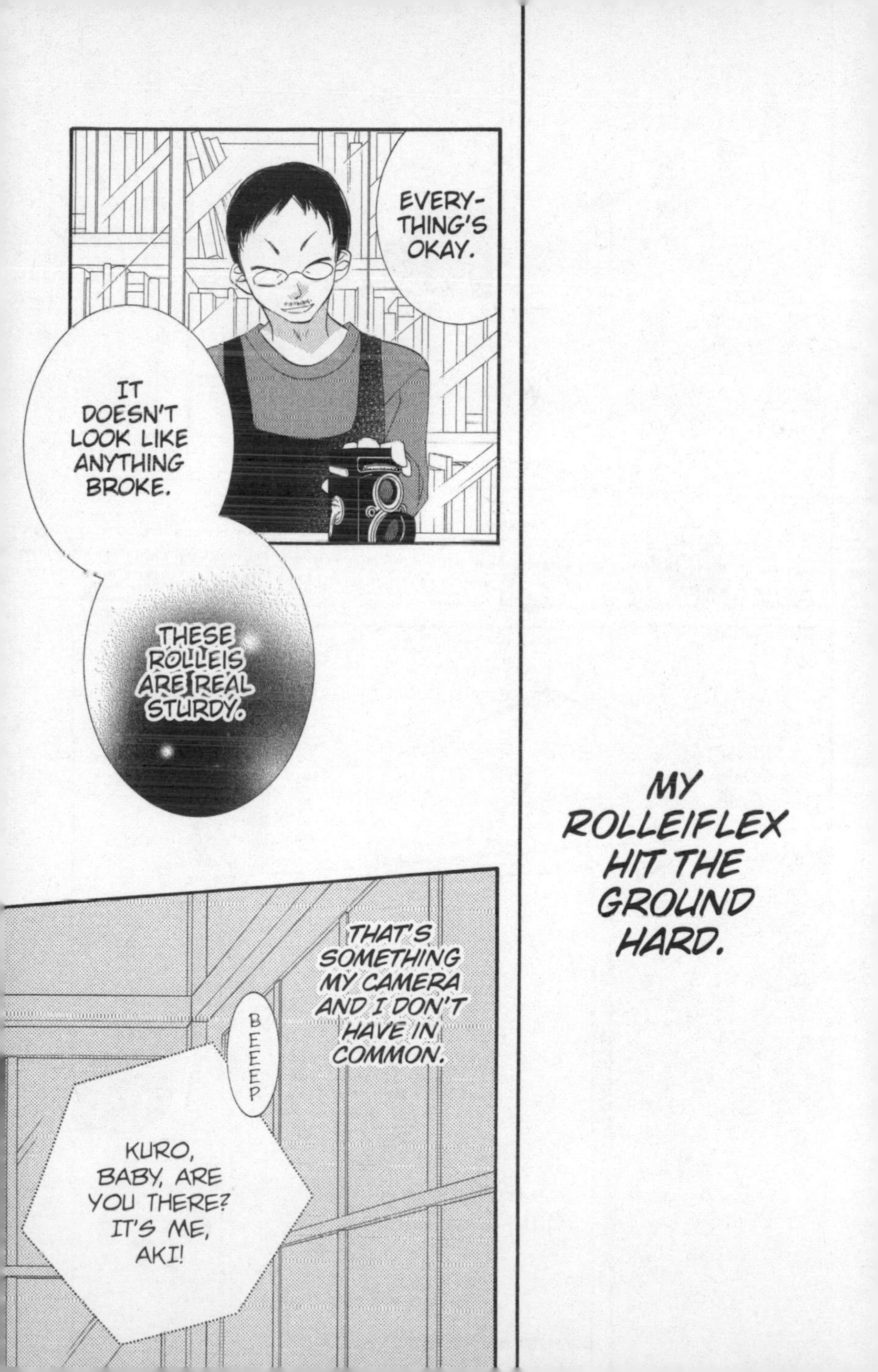
MY ROLLEIFLEX HIT THE GROUND HARD.
EVERY-THING'S OKAY.
IT DOESN'T LOOK LIKE ANYTHING BROKE.
THESE ROLLEIS ARE REAL STURDY.
THAT'S SOMETHING MY CAMERA AND I DON'T HAVE IN COMMON.
BEEEP
KURO, BABY, ARE YOU THERE? IT'S ME, AKI!

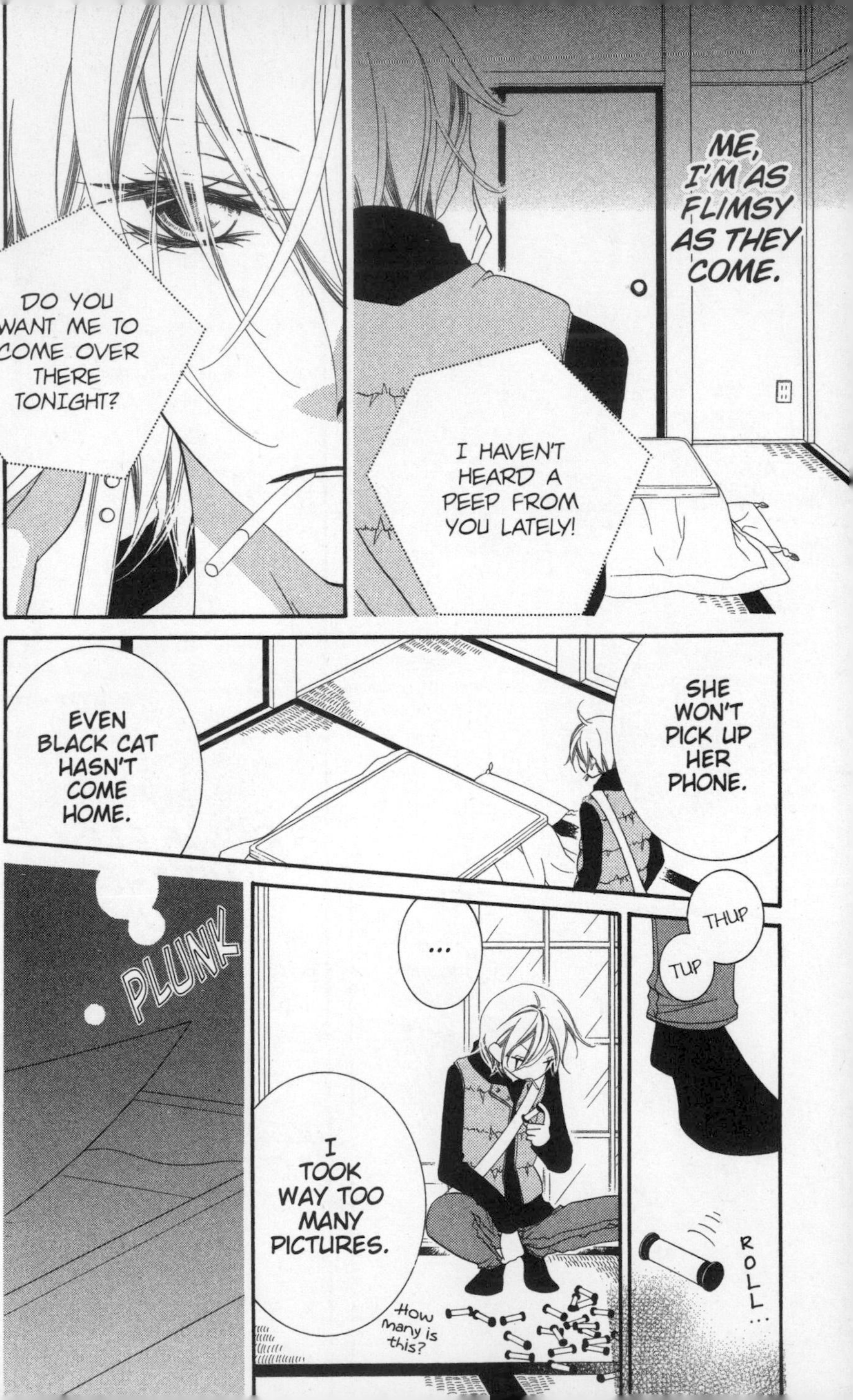
ME, I'M AS FLIMSY AS THEY COME.
I HAVEN'T HEARD A PEEP FROM YOU LATELY!
DO YOU WANT ME TO COME OVER THERE TONIGHT?
SHE WON'T PICK UP HER PHONE.
EVEN BLACK CAT HASN'T COME HOME.
THUP
TUP
...
ROLL...
I TOOK WAY TOO MANY PICTURES.
How many is this?
PLUNK

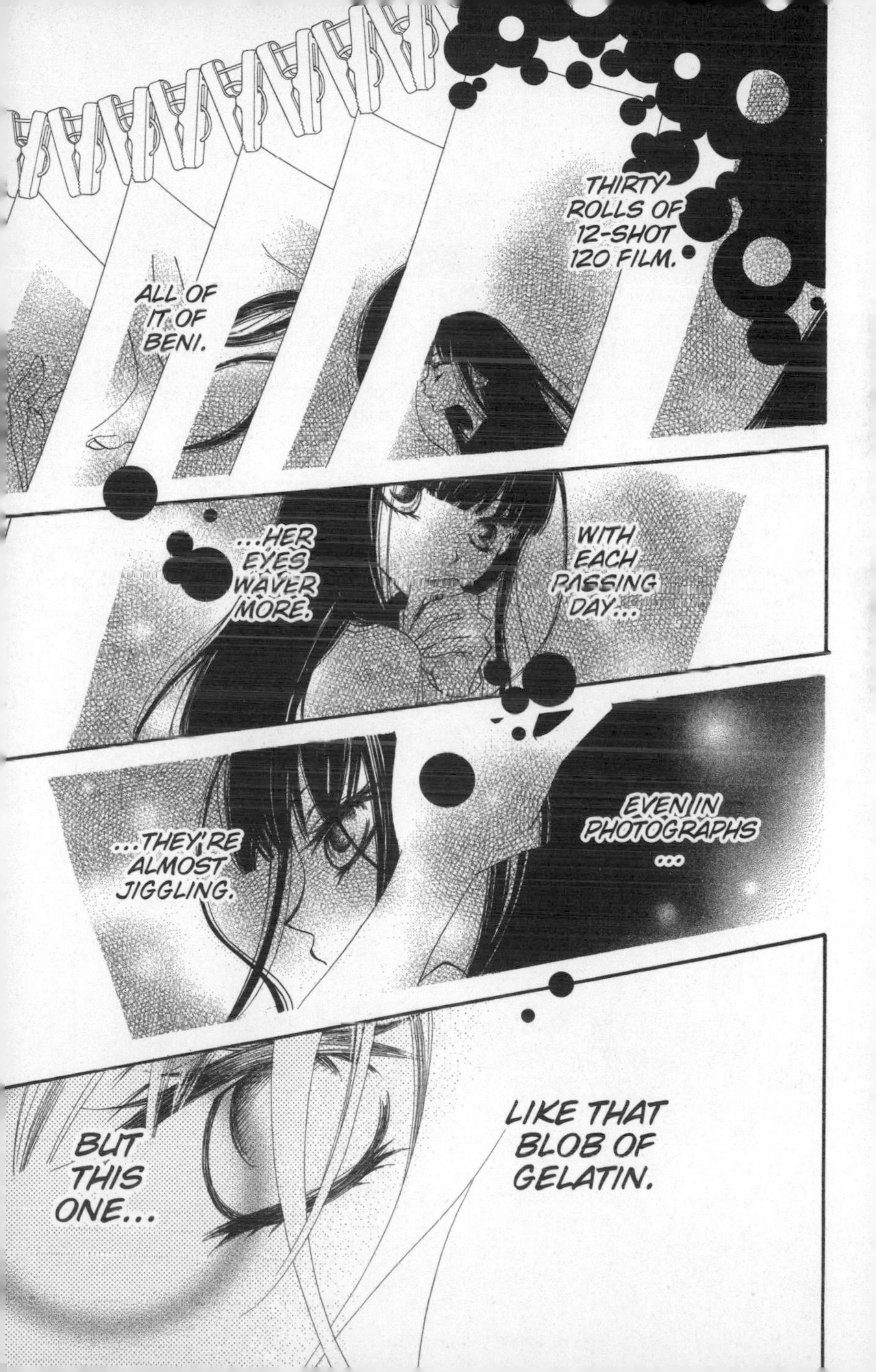
THIRTY ROLLS OF 12-SHOT 120 FILM.
ALL OF IT OF BENI.
WITH EACH PASSING DAY...
...HER EYES WAVER MORE.
EVEN IN PHOTOGRAPHS ...
...THEY'RE ALMOST JIGGLING.
LIKE THAT BLOB OF GELATIN.
BUT THIS ONE...

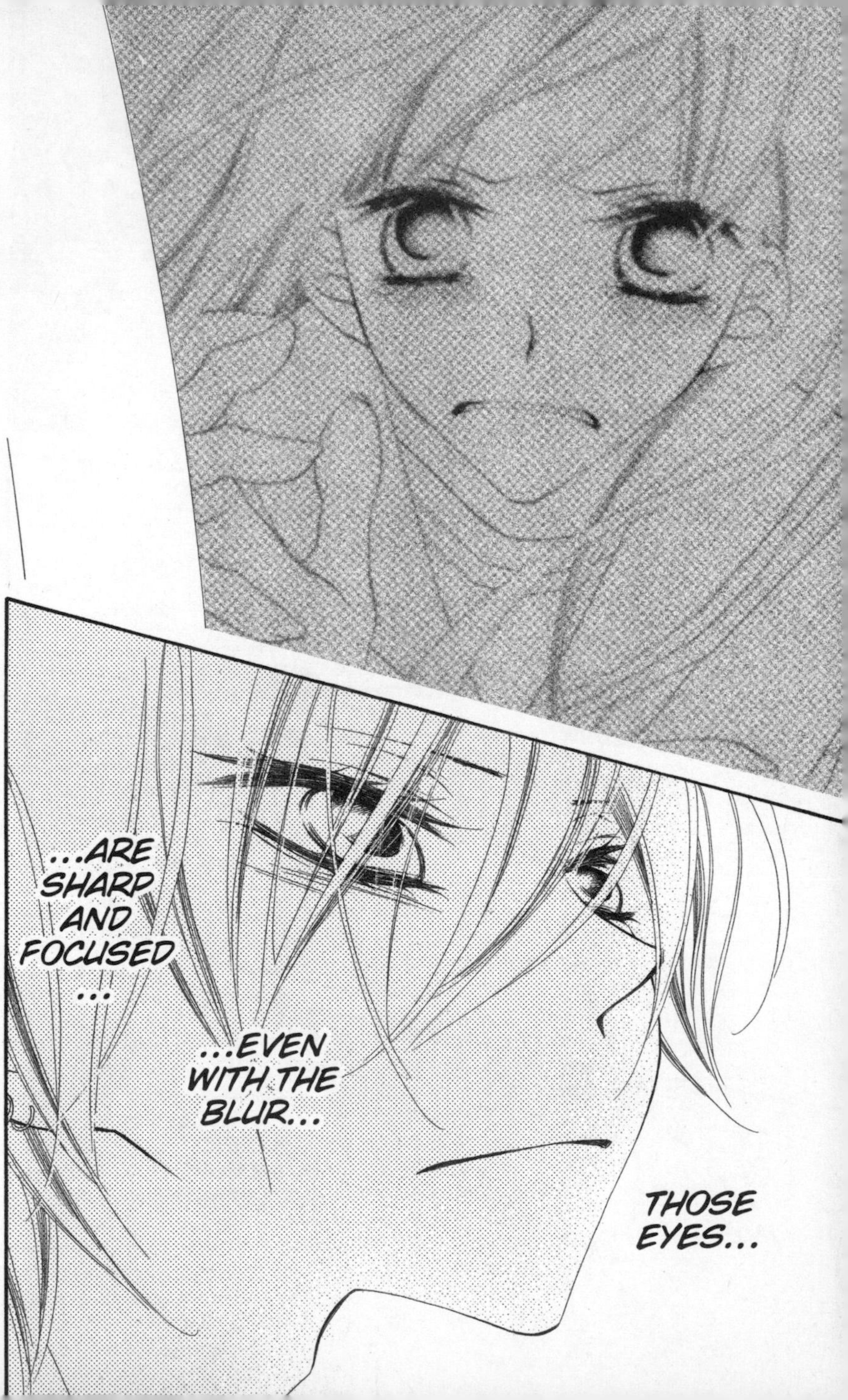
THOSE EYES...
...EVEN WITH THE BLUR...
...ARE SHARP AND FOCUSED...

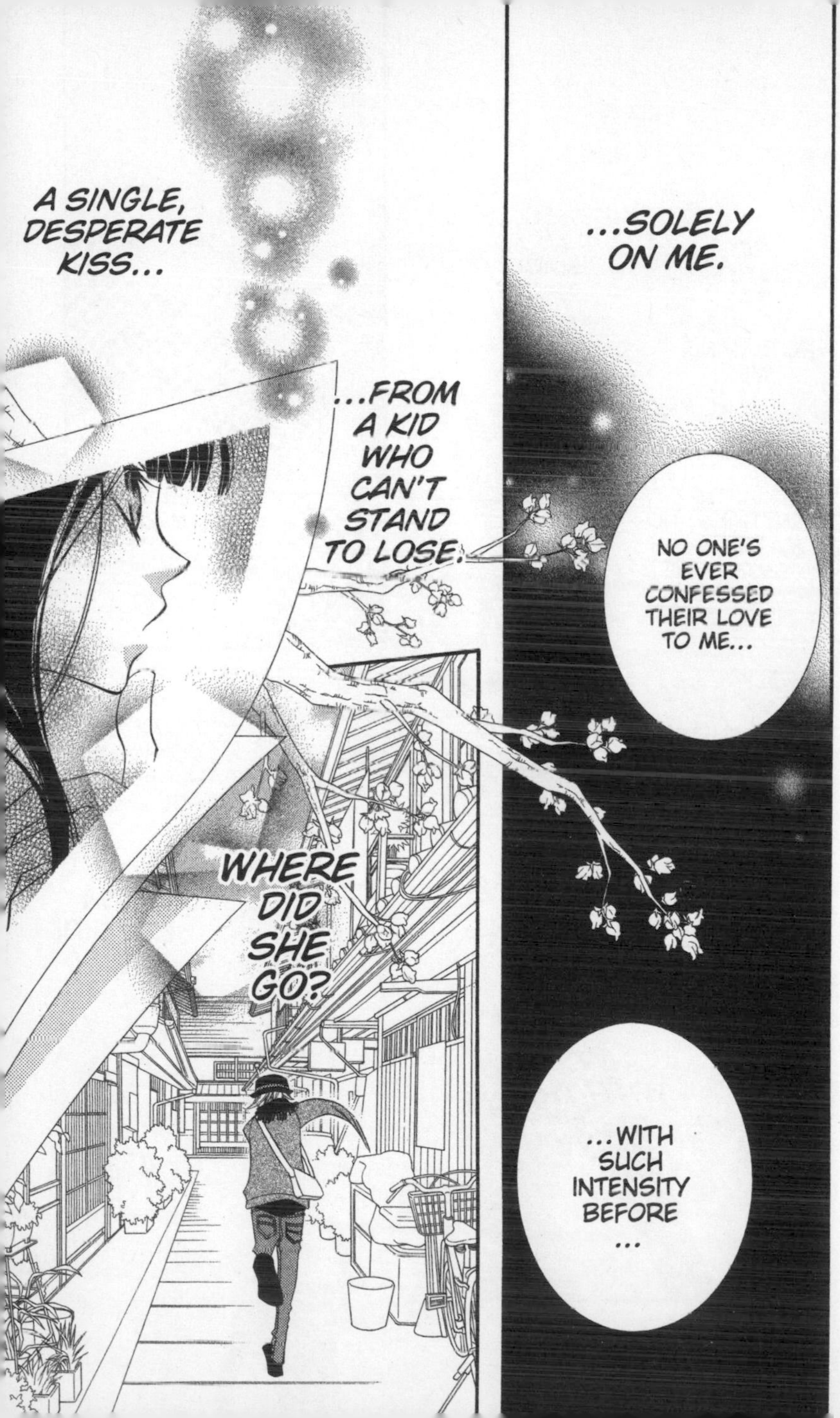
...SOLELY ON ME.
NO ONE'S EVER CONFESSED THEIR LOVE TO ME...
...WITH SUCH INTENSITY BEFORE ...
A SINGLE, DESPERATE KISS...
...FROM A KID WHO CAN'T STAND TO LOSE.
WHERE DID SHE GO?

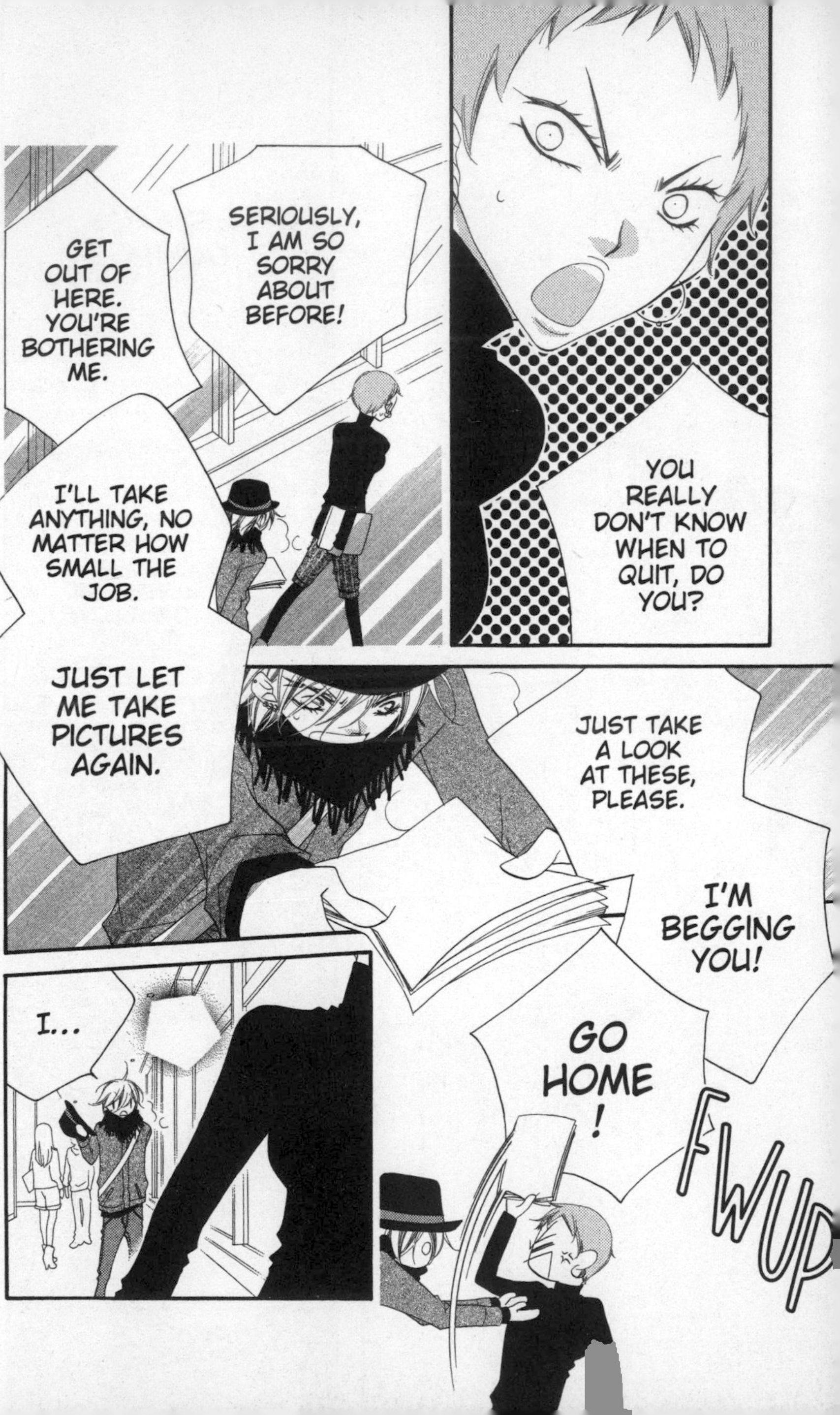
YOU REALLY DON'T KNOW WHEN TO QUIT, DO YOU?
SERIOUSLY, I AM SO SORRY ABOUT BEFORE!
GET OUT OF HERE. YOU'RE BOTHERING ME.
I'LL TAKE ANYTHING, NO MATTER HOW SMALL THE JOB.
JUST LET ME TAKE PICTURES AGAIN.
JUST TAKE A LOOK AT THESE, PLEASE.
I'M BEGGING YOU!
GO HOME!
FWUP
I...

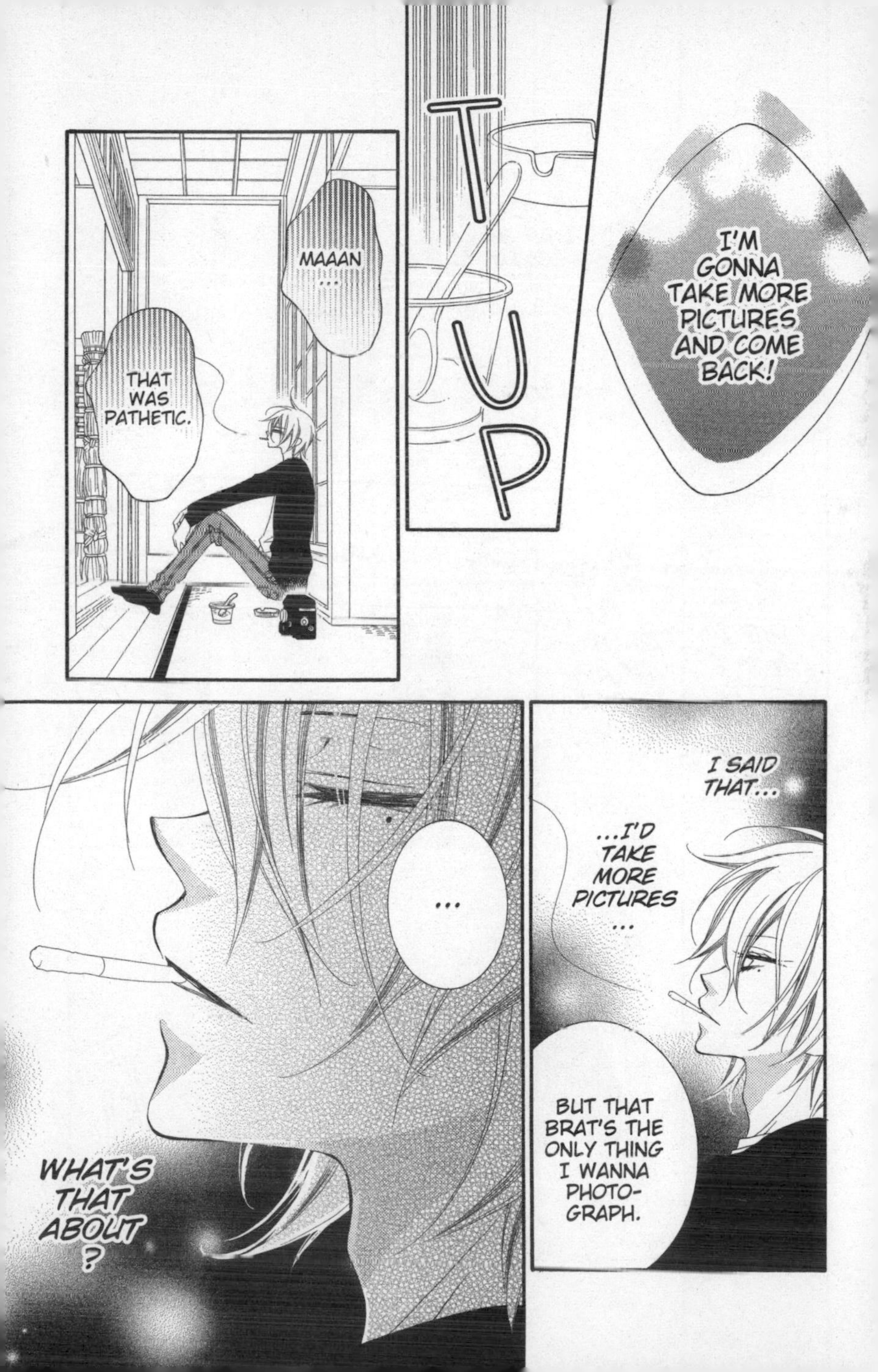
I'M GONNA TAKE MORE PICTURES AND COME BACK!
TUP
MAAAN...
THAT WAS PATHETIC.
I SAID THAT...
...I'D TAKE MORE PICTURES...
BUT THAT BRAT'S THE ONLY THING I WANNA PHOTO-GRAPH.
...
WHAT'S THAT ABOUT?

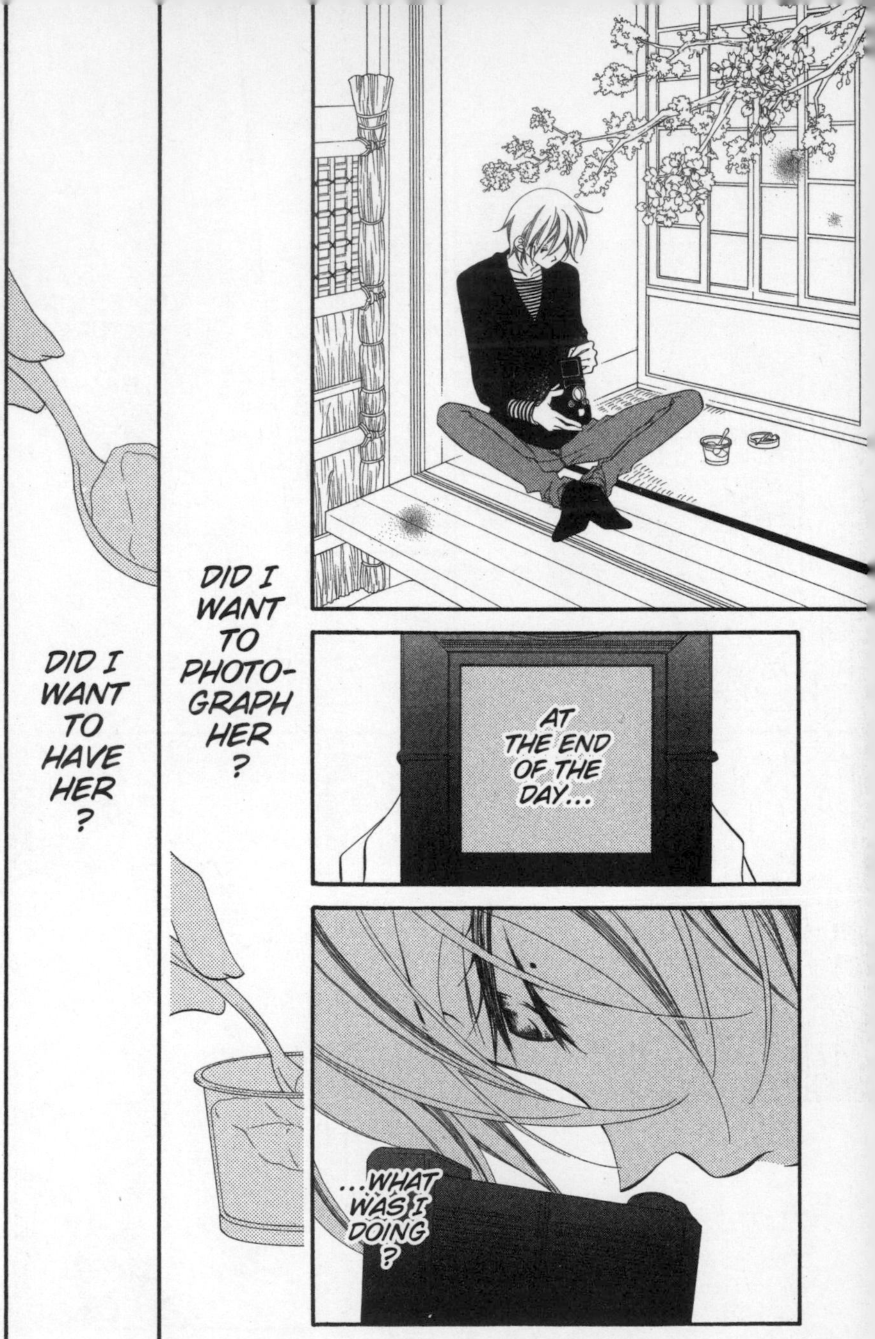
AT THE END OF THE DAY...
...WHAT WAS I DOING?
DID I WANT TO PHOTOGRAPH HER?
DID I WANT TO HAVE HER?

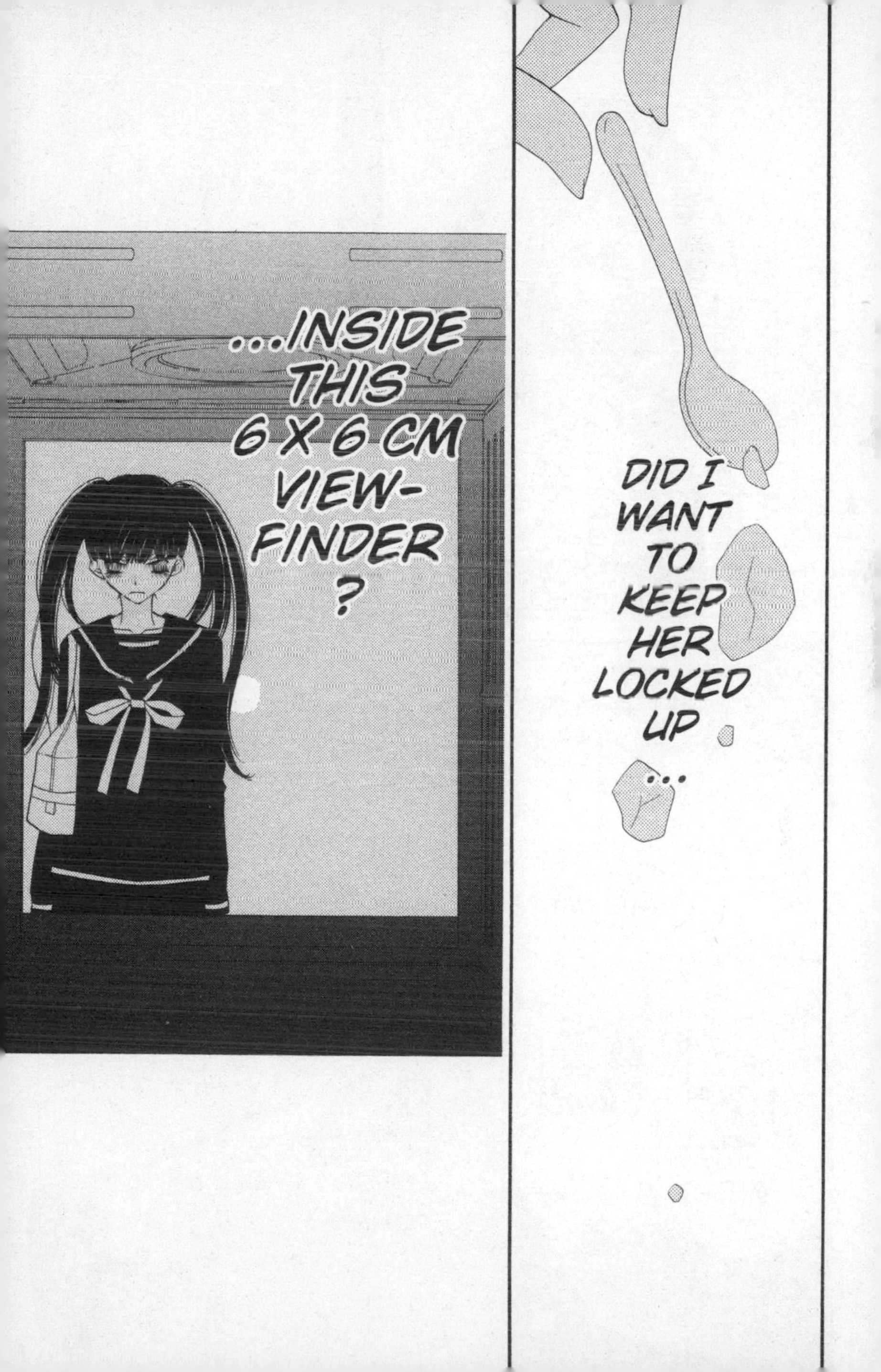
DID I WANT TO KEEP HER LOCKED UP ...
...INSIDE THIS 6 X 6 CM VIEW-FINDER ?

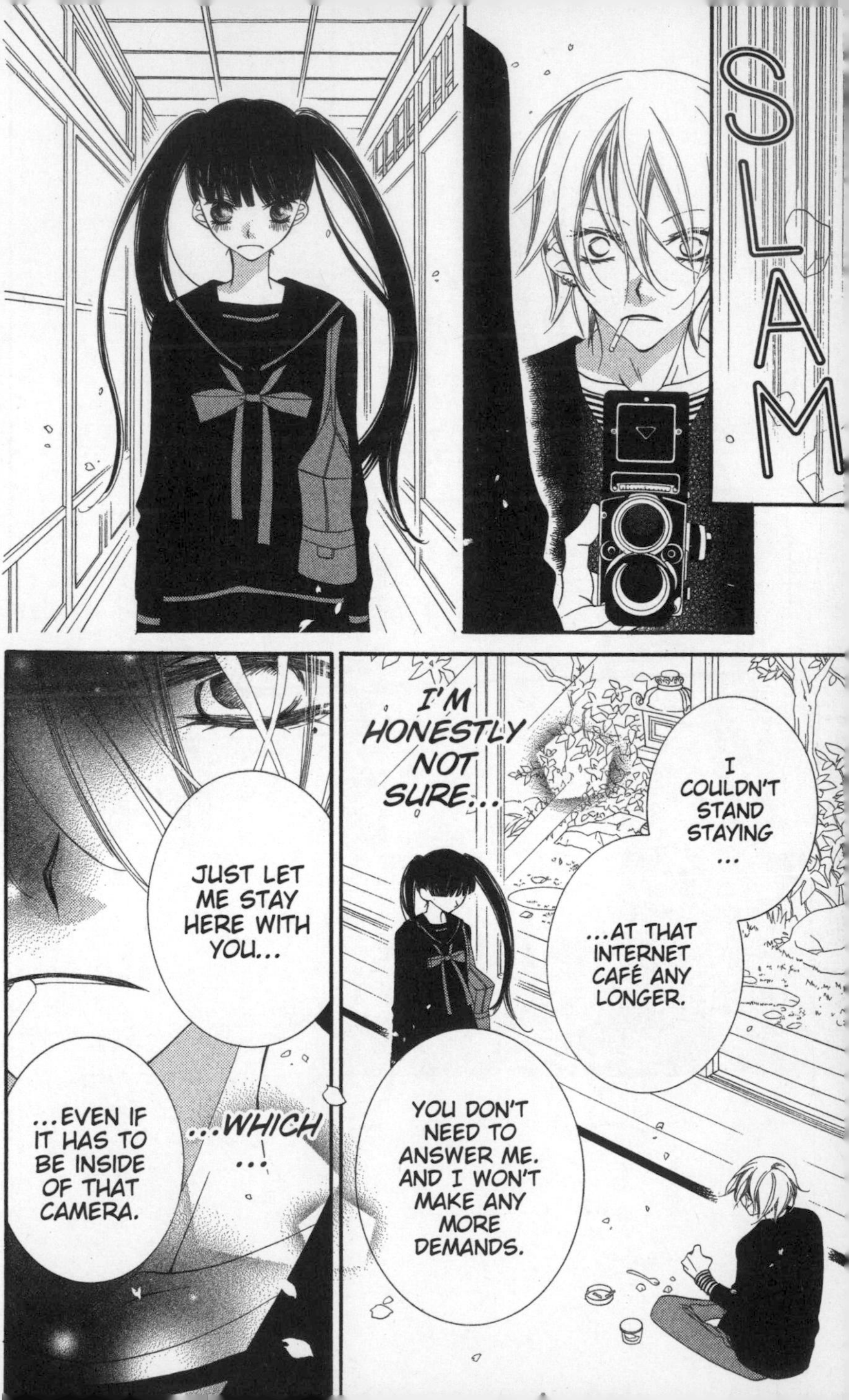
SLAM
I COULDN'T STAND STAYING ...
...AT THAT INTERNET CAFÉ ANY LONGER.
I'M HONESTLY NOT SURE...
YOU DON'T NEED TO ANSWER ME. AND I WON'T MAKE ANY MORE DEMANDS.
JUST LET ME STAY HERE WITH YOU...
...WHICH ...
...EVEN IF IT HAS TO BE INSIDE OF THAT CAMERA.

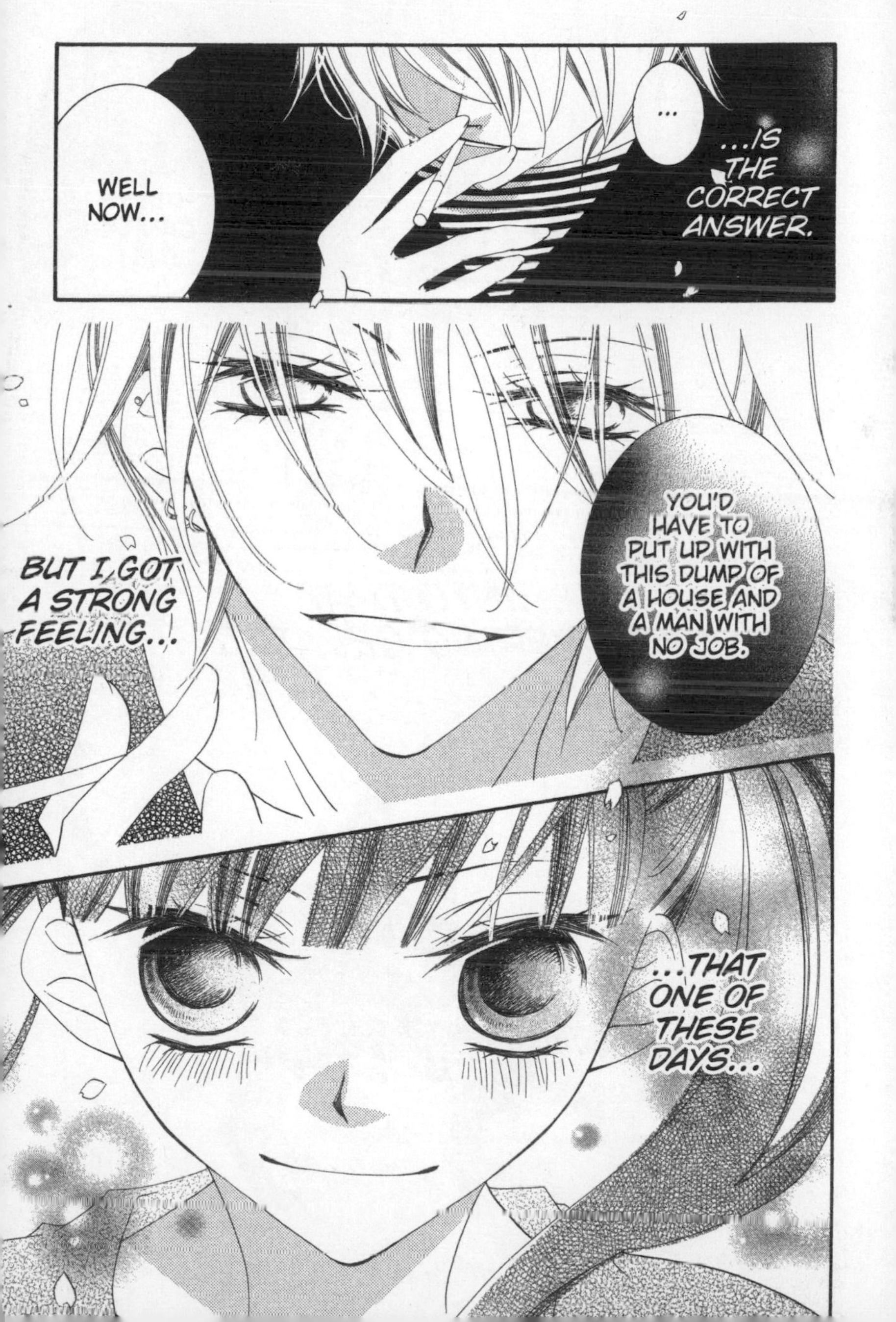
...
...IS THE CORRECT ANSWER.
WELL NOW...
YOU'D HAVE TO PUT UP WITH THIS DUMP OF A HOUSE AND A MAN WITH NO JOB.
BUT I GOT A STRONG FEELING...
...THAT ONE OF THESE DAYS...

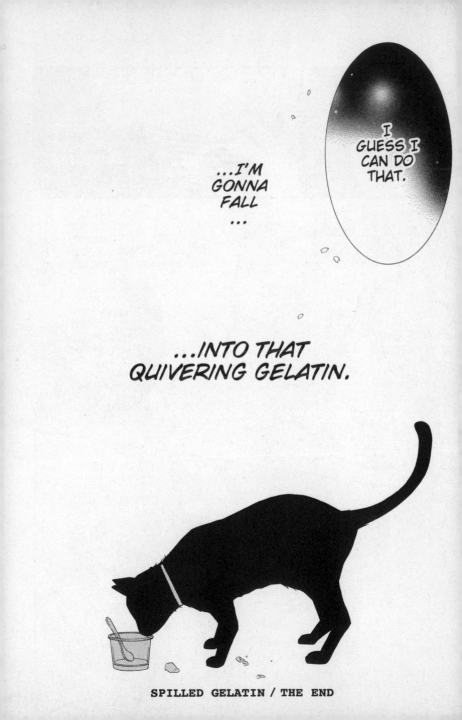

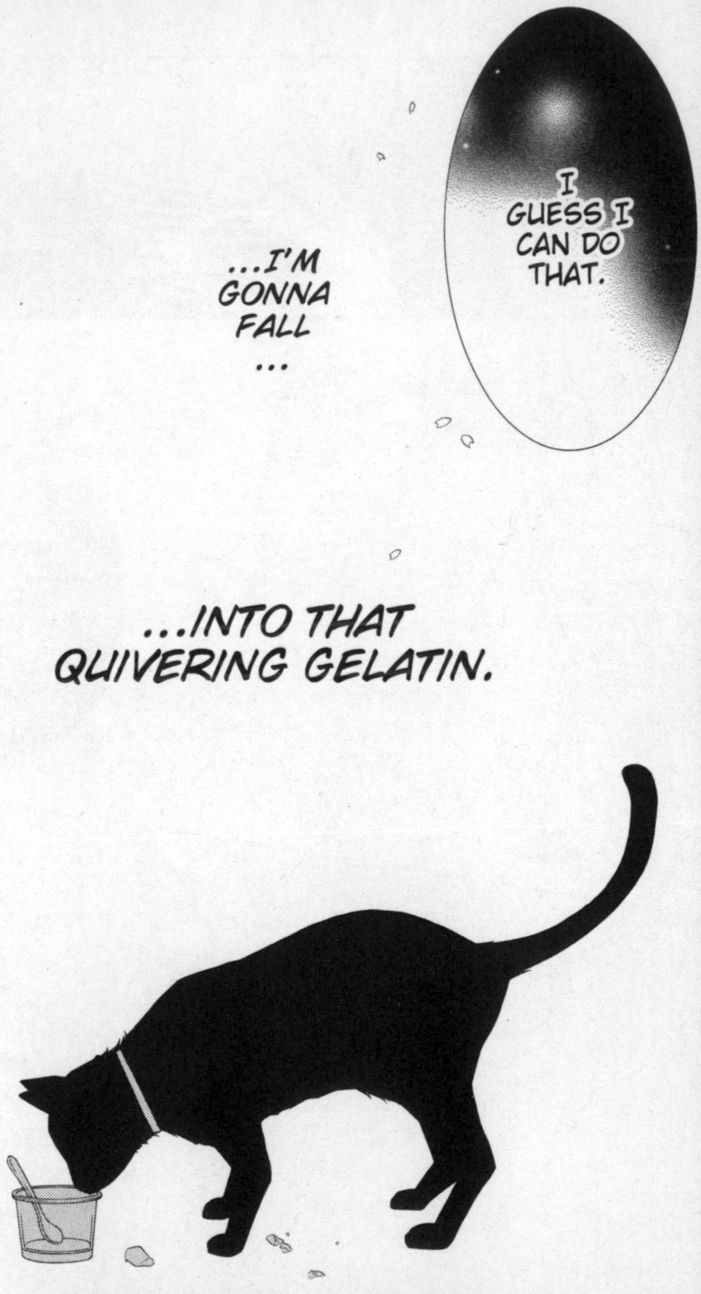
I GUESS I CAN DO THAT.
...I'M GONNA FALL ...
...INTO THAT QUIVERING GELATIN.

SPILLED GELATIN / THE END

I want to express my gratitude to all the concert venue staff members who took time out of their busy schedules to answer my requests for Tokyo Sailing reference materials. I'll be thanking you all by name in the next volume!

- Ryoko Fukuyama

Born on January 5 in Wakayama Prefecture in Japan, Ryoko Fukuyama debuted as a manga artist after winning the Hakusensha Athena Shinjin Taisho Prize from Hakusensha's *Hana to Yume* magazine. She is also the author of *Nosatsu Junkie*. *Anonymous Noise* was adapted into an anime in 2017.

ANONYMOUS NOISE
Vol. 13
Shojo Beat Edition

STORY AND ART BY
RYOKO FUKUYAMA

English Translation & Adaptation/Casey Loe
Touch-Up Art & Lettering/Joanna Estep
Design/Yukiko Whitley
Editor/Amy Yu

Fukumenkei Noise by Ryoko Fukuyama
© Ryoko Fukuyama 2017
All rights reserved.
First published in Japan in 2017 by HAKUSENSHA, Inc., Tokyo.
English language translation rights arranged with HAKUSENSHA, Inc., Tokyo.

Printed in the U.S.A.

Published by VIZ Media, LLC
P.O. Box 77010
San Francisco, CA 94107

10 9 8 7 6 5 4 3 2 1
First printing, March 2019

VIZ MEDIA
viz.com

Shojo **Beat**
shojobeat.com